HUMAN COMMUNICATION

HUMAN COMMUNICATION: The New Fundamentals

L.S. HARMS
University of Hawaii

HARPER & ROW, PUBLISHERS
New York, Evanston, San Francisco, London

Under the advisory editorship of J. Jeffery Auer

Sponsoring Editor: Voras D. Meeks
Project Editor: Duncan R. Hazard
Photo Editor: Myra Schachne
Designer: Jared Pratt
Production Supervisor: Stefania J. Taflinska

HUMAN COMMUNICATION: The New Fundamentals

Copyright © 1974 by L. S. Harms

Library of Congress Cataloging in Publication Data
Harms, Leroy Stanley, 1928–
   Human communication: the new fundamentals.

   Bibliography: p.
   1. Communication. 2. Mass media I. Title.
P90.H33 1974 301.14 73-8371
ISBN 0-06-042643-8

FOR JAKE, BILL, KATE, TINA,
AND THEIR FRIENDS

CONTENTS

IV COMMUNICATION IN THE FUTURE 179

PREFACE

The purpose of this book is to advance the right of man to communicate.

By *man* I mean we humans—you, me, all of us—who share the fragile resources of our spaceship°°earth both now and in the future.

By *right* I mean what the United Nations means in the preamble and the thirty articles of the Universal Declaration of Human Rights.□

By *communicate* I mean social interchange for a mutual purpose, rather than the more limited individual freedoms of speech, expression, information, and association. In the space age, the right of man to communicate□□will be made possible by the global interplay of technology, culture, *and* communication.

By *advance* I mean a *change* from the way we now communicate to a better way of communicating that vibrates in harmony with the vast new possibilities of the space age. For each of us, such an advance requires new communication attitudes, new communication skills, and new questions that probe the future of man as space age communicator.△

For most of us, the space age revolution in communication began abruptly on July 20, 1969, when we heard Neil Armstrong say, "One small step for man, one giant leap for mankind." We heard; we saw; the communication possibilities of man changed.

We are in the early stages of a worldwide revolution that has begun to transform all areas of communication. Human communication, a subarea of communication, is being rapidly transformed in fundamental ways. This book sets forth those new fundamentals of space age human communication.△△

This book had its beginning in 1963 as part of the Ford Foundation International Curriculum Project at the University of Kansas. A programmed trial draft was completed and tried out in 1964. That draft was completely reworked during the following year at the East-West Center in Honolulu. Portions of those materials were used in a variety of courses over the next few years. A course employing materials similar to the ones now in

° "Human Rights" cannot be discussed merely as an abstract matter . . . but only as the day-to-day experience of men and women everywhere.
Human Rights: The Dignity of Man, 1963:1.

°° We travel together, passengers on a little space ship, dependent on its vulnerable reserves of air and soil; all committed for our safety to its security and peace; preserved from annihilation only by the care, the work, and, I will say, the love we give our fragile craft.
Adlai E. Stevenson, 1965:151.

□ . . .recognition of the inherent dignity and of the equal and inalienable rights of all members of the human family is the foundation of freedom, justice and peace in the world.
Human Rights: The Dignity of Man, 1963:51.

□□ The time will come when the Universal Declaration of Human Rights will have to encompass a more extensive right than man's right to information, first laid down . . . in Article 19. This is the right of man to communicate.
Jean d'Arcy, 1969:14.

△
Human Communication
Individual Communicator
Home Community
World Community

△△
New Fundamentals (See Section 2.5)
Information Abundance
Equal Access to Information
Real-time Communication
Two-way Communication Systems
Association Variety

this book was offered in 1970. That entire course was tape recorded and analyzed. A dictated "trial draft" was prepared in 1971. That trial draft was used in three college and university settings. The book you now hold was completely rewritten in 1972 during a sabbatical leave from the University of Hawaii. But even after a decade of effort on my part, the book is not complete. It must be completed by you.

To be complete, the book requires three major contributions from you.

- Attitude. From time to time, there will be some simple attitude scales° in the margin. As you read, mark these scales. Discuss your attitudes with persons who are reading the book and with others who are not. Where you find the text differs from your view, *change the text.* Cross out a sentence; write one that is better for you. Illustrate. Add material. Doodle. Draw charts that show relationships. Compose a poem. Make the book consistent with your attitude.
- Skill. The projects°° at the end of each chapter enable you to test your present communication skill levels. On most of the projects, continued practice will help you improve your communication skill to any level you choose for yourself.□
- Questions. Each chapter ends with a few questions. The first questions are relatively easy; the later ones are more difficult. These questions do not have answers at the end of the book, nor are answers neatly assembled anywhere else in the world. They are real questions that arise from our purpose: to advance the right to communicate. The answers *we* develop for these questions will advance or retard that human right.

The book contains a *method* for improving human communication.□□ It is a "how to" and a "when to" book. It is also a "when not to" book. The method focuses on *A*ttitudes, *S*kills, and *Q*uestions. For short, it is the *ASQ method.* ASQ is pronounced in the same way as the word *ask.*

The ASQ method is *cybernetic*△ in philosophy. You may find it useful to look at Norbert Wiener's little book on cybernetics, *The Human Use of Human Beings.* The central concern of the present book is with the individual human communicator. Many of the illustrations and examples found in the margin are drawn from "the day-to-day experiences of men and women everywhere."△△

Human communication is a social process. For this reason, it becomes necessary to expand outward from the individual communicator to his home community and to extend on into the world community. Human communication is an individual and home community and world community process.✩

°
Attitude Scale
- 1 2 3 ? 5 6 7 +

°° See Projects at ends of Chapters 3–10.

□ Effectiveness in a free society is now seen to be proportionate to how well one understands the process of speech-communication and how skillful one is in its use . . . .
William S. Howell, in Fred Casmir and L. S. Harms, 1970:vi.

□□ The more skilled at communication are the people whose goal is a just and good society, the greater the chances that we will have that sort of society. . . . with that goal, you have the responsibility to develop to the maximum your abilities to communicate in order to help your society toward that goal. This is true whether your society is made up of two persons or a total community. . . .
A. C. Baird, F. H. Knower, and S. L. Becker, 1971:5.

△ Cybernetics . . . does not ask "What is this thing?" but "What does it do?" . . . Cybernetics

The book contains a "simple and practical story" of man as space age communicator. I've enjoyed writing this book; I hope you enjoy rewriting it.✩✩ There is space in the margin for you to add to or change the book. Become a co-author!

But we need a larger purpose or a general goal for this co-authorship. Permit me to suggest this challenge:

- Let us declare the right of man to communicate to be a long-range goal° of mankind
    for you,
    for me,
    for all of us.
- If not us, who?
- If not now, when?°

Aloha.

L. S. Harms

deals with all forms of behaviour insofar as they are regular, or determinate, or reproducible.
W. Ross Ashby, 1963:1.

△△ I would like therefore to ask the indulgence of my honorable and learned readers . . . into whose familiar provinces I have wandered at times in the telling of my simple and practical story.
R. G. H. Siu, 1957:viii.

✩

Human Communication
Individual Communicator
Home Community
World Community

✩✩ It is the thesis of this book that society can only be understood through a study of the messages and the communication facilities which belong to it. . . .
Norbert Wiener, 1954:18.

° By long-range goal, I mean some desired future state of affairs whose realization would require an effort lasting over many generations. . . . To qualify as a long-range goal for mankind, a goal must involve a large number of people, probably a considerable fraction of the human race.
Gerald Feinberg, 1969:4.

° There was once a rabbi who had the reputation for knowing what was in a man's mind by reading his thoughts. A wicked boy came to see him and said: "Rabbi, I have in my hand a small bird. Is it alive, or is it dead?" And the boy thought to himself: If he says it is dead, I will open my hand and let it fly away; if he says it is alive, I will quickly squeeze it and show him it is dead. And the boy repeated the question: "Rabbi, I have in my hand a small bird. Is it alive, or is it dead?" And the rabbi gazed steadily at him, and said, quietly: "Whatever you will; whatever you will."
Daniel Bell, 1967:697.

ACKNOWLEDG- MENTS

This book has multiple origins and an involved history. My debt to other persons and institutions is large and must be acknowledged.

The basic notions of the book arose out of leisurely discussions with Manfred Schröder and many others during my student days in Paris about the needs and possibilities and rights of man. A bit later in graduate school, the guidance of Dr. Franklin H. Knower was particularly helpful; and through long discussions with Dr. Robert E. Dunham, the special importance of dialog and the dyad were reconstructed and rediscovered.

The Ford Foundation, through an International Curriculum Project administered at the University of Kansas by Dr. Francis Heller, provided support for a first programmed draft of the book under the title *Oral Communication: An International Emphasis;* a second draft was prepared at the East-West Center in Honolulu under the title *Person to Person International Communication.* That draft had become two books and it has taken quite a while to separate them.

The first of these two books, *Intercultural Communication,* has also been published by Harper & Row. The second is this present more general book, entitled *Human Communication: The New Fundamentals.*

This book was cast in yet another form as *The New Fundamentals of Speech Communication in the Space Age.* That draft was tried in classes by Professor Harold Svanoe at Luther College in Decorah, Iowa; by Mrs. Kay Yamada at Leeward Community College in Pearl City, Hawaii; and by the author at the Manoa Campus of the University of Hawaii. Professor Svanoe, Mrs. Yamada, and their students suggested many improvements, as did my students at Manoa in some fifty hours of interviews. My thanks to all of you.

The present book was drafted and redrafted in Honolulu while I was on sabbatical leave from the University of Hawaii. Many persons have read one part or another of the book and suggested improvements. In particular, I would like to thank Professor E. C. Buehler, Mr. Dan J. Wedemeyer, and Dr. Paul J. Heinberg for their helpful suggestions.

Voras D. Meeks and the staff at Harper & Row also deserve a special thank you.

Finally, to Mrs. Jill Bennett Elkins, student assistant *par excellence* who attended to the 2001 details of book preparation—Mahalo and Aloha.

Grateful acknowledgment is made to the following publishers and authors who granted permission to reprint from the following material.

Ben H. Bagdikian, *The Information Machines: Their Impact on Men and the Media* (New York: Harper & Row, 1971). Copyright © 1971 by the RAND Corporation.

G. A. Borden, R. B. Gregg, and T. G. Grove, *Speech Behavior and Human Interaction* (Englewood Cliffs, N.J.: Prentice-Hall, 1969). Copyright © 1969 by Prentice-Hall, Inc.

Colin Cherry, *World Communication: Threat or Promise?* (New York: Wiley-Interscience, 1971).

Conference Board, *Information Technology:Some Critical Implications for Decision Makers* (New York, 1972). Published by The Conference Board and sponsored by the Senior Executives Council. Reprinted by permission.

Douglas Jones, *Communication and Energy in Changing Urban Environments* (Hamden, Conn.: Shoe String Press, 1971). Reprinted by permission of the Colston Research Society, from Volume 21 of the Colston Papers.

Daniel Lerner, *The Passing of Traditional Society* (New York: The Free Press, 1958). Reprinted with permission of the MacMillan Company. Copyright © 1958 by The Free Press.

John McHale, *World Facts and Trends* (New York: The Free Press, 1972). Reprinted with permission of the MacMillan Company. Copyright © 1972 by John McHale.

James Martin, *Telecommunications and the Computer* (Englewood Cliffs, N.J.: Prentice-Hall, 1969). Copyright © 1969 by Prentice-Hall, Inc.

Magoroh Maruyama and James A. Dator, eds., *Human Futuristics* (Honolulu, Hawaii: Social Science Research Institute, 1971).

Bill Moyers, *Listening to America* (New York: Dell, 1971). Copyright © 1971 by Bill Moyers.

NASA, Apollo 11 and skyland photographs (Washington, D.C., Public Information Office).

James Nelson, ed., *Wisdom for our Time* (New York: W. W. Norton, 1961). Copyright © 1961 by National Broadcasting Company, Inc.

Y. V. Lakshmana Rao, *Communication and Development* (Minneapolis,

Minn.: University of Minnesota Press, 1966). Copyright © 1966 University of Minnesota.

Carl Sagan, plaque for Pioneer 10 (Ithaca, N.Y., Cornell University).

Harold Stewart, *A Net of Fireflies* (Rutland, Vt.: Charles E. Tuttle, 1960).

Twentieth Century Fund, "The Future of Satellite Communications: Resource Management and the Needs of Nations," second report of the *Twentieth Century Fund Task Force of International Satellite Communications* (New York: The Twentieth Century Fund, 1970).

Gerald Weinstein and Mario D. Fantini, *Toward Humanistic Education: A Curriculum of Affect* (New York: Praeger, 1970).

Frederick Winsor and Marian Parry, *The Space Child's Mother Goose* (New York: Simon and Schuster, 1963). Copyright © 1956, 1957, 1958, 1963 by Frederick Winsor and Marian Parry. Reprinted by permission of Simon and Schuster, Inc.

Grateful acknowledgment is also made to the following sources for permission to reproduce the photographs appearing throughout the text.

American Airlines
AT & T Photo Services
Camera Craft, Inc.
Ford Foundation
GM Photography
IBM
Morton Beebe and Associates
NASA
National Broadcasting Company
New York Public Library
New York Stock Exchange
The Port of New York Authority
RCA Corporation
Science Research Associates, Inc.
Tom F. Walters
United Nations
Whitestone Photo

Cover and title-page photographs: Courtesy of The New York Public Library

c 1500

c 1900   1950's   1960's   1970's

This world is but a single dewdrop, set
Trembling upon a stem; and yet . . . and yet . . .
 Issa *in Harold Stewart, 1960:66.*

happened in other communities at times of rapid and widespread change. Appendix A.2 contains five accounts or stories of rapidly changed communities.

The first of these accounts is set in Balgat,[°] a small village some ten kilometers outside of Ankara, Turkey. Balgat was a traditional village like thousands of others in the world *until* the road to Ankara was built and low-cost hourly bus service to Ankara was begun. The men of the village were then able to work "in town," and for the first time, they were able to earn money. They used money to buy tickets to see exciting movies, and they bought radios. In the short span of four years, the two technologies of communication—transportation and telecommunication—transformed nearly every cultural tradition in the village.[°°] Whether that change was an advance is a question of value. There is probably no single question which is more important to us as we begin to build a space age culture. We too live in Balgat. The road has been built; the buses are running.

The second account is set in two villages in South India. One is a traditional village; the other is a village that is on the way to becoming "modern."[□] The author lived in each of the villages for some months, conducted interviews, and "absorbed" the patterns of communication. His account makes particularly clear the widespread change that occurs in cultural patterns as a direct result of the availability of new information from a variety of sources. The same pattern will be repeated on a much larger scale in India as direct satellite telecasts begin to reach thousands of traditional villages.

The third story is told by Peace Corps volunteers[□□] who went to the villages in the Philippines to "help out." The account is based on reports from the volunteers. The volunteer "communicators" progressed through several stages. They began as the newly arrived "reformer"; grew into "mutual acceptance"; and went on to a satisfying and "productive relationship." The volunteers reported that as a result of their attempts to communicate they felt they had gained more from their hosts than they had been able to give. Some of the volunteer "communicators" were more than a little surprised at their own conclusions. Such is the risk and the reward of intercultural communication; both risk and reward are at times unexpectedly large.

The fourth account is the work of a journalist who traveled across mainland America with "notebook and tape recorder"; he reported what he heard people talking about. There is more than an occasional reflection of the tension between the home community and the world community—the very personal ethnic enclave and the very impersonal global village. He reports that people have a story to tell and they wish to be heard.

emphasis at this point in time is similar to telling the owner of a horse that has just won the Kentucky Derby that he has a "pretty fast" horse.
L. L. Barker and R. J. Kibler, 1971:2.

[°] What clues existed were in a few words spoken by the villagers. These words we collated with the words that had been spoken to the interviewers by hundreds of villagers and townspeople. . . .
Daniel Lerner, 1958:20.

[°°]

> A major change in patterns of communication usually improves a community.
>
> Disagree 1 2 3 ? 5 6 7 Agree

[□] Our choice of villages was governed by the single overriding hypothesis that communication patterns . . . will differ as between the traditional village and the "developing" village.
Y. V. Lakshmana Rao, 1966:10.

[□□] I was whole and the bonds and patterns of communication were whole. . . . The important idea to me is mutualness.
Lawrence H. Fuchs, in D. Lerner and W. Schramm, 1967:253

nological culture.° Others point to the growing interest in the local cultures in the home community, we are each of us members of a family and live in a small community with others of similar ethnic°° origins and cultures; and that culture must be maintained and passed on to the next generation. These feelings of "global village" and "ethnic enclave" represent diverse views of culture. Agreement there is not.

The bi-cultural view□ is helpful at this time. This view allows us to distinguish between the home community and the world community. In the home community the members evolve a specific or unique culture; in the world community, the members shape a general or global culture unlike any specific culture but reflecting elements—ideally the better ones—from many of them.

Many of us recognize that we live in both a home community and a world community. We are of two cultures. We are bi-cultural. But a certain tension□□ sometimes arises. Serving two masters is seldom easy.

Our developing space age attitude is shaped in the meeting of cultural patterns and communication patterns.△ The technologies of telecommunication and transportation make it possible and often make it necessary for us to engage in communication with persons who are culturally unlike us. We distinguish between *inter*-cultural and *intra*-cultural communication. Inter-cultural communication moves us toward a world cultural community; intra-cultural communication moves us toward a home cultural community. Inescapably, as inter-cultural communication increases, intra-cultural communication decreases.△△ The reverse is also true. The time available per day for communication changes very little.

1.2.3 Communication

Human communication☆ may be viewed as a form of social interchange engaged in for some mutual purpose. Two persons conversing in a living room, two persons talking over the telephone, a committee meeting, a conference call, a public speaker and his audience, a radio newscaster and his listeners—all are examples of human communication. In each of these examples, as we shall see in detail later, communicators organize a communication system to achieve a purpose; each of the systems is joined by a link in either the transportation or telecommunication networks.

The major focus of this book is on human communication.☆☆ It is appropriate, therefore, that we examine human communication, technology, and culture from that point of view. To glimpse what may be happening to us at this time, it is helpful to examine what is known to have

° Today, electronics and automation make mandatory that everybody adjust to the vast global environment as if it were his home town.
Marshall McLuhan, 1968:11.

°° The term "ethnic group" usually refers to those who possess a shared tradition, an idea of common destiny, and a feeling of spiritual togetherness, all of which may exist even if they possess no common territory or political organization.
Arthur L. Smith, in L. L. Barker and R. J. Kibler, 1971:306.

□
Bi-cultural View
Home Community Culture
World Community Culture

□□ Our sense of belonging to one world has never been keener than at present. Yet the emphasis on this evident fact itself implies that while every individual is affected by the quickening flow of world events, he is still strongly influenced by the ways of living . . . in his own . . . culture.
Hajime Nakamura, 1964:3.

△ For I believe we are on the verge of developing a new kind of culture . . . I call this new style *prefigurative,* because in this new culture it will be the child—and not the parent or grandparent—that represents what is to come.
Margaret Mead, 1970:68.

△△ To be a good communicator one must understand the culture in which he communicates. His message systems must be so organized that they are supported by cultural mores and motivations.
A. C. Baird, F. H. Knower, and S. L. Becker, 1971:24.

☆
Communication

☆☆ Most texts on communication begin by emphasizing the importance of communication on contemporary society. We feel that such an

I

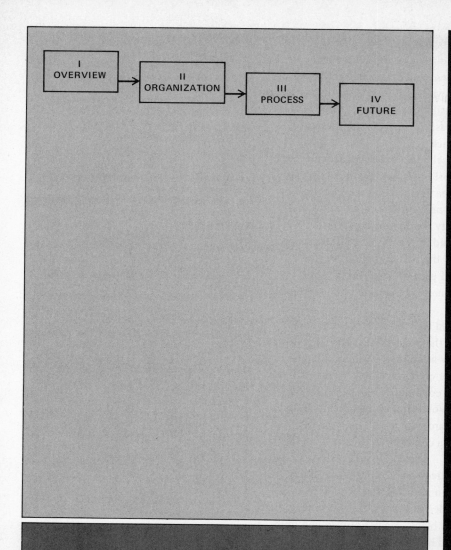

I
OVERVIEW

We live at the dawn of a new age. Call it the space age.° We enter the space age enmeshed in ageless problems unsolved during a half million years of human history. Yet, new possibilities to invent and create and plan open up for us. If we evolve our mutual possibilities wisely, these can become the best of times; but if we exploit our new possibilities unwisely, these could be the worst of times. The dangers are ageless; the new possibilities unfold as we invent and create the future in the space age.°°

Each of the many communities in the world encourages a particular view of the immediate community and of the world that lies beyond. Like the tourist who visits Hawaii, I appreciate the sea and sun and the mountain peaks and the volcanoes that erupt and add new earth. Unlike the tourist, I also appreciate that the Hawaiian community is an important world communication center. We are much involved in the use of communication satellites, for instance. Hawaii is also one of the first communities to become seriously interested in the future.□ I provide these background comments because, like everyone else, the message I choose to communicate is much influenced by where I live.

But then, you too are similarly influenced by your home community. And for your purposes as a communicator, the essential resources are also at hand in your community. Out of your daily association with family and friends, you develop your basic purposes for communicating. Some of those purposes will take you far from your home community as you seek new information. In turn, the new information you acquire must be integrated into the web of attitudes and values you share with your family and friends. In the space age, the home community has a central role to play in all of human communication.

To begin to appreciate the new possibilities open to us, it is necessary to sketch a design of human communication on a canvas that is millions of years long and millions of miles wide. The design travels through time and stretches across space. Most of the canvas is blank. Man as human communicator has only a half million year past and he has a future that may yet extend for billions of years. Man is very young; his experience as a communicator is limited. Most of that experience was acquired in small, traditional communities. Almost all of man's experience as a communicator is pre-space age.

The chart on page 5 identifies the four major sections □□ of the book: Overview, Organization, Process, and Future. There are fourteen chapters. Each chapter is divided into about seven units.

The Overview section contains two chapters. Chapter 1 sketches the growth of communication and locates the space age within human history. Chapter 2 introduces the space age study of human communication. Taken

° A new era in human communication . . . like other aspects of the space age, has arrived abruptly. It still carries with it an aura of science fiction, yet is a reality which progressively and with dramatic speed will influence our daily lives. Decisions taken now may be crucial in shaping the future of . . . communication for many years to come.
UNESCO, 1968:Preface.

°° I have no doubt that in reality the future will be vastly more surprising than anything I can imagine . . . we shall come to see that the use, however haltingly, of our imagination upon the possibilities of the future is a valuable spiritual exercise.
J. B. S. Haldane, in Arthur C. Clarke, 1967:300.

□ From August 5 through August 8, 1970, some seven hundred delegates and guests of the Governor's Conference on Hawaii 2000 met in the Ilikai Hotel in Honolulu and wrestled with problems of the future of Hawaii.
J. A. Dator, in M. Maruyama and J. A. Dator, 1971:131.

Human Communication

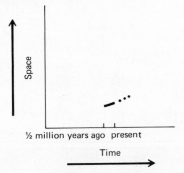

½ million years ago   present

Time

□□ *Major Sections*
Overview
Organization
Process
Future

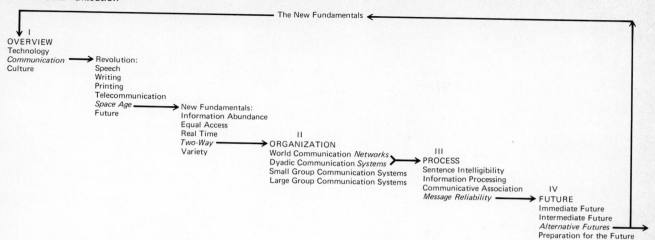

together, the two chapters outline the new fundamentals of human communication. As you read, you will need to add details to that outline.

The book introduces the ASQ method° (*A*ttitudes, *S*kills, and *Q*uestions). To help you display your attitudes to yourself, simple attitude scales will be placed in the margin. The usual form of the scale will be − 1 2 3 ? 5 6 7 + . You can define the − and + signs as you wish. Some possibilities are sketched in the margin.°°

Sometimes, only a word or phrase will appear above the scale. At other times longer statements will be used. Some of these longer statements will be "quotations" from other communicators.

At the end of each chapter, you will find a project that will help you advance your communication skill. Each chapter ends with a few questions. These questions are related to the right of man to communicate.

If you have read the Preface, please go on to Chapter 1.

°
ASQ Method
Attitudes
Skills
Questions

°°

BASIC ATTITUDE SCALE
− 1 2 3 ? 5 6 7 +
SOME ALTERNATE SCALES
1 2 3 ? 5 6 7

NO No no ? yes Yes YES

Bad   1 2 3 ? 5 6 7 Good
Weak   1 2 3 ? 5 6 7 Strong
Slow   1 2 3 ? 5 6 7 Fast
Disagree 1 2 3 ? 5 6 7 Agree

1

ON
COMMUNICATION

This chapter introduces the story of man as space age communicator. It explores the cybernetic relationships between technology, culture, and communication. The major communication revolutions are charted. Some consequences of accelerating change are noted. The chapter ends with a first statement of the right of man to communicate.

I
OVERVIEW →

1.1 INTRODUCTION

We are probably the first humans to see our planet through the eye of a spaceship camera; and, as a curious consequence, we have come to call the blue planet our spaceship earth.[°] We now talk of life support systems and interstellar communication systems as casually as we talk about hamburgers and recorded music. We expect that before the year 2000, the first human child will be born on the moon. We begin to develop a space-age attitude.[°°] Space age technology changes the way we communicate about our earth spaceship and our earthman culture.

[°] The most important fact about Spaceship Earth: An instruction book didn't come with it.
R. Buckminster Fuller, 1970:6.

[°°] The Earth is indeed our cradle. . . . The Solar System will be our kindergarten.
Arthur C. Clarke, 1972:81.

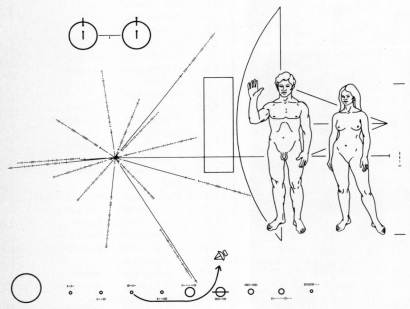

By permission of Carl Sagan

    Pioneer 10 provides an example of our space age attitude. That space "probe" was programmed to pass Mars and Jupiter and, then, to swing out of the solar system and continue its journey—forever. Pioneer 10 is a missile that carries a message from us earth people. The informational plaque attached to Pioneer 10 shows a friendly Adam and a demure Eve; it also gives our earth address. Beyond that, it represents a major attempt on our part to establish communication with "those quaint folks" who live out there.[□] The Pioneer message further

[□] . . . the idea that *we* are the only intelligent creatures in a cosmos of a hundred million galaxies is so preposterous that there are very few astronomers today who would take it seriously.
Arthur C. Clarke, 1972:94.

assumes those "folks" are able to do things we can't yet do. Namely, retrieve such a probe, make sense out of its message, and send an answer. What do you suppose will happen on earth when we receive such an answer? Of course, a mishap may occur; the probe may self-destruct. Yet . . . °

Let us review where we are. Our planet has an estimated life expectancy of nine billion years. Spaceship earth is more than four billion years old. Some form of life has been supported on earth for about two billion years.

Man evolved slowly and, for a brief four million years, lived quietly on earth. Then, by some chain of still unknown circumstances, man became able to speak;°° he got the "word." Talking man is a newcomer on a middle-aged planet.

For millions of years our honorable ancestors were speechless. Then, about 500 thousand years ago, man began to evolve the capacity to communicate through speech. The transition from man as "animal"□ to man as "human" occurred as a system for speech communication evolved. Thus, human history begins. Every child who develops through the stages from birth cry to articulate speech relives in five years that process which originally took thousands of years to evolve. Each human on this earth is now man the communicator.

We can only speculate about the details of the full relationship between being a communicator and being human.□□ We do not yet find a good example of one without the other. The so-called wolf-child demonstrates the absence of both communication and humanness. As man communicates, he becomes human; that much is clear. Humans communicate each other into humanness.△

Today we claim that the capacity to communicate through speech is the single most distinctive characteristic of humankind. But our man-made claim to distinction is now challenged by the dolphin and the computer here on earth, and by our recognition that—just perhaps—beings more intelligent than earthman communicate among themselves on the planets of the distant star systems. We once claimed that our flat earth was the center of the universe. We know different now. Perhaps we shall have also to revise our claim about human communication.△△

We can continue to believe, at least for a time, that man's humanness is inseparably interlinked with his individual capacity to communicate. However, the space age which just

°

HUMAN COMMUNICATION	
Difficult 1 2 3 ? 5 6 7 Easy	
Safe 1 2 3 ? 5 6 7 Risky	
Bad 1 2 3 ? 5 6 7 Good	

°° Speech is such a peculiarly human activity that it is not even approached by man's closest relatives and his most active imitators.
Norbert Wiener, 1954:82.

□ For . . . millions of years man-like primates lived upon earth. . . . Somewhere in this timeless past, some of these naked stone-using animals rose apart from their fellows and became men . . . in a sense we can say exactly when it was. . . . It was when they began to talk. With that event timelessness was ended.
Dan Lacy, 1961:1.

□ □ No human infant could survive without other people, and no member of *Homo sapiens* develops into a *human* being unless he experiences interactions with human beings. Each of us has identity in relation to mankind. An infant cut off from human interaction may develop physically, but he may not become fully human.
John W. Keltner, 1970:290.

△

Being Human Has Nothing To Do With Communication	
Disagree 1 2 3 ? 5 6 7 Agree	
A man becomes human as he learns to communicate.	
Disagree 1 2 3 ? 5 6 7 Agree	
The better communicator a man is, the more human he is.	
Disagree 1 2 3 ? 5 6 7 Agree	

△ △ We ordinarily think of communication . . . as being directed from person to person. However, it is quite possible for a person to talk to a machine, a machine to a person, and a machine to a machine.
Norbert Wiener, 1954:76.

now opens before us promises to change human communication in far-reaching and *irreversible* ways. This change appears likely to be equal to or greater than the one that occurred when man first developed the capacity for speech communication. We shall each learn what it means to be a space age communicator, and we shall change as we learn.

The space age revolution in communication appears likely to unfold within a timespan of 50 years or less rather than 500 thousand years or more.[°] To put the matter differently, a twenty-year-old human stands at the midpoint in communication history; he will personally experience as much change in human communication in the next fifty years as was experienced by mankind during the last 500 thousand years. The purpose of this book is to help you cope with that change. Or to say the same thing in another way, the purpose[°°] of this book is to advance the right of man to communicate.

1.2 OUR CYBERNETIC WORLD

We can choose to be most interested in the past, the present, or the future. Our attention shifts to the consequences of present change for the immediate and intermediate future. We also begin to ask: What changes should we now plan to make at what future time? We begin to develop a space age attitude toward change. This is a new course in human history.

Our space age attitude is best described as cybernetic. We employ cybernetic methods. Cybernetics[□] is defined as the processes of control and communication in man and machine; cybernetics includes both communication facilities and messages. The term *cybernetics*e most often appears along with terms such as technology, communication and culture—our concerns in this section of the book. The term *cybernetics*[□□] also is related to communication networks and communication systems, purpose and feedback, synergy and serendipity. These concepts and other closely related concepts will be explored more fully in later sections of the book. The ASQ method for the study of human communication (*A*ttitudes-*S*kills-*Q*uestions) is based on cybernetics.

From our cybernetic view of human communication, we find that technology and communication and culture are so closely related that it often is difficult to deal with them separately.[△]

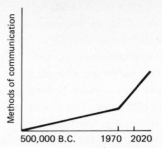

[°]   We are at the beginning of a chain reaction. The ingredients already exist. The fuse has been lit. It is clear that we now have a [communication technology] so powerful that it will take many decades for us to use it to its full potential. But its full potential is far beyond our cleverest imagining today.
James Martin, 1969:28.

[°°]   When you get the purpose-sentence, remember that it is primarily for you. . . . Like a ship's compass, it can be checked occasionally to make sure that your course is steady toward your goal.
J. Jeffery Auer, 1967:94.

[□]   We have decided to call the entire field of control and communication theory, whether in the machine or in the animal, by the name Cybernetics.
Norbert Wiener, 1961:11.

[□□]   The term "Cybernetics" derives from the Greek word *kybernetes*, which means steersman. . . . The Latin term *gubernator* is derived from the Greek, and hence also our word governor.
Charles R. Dechert, 1967:11.

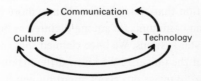

[△]   The sum total of values, beliefs, and practices of a civilization may be called its culture. Because communication is the primary means by which culture is transmitted from one

But we must separate technology and culture from communication just enough to help us discover how communication does what it does. That separation or analysis provides a starting point for the study of human communication in the space age.

1.2.1 Technology

Technology° may be viewed as those inventions of man that become widely useful through the process of manufacturing. Communication satellites and telephones are good examples; so are spaceships and jet planes. Technology°° is inanimate and nonliving.

Technological devices, taken one by one, amount to rather little.□ A disconnected telephone mechanism in a new home is only a fair paperweight. But wire that same telephone mechanism into the telephone network of the community, and it suddenly has a thousand known and potential uses. The home community network can also be connected to a satellite; and three properly positioned satellites provide a world network. Each home community can be connected to any other community; any telephone can be connected to any other telephone in the world; any person can talk to any other person.□□ How many digits would be required for worldwide direct dialing?

A car parked in a garage is a big toy for a small child. But decide to go—rather than telephone—to a destination anywhere in the world. Drive your car to a nearby airport. From that airport board an airplane and fly to any other airport in the world, rent a car, and drive to your destination. All road networks lead to a nearby airport. Each airport is a ground station in a worldwide air transportation network.△ How many airline passenger seats are needed? Where? When?

Our use of communication technology often creates both problems and possibilities on a world scale. Fifteen digits are required for worldwide direct dialing. But when each person learns to want his own mobile telephone, the problem changes again. How many airline passenger seats are needed? All of us know we sometimes can't reserve a seat at the exact time we wish to travel; other times, we are one of but 20 passengers on a 200 seat airliner for a 2,000-mile flight. We have problems to solve.

Telecommunication technology and transportation technology encircle the globe.△△ The telecommunication technology—satellites, telephones, radio, television—makes possible a worldwide telecommunication network; the transportation technology—airplanes, automobiles, trains, ships—make

generation to the next . . . it is not surprising to find the culture of a civilization revealed in its communication. By studying communication within a society it is possible to enhance our understanding of that society's culture.
T. Clevenger, Jr., and J. Matthews, 1971:1.

°
(Technology)

°° There is nearly universal agreement that technology includes physical artifacts such as power plants, telecommunication systems, and airplanes, as well as the physical actions that alter the environment. . . .
Joseph F. Coates, 1971:225.

□ Technology is not comprehensible in isolation but only within a social political environment.
Colin Cherry, 1971:xi.

□□ Inventions that increase speed and immediacy of information have always changed the nature of their world. The introduction in Europe of printing by movable type in the fifteenth century helped to produce the Renaissance, the Reformation. . . . Television in the 1950's crystallized the civil-rights revolution, rebellion on the campuses, and a dislocation between those who were shaped by the new machine and those who were not.
Ben H. Bagdikian, 1971:xii.

△ Whereas tribal man became disoriented when separated from his local group and surroundings, and early city/local state man could barely conceive of any larger territory, we are now in a period when many men think casually in terms of the whole earth.
John McHale, 1969:12.

△△ In particular, our global communication network, though as yet largely confined to Western traffic usage, at last offers the beginning of practical means for realistically operating the International Organizations, without requiring people to shed all their national and cultural identities
Colin Cherry, 1971:202.

possible a transportation communication network. Taken together, the two world networks create new choices and open new opportunities for man.

Both the telecommunication and transportation networks are *demand limited.* Their present size is limited by present demand. We can now manufacture more satellites and airplanes, for instance, than our world can use. The supply can exceed the known demand. But how can we predict the demand for major worldwide services when such services have not been available before? The use of technology is strongly influenced by culture.[°]

We turn now to the matter of human cultures.

1.2.2 Culture

Culture[°°] can be considered to be everything man learns from and creates through experience that he values enough to pass on from one generation to the next. Speech communication patterns and dramatic literature are convenient examples; so are human institutions such as local political parties and the United Nations. Cultural heritage contrasts with biological inheritance. Culture[□] is not inherited; it is relearned by each man.

Technological change in the world leads to a change in culture; it may promote cultural variety or cultural similarity. Machines make time for more human leisure. Greater leisure time may provide the opportunities for development of new patterns of human experience that move through the stages from fad to cult to subculture. Worldwide television news broadcasts and other informational programs can lead on to cultural similarity.[□ □] The question before us is this: in any culture, to what extent should communication introduce variety and to what extent should it promote similarity? What mix of variety and similarity is best for us as we live in our world? [△]

Today a man may become mono-cultural, bi-cultural, or multi-cultural. Culture can be viewed as something that can be ordered on a line from one to several. A man may consider himself to be a member of one, two, or several cultural groups. Culture may also be viewed as something more fluid. A man may consider himself at one time to be a member of a single cultural group; at another time, of several groups; or he may not wish to look at the matter of cultural identity that way at all. There are choices today, and increasingly persons feel strongly about those choices they have.

The possible viewpoints about culture are as varied as the cultures that develop them. McLuhan, for instance, insists that the technologies of telecommunication and transportation make all of us members of the same global village; we are, one and all, members of a single worldwide tech-

[°] The world we now live in, with its particular qualities of speed, mobility, rapidity of change and communication, has no historical precedent as a cultural context. Man can now see farther, move faster, produce more than ever before. Devices such as high-speed cameras, radio telescopes, and the orbital satellites have extended the range of our sensory experience far beyond that ever imagined. Besides enormously enlarging the extent of the physical world available to our direct experience in an ordinary lifetime, such new means provide us—through the multimedia, TV, motion pictures, picture magazines and newspapers—with what is virtually an extension of our culture world. A constant stream of moving, fleeting images of the world is presented for our daily appraisal. Through these means we extend ourselves physically, telescoping time, moving through history, spanning the world through unprecedented visual and aural means of experience.
John McHale, 1969:295.

[°°]
Culture

[□] A culture consists of the shared meanings and values that the members of a group hold in common. Culture is acquired through the interaction and communication that goes on among the members of a group.
Caroline B. Rose, 1965:54.

[□ □] A common culture, then, is a common set of stable, habitual preferences and priorities in men's attention and behavior, as well as in their thoughts and feelings. Many of these preferences may involve communication; it is usually easier for men to communicate within the same culture than across its boundaries.
Karl W. Deutsch, 1966:88.

[△]

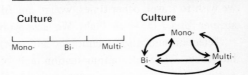
We are all members of the same global village.

Disagree 1 2 3 ? 4 5 6 7 Agree

Culture

| Mono- | Bi- | Multi- |

Culture

Mono-
Bi-
Multi-

The fifth account is by a man who heads one of the most remarkable institutions of man, the East-West Center in Honolulu. Its full title is the Center for Technical and Cultural Interchange Between East and West. The institution supports programs that enable men to interchange their cultural and technological heritage. Briefly, interchange describes a way of communicating that enables men of diverse cultural backgrounds to share information for some mutual purpose. This important concept of interchange will be developed more fully in a later chapter.

The five accounts show the patterns of change in the communities of man.° They show the simple and powerful relationship between technology, communication, and culture:

- The communication technologies enable man to travel and to hear and see further than ever before.
- Humans communicate with a growing variety of other humans as they seek to obtain information.°°
- Human cultures shift and grow from the dual influence of technology and communication.

The availability of great quantities of new information is the fundamental key. Information unlocks the door that leads on to change in technology, culture, and human communication.□

1.3 COMMUNICATION REVOLUTIONS

The major communication revolutions of the past continue to evolve and reshape the fundamentals of human communication in the present and for the future.□□ In the sections that follow, communication by speech, writing, print, and telecommunication will be briefly examined. Finally, the special significance of the space age for human communication will be discussed and some possible future revolutions will be identified.

The term *revolution* often describes a large and sudden change. A government is removed by the revolutionary forces at 2:30 on Thursday afternoon, and by 2:35 the revolutionary government is installed and collecting taxes. In political revolutions, the underground can replace the existing government and can itself become the establishment in a matter of minutes. The so-called *communication revolutions* have not and do not turn out that way. Rather than replace what existed before, the changes introduced by a communication revolution make a place for themselves along with the patterns and possibilities for communication that exist at the time. The revolutions in communication weave new possibilities into a

° Most importantly, these changes have taken place almost simultaneously—within the lifetime of one generation—and the impact of knowledge of the change is world wide. . . . Until yesterday, the village dwellers everywhere were cut off from the urban life of their own country; today radio and television bring them sounds and sights of cities all over the world. *Margaret Mead, 1970:56.*

°° It is the maximal use of communications and the willingness to learn from experience which we see as the routes into the future. . . . *R. Theobald and J. M. Scott, 1972:16.*

□

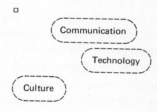

□□ New methods of communication usually create new cultures, disrupting old assumptions and causing revolutions. *Ben H. Bagdikian, 1971:204.*

half-million-year long trend. There are only revolutionary breakthroughs in the long evolutionary trend of human communication.

Evolution would, of course, be a better term than communication revolution.[°] But evolution does not make headlines. Because of the turtle-like pace of evolution, daily attention over long periods of time is required to discover a trend and to determine where it leads. The first telephone conversation was hailed as revolutionary. A hundred years later, the telephone grows in importance in areas as diverse as teenage dating and multinational business.[°°] The other misnamed communication revolutions evolve in much the same way. In human communication, there is change, a growing accelerating change, and much of it is for the betterment of man. The term *communication revolution,* then, is best understood within its own special context.

1.3.1 Communication Through Speech

How man first learned to communicate through speech remains a mystery.[□] There are, as you may know, dozens of theories about the origins of speech. The names given these theories suggest something of their content: Divine Origin, Echoic, Vocal Play, Oral Gesture, Social Pressure, and Social Control.[□□] When did speech originate? Many scholars have guessed. Five hundred thousand years ago seems a reasonable estimate.

Speech communication is the first and probably the greatest of the several communication revolutions. Speech either made coordinated group life possible or added a major new dimension to it. Speech also enabled groups of men to share their individual stores of knowledge; that sharing develops the powerful "group intelligence" we now call culture.

From the earliest times to the present day, there have been two major themes in the study of speech communication.[△] Each of these themes develops attitudes, requires skills, and generates questions. Today, the most descriptive names for these two themes are:

- Information theme
- Association theme

In our varied history, in our diverse practices in the present, and in our alternative futures, a tension between information and association sometimes arises.

The two speech communication themes center in man's most basic requirements. Man requires information to achieve those purposes that arise out of the problems and possibilities inherent in his family and home community.[△△] Man requires association to build and maintain those interpersonal relationships that permit him to be an intimate member of his

[°] In its most general sense, the word "evolution" means the progressive transformations of a system in the course of time. *Rene Dubos, 1968:63.*

[°°] There were about a million overseas telephone calls in 1950. By 1960 the figure had jumped to nearly four million. And six years later the number was up to ten million. Data communications are increasing even faster. *Hal Hellman, 1969:62.*

[□] If we search through the most primitive and the most ancient evidence of intellectual activity, through myths, magic, or religions, we find one question that is repeated over and over: from what source comes the power of speech? *Eric H. Lenneberg, 1967:1.*

[□□] There is no record of when man began to speak or of the steps by which he advanced to the stage where even the idea of recording his speech was possible. . . . It is quite possible that all of the theories which have been advanced contain elements of truth . . . it is equally certain that none of them has satisfactorily told the whole story. *Giles W. Gray and Claude M. Wise, 1959:456.*

[△] Human Communication
Information theme
Association theme

[△△] All communication has for its purpose the transmission of information to produce a response. The purpose of a communication system is the efficient transmission of information. *John P. Froehlich, 1969:1.*

family and home community.° Information and association both touch every aspect of man's humanity.

Up until about 1750 or 1800, most men lived out their lives in the traditional village community. They learned to communicate within the family circle in the home community. All or nearly all of their communication occurred within that community setting with persons who lived nearby and were well known. Communication was speech communication. Under these circumstances, members of a community become specialists in communicating with one another. Had most humans continued to live out their lives in the community of their birth, isolated from outside influences, the world would most likely have continued to be much as it was from the beginning of agriculture up to about 1750.

In the traditional community,°° a harmony evolves between information and association. Within the family setting, Son learns from Father, and Daughter learns from Mother. A basic family and community culture is transmitted. And it is maintained by the new generation. The cycle repeats with little variety.

In any community, new information changes old associations. The traveler brings information on how people in other communities live. Odysseus, Marco Polo,□ and the mythical Gulliver are well-known examples. Today, men who return from a journey in space bring rock samples and tell of the sights along the way. Thus, information flows and associations evolve.□□

Information from the "outside" flows into a community in one of two ways. A member of the community leaves the community, lives elsewhere for a time, and returns to his home community differently informed. A college student who studies abroad is a good modern example. Or a traveler from the outside associates for a time within a community. He informs community members of other ways of doing things. Community members thereby acquire information. And they try and test that information within their community. The Peace Corps volunteer is an example. The college student and the Peace Corps volunteer both are agents of a community-based interchange.

At each stage along the way, a traveler communicates through speech. He talks with the people he meets. He *both* informs and is informed. He participates in new types of *inter*cultural human associations.△ He is an agent of change in a particular sense. Change is a two-way process. Change through speech communication, then, is quite often interchange.

From time to time, speech communication has been viewed as either information *or* association. The logic of Aristotle predisposes us to seek the either/or type of logical category. In another discipline, for example, much

° . . . human communication, wherever it is genuine, is always a person-to-person call—never a transcribed message from an anonymous answering service to whomever it may concern. *Floyd W. Matson and Ashley Montagu, 1967:6.*

°° A postfigurative culture is one in which change is so slow and imperceptible that grandparents, holding newborn grandchildren in their arms, cannot conceive of any other future for the children than their own past lives. *Margaret Mead, 1970:1.*

□ . . . Marco Polo . . . narrated his success to a cellmate in a Genoese prison, and the account was written in a kind of French. *John W. Black, in Frank Geldard, 1965:101.*

□□ Subcultures within the dominant pattern of a culture may be shown to have people with vastly different *images* of what is desirable in communication, different *attitudes* toward communication, different *value systems* in some respects, and different *habits* of communication. *A. C. Baird, F. H. Knower, S. L. Becker, 1971:24.*

△ In addition, I suggest that you analyze your behavior patterns vis-à-vis people from other cultures. You tend to treat them as "culture types" and sources of cross-cultural information rather than individual personalities. I know from your computer-record that you have already half-perceived this pattern, but so far you have failed to act on this perception. *R. Theobald and J. M. Scott, 1972:43.*

discussion centered on whether heredity *or* environment determined the intelligence of a young adult. Today, as in many earlier times, discussion centers on whether association or information should be the goal of speech communication. Those who urge emphasis on association insist that the end purpose of speech communication is better interpersonal relationships. If people loved each other more, the reasoning goes, all problems of communication would evaporate. Those who urge emphasis on information point out that most of man's difficulties in communication arise out of ignorance. If he knew more about communication, knew more about the world, the main problems in human communication would disappear. And so it goes.

The ASQ method we follow in this book seeks to clarify the relationship between information and association. It is not a particularly easy task, but it is an important one.

1.3.2 Handwriting

In the beginning° the written word was an instrument to provide a permanent record of the word that had been spoken. One of the earliest written records, as you might guess, turns out to be a set of instructions prepared by a father to guide his son on ways of talking with people. Such early written documents reveal the several levels of close relationship between speech and writing. The human urge to make marks that will guide the future action of family and friends shows through, too.

The early written records serve to date human writing as coming into use around 3000 B.C. Clay°° tablets filed in dry cave storage libraries were available for later use by the archeologist who had the time to search them out and the turn of mind to learn to read them. The origins of writing are themselves recorded in writing. By 3000 B.C., then, writing was quite well developed.

An invention as important as writing did not remain only a means of recording speech, though that use still is a major one. In time, writing also became a means for working with words to create a message that had not yet been spoken. The shaping of a written history of a community, for instance, goes beyond the possibilities of an oral history. The communicator who writes out what he plans to say at some future time uses writing in another important way.

Some 5,000 years later, most adults can make a mark on paper that stands as their signature. But many cannot write a simple instruction or a personal letter. In the traditional village, in many communities of the world, the letter writer does a thriving business. He sets down on paper those words, that message, an individual wants transmitted beyond a distance or during a time that he does not choose to travel.

° But if men are human because they can talk, they are civilized because they can read. . . . Until there were words that could be preserved exactly and indisputably beyond the limits of memory, there could not be laws and . . . administration complex enough to organize a city. . . . This was possible only with the second revolution in communication, the invention of writing.
Dan Lacy, 1961:1.

°° It was probably . . . about five thousand years ago, that the Sumerians . . . came upon the idea of writing on clay. Their first attempts were crude and pictographic. . . .
S. N. Kramer, in Jacquette Hawkes, 1963:373.

Petroglyph, Island of Hawaii

Photo by Jill Bennett Elkins

On the receipt of the reply to the letter, the professional letter writer becomes the letter reader. The letter writer–reader is an instructive man to observe. The hand writes a message to be transmitted to some other place at some future time.

We appreciate now that what handwriting introduced was an external form of message storage.° Thus, it became possible to store a message for periods of time longer than a man's life. At first, only a few persons could read and write. Those few were able to control access to that information. While speech communication skills were learned within the family by everyone, only a few learned to read and write. "Readin' and Ritin' " are learned, if they are learned at all, in school.

1.3.3 Printing

More than four thousand years after handwriting systems were developed, printing was invented. The work of Gutenberg in the early 1400s is often used as the reference date for the start of printing. Like other inventions at that time, printing took several hundred years to become widespread. It has only been within the last decade that easy access to a printing press has been possible for individual communicators. Anyone with access to a copying machine has a private printing press.

The print revolution introduces a *multiplier* effect°° into human communication. Print makes it possible to transmit a message across time and distance and, most importantly, to do so on a large scale. The making of many copies of a single message introduces a new possibility into human communication. But it only introduces a possibility, for it requires reading skill to complete the communication cycle. Many adults cannot read, and many others read so poorly that they probably misunderstand more than they understand. This, of course, is as unfortunate as it is unnecessary. Children, almost without exception, learn to communicate through speech before age five. The home is also an excellent setting for learning to read *before age five.*

Printing also introduces a major imbalance into human communication. For every sender, there are many receivers. This opens the way for a few communicators to transmit their messages to a great many receivers—and the normal corrective feedback processes operate poorly when they operate at all. Errors as well as information are transmitted.

1.3.4 Transportation and telecommunication

As we begin the space age, it is helpful to look backward in time. We can trace the origins of the two great communication networks. Then, as now, communication networks "carry" human information.

° Writing, even more than speech, made possible the creation of a storehouse of knowledge, and the supplementing of memory by means of records. It was this facility of preserving what individuals had found out that, more than anything else, made human progress possible.
Bertrand Russell, 1961:8.

°° Within little more than a half century after the first European printing, substantially the whole corpus of Western knowledge had been reduced to print . . . within a couple of generations the number of people able to . . . make use of the new knowledge . . . became hundreds of times as large.
Dan Lacy, 1961:6.

Daily Newspapers, per 100 inhabitants

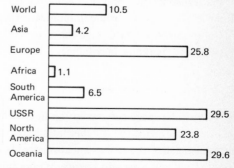

World	10.5
Asia	4.2
Europe	25.8
Africa	1.1
South America	6.5
USSR	29.5
North America	23.8
Oceania	29.6

Conference Board, 1972:231

The evolution of the "power" of speech communication coincides with the beginning of human history. The year 500,000 B.C. serves as an approximate date. At that time, all human information was stored in the human memory. "Word of mouth" information was transported by the man on foot. Somewhat later, the alternatives of drum talk and smoke signals came into use; these inventions are the fundamental forms of telecommunication. Earth distance is the critical matter.°

From the human viewpoint, the linkages provided by the technologies of transportation and telecommunication shrink the size of the world. A man walks to a nearby community. He associates with members of that community and exchanges information with them. Later, he may engage in drum talk with them. Or, the events may occur in reverse order. The drum network may carry the message, "Come to the meeting." Either way, humans are linked by their networks of communication.°°

So far as we know, from 500,000 B.C. up to about 1750 A.D., change was rather slow. A few of the traditional villages had become cities. Paris, London, New York, and Tokyo are among the early cities that are "world cities" today.□ They were then and are now *communication centers* for their regions. In and around these cities, communication facilities were invented and developed. The period from 1750 to about 1900 saw transoceanic steamboats and telephone, trains and telegraph, automobiles and wireless radio come into use. By 1900, the transportation and telecommunication technologies had gathered force to the point of becoming a communication revolution.

The transportation and telecommunication revolution unfolds in a seventy-year period from about 1900 to about 1970.□□ By 1900, national rail and telegraph networks exist. The nation state is created by the telegraph and the train. International telephone service is in operation. The International Telecommunication Union works out the agreements necessary for the later emergence of world communication networks.

At the beginning of the space age in 1970, the separate national linkage of the transportation and telecommunication technologies were taking shape as full-service world communication networks. The jet plane and the communication satellite forge these networks and make a world community possible and, perhaps, inevitable.

1.3.5 Space Age Communication

In a word, the space age revolution in communication is *cybernetic*. More precisely, the space age is cybernetic in method.△ The space age is sometimes also called the communication era. Thus, the usual definition of cybernetics as the art and science of communication and control in man and

° The expression "this shrinking world" is commonplace today but it is another deceptive one. . . . That is, the world has shrunk as a result of faster communication, but only in *time scale.*
Colin Cherry, 1971:xiii.

°° As world communication networks expand, which they are doing rapidly, so we must increasingly come to see other peoples and nations in terms of their various institutions. Further, if we have no personal acquaintances whatever, we can see them only as collections of institutions.
Colin Cherry, 1971:175.

□ Government and trade were invariably the original [reasons for] . . . the world cities. But these places early became the centers where professional talents of all kinds congregated. . . . Students and teachers are drawn to the world cities; they commonly contain the great universities. . . . Inevitably, the world cities have become the places where information is gathered and disseminated . . . In this century also the world cities have naturally become the headquarters of the great national radio and television networks.
Peter Hall, 1966:7.

□□ We have come a long way since the days when information and man moved at the same rate. . . . The movement of information has been equal to the speed of light for a number of years—since the advent of broadcasting.
A. C. Baird, F. H. Knower, S. L. Becker, 1971: 191

△

The real objective of the space program, though not stated or even fully recognized by its participants, may ultimately be to make us a society of the universe rather than of the earth alone.
Simon Ramo, 1970:59.

Impossible 1 2 3 ? 5 6 7 Possible

machine seems doubly appropriate. Space age developments in communication are intertwined with cybernetic theory, or method, or approach, or viewpoint.

As indicated earlier, a cybernetic view of communication leads to a concern with communication networks and communication systems.[°] Fortunately, a cybernetic approach to the study of communication helps us to make matters quite simple. For instance, only two networks and three systems provide the foundation for all of human communication. The concept of purpose provides a focus for our discussion. It also provides a simple means of testing how well human communication works.

In the space age, the central question is: What does human communication do? What communication does, and what happens as a consequence of human communication are the basic matters. Notice the different directions on which the basic question leads the asker:

- What *is* communication?
- What *does* communication do?

The "is" question leads on to classification; for example, "There are twenty-two types of public speeches." The "does" question leads on to the study of purpose, network, system, and messages. Communication systems operate to achieve a purpose—that is what they *do*.[°°]

In the space age, there are three milestones of importance to us. The Telstar communication satellite demonstrated international television capabilities; Apollo II demonstrated that man could travel to another "planet;" and Pioneer 10 demonstrates our interest in engaging in communication with "intelligent life" on other planets. The "message" of Pioneer 10, in some ways, is the most profound of all. Pioneer 10 documents the emergence of a space age attitude. It is this attitude that leads us to extend our communication skills and to pose the searching new questions required by our changing situation. In short, the ASQ method starts from this attitude.

A large portion of the book centers on the influence of the space age on the day to day communication of men and women everywhere. That space age influence is both simple and practical. While that space age cybernetic approach creates some new problems, it will enable the solution of many others; and it opens many new possibilities.

The major change[□] brought about by the space age revolution in communication is deceptively simple. At first glance some persons even assume it is just another word game. But the larger message is that cybernetic concepts enable men to "hook their brains" together in new ways and thereby achieve mutually shared purposes beyond those that could be achieved by a single individual.[□□]

[°] The communications revolution will have the most profound influence upon that fairly recent invention the nation-state. . . . What the railroad and the telegraph did to continental areas a hundred years ago, the jet plane and the communications satellite will soon be doing to the whole world.
Arthur C. Clarke, 1972:162.

[°°] The most fundamental concept in cybernetics is that of "difference," either that two things are recognizably different or that one thing has changed with time. . . . All the changes that may occur with time are naturally included, for when plants grow and planets age and machines move, some change from one state to another is implicit.
W. Ross Ashby, 1963:9.

[□] A very important change, even a "revolution," in communications can take place without necessarily being based on major changes in technology. All that may be required is a change . . . under which the technique of communication is employed.
Dan Lacy, 1961:6.

[□□] The mutualistic view . . . is that there are only parts, and parts create a system of interaction. There is no "whole" prior to the parts.
M. Maruyama and J. A. Dator, 1971:15.

In Chapter 2, the special significance of the space age revolution for human communication will be examined.

1.3.6 Future Revolutions

Even before the space age cybernetic revolution in communication runs its course, several more revolutions may occur. As we shall see in the last section of the book, a number of breakthroughs are possible. We shall mention only three such "changes" here.

1.3.6.1 Micro Communication Technology

Communication technology grows smaller, faster, cheaper, and smarter.[o] The first radio receivers were packaged in boxes that took two men to carry. Bigger was better. Year by year the radio has been reduced in size and increased in portability. Some radios now are hearing-aid size. Next ones may be implanted, as the heart pacemakers now are, under the human skin. But instead of a receive-only radio, such a device could be a transceiver— both transmit and receive—for both audio and visual signals. The visual device could be in the eye, the audio in the ear.[oo] Connected directly to satellite, such a device would augment human intelligence in difficult-to-predict ways; it would also open the possibilities of control. What consequences would you expect from such a transceiver?

1.3.6.2 Man–Machine Communication

In the immediate future, we humans will spend more time talking with intelligent machines.[□] We have grown accustomed to receive "prerecorded" time-of-day, weather, airflight arrival, and stock report messages. We also respond when we are "asked by a machine" to leave a message. At some medical centers, basic medical information is obtained from a patient by a computer. More than half of the persons so interviewed refuse to believe that they were not in contact with a real human being. In time, might we humans come to prefer to communicate with a friendly machine[□□] rather than another human? If so, what might the consequences be?

1.3.6.3 Earthman–ETI Communication

A third possibility[△] for a next communication revolution arises from the possibility of earth contact with intelligences from a distant galaxy, an extraterrestrial intelligence or ETI. Planets other than earth appear suitable for life. Such being the case, at least some of that life might well be more intelligent than earthman. We are more likely to contact, or be contacted by, the more rather than the less intelligent of those beings. When such

[o] . . . at this very moment there are appearing simultaneously, on the twin horizons of the infinitely large and the infinitely small, unmistakable signs of a breakthrough into a new order of creation. . . .
Arthur C. Clarke, 1972:80.

[oo] All these communication media basically do one thing: they remove certain constraints which hitherto existed upon the *possibilities* for better international co-operation.
Colin Cherry, 1971:169.

[□] In the world of the future, then, we feel that the computer will become invisible, as the telephone now is. . . . In short, computers will gradually cease to be amazing, although the things they will be able to do would astound us today.
Charles T. Meadow, 1970:413.

[□□]

> **I'd rather communicate with a friendly machine than with a hostile human.**
>
> **Never 1 2 3 ? 5 6 7 Always**

[△] The possibility of life beyond the Earth evokes today strong and partisan emotions. There are some who want very much to believe that extraterrestrial life—particularly the intelligent variety—is common throughout the universe; and there are those who are committed to the view that extraterrestrial life is impossible, or so rare as to have neither practical nor philosophical interest.
I. S. Shklovskii and C. Sagan, 1966:13.

contact is made, it seems certain communication on earth will change. The question is, in what ways?[o]

Three possible upcoming revolutions in human communication have been hinted at above. They along with other possibilities will be explored more fully in the final section of the book. We turn now to examine some of the consequences of change that changes faster today than it did yesterday.

1.4 ACCELERATION OF CHANGE[oo]

The human, it is said, is the only animal who knows that a day will come when he no longer lives. He is told of the day he was born; he celebrates that day each year as family and friends honor him on his birthday. He knows in a general way how many birthdays he will celebrate. He knows he has a lifespan, but he has no sure way at this time of knowing how great that span will be.

Human communication develops, and from time to time, redevelops during the full lifespan of everyone. For an individual,[□] looking at his own communication activity, it is helpful to consider that communication in a lifespan framework. To appreciate the tides of change that affect human communication, a look two generations into the past and two generations into the future will be helpful.

The birth of your grandparents and the death of your grandchildren provides a family-span of nearly a hundred years into the past and a hundred years into the future—the better part of the two great centuries in the story of human communication.[□□]

Man is the animal who communicates. Quite clearly, if by some misfortune, he does not develop the skill necessary to communicate with his fellow man, he lives as a stranger in his home community, and he does not fully develop as a human. If you grant this much, does it not also follow that the better communicator a man is, the more human a man he is?

The acceleration of change can be observed in many areas. Means of transportation are a case in point. For most of human history, a man could travel no further in a day than he could walk. A man can walk ten to twenty miles a day. If he extends himself he can cover as much as fifty miles a day. Now even the slower forms of surface transportation—cars, trains, and ships—exceed that distance per hour. Traffic jams are, of course, a different and instructive matter.

A similar acceleration in change[△] is obvious throughout the field of communication. For thousands of years after man learned to communicate through speech, no major new developments are evident.[△△] Handwriting comes about 3000 B.C. Printing follows at about 1400 A.D. Telecom-

[o] Think of the questions we might ask of *homo superior,* questions of creation, of immortality, of purpose. Or the upsettingly simple answers we might receive to questions unasked, the gaps of theory that might be bridged or the deadend theories that need never develop, the variety of ways such intelligence might transmit its information to us.
Neil P. Ruzic, 1970:217.

[oo]
Solomon Grundy
Walked on Monday
Rode on Tuesday
Motored Wednesday
Planed on Thursday
Rocketed Friday
Spaceship Saturday
Time Machine Sunday
Where is the end for
Solomon Grundy?
Frederick Winsor and Marian Parry, 1958:22.

[□] . . . man retains a large part of his brain unused, unidentified for specific function, awaiting something.
Neil P. Ruzic, 1970:221.

[□□]

Generation	Probable Life-span
Your grandparents	1905–1975
Your parents	1930–2005
Your own	1955–2030
Your children	1980–2060
Your grandchildren	2005–2085

[△]

> **CHANGE**
> **Uncomfortable** 1 2 3 ? 5 6 7 **Comfortable**

[△△]

Speech	500,000 B.C.
Writing	3000 B.C.
Printing	1400 A.D.
Trans./Tele.	1900 A.D.
Space age	1970 A.D.
Next revolution	1985 A.D.?

munication and transportation can be dated at about 1900 A.D. Space age communication begins at about 1969. It seems likely the next communication revolution(s) will be underway well before the year 2000. We live at a time made distinctive and, sometimes, uncomfortable by its rate of change.

1.5 THE RIGHT TO COMMUNICATE

The right to communicate develops from a foundation of *mutuality*:[°]

Any two (or several, or many) humans have the right to communicate

- For any mutual purpose
- At some suitable time and place
- Under mutually agreed on conditions
- With appropriate communication facilities

This statement is a first attempt to put into words the right of man to communicate.

1.5.1 The Universal Declaration of Human Rights

The Universal Declaration of Human Rights was approved in the United Nations on December 10, 1948. These articles set a code of conduct for all men. There are thirty articles in the code. In the preamble, the code recognizes "the inherent dignity and the equal and inalienable rights of all members of the human family. . . ." The articles support the individual man against undue and illegal pressures and powers of the state.

Article 19[°°] bears most directly on the right of man to communicate. The phrase "right to freedom of opinion and expression" refers to basic rights of an individual to his own views on any matter and of his right to express those views. Equally, the individual has the right "to seek, receive and impart information." The case for the individual is well stated. But communication is a social activity. At least two persons must participate to make communication possible.[□] The right of the individual is bounded by the rights of other individuals.

While Article 19 sets forth a right to information, Article 20[□□] concerns the right of association. The individual is free to join an association; he is also free not to join an association. The right to associate and *not* to associate is vitally important.

1.5.2 The Right of Association

The right to communicate is a *mutual* right. An individual must be free to enter into a communicative association, and he must be free to *not* enter into a communicative association.[△] Mutuality rests on freedom of choice.

[°]   A genuine dealing with one another in which it must occur that a working together—I do not say, a coexistence, that is not enough, I say and mean, despite all the monstrous difficulties, a cooperation—must be preferred to the common destruction.
Martin Buber, 1967:58.

[°°]   Everyone has the right to freedom of opinion and expression; this includes freedom to hold opinions without interference and to seek, receive and impart information and ideas through any media and regardless of frontiers.
Article 19.

[□]

The right to communicate is a *mutual* right.

Seldom 1 2 3 ? 5 6 7 Always

[□□]
1. Everyone has the right to freedom of peaceful assembly and association.
2. No one may be compelled to belong to an association.
Article 20.

[△]   Relationships are said to be *nonvoluntary* when an individual is constrained to a relationship in which his outcomes are relatively poor and/or is excluded from alternative relationships in which his outcomes are relatively good.
J. W. Thibaut and H. H. Kelley, 1967:186.

Article 20 states that an individual cannot be compelled to join an association. In the sense intended here, he cannot be coerced into a communicative association. It is a violation of his human rights. In a similar way, the U.S. Constitution specifies that a man must be advised that he need not testify against himself. Even when he is required to be physically present in a court, he cannot be compelled—by threat or torture—to testify against himself. He need not associate for any purpose of communication. The individual communicator, then, has the right to remain silent in certain instances.

The right *not* to communicate, if widely practiced, could defeat the right to communicate.° Elected officials for example, exchange part of the right not to communicate for the privilege of holding office. However, the abundance of information and the several ways of obtaining that information reduce the problem that arises when one individual wishes to communicate and another individual does not. When alternate action routes are readily available, the difficulty is not likely to become a serious one.

The right not to associate could reduce the instances of abuse that arise in some attempts to communicate. One suggested test comes from Albert Einstein, by way of the writings of Norbert Wiener.°° Einstein was fond of observing that "nature was subtle but not mean." A scientist attempting to discover the laws of nature could expect a challenging but not an impossible task. Nature would not bluff or lie, nor would nature create distracting noises. In other words, the tone of the scientist's research venture is cooperative rather than competitive. Nature is not an adversary. There seems no valid reason for assuming that human communications should be made *artificially* difficult by bluffing and noise making, that is, by competition or an adversary approach.□ Given the limited amount of time in the life of any human, he must have the right to avoid those communication situations which proceeed from an artificially difficult adversary base; and he must be free to *dis*-associate himself from communication situations that transform themselves into competitive communication. Every communicator has alternatives open to him for communication which may be "subtle but not mean." In a word, there are always cooperative alternatives and these can lead on to synergy and serendipity.□□

1.5.3 The Right to Information

As we move toward equal access to the world's information, the individual has more alternatives available to him. As the individual communicator seeks information for any particular purpose, he can gain access to it through other communicators who "know it" or he can obtain information through many other impersonal routes.

°

> **The right *not* to communicate, if widely practiced, could defeat the right to communicate.**
>
> **Disagree 1 2 3 ? 5 6 7 Agree**

°° This distinction between the passive resistance of nature and the active resistance of an opponent suggest a distinction. . . . The [researcher] need not fear that nature will in time discover his tricks and method and change her policy. Therefore, his work is governed by his best moments, whereas a chess player cannot make one mistake without finding an alert adversary ready to take advantage of it. . . . The chess player is governed more by his worst moment than by his best moments.
Norbert Wiener, 1954:36.

□ We realize, for example, that man does not, in the end, master nature in the nineteenth century sense but collaborates within the natural world; his very existence depends upon an intricate balance of forces within which he is also an active agent.
John McHale, 1969:5.

□□ For I speak of nothing else but the real man, of you and of me, of our life and of our world. . . .
Martin Buber, 1958:13.

In practice, the right "to seek, receive, and impart information" is a receive-only right. Information presented as "news" on radio, television, and papers reduce the need to seek information. Thereby, to a large extent human choice is restricted.° Many communicators receive several hours of information and entertainment each day. They do not have the opportunity to impart information on a comparable scale. If the right to impart information was increased through appropriate technology, it could more than offset any local inconvenience that might arise from the right *not* to communicate. The right to communicate must come to mean a balance between the "seek, receive, and impart" operations. This appears to mean that the individual communicator must be free to choose among a suitably large set of potential cocommunicators.

The communicator who listens to anything anyone wishes to say to him is as ill-informed as the communicator who expresses the same view for the forty-third time to the forty-third listener. The notion of seeking (or selecting, or choosing an alternative) is an important part of the right to communicate. The mass media severely restrict the right to *seek*.

1.5.4 Some Requirements

The right to communicate begins with *mutuality*. In much of human communication today mutuality is not the point of departure. For all of us, some new attitudes,°° skills, and questions will be required. Attitudes relating to the role of communication in the life of the individual communicator assume a new importance. Dialog skills in communication become increasingly important; preparing and transmitting a message—a public speech or a newscast, for example—less so. Searching questions about what we humans can together accomplish through communication must be posed and their answers sought. Communication in the world community requires some shifting by you, me, and all of us.□

A few men now enjoy the right to communicate most of the time. Many other men do on rare occasions. Most men do not yet have the right to communicate; we can change that.□□

1.6 SUMMARY

This chapter has sketched a design of human communication through time and across space. The relationship of technology, culture and communication was examined. The five major communication revolutions were sketched. Some of the consequences of change were mentioned. Finally, the right to communicate was discussed.

°
. . . we are in an age where the enormous per capita bulk of communication is met by an ever-thinning stream of total bulk of communication. More and more . . . a product, like the white bread in the bakeries, is made rather for its keeping and selling properties than for its food value.
Norbert Wiener, 1954:132.

°°
The right to communicate requires new:
Attitudes
Skills
Questions

□
If our present troubles can be conquered, Man can look forward to a future immeasurably longer than his past, inspired by a new breadth of vision, a continuing hope perpetually fed by a continuing achievement.
Bertrand Russell, 1961:127.

□□

RIGHT TO COMMUNICATE		
Weak	1 2 3 ? 5 6 7	Strong
Slow	1 2 3 ? 5 6 7	Fast
Passive	1 2 3 ? 5 6 7	Active
Bad	1 2 3 ? 5 6 7	Good

1.S SKILLS: COMMUNICATION IN YOUR HOME COMMUNITY

PURPOSE

To survey the communication facilities in your home community:

- Investigate local communication facilities.
- Discuss among yourselves the state of communication in your home community.
- Update the "message" of Chapter 1 by deleting, revising, and adding to each of the units.

PROJECT

Work with a cocommunicator, or partner. Examine the topics listed below:

- Select one not selected by others.
- Indicate your selection to your instructor.
- Agree on a time to present your report.

Develop a plan:

- Decide what information you will require.
- List likely sources for acquiring that information.
- Interview, discuss, and read as necessary.
- Prepare a brief report appropriate for your purpose.
- Indicate *precisely* what units in Chapter 1 should be updated by the information you obtain.

TOPICS

Space Age Perspective
  One justification for spending money on space exploration is that such adventures demonstrate what men can accomplish when they work together. Can you identify any major changes in outlook or perspective or cooperativeness in your commumity that result from space age developments? Do you detect a space age attitude?
Culture-Technology-Communication
  The global interplay of culture, technology, and communication is evident in some institutions in every home community. Select a local branch of a multi-national business: airline, hotel chain, travel agency, business machines, telephone, telegraph, radio station, TV station, etc. What changes occurred in the last five years? What changes are anticipated in the next five years?

Humanness and Communication

Several academic fields study the relationship between humanness and communication. Interview professionals and students in areas such as anthropology, sociology, information science, English, as well as speech communication. Are the perspectives from the several people working in these fields similar or different?

Speech Communication Pathology

What services are available in your community for those persons who do not develop speech in the normal way? Speech clinics? Speech correction centers? Communication disorders clinics? What tests are applied for admission? What training procedures are used? What tests are applied for "graduation"? What is the major consequence of not getting help when it is needed?

Speech Communication Training

Beyond the informal learning of speech communication in the home, what training programs are available for the normal child? Check language arts programs in pre-school, elementary, and secondary schools. By the time he enters college, how much of what type of speech communication training has the typical freshman had?

Communication Skills

What relationship exists between the four basic communication skill areas of listening, speaking, reading, and writing? Is deafness, or blindness most handicapping? Why?

Writing

Is it any longer necessary to learn to write by hand? Would it be better to begin by learning to typewrite? Or would it be better still to learn to use and make cassette recordings?

Print

List several activities in your community that appear to depend on print. Check to find how many of these activities could be carried out by alternate means of communication. McLuhan claims, "The age of print is passing." Do you agree?

The News as Printed

Collect about seven news reports (from radio, TV, and newspapers) on persons who live in your community. Check in person or by phone with the persons reported on. Ask them what information is accurate and what is inaccurate. Do you find what you expect to find? How do you interpret your findings?

Radio and Television

What are the major consequences of radio listening and television viewing? Work out five questions you think important. Go forth and interview. What patterns do you find? Did you expect to find these patterns?

Cybernetic Approach

The concept of cybernetics is used in a wide variety of areas. Is its meaning similar or different in areas such as education, electrical engineering, business, communication, sociology, biology, and information science? What is general systems theory?

Future Communication Revolutions

What do you expect will be the next major communication revolution? When and how will it begin? What will the consequences be for your home community?

Right to Communicate

Do most people in your community enjoy the right to communicate? Check with your local United Nations Association chapter. Talk with a lawyer interested in free speech, or censorship, or communication law. Ask your family and your friends. What do you find?

1.Q QUESTIONS

1.Q.1 How did you learn to communicate?

Identify the major influences on your present style of communicating. Were you most influenced by your parents? Brothers and sisters? Teachers? Friends? Do you have a communication style that identifies you as a member of a particular home community? Or is your communication style more general?

1.Q.2 Do you enjoy the right to communicate?

Do most persons in your community? What changes would you expect in the world community, if most persons had the right to communicate?

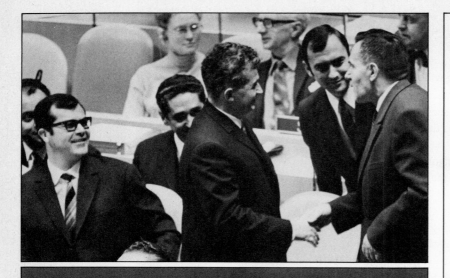

In this chapter, human communication is located within the larger perspective of the space age revolution in communication. This chapter outlines the book and introduces most of the basic concepts. These concepts are developed more fully in the later chapters of the book. Please read this chapter with care before going on to the rest of the book.

```
    I
OVERVIEW  →
```

2

INTRODUCTION TO HUMAN COMMUNICATION

2.1 INTRODUCTION

We live at the dawn of the space age. The winds of change that sweep across the sea of space now catch our ship, The S.S. Earth. Whether we wish it or not, it falls to our lot to steer a safe course through that uncharted sea.° The ports of the past are closed to us. In the dawn hours of the present, together we invent our future in the space age.

Every present contains at least three futures.°° One of these futures is a simple extension of the present; things are as they will be. Another is a much worse future; things go from bad to worse and continue on to the final downfall of mankind. The third future is much better than the present; things become good and continue to get better for all of us. By our actions in the present, together we invent one of those three futures.□

At this moment in time, words do not come easily for me. In myself, and in many others I talk with, I find a sense of wonder, a feeling that there is now more to be said than can yet be spoken. I suspect you too feel this way at times.□ □

For those of us who saw our earth afloat in space, the familiar has also become strange. The earth is not flat like a map. Nor does it have the North and South poles firmly anchored in a frame. The earth floats in the great sea of space. The once familiar ground we walk on, the once familiar words we speak, now have a new dimension.△ We sense that space dimension and feel it even though we cannot yet articulate it. We are shaping a new attitude. For lack of a more exact term, let us call that new attitude the *space age attitude*.

As you clarify and articulate a space age attitude for yourself, you will find that many of your most basic attitudes toward human communication also change.△△ For instance, a new attitude will influence

- The purposes you seek to achieve by communicating.
- When you choose to communicate and when you choose not to communicate.
- The persons with whom you choose to communicate.
- The level of communication skill you will need.
- The questions you seek to answer.☆

The above areas will be reshaped as your new attitude emerges.

It becomes clear that all of us will change some of our basic attitudes toward communication. The space age revolution in communication promises to transform speech communication *at least* as much as the printing press transformed handwriting. We shall next examine two areas where shifts can be expected in present attitudes about communication.

° We are still in the position of the medieval cartographers with their large areas of "Terra Incognita" and their "Here be Dragons." . . .
Arthur C. Clarke, 1972:75.

°°

I expect human communication will change dramatically by the year 2000.

Disagree 1 2 3 ? 5 6 7 Agree

□ . . . what conditions will have to be fulfilled if men are to continue to exist for a long time. So far as physical conditions are concerned, there seems to be no good reason why life, including human life, should not continue for many millions of years. The danger comes, not from man's physical or biological environment, but from himself. He has survived, hitherto, through ignorance. Can he continue to survive now that the useful degree of ignorance is lost?
Bertrand Russell, 1961:69.

□ □
Probable-Possible, my black hen,
She lays eggs in the Relative When.
She doesn't lay eggs in the Positive Now.
Because she's unable to Postulate How.
Frederick Winsor and Marian Parry, 1958:1.

△
The Spring Sea
All day, with gently undulating swell,
The spring sea rose and fell, and rose and fell. . .
Buson, in Harold Stewart, 1960:14.

△ △ We need to face up to a world that has been made into one interdependent community, less by political or ideological ideas than by scientific and technological facts.
John McHale, 1969:14.

☆ Many questions are raised: will world communication help unite or divide us? Do radio, T.V. and the Press control us or not? Is T.V. really increasing juvenile delin-

2.1.1 Common Sense

For the most part, our common sense understandings of communication have evolved slowly over tens of thousands of years. A child is born into a family. He learns to walk and talk. Before age two, most children walk and climb; by five, they run well. By age two, most children begin to form two-word sentences; by five, the child communicates for a wide variety of purposes.° He answers questions, and he asks questions that an adult at times finds difficult to answer. The world over, by age five, more than nine out of every ten children are skilled communicators within the family circle. A child just learns to talk and walk. Everyone knows that. It's common sense.°°

The child learns to communicate in the style of his family and friends and neighbors. At first, talking is as natural for the child as walking. A little later, at school perhaps, he notices a teacher or fellow student from somewhere else "talks funny." Children often mimic and ridicule any child that speaks in a noticeably different way. If you were ever the "new kid at school" you will remember incidents of this nature. Out of experiences of this kind basic attitudes are shaped.

Up until about 1750, most humans lived out their lives in traditional village communities. These were usually quite stable groups. Few members left the community and few entered the community. Those who did travel to and from a community were treated with caution. If you grew up in an old-fashioned community, you have some definite attitudes about talking to strangers.

Our basic human communication skills are still shaped in a home community.□ So are basic attitudes toward human communication. Both skills and attitudes are shaped at an early age, and they are often maintained long after they cease to be appropriate as an unexamined part of the common sense, the shared culture, of the home community.□□

In the space age, fundamental changes in human communication are underway. A community member will associate with a wide range of other persons from outside the community. He will seek information from a wide variety of information storehouses. For purposes of importance to himself and his community, he will communicate with strangers who have different expectations than the good people he grew up with. To achieve his purposes, he must at this point develop an *un*common sense about communication.

2.1.2 Natural, Seminatural, and Unnatural Communication

Man has been able to communicate with his fellow man through speech for only a half-million of his four million years on earth. Over a period of time,

quency? . . . What is modern communication doing to us and what new media are around the corner, yet to come?
Colin Cherry, 1971:xi.

° While the beginnings of human speech are lost in antiquity, the development of speech in children is observable and well understood. . . . Speech, therefore, develops in the child for the same reason that language developed in the race—in order to meet a social need.
A. H. Monroe and D. Ehninger, 1967:14.

°°
> **As a communicator, I am better than average.**
>
> **Disagree 1 2 3 ? 5 6 7 Agree**

□
> **Communication skills and attitudes appropriate in the past may be inappropriate in the future.**
>
> **Disagree 1 2 3 ? 5 6 7 Agree**

□□ . . . it is the purpose of this book to make some examination of the nature of human communication itself, if only to get away from the naive idea that it consists of people sending messages to one another, and then to look at various aspects of today's so-called communication explosion and its implications for the future.
Colin Cherry, 1971:xiii.

man—in many tribal communities of the world—*learned* to communicate.[o]
To the tribe that did not yet communicate, the act of speaking must have
seemed unnatural indeed—a strange, buzzing noise. Only much later,
probably after writing systems were invented, man could discover that
different languages existed. A child speaks well without being aware that he
speaks a language.[oo]

Learning to communicate in a first language in the home community
evolves in what is now quite a natural fashion. The mother and other family
members through patterns of daily interaction enable a child to learn to
speak. Neither the "teacher" nor the "pupil," in this case, need be aware of
the learning process. The child who reaches adolescence will likely be an
effective communicator in his own home community on purposes of
importance in that community. He will be a specialist in that particular
community. And he will have reached the limits of development of speech
communication that can be achieved by natural means within his home
community.[□]

The school environment shapes and further develops speech
communication. But the school environment is at best only seminatural
when compared with the natural home environment for the further
development of speech[□□] communication or for learning to communicate in
a new language. Finally, any young adult who has spent part of his life
outside his home community demonstrates the consequences of that
additional experience in the way he communicates *within* his home
community. Now let us push the matter a step further.

Suppose you agree to participate in a communication experiment with
Mr. Turing. You meet each day for half an hour in a small room. Mr. Turing
is a clever Britisher with a wry sense of humor. Toward the end of the first
meeting, Mr. Turing divides the room with a screen. You can hear him
perfectly well but you can no longer see him. Thereafter, you enter from
one side of the room, he from the other. The second morning he announces
that he has brought his Turing machine with him. Mr. Turing lowers the
screen for just a moment to show you the machine. He explains to you that
his machine is a completely general machine that can be programmed to be
any specific machine. In particular, he intends to program that machine to
communicate with you in exactly the same way that he communicates with
you. You ask if he really considers himself to be some kind of communication machine.[△] He replies, "That is for you to decide."

Mr. Turing, on the third morning, suggests a simple test. He suggests that
you attempt to determine from the communication exchange the first
moment that he is no longer in the room with you. He encourages you to
ask questions. When you think you know, you are to lower the screen to

[o] It is a world in which clusters of settle-
ment, nodes of transport, centers of culture,
areas and centers of language, divisions of caste
and class, barriers between markets, sharp
regional differences in wealth and interdependence, and the uneven impact of critical
historical events and social institutions all act
together to produce a highly differentiated and
clustered world of regions, peoples, and
nations.
Karl W. Deutsch, 1966:187.

[oo] Speaking may seem as common as
breathing, but words carefully chosen for
special purposes may bring forth hidden power,
be it at the family breakfast table or at the
United Nations. . . . The spoken word, likewise,
may exert strong influence on human destiny.
The society we live in today is largely
attributable to what people have said to one
another.
E. C. Buehler and W. A. Linkugel, 1969:5.

[□] The real essence of community is
undoubtedly to be found in the—manifest or
hidden—fact that it has a center. . . . the circle
is drawn from the radii, not from the points of
the periphery. . . . The "social" belongs to it.
Martin Buber, 1967:89.

[□□] Most people, when they anticipate taking a
"speech" course, think immediately of learning
to get up in front of an audience of a number
of people to produce a one-way transmission of
ideas, or monologue. As we have tried to show
in this book, the essence of speaking for most
of us is found in the more private and
interpersonal situation and involves the dialog,
or more extrinsic two-way interaction.
John W. Keltner, 1970:321.

[△]

Quite simply, a human is an advanced
communication machine.

Disbelieve   1 2 3 ? 5 6 7   Believe
Impossible   1 2 3 ? 5 6 7   Possible

check to see if you find Mr. Turing alone, Mr. Turing and the machine, or just the Turing machine.

You converse with "Mr. Turing." You ask questions about your major academic interest, the weather, British humor, and, from time to time, you ask when he is going to try to get his machine to enter the conversation.

The days fly and the weeks pass. One day you discover that you have been asking "Mr. Turing" questions for more than twenty hours. While the association has been both pleasant and informative, the experiment had taken a long time. The next morning you ask when the experiment will be over. "Mr. Turing" suggests that you lower the screen and see for yourself. On the table is the Turing machine. Beside the machine, in neat handwritten form, is a note from the "real" Mr. Turing.[°] He has written, "I did not return on the third day."

You are a little embarrassed and slightly angry. There are many uncomfortable questions. If the machine is general, could it also be programmed to "sit in" on conversations for you? Could it at least answer the phone for you? Did you most enjoy talking to Mr Turing or to his machine? If speech communication is a major distinguishing characteristic of the human . . .

The natural, the seminatural, and the unnatural in human communication are changing. The child learns to communicate in his home community by natural means. The young adult by seminatural means extends his ability to communicate in college by taking courses in communication; formal education is aimed at changing human nature. But the "talking machine" is another matter. It is not natural or even seminatural; it is an unnatural, or artificial, communicating intelligence. As the space age continues we humans will have to learn to come to terms with intelligent communication machines. How do you plan to do it? When you can answer that question, you will probably also know how to communicate with super intelligent beings from outer space![°°]

2.2 CONCEPT OF PURPOSE

The everyday meaning of the term *purpose* serves as a starting point.[□] Men and women everywhere establish purposes to serve as *guides* to help them get from where they are to where they wish to go. For instance, a young adult may choose the alternative of going to college. He does so for many purposes: to get a college degree; to obtain an education; to get married; to expand his outlook; to get away from home; or to develop a space age attitude. A college diploma, a marriage license, and a new address show that certain of these purposes have been achieved. There are no easy ways of

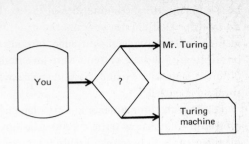

[°] The problem of testing a machine to see whether it is intelligent was first discussed by the great British logician and computer pioneer, Alan Turing, who died in the early 1950's. It was from my personal association with Turing during the war and the early post-war years that I acquired my interest in the possibilities of using digital computers to simulate some of the higher mental functions that we call 'thinking'. Turing proposed the following test. The machine was to be placed on one side of a screen and a human examiner on the other side. Conversation between man and machine was permitted through the medium of a teleprinter. If after an hour or two's typewritten conversation the machine has managed to fool the examiner into thinking that he had been conversing with a human being, then according to Turing the machine's claim to intelligence should be conceded.
Donald Michie, in Jasia Reichardt, 1971:191.

[°°] I assume here that any intelligent creatures we might find are superior to us simply because our advances are so recent in the lifetime of our species.
Neil P. Ruzic, 1970:217.

[□] Our society is filled with attempts to achieve goals through civilized communication. It is also continuously bombarded with attempts to reach goals through direct physical force. Hopefully, increasing man's communication effectiveness will dull the attractiveness of force as a way of fulfilling his purposes.
T. A. Welden and H. W. Ellingsworth, 1970:17.

establishing that a young adult is educated, has an expanded outlook, or a space age attitude. Usually, the more specific and exact a purpose, the easier it is to know when the purpose is achieved.

Every individual communicator has a set of problems and possibilities. Quite often, in his home community, other individuals share some of those same problems and possibilities. Equally, other individuals in other communities in the world *also* share some of these very same problems and possibilities. The problems of population and pollution are common to most of the communities in the world. Some of the purposes for human communication arise out of shared problems. The possibilities brought about by new technology are also shared by individuals in many communities in the world. Some of the purposes of communication also arise out of shared possibilities. Both shared problems and shared possibilities lead on to communication for some *purpose.*

The concept of purpose is very general.° In fact, like the concept of cybernetics with which it is closely associated, the concept of purpose is sometimes uncomfortably vague. As employed in this book, purpose includes most of the usual meanings of the terms *goal,*°° *objective, intent, aim,* and *teleology.* Purpose is a general concept, and, as we shall see, a useful one.

Purpose stands in contrast to purposelessness; more directly, "purpose" contrasts with "random."□ It is very difficult for a human to do anything for a period of time in a random or nonordered or nonorganized fashion. For instance, write a string of 100 one-digit numbers. Try to keep the order random. When you have finished, ask a friend to look back over the string of numbers with you. Chances are very good that both of you will detect patterns in the string of numbers. That tendency to build patterns is one element in the concept of purpose.

Next write or tape record 100 words. Try to produce the words in random order. Again, both you and your friend will detect patterns. Some of these patterns will reveal rudimentary grammatical structures. Others will reveal word association tendencies, and so on. By these tests, and others you can easily invent, you can reveal to yourself how difficult it is for a human to do anything in a random fashion. It is impossible, as we shall repeatedly see, in the case of human communication.□□

A first clue to purpose in a communication system comes from the way feedback operates. More simply, all purposeful communication requires feedback. Any communication element, say a word or sentence, that does not contribute to the system purpose is "corrected" by feedback. It is either eliminated or revised. Each element, then, is tested against the system purpose.

° When we perform a voluntary action what we select voluntarily is a specific purpose, not a specific movement.
A. Rosenblueth, N. Wiener, and J. Bigelow, in Walter Buckley, 1968:222.

°° Goals are *generated* by people. Goals are empirically built *inductively* by the opinions of people. Engineers work from a given goal downward, while human futuristics need to operate upward from people at the *grass-roots.*
M. Maruyama and J. A. Dator, 1971:1.

□ Active behavior may be subdivided into two classes: purposeless (or random) and purposeful. The term purposeful is meant to denote that the act or behavior may be interpreted as directed to the attainment of a goal—i.e., to a final condition. . . .
A. Rosenblueth, N. Wiener, and J. Bigelow, in Walter Buckley, 1968:221.

□□ We believe, however, that the notion of purpose is not absolute, but relative; it admits degrees. We further believe that it involves a human element, namely the attitude and objectives of the observer.
A. Rosenblueth and N. Wiener, in Walter Buckley, 1968:234.

2.2.1 Tests of Purpose

Consider a dyadic human communication system. There are two communicators, Communicator A and Communicator B. There is also one interested onlooker, Observer O. Under these circumstances, the two communicators and the one observer ought to agree on the following:

- A one-sentence statement of purpose. Any one of the three ought to be able to say what the system purpose is in a single sentence. That statement must be acceptable to the other two.
- An appropriate specificity of purpose. A purpose needs to be specific enough to enable the communicators and the observer to determine when the purpose has been achieved or when the purpose is unlikely to be achieved.
- Appropriateness of items of information and communicative association. Every purpose selects its information from that shared by the communicators; at the same time, the purpose suggests the type of association or relationship between the communicators that will facilitate the achievement of that purpose.

In human communication systems, as in cybernetic theory, the concept of purpose plays a key role.[°] We look next at the levels of purpose.

2.2.2 Levels of Purpose

The individual child is born into a family that lives in a home community which in turn is part of the world community. The individual child is not consulted before birth about when and where he would like to be born, how tall he would like to grow, how much he would like to weigh, or what color he prefers for his eyes, hair, and skin. The individual human starts where he is born with what he inherits. A major part of his inheritance is the culture of his home community with its unsolved problems and yet-to-be-developed possibilities.

Much of our common sense about human communication is a useful guide only to the edge of the home community. We declare that the purposes of communication are the business of only the persons directly involved. With a tight upper lip, we proclaim, "We are free to speak. It's our right." And so, of course, it is.[°°] But the dynamics of the space age movement of men and messages make it necessary for us to reexamine our common sense attitudes.

Over nearly all of our communication history, a man lived out his life in the community in which he was born. His opportunity to communicate with others outside his community was severely limited. Likewise, he had little opportunity to communicate with the traveler from the outside. He communicated with persons he knew well. His purposes for communicating

[°]

Two or more communicators always communicate to achieve some purpose.
Disagree 1 2 3 ? 5 6 7 Agree

[°°]

FREEDOM OF SPEECH		
Restricted	1 2 3 ? 5 6 7	Unrestricted
Weak	1 2 3 ? 5 6 7	Strong
Passive	1 2 3 ? 5 6 7	Active
Past	1 2 3 ? 5 6 7	Future

arose from the daily activity of his community. He exchanged information with other persons with access to a similar cultural store of information. In such a community, there are a number of checks and balances at work.

Two or more individual communicators communicate to achieve some purpose. As they do so, they also produce a message. "Excerpts" from that message are stored in the memories of the communicators. Each of these communicators is free to use items from that message as information in the future when he communicates for other purposes. Potentially, any two communicators from any two communities can communicate with each other to achieve some purpose. In so doing, they rely on messages, the informational items, stored in their memories. A message can have a second-level consequence. It can also have a third- or a fourth-level consequence as well.

As communities and the individual communicator become more interdependent, the consequences of any particular message become more difficult to anticipate. For instance, as an individual feels more strongly the tension between the world community and the home community, he may respond in one of two ways. He may overvalue the world community and devalue the home community. Or he may do the opposite. An attitude shift will be reflected in the purposes for which he chooses to communicate. If, for instance, the individual communicator chooses to communicate for purposes of building a better home community, he may seek to communicate with persons he believes similar to himself. He may avoid communicating with all others. By so doing, he may deprive himself of access to the information he most needs to achieve his purpose of building a better community. The choice of purpose seldom has a single consequence. Every message becomes part of the world message stream; it either purifies that stream or pollutes it.

In the space age, it is useful to examine the purposes of human communication at four levels

- *Individual.* An individual communicator shapes his own purposes for communicating. The purposes he seeks to achieve by communication, over time, determine the "kind of human" he will become. As he achieves his purposes, he also stores messages in his memory. He uses parts, or items, or excerpts of those messages in the future when he communicates for other purposes.
- *Communication System.* Two or more individual communicators organize a communication system to achieve a mutual or system purpose. A system purpose results from the combination of individual purposes, or it results from one communicator controlling a commu-

nication system in a way that permits him to achieve his individual purpose.

- *Home Community.* How a community solves its problems and develops its possibilities depends on the mixture of communication systems. A community that selects its information from that presented by "mass media" charts a different course from the community that seeks the specific information required to achieve its mutual purposes.
- *World Community.* Either as a series of interdependent communities or as a single unified community, the quality of communication at the world community level is determined by the other three levels. In a basic sense, the purpose for which any two persons choose to communicate affects the course of the world.

Recall that Einstein believed that "nature was subtle but not mean."° The same observation can be made about a purpose for communication. In addition to the immediate consequences, a purpose may have other, subtle consequences. As the communities of our world become more interdependent, it becomes necessary for a communicator to choose purposes and build messages that are not only effective within a particular communication system, *but also* are *not* "mean" at some other level.

Buber has pointed out that the only new thing man has introduced into nature is the *lie.* He also urges us not to speak to each other as things or objects, as an *It.*°° In Einstein's terms, the lie distorts information, and the It distorts human associations. The lie□ and the It are part of the "meanness" that man sometimes adds to nature. They need not be part of human communication because man the communicator always has alternatives available to him. There are genuine alternatives to the adversary approach.

If, as we enter the space age, we communicate for purposes and build messages that are valid beyond a particular communication system, we can begin to shape a new world attitude. More directly, how you choose to communicate, and when, will make a difference to you, to me, to all of us. Each of your communication purposes is a declaration of your personal values.

2.3 DEFINITION OF HUMAN COMMUNICATION

If you ask the next person you meet to define communication, the chances are very good that he will be able to do so—to his satisfaction.□□ If you ask several persons, you are likely to get several different definitions. If you try to summarize the definitions you are given, you will have a difficult task. If you look over some of the thousands of books and articles on communica-

°
> Nature is subtle but not mean.
> Disagree 1 2 3 ? 5 6 7 Agree

°° As *experience,* the world belongs to the primary word I-It.
The primary word I-Thou establishes the world of relation.
Martin Buber, 1958:6.

□ The lie is the specific evil which man has introduced into nature. . . . the lie is our very own invention, different in kind from every deceit that the animals can produce. . . . It was possible only as directed against the conceived truth.
Martin Buber, 1953:7.

□□ What, then, is 'human communication?' Strictly, the word communication comes from the Latin *communico*—meaning *share. Share,* notice, not 'I send messages'. Communication is essentially **a social** process.
Colin Cherry, 1971:2.

tion, you can easily find a hundred or more different definitions of communication. You will discover that these definitions differ in three main ways. Some definitions attempt to include all living things; others limit themselves only to human beings. Some definitions limit themselves to communication undertaken for some purpose or intent; others do not. Some definitions include only communication that is successful in achieving its purposes; others include failures as well.

If you *observe* people who are engaged in communication, the problem of definition becomes a great deal simpler. For instance, suppose you observe and tape record two persons who meet at an airport. They stop, they stand and talk, and they go their separate ways. You note that they appear to agree on a starting point and stopping point. On playing back your recording, you hear one person say to the other, "What's that?" and note that a word is repeated. A bit later, the other person says, "I don't quite understand what you mean," and you note that some of what had just been said was repeated and elaborated on. Just before the two persons stop communicating, you hear one person say, "I think we've a good idea here," and the other says, "I agree. Let's meet at my place tomorrow for lunch and work out a plan. O.K.?" "O.K." The entire meeting, you note, has taken exactly 2 minutes and 50 seconds.

In the manner of your favorite detective, you then deduce that the meeting you had observed contained the basic patterns of human communication. It displays organization. Some details were modified while communication was in process. It appeared to be purposeful. In this case, it appeared to achieve a purpose, or achieve success. That, you conclude, is representative of what happens when people communicate with each other.

2.3.1 A Working Definition of Human Communication

In slightly more formal terms, a working definition of *human communication*° may be stated as follows:

- By definition, any human communication *system* operates for some *purpose* within a communication *network*.
- A human communication system is always *organized* by two or more communicators to achieve some purpose and is, therefore, a *self*-organized system.
- The feedback-guided *process* of human communication within a system enables communicators to achieve their purpose.
- As communicators operating within a human communication system achieve their purpose, they also develop a *reliable message*.
- A reliable message in the space age often serves purposes beyond those of the communication system in which it was *developed*.

°
Human Communication
Purposeful
Organized
System
Network
Process
Reliable Message
Development
Synser
Future

- When conditions are appropriate, "synser" communication becomes possible.
- By definition, any definition of human communication (including this one) will change in the *future*.

This working definition focuses on human communicatin which is purposeful. Human communication to achieve a purpose must be organized. The process through which a purpose is achieved occurs only in an organized system.

2.3.2 Some Consequences of the Definition

From time to time, human communication is defined as a "complex process" or an unpatterned set of unintended activities. Those who define communication in this way often get swamped by their own definition, abandon ship, and urge others to do the same. We need not do so.

It is important to note that the definition *excludes* nonhuman communication. It also excludes off-time human communication such as handwriting. Beyond that, it bypasses the problems of nonintentional and purposeless communication. It also ignores the question of whether a machine can have a purpose for communicating with a human. While it acknowledges that failure can and does occur, the approach to communication embodied in the definition is success-oriented; it implies a concern with serendipity rather than errors and with synergy rather than barriers.

This working definition intends to cut human communication down to a manageable size. Even so, it covers enough important territory to keep us busy. It permits us to extend beyond human speech communication when we wish to do so. The definition also facilitates relating human communication to other areas of study where a system approach is prominent.

2.4 REFERENCE MODEL

To bring the definition presented in unit 2.3 into sharper focus, a reference model may prove helpful. The model displays a two-node communication network and a dyadic communication system.°

2.4.1 Two-Node Network

A communication network provides the necessary *linkage* for any human communication system. In the case of a dyadic system organized by Communicator A and Communicator B, the necessary linkage can occur in one of two ways. In a telecomnet (telecommunication network), the link for A and B can be provided by cable, radio signals, or by satellite. The

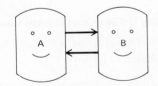

Communicator A   Communicator B

°   Our bias on this point is apparent: we assume that if we can achieve a clear understanding of the dyad we can subsequently extend our understanding to encompass the problems of larger and more complex social relationships.
J. W. Thibaut and H. H. Kelley, 1967:6.

telecomnet link permits both A and B to remain in their home communities and communicate across space. In a transcomnet (transportation communication network), the necessary link is provided by transporting A from his home community to the home community of B. In this case, one communicator is moved across space by car, train, boat, or plane.

2.4.2 Dyadic Human Communication System

The dyadic system is basic for human communication.° It is the smallest, most general, and most important system. It is organized by two and only two communicators. In the model, the two communicators are identified by the letters A and B; the two arrows show that they communicate with each other—they communicate as equals.

Later on, we will develop the notion that the purpose of a system of this type is to process reliable messages.

The special characteristics of the space age require that each of us be able to participate in a communication system and observe accurately what happens in a communication system when others participate in it. A space age communicator needs to be able to do both at the same time, that is, to participate and observe simultaneously.

2.5 THE NEW FUNDAMENTALS

The space age revolution in communication has changed and will continue to change the fundamentals of human communication. The term *fundamentals* means the foundations, the basic elements, or the essentials.°° Five changes of fundamental nature are discussed below.

2.5.1 Information Abundance Versus Information Scarcity

For most of human history, information has been scarce. But the tide has turned from scarcity to overwhelming abundance. What was at first called an information explosion turns out to be an ever increasing spiral of information. More than 90 percent of the trained researchers who have ever lived in the world are alive today; more importantly, they are busy in thousands of settings conducting the research that produces still more new information.□ The space program alone in its brief history has produced over 100,000 major research documents. No human could even read those documents at the rate they are currently being produced. Other new information is generated by interchanges between human communicators. There is more new information produced today than yesterday; tomorrow more will be produced than today.

The result of information abundance is such that even a full-time scholar

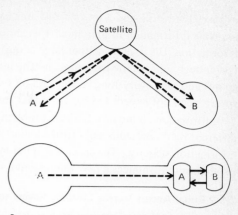

° The main point of departure for this discussion will be the two-person communication group, because in these *dyads,* as they are called, the basic processes and relations are most clearly evidenced.
T. Clevenger, Jr., and J. Matthews, 1971:115.

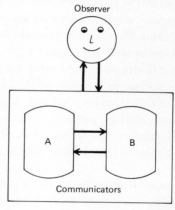

Observer

Communicators

°° A fundamental of speech is a property of speech universally present in situations of oral communication, i.e., voice, articulation, listening, . . . bodily action. . . .
John F. Deethardt, Jr., in Fred Casmir and L. S. Harms, 1970:71.

□ A major assumption underlying all communication research is that communications is essentially purposeful and functional and therefore affects behavior.
G. A. Borden, R. B. Gregg, T. G. Grove, 1969:224.

or specialist working in a very narrow area can now only sample the available information in that area.° He cannot acquire all of the available information. His brain is neither large enough, his rate of information input fast enough, nor his life long enough. The instructor who tells a student to go out and read everything he can find on topic X before presenting a speech need not expect to hear from that student again!

Information abundance is a new problem.°° It requires fundamentally different methods, skills and attitudes than were appropriate in a time of information scarcity. The space age spiral in the production of new information introduces a new fundamental of human communication.

2.5.2 Equal Access Versus Limited Access to Information

Access to information created by man 'and stored in our world can be limited in a number of ways. The game of control begins at an early age. One child whispers some bit of information into the ear of a second child. A third child doesn't hear and asks, "What did you say?" The other two children giggle and shout in unison, "We won't tell you; it's a secret." If the third child persists in playing the game, the first two children often appear to be exchanging "secrets" when they are only making noises out of earshot of the third child. The exchange of secret information often gives way to the appearances of such an exchange in the playgrounds of the world, be they attached to elementary schools or national capitols.

As every child seems to know, information—and sometimes the appearance of having information does even better—makes possible most kinds of power. Military, political, social, and academic power depend on access to information. Even school grades depend on information, but the appearance of having information often does even better, as many students know.

The question of power figures in the procedures for processing information. Many governments censor the information that is permitted into their countries and that which is allowed out. The military establishment classifies its informational documents and then develops elaborate procedures for determining who may receive what information. Some university professors refuse to have their lectures tape recorded or filmed for television and preserve temporarily by this means the appearance of possessing "secret" information. The college student home for a holiday brushes his young brother's question aside with a superior, "You're too young to understand that." That young boy back in the school playground appears to whisper something in the ear of one of his friends. The round continues.

There are so many "good reasons" for controlling access to information.□

° Almost all of the prescriptions that a fifty-year-old doctor writes are for drugs unknown when he was in medical school, and most of the methods of treatment he now uses are novel or greatly changed.
Dan Lacy, 1961:14.

°°

ABUNDANCE OF INFORMATION		
Bad	1 2 3 ? 5 6 7	Good
Unhealthy	1 2 3 ? 5 6 7	Healthy
Ignorance	1 2 3 ? 5 6 7	Knowledge

□

CONTROL OF INFORMATION		
Bad	1 2 3 ? 5 6 7	Good
Helpful	1 2 3 ? 5 6 7	Useless

National security, governmental strategy, academic standards, personal importance are but a few that are cited in one place or another. The list is long; each item is individually sanctioned by its own tradition.

Equal access also depends on a number of factors beyond the usual procedures for control. As the store of information gets larger it becomes more difficult to control. New means for disseminating information come into use. Worldwide satellite broadcasts—the first man on the moon, for instance—are difficult to block out or jam. Copying machines with increasing frequency are used to make additional "public" copies of secret documents. It becomes increasingly difficult to control access to information. The cost of controlling access is becoming prohibitive.

For several decades now, there has been a trend toward equal access to information.° International and national guarantees of freedom of information help. Widespread opportunity for education helps. The growing worldwide understanding that equal access to information is a vital human right is of greatest importance.

In the future, perhaps we can devote the resources we now use to control access to information to make possible equal access to information. We must find ways for each human to obtain the information he needs at the time he thinks he needs it in a form he can use at a price he can easily pay. That is no easy task.

Communication through speech has a vital role to play in a shift to equal access to information. As that change occurs, human communication itself will change and grow in a fundamental way.

2.5.3 Real-time Versus Off-time Communication

Time figures in a central way in human communication. Technologies make more different times available to human communicators. For instance, dialog recorded at 45 rpm can be played at a *real-time* 45 rpm, a slow-time 33 rpm or a fast-time 78 rpm on most record players; in films the dialog and/or picture motion can be in slow, speeded, or reversed motion with bizarre and often humorous effects. Slow-time and fast-time stand in a particular relationship to real-time human communication. The instant replay permits the second look.

Print communication is off-time. There is no necessary relationship between the amount of time it takes to write a book and print it and the time it takes to read it and make use of it. The revolutions brought about by handwriting and print were off-time developments.

Real-time human communication increases in importance as the communities of the world become more interdependent.°°Much of the most useful information is *perishable.* Travel in space is well planned, but a lot of

°   . . . to create social and political institutions appropriate for a world in which all populations will begin to have access to the total knowledge of mankind.
Ben H. Bagdikian, 1971:27.

°° What you will say, you cannot unsay; you may of course withdraw the remark, or apologize, or correct yourself, or bite your tongue, or wish to sink through the floor. But nevertheless it has been said and thus your relationship will . . . be changed for better or worse.
Colin Cherry, 1971:11.

small midcourse corrections are required. "Hot lines" are installed to facilitate real-time communication before irreversible forces of war are set in motion. As we come to view our world as a spaceship with life-support systems, the need for real-time communication increases both for coordination and planning.

A shift from off-time to real-time communication blends the space age and speech revolutions. This blend, of course, fundamentally alters human communication.

2.5.4 Two-Way Versus One-Way Communication Systems

The most fundamental change occurs in human communication as new technology makes it possible to shift from a one-way system to a two-way system.[°] On the surface, the change appears small. A more detailed examination shows the surface appearances to be misleading.

In a one-way communication system, there is a sender and a receiver or receivers. The sender transmits a prepared message to a receiver; the message is intended to accomplish a sender-determined purpose. The receiver either receives the message or he does not. He makes such use of the message as seems appropriate to him.

In a two-way communication system, there are two or more communicators. The communicators decide on a mutual purpose and develop a message to achieve that purpose. They separately make such additional use of the message as seems appropriate to them.

A two-way communication system enables communicators to combine their informational resources.[°°] To be able to do this, they must associate with each other. The interplay between information and association enables the communicators to build a reliable message. The more reliable the message, the more skillful the communicators demonstrate themselves to be.

Two-way communication assumes communicators have access to quantities of different but relatable information. It presumes that communicators have attitudes and skills which facilitate real-time message development. Given these conditions, it will follow that communicators can profit from communicating with each other in the sense that they amplify what each previously knew and that from time to time they will create or discover new information of high value to themselves.

As two-way communication systems become preferred by an increasing percentage of the world's communicators, we advance the right of man to communicate in a fundamental way.

2.5.5 Association Variety Versus Association Similarity

As a community shifts from a traditional to a modern to a space age outlook, the patterns of association or interpersonal relationships also

[°] There are organizational and cost barriers to some of these two-way functions . . . but the technology for their implementation already exists.
Ben H. Bagdikian, 1971:xxv.

[°°] But improving the system's capacity to respond to individual needs will not in fact improve its content unless that is what the individual demands.
Dan Lacy, 1961:92.

change. As the individual communicator seeks information from a wider circle of information sources, at the same time he associates with a wider number of different communicators.° As this shift occurs, the individual communicator spends less time engaged in communication with family members and friends. The consequences of this trade-off are profound. A later chapter is devoted to this fundamental shift.

2.6 ORGANIZATION

Though we humans communicate with each other for several hours every day, we do not communicate with every one all the time. For the most part we are silent when we sleep. Most of us require some hours of silence when we are awake to maintain what passes as sanity in our culture. During a day and across a lifespan, we choose to communicate or choose not to communicate. To communicate, or not to communicate, that is a matter of choice.°°

As will become more apparent in the next section of the book, human communication requires organization to achieve any particular purpose. In the space age, there are so many possible forms and patterns of organization in human communication that it becomes necessary to simplify matters.□ The ASQ method was devised to make things simple; all human communication is viewed as occurring in one of *three* communication systems operating in one of *two* world communication networks. Six system/network patterns are possible.

2.6.1 World Communication Networks

All human communication is made possible by one of two worldwide communication networks. The first of these networks is a tele-communication network (telecomnet). It is best symbolized by the communication satellite. The second worldwide network is the transportation communication network (transcomnet). It is best symbolized by the jet airplane. Taken together, these two networks make all of human communication possible by two means. In the telecomnet, message elements are exchanged between communicators who are separated in space. In the transcomnet, the communicators are transported into a single communication space. These two networks are examined in detail in the following chapter.

2.6.2 Human Communication Systems

There are three major human communication systems: they have existed since earliest times. These are:

° What is unfolded in interpersonal communication . . . is increasingly more personal information about the way the other thinks, the way he acts, his values, his beliefs, his interests, his idiosyncratic habits—good and bad.
G. A. Borden, R. B. Gregg, T. G. Grove, 1969:82.

°°

> Communication is usually a matter of individual choice.
>
> Disagree 1 2 3 ? 5 6 7 Agree

□ The scale of our global systems of . . . communication and transportation, has now gone beyond the capacities of any single national or regional group to sustain or operate wholly. . . . Each system is complexly interlocked with all others.
John McHale, 1969:14.

- The dyad organized by two communicators
- The small group of 7± 2 communicators
- The large group of $(7x2) + n$

These are the major system sizes—2, 7, and 15+ communicators. Each of these systems can operate in either the telecomnet or the transcomnet. The three systems are closely related.° Each has special advantages and particular limitations.

Human communication, then, requires organization. The two networks and three systems will be explored in detail in Section II.

2.7 PROCESS

Human communication is a process that unfolds within an organized system. In the space age, the communication process moves at a conversational or real-time rate. Quite often, communicators work under conditions of information overload and interpersonal stress. Frequently, the purpose for communication is critical to the survival of the communicators. Failure is punishing and destructive. Uncertainty is high.°° Under these conditions, communication needs to be failsafe.

Failure can be reduced and success can be increased by skillful modifications of the details and patterns of the communication process. Four chapters are devoted to the critical aspects of real-time human communication process.

2.7.1 Sentence Intelligibility

Many of the major barriers to communication can be reduced or eliminated by careful attention to the details of communication. In particular, the intelligibility or accuracy of saying and hearing words must be maintained at a high level. Equally, the length and other details of a sentence make it a contributor to or a distractor from successful communication. The details of sentences are especially important in a telecomnet linkage where communicators are culturally different.

2.7.2 Information and Association

The patterns of information processing and communicative association will be examined within human communication systems.□ The interdependence of these two patterns turns out to be much greater than previously expected. The more skillful the interchange of information between communicators, the better their communicative association is likely to be.□□ The relationship of information and association is particularly interesting in the case of intercultural communication.

° Thus, there is mutual effect. In this sense, all who are involved in a communication situation are both senders and receivers of messages and, sometimes more important, one is doing both simultaneously. . . . In many communication situations, each individual is simultaneously source and receiver most of the time.
A. C. Baird, F. H. Knower, S. L. Becker, 1971:12.

°°

Uncertainty		
Bad	1 2 3 ? 5 6 7	Good
Comfortable	1 2 3 ? 5 6 7	Uncomfortable
Sad	1 2 3 ? 5 6 7	Happy

□ In a very real sense, information is the glue that holds society together.
Hal Hellman, 1969:9.

□□ The truth is that communication is an art, . . . the art of cooperation in purest form.
Ashley Montagu, in Floyd W. Matson and Ashley Montagu, 1967:445.

2.7.3 Message Reliability

All human communication systems are organized to achieve some purpose. A message processed by a communication system must be reliable. The reliability of the message is tested against the communicators' purpose. In the space age, it is often difficult to create reliable messages and it is especially important that we human communicators be able to do so. Our survival on spaceship earth depends on it.

The four chapters in Section III treat the details and patterns of the human communication process.

2.8 FUTURE

Human communication in the future will differ in important ways. Some major trends that we know about today can be expected to extend into the future. But breakthroughs that we do not expect can radically alter present trends or start entirely new ones.° The ways we humans communicate with each other will change, and with a proper mix of serendipity and synergy, communication will change for the better.

2.8.1 Immediate and Intermediate Futures

In the immediate future, the videophone, talking computer, and the Home Communication Center will make it possible for you to "communicate to work."°° In the intermediate future, say at the year 2000, the capacity of the human brain may be greatly increased, and each human may have complete and instantaneous access to the world's storehouse of information.□ We will have greatly advanced the right of man to communicate.

2.8.2 Alternative Futures

Every present invents one of three very different futures. Scenarios for a worse, a similar and a better future are *sketched out* (see Chapter 13). The larger questions of valid purposes and reliable messages are reconsidered. The right of man to communicate is further explored.

2.8.3 Preparing for the Future

It is possible today to develop communication skills, understanding and attitudes for the probable futures.□□ The main message of this book is that it is not only possible to do so but necessary. Our survival on this planet depends on our increasing our capacity to communicate with one another. We must learn to increase the reliability of the messages in the world stream of human communication. In this manner, we advance the right of man to communicate.

° Perhaps we enter now a new stage of evolution. Perhaps man's next adaptive act lies in other stellar systems. Perhaps there he will find a meaning to existence, to life and death, a purpose to evolution beyond random accident, an end higher than man the consumer. If so, he will be unique in the species of earth, for no other organism on that planet in the past billion years has existed for any other purpose.
Neil P. Ruzic, 1970:216.

°° During the next decade we will see coming into the home a general-purpose communications console comprising TV screen, camera, microphone, computer keyboard, and hard-copy readout device.
Arthur C. Clarke, 1972:160.

□ There was an old man in a Time Machine Who borrowed a Tuesday all painted green. His pockets with rockets he used to jam And he said, "I have thunk, so I cannot am!"
Frederick Winsor and Marian Parry, 1958:6.

□□ I think we will have two essential levels of government. One will be local and involved in immediate decision making. The other will be international. We will be well on our way towards such a reorganization by 1980.
Robert Theobald, 1970:52.

2.9 SUMMARY

In this chapter, the major concepts of human communication in the space age were introduced. The problem of relying exclusively on common sense was indicated. Alternative views of human communication as natural, seminatural and unnatural were briefly discussed. A space age definition of human communication was presented along with a reference model. The five new fundamentals of information abundance, equal access, real time, two-way communication, and association were set forth. The basic concepts of organization, process, and future were sketched out.

In the next chapter, the two world communication networks are examined.

2.S SKILLS: COMMUNICATION IN YOUR CAREER AREA

PURPOSE

To discover the ways human communication facilitates work in your career area or in one of your probable career areas.

PROJECT

Arrange to observe and interview three persons who now work in your career area. These persons should be at different career stages:

- One of these persons should be in his first year or two on the job.
- Another should have about ten years experience in the area. A decade is long enough for him to receive a major promotion and experience a "career shift."
- Another should have twenty or more years experience in the area. This person will have experienced several major changes and will have developed ways for coping with change.

With a partner, draw up a list of seven questions:

- These questions should be specific and brief. They should permit you to obtain answers either by observing or by interviewing.
- The questions should cover what you consider to be the major relationships between human communication and your career area. Discuss the wording of the questions with your partner. Review Chapters 1 and 2. Browse through the rest of the book.
- During most job interviews, a candidate is rated on his communication skills. Find out what the communication skill expectations are for your career area. What are the rewards for high levels of communication skills? What are the penalties for inadequate skills?
- Quite often, when an employed person takes a course in

communication, he is trying to develop attitudes and skills that are vitally important to the work he does. Some of your questions ought to help you find out what you would want to learn now if you had the benefit of a few years work in your area.

- After you draft the questions, try the questions out on your partner and perhaps on one or two other persons. When you are satisfied that the questions get useful answers, write them in the space below.

QUESTIONS

Be sure to discuss these questions with your partner. As you collect information, tape record or take notes.

1.

2.

3.

4.

5.

6.

7.

RESULTS

1.

2.

3.

4.

5.

6.

7.

Be prepared to share these results in a small group discussion or as a short oral report before the entire large group.

GENERAL CONCLUSIONS

After you have discussed your results or heard others report their results, draw the appropriate conclusions. Be sure the conclusions relate to the original purpose.

1.

2.

3.

2.Q QUESTIONS

2.Q.1 Within your career your career area, what do you anticipate will be the required new human communication attitudes and skills:

- In five years?
- Ten years?
- In twenty years?

There was a time when skill in speaking in public was regarded as highly important. At another time, good listening was thought to be the key to effective communication. Did you find indications of the need to be able to talk to machines? What role does the telephone, conference television, and other telecomnet equipment play?

2.Q.2 Which of the new fundamentals seems likely to most influence:

- Your career area?
- Your life in your home community?

The five new fundamentals are: information abundance, equal access to information, real-time communication, two-way communication, and association variety.

2.Q.3 Is it possible to move away from an adversary approach to communication and on to an approach more in harmony with nature:

- In your own communication?
- As a dominant pattern in your home community?
- As a dominant pattern in the world community?

An adversary or competitive approach to human communication imposes severe limits. What one communicator gains the other loses. But from a larger view, both communicators lose because they deprive themselves of the possibility of both synergy and serendipity.

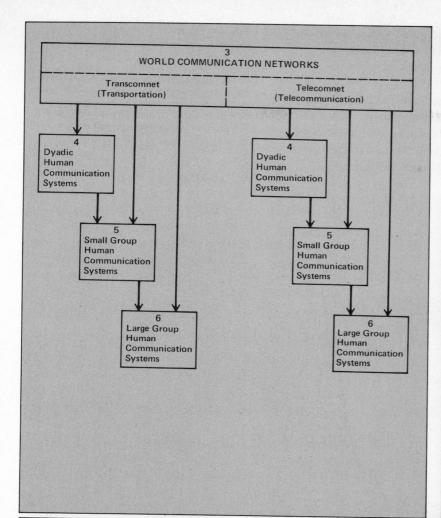

3 WORLD COMMUNICATION NETWORKS

Transcomnet (Transportation)

Telecomnet (Telecommunication)

4 Dyadic Human Communication Systems

5 Small Group Human Communication Systems

6 Large Group Human Communication Systems

II

ORGANIZATION FOR HUMAN COMMUNICATION

3 WORLD COMMUNICATION NETWORKS
4 DYADIC SYSTEMS
5 SMALL GROUP SYSTEMS
6 LARGE GROUP SYSTEMS

II ORGANIZATION →

Synergy is the key concept in this section. Sometimes one times one equals three; when that happens, synergy is operating. Quite simply, synergy means augmentation, amplification, or multiplication. Synergy requires organization.°

A system is usually defined as a whole that is greater than the sum of its independent parts. In the case of a human communication system, the communicators achieve a purpose they could not achieve individually by that kind of self-communication called thinking. That extra achievement that comes from combining two (or several) brains through human communication is a form of synergy.

° All the media of communication which are today pouring from the cornucopia of modern technology offer power to relate one set of human activities, at one place, to other sets of activities, at other places: i.e. to *organize*.
Colin Cherry, 1971:x.

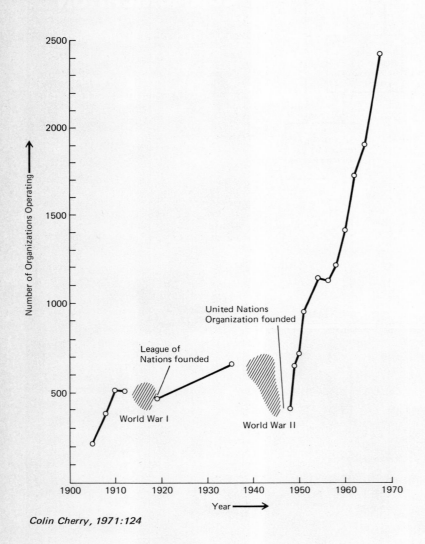

Colin Cherry, 1971:124

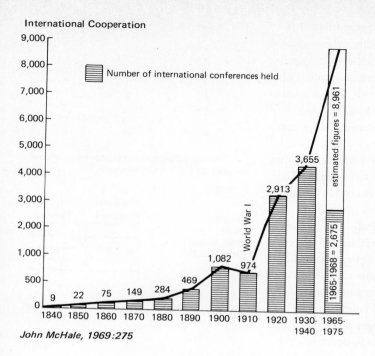

International Cooperation

⬛ Number of international conferences held

John McHale, 1969:275

All human communication occurs in a world communication environment.[°] The world is encircled by two communication networks; one of these networks is a telecommunication network and the other is a transportation network. Taken together, these two networks provide the necessary linkage for the three human communication systems[°°] These three systems are the dyad, the small group, and the large group. Each of these three systems can operate in either of the two networks. There are six system/network combinations.

The three-in-two—three systems in two networks—model is intended to be simple enough to be useful and complex enough to be interesting. The model includes those areas of interest to the individual communicator; it leaves no large area uncovered. The model is essentially complete.

There are two magic numbers in this model: *two* and *seven*.[□] There are two networks. The dyadic system has two communicators; the small group has seven plus or minus two communicators; and the large group has seven times two plus *n* communicators. The three systems can operate in the two networks to give six possibilities—which is clearly seven minus one. The model is simple; the numbers are all small.

The organization of the communication networks and of communication systems differ markedly. The two communication networks are built up from technological devices. They are formally organized and formally

[°]   How is world communication organized and operated? By its very nature it is international: the post, telephones and telegraphs, airways, connect together countries which have different political and economic systems. . . World communication has essentially forced the various governments to get together and agree upon how it shall be done, whether they like each other or not.
Colin Cherry, 1971:126.

[°°]   The essence of our message to the reader is that communication is the matrix in which all human activities are embedded. In practice, communication links object to person and person to person; and scientifically speaking, this interrelatedness is understood best in terms of systems of communication.
J. Ruesch and G. Bateson, 1968:13.

[□]
Model
Networks: 2
Dyadic System: 2
Small group system: 7 ± 2
Large group system: (7 × 2) + *n*
Systems and networks: 7 − 1

controlled. Communication networks exist even when no communicators are using them. The case is the opposite for human communication systems. Such systems require no technology beyond that of the network linkage. They are informally organized or *self*-organized by the communicators who participate in them. They become disorganized and cease to exist as soon as the communicators stop communicating. It is important to distinguish between communication networks and communication systems in the case of human communication.

The individual communicator has a purpose° for communicating. Within the linkage capacity of the two networks, he is then free to organize a communication system with other communicators who choose to communicate with him. In this sense, a communication system becomes *self*-organized; it is organized by the participating communicators themselves.

Any communicator can participate in only one communication system at a time. There are only a few exceptions. Likewise, that one system utilizes a single link in only one of the two networks. From the view of the individual communicator, he is free to choose from one of six system/network combinations. Once he chooses, however, the individual communicator is, for the time that system operates, subject to its advantages and limitations.

The individual communicator has a purpose. He seeks to communicate with one or more other persons to achieve that purpose. By so doing, he acknowledges that he needs help to achieve that purpose. He also anticipates a certain cost in time and other resources.

° The individual communicator must choose the appropriate system/network.

Purpose:

Systems	Networks	
	Transcom	Telecom
Dyad		
Small Group		
Large Group		

3
WORLD COMMUNICATION NETWORKS

Chapter 3 contains maps of the two world communication networks. As was pointed out earlier, human communication occurs in communication systems that operate for some purpose in one of the two world communication *networks*. Taken together, the two world networks provide the required linkages for all human communication systems. Communication technologies of all types form the two world networks.

3	
WORLD COMMUNICATION NETWORKS	
Transcomnet (Transportation)	Telecomnet (Telecommunication)

3.1 INTRODUCTION

There are two world communication networks:[°] the telecommunication network—shortened to *telecomnet*; and the transportation communication network—shortened to *transcomnet*. The telecomnet enables a communicator to hear and see at any desired distance; it provides a *telelink*. The telecomnet permits a communicator to "transport" message elements back and forth between himself and another communicator. The transcomnet enables a communicator to transport himself to some other location. The telecomnet transports the message; the transcomnet transports the messenger. For some purposes, the two networks are equal: for others, of course, they are not.

Nearly everyone in the world makes some use of both networks.[°°] There are some exceptions. For instance, consider the person born at home who never leaves that home during his entire life and never talks to a stranger from a distant community and never hears a radio or talks on a telephone. There are still some persons in the traditional villages of the world who live that way. Some persons, then, still make little use of and are little influenced by the linkages provided by either of the world communication networks.

Most of us depend on the two networks many times every day. Even nations at war with each other continue to cooperate with each other in the maintenance of the communication networks. Not only conflict, but most of man's activities depend on the communication networks. To understand why this is so, we need a world map.

Imagine that you have just stepped out of a space shuttle and into a skylab.[□] You find yourself in the company of half a hundred persons from twenty different countries. One team is observing the movement of fish in the world's oceans. Another team is observing the world weather patterns. Still other teams are examining the geological structure of continents. You join a newly formed team that undertakes to *map* the two world communication networks.

You begin your examination of the earth's surface. Your first observation is devastatingly simple. You cannot tell where national boundaries are. You can clearly distinguish ocean from land; but you cannot tell France from Germany nor the United States from its American neighbors. The nation states of the United Nations are not visible as independent national islands. Japan and England are exceptions that underscore your simple observation. But then you ponder the ocean and the weather patterns; the tides and the winds are unbounded by the lines men draw on the surface of the earth.

[°] *World Communication Networks*
Telecomnet
Transcomnet

[°°] It is utterly useless, in the writer's opinion, to theorize or speculate about the future of world communication in terms of these Western images alone, as though "Western man" were "the world."
Colin Cherry, 1971:201.

[□] Enough of ants. Let us now put on our wings like angels and fly up to Heaven, to gaze down upon the human race. Millions and millions of people scurrying about in all directions, very busily doing millions of different things; we shall have to watch them for a very long time before we can see any overall pattern in all this business.
Colin Cherry, 1971:1.

Your team begins the month-long task of mapping the communication networks. Your skylab is in orbit over the equator at 271 miles. You can take a wide angle view and see about 40 percent of the earth's surface. Or you can focus in on any two communicators precisely enough to both see and hear them. You find both views necessary.

As you scan the surface of the earth, your first reaction is that the earth is encircled by two great fishnets. The net is uneven. In some areas, the pattern seems to resemble a spider web; the links seem to be organized around a center.° In other areas, the holes in the fishnet appear large enough for whales to swim through. The nets are worldwide, but some links are much heavier than others; some areas are only lightly covered.

From your skylab observation post, you note a number of communication satellites located at 22,300 miles above the equator in geostationary orbit. The instruments available in the skylab enable you to observe the interconnections between the satellite in orbit and the satellite ground stations located in the thousands of home communities distributed around the world. You further detect that each ground station connects to telephone lines and underground cables. These lines and cables in turn connect into the homes, schools, offices and other locations in each of the thousands of communities. As·you sketch out the network, you notice that it also looks like a diagram of a network of the human nervous system. You have one basis for comparison. Perhaps you will find a better one.

From your skylab post, you observe the great jetliners speeding along the air routes of the world. The planes start from and return to airports that are located near the cities of the world. You note that the passengers who leave the airplanes continue their journeys by ground transportation—train and car—to homes, schools, and offices. Again, as you sketch, a simple pattern emerges. It looks more than a little like the first.

You look over at a communication satellite and decide it best symbolizes the first network. You look down at a jetliner and decide it provides a symbol for the other network. Via satellite you report your observations to your earthbound friends. Via space shuttle—an advanced airliner—you return to your earthport. You again stand on the good earth, but there is a difference. You can visualize the great networks that circle the entire earth, and you can examine any link of either network that happens to interest you.

3.2 ON NETWORKS

The world communication networks are not fully developed at this time. They are, however, complete enough to enable us to imagine a world in

NASA

° The improvement of communications will also render obsolete the city's historic role as a meeting place for minds and a center of social intercourse.
Arthur C. Clarke, 1967:176.

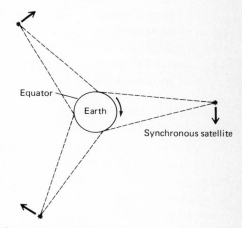

Equator

Earth

Synchronous satellite

James Martin, 1969:352

Earth

James Martin, 1969:352

which any man can communicate with any other man. To bring this about, a more nearly equal distribution of technological resources is necessary.°

There are two trends in the development of both the telecomnet and the transcomnet that deserve examination. First, local network links become integrated into the world network. Second, network links that are developed for a single use begin to serve additional uses.

3.2.1 Local Links Form a World Network

The world communication networks have been pieced together from communication links first developed in particular communities. The problem of fitting together telecommunication equipment into a serviceable network has required both ingenuity and cooperative planning.

If you have ever put together a music system from off-the-shelf components and assembly kits you will have a feel for the problem. Loud speakers from Germany, an amplifier from Japan, a tapedeck from America, a record player from England suggest the possibilities and problems.

The problem of transportation links is similar. Roads get cut into the surface of the earth where foot paths run and ox carts travel. The road which is good for the hooves of a horse is seldom equally good for the tires of the latest Italian sports car. Airstrips which are excellent for the Alaskan bush pilot are unworkable for the international jet liner. Adjustments are made.

In both networks, the first problem has been to integrate local links into a workable world network. To a large extent this has already been done. But the lines of linkage in the networks reveal more than a little of our past history. To send a telegram a few miles, say from across the border between Indian and Pakistan, it has been necessary to "go through" the several thousand mile linkage to and from London, England. The lines of communication set up by the Empire outlived the Empire. To fly from Honolulu to Geneva, until recently, it was necessary to fly over the U.S. mainland. Now, the more direct link through Anchorage and "over the top" has been opened up. The fitting together of local communication links creates a world network which, at least in its early stages, is quite uneven.

The two world networks are now complete enough for each of us to think of being able to talk by telephone to any other person in the world. There are practical difficulties of language and time zone differences. Some important difficulties, of course, are political. It is also becoming possible for almost any two persons to be able, at least, to meet at an international airport in a neutral country to communicate with each other.°° Again, there are practical difficulties of obtaining passports and travel funds. But in both

°

Poor countries should be given communication technology by rich countries.

Disagree 1 2 3 ? 5 6 7 Agree
Unfair   1 2 3 ? 5 6 7 Fair

Network Linkages

°°

Those persons who might say things that would embarrass their government should not be allowed to travel outside their country.

Disagree 1 2 3 ? 5 6 7 Agree

cases, it is now technically *possible* for almost any two persons to communicate with each other by means of a telecomnet link and/or a transcomnet link. It must be emphasized that the two networks create new possibilities.

Distance has been a major determiner of cost in both networks. As the local links are fitted into a world network, a fundamental change occurs. The satellite either makes all telecomnet communication long distance *or* local depending on how you choose to view the matter. The *uplink* from earth to satellite is 22,300 miles and the *downlink* from satellite to earth is 22,300 miles. The uplink–downlink distance is about 45,000 miles. By earth distance, 45,000 miles is almost two times around the world. But the uplink–downlink distance changes very little for a "telephone call" between two communicators who live a few feet apart on opposite sides of a street or a few thousand miles apart on opposite sides of a continent or ocean. In a comparable way, the greatest costs in a jetliner are associated with getting the passengers into the plane and off the ground and landing the plane and unloading the passengers. The low-cost, long-distance charter flight illustrates the decreasing effect of earth surface distance on cost of air travel. Earth distance as a real cost diminishes in importance in both world communication networks.

3.2.2 Single Purpose into Multi-Purpose

As the world networks take shape, the variety of uses for each of the networks increase. Human communication needs are but one force that stimulates network growth. There are several other uses. For instance, the telecomnet is increasingly used for data transmission. The multinational businesses provide a convenient example. Business data stored in several different computers can be transmitted to a central computer in some other country for processing. That processed data can be retransmitted to the original computers. Hotel reservations, space availability on airlines and dozens of other uses also employ the linkage capacity of the world telecomnet.

The transcomnet has always carried items for "trade" along with the passengers. The airlines increasingly carry cargo *and* passengers. A wide variety of items that would perish in transit by boat or rail—fresh pineapple, for instance—now share space with passengers in the air links of the transcomnet.

The two networks now make services available on a worldwide basis that even a few years ago were only possible within a single community.° The trend is strong. Both networks are adapted to serve additional human purposes.

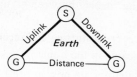

Ground to Satellite to Ground

Uplink · S · Downlink · Earth · G—Distance—G

Increased communication among persons from different parts of the world increases the prospects for world peace.

Disagree 1 2 3 ? 5 6 7 Agree

3.3 TELECOMNET

The telecomnet has four basic components. These are:

- The communication satellite
- The satellite ground station located in the home community
- The connecting "cable" between ground station and home (or office, etc.)
- The transceiver (transmitting and receiving devices such as a telephone) located in the home

The necessary satellites are now in orbit. Only some of the world's communities have the necessary ground stations. In the communities that do have ground stations, only some of the homes have transceivers. The use made of the telecomnet by those who have full access to it varies considerably. The cost of the telecomnet services is the basic limiter.

Basic Telecomnet Components

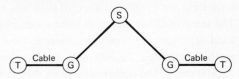

World Telecommunication Network

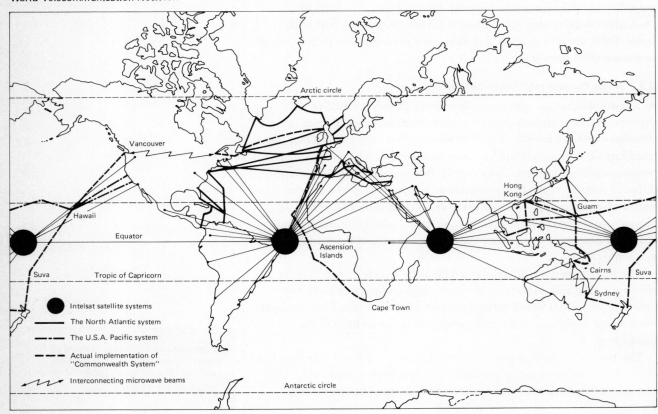

Colin Cherry, 1971:62

3.3.1 World Telecomnet

The communication satellite is the key component in the world tele-comnet.[°] The satellite makes the full network possible. The ground station, cable, and transceiver each serve a vital function. But it is the satellite which makes a full range of worldwide communication facilities possible.

The communication satellite, then, makes a world telecomnet possible. In most general terms, the satellite receives messages (or signals) from a ground station, amplifies these messages (makes them stronger) and sends those amplified messages to some other ground station. There is an essential relationship between the ground station and the satellite.

The relationship between the ground station and the satellite is of this order. A small, weak satellite requires a large, powerful ground station. When a satellite serves only a very few ground stations during a very short satellite life, it is preferable to have a small, weak satellite and a large, powerful ground station. The first satellite was a small, weak one. However, the relationship between ground station and satellite is changing.

Within the last decade, the useful life of a satellite has been greatly extended. The capacity of a satellite to serve large numbers of ground stations has been increased from twelve two-way telephone voice links to more than 100 times that number. Given these changes in length of life and in linkage capacity, it becomes preferable to have a large, powerful satellite and a small, weak ground station. That change reduces the price of ground stations from several millions of dollars to a few thousands of dollars. Thus, the reduced cost of a ground station makes it possible for any community to have one.

At present, the existing satellite ground stations are usually connected to telephone exchanges and broadcast stations. One heavy use of the satellite and its ground station is to provide telecomnet linkage for telephone traffic.

[°] The very capabilities that telecommunications will offer in the future will affect not only the design of dwellings and their layout, but may lead us to question existing ideas about the need for cities as we understand them, and their location.
J. S. Whyte, in Douglas Jones, 1971:97.

Point to point

Data relays

Mars

Direct broadcast-voice and TV

Radio   TV

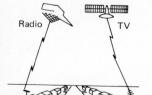

NASA

Navigation/Traffic control

Multiple access

Community TV

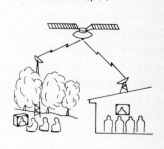

The telephone company in nearly every country is one of the largest businesses. Another heavy use of the satellite and ground station is by television and radio broadcasting stations. The "live via satellite" designation is now familiar to all of us. The broadcast companies are in many nations also among the largest businesses. The telephone and broadcast uses are now well established. Important as the telephone and broadcast services are, in the immediate future, the telecomnet is likely to be more widely used for other purposes.

In some communities, coaxial cable, CATV, or community antenna television has been in use for a number of years. The *cable* has been used to "deliver" television into homes in communities where the usual broadcasting transmission towers have been inadequate. As so often is the case with a piece of technology, suddenly the cable has a different set of possible uses.°

The cable has the possibility of bringing about forty *two-way* channels or links into any home. A few of these channels could be used as they now are for television, for FM radio, telephone, and other similar uses. The additional links could be used for two-way connection to computer information systems, "open university" educational centers, news centers, and a wide variety of other services including "communicating to work." The community cable can be connected directly to the satellite ground station.

To review for a moment, the communication satellites are positioned 22,300 miles above the equator. Satellites are under international, or world control. To a large extent, the ground stations and the cable are under community control. The possibilities that develop in any particular community depend on the actions of the members of that community.

When the ground station and cable facilities are installed, another development becomes possible. Look around a home. Gather up the telephone, television, radio, typewriter, newspaper, magazines, books, adding machine, timing devices, and related communication facilities. Imagine a single transceiver device that could perform all of the services these separate devices now perform—and more. Call that transceiver a Home Communication Center. In the immediate future, such a device will become available. The capacity of the satellite, ground station, and cable requires it.

The world telecomnet begins to be an organized network. The communication satellite is the key component. Unlike the long-distance wire and cable lines, the satellite can be easily moved from one location to another. The hundreds of two-way voice linkages can be allocated as required. Thus, the satellite can serve a small village on a remote island as easily as it can serve a major city; the wire-based networks most often link

° The long-range significance of cable is not its ability to duplicate existing television programs. It is the potential for two-way communications between the home and a vast array of information services: twenty-channel cable has forty thousand times more capacity than telephone wires. Such a high-capacity installation in each home, interconnected with computers, is capable of handling information far beyond voice telephone.

Ben H. Bagkikian, 1971:xxv.

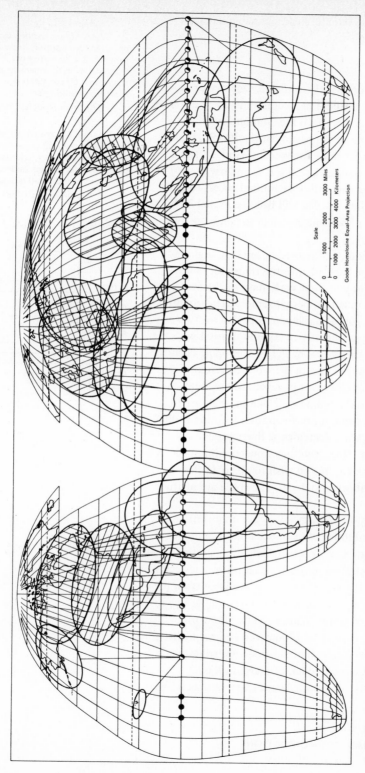

A distribution of regions served by and parking spaces for communication satellites that could satisfy the projected world demand for satellite communications in 1985. Parking spaces are circles on equator, fully shaded for Intelstat system, partly shaded for regional TV and data systems. Shaded regions are served by six satellites, unshaded regions by one satellite.

W. R. Hinchman and D. A. Dunn, 1970:78–79

Goode Homolosine Equal-Area Projection

Scale

0   1000   2000   3000 Miles

0 1000 2000 3000 4000 Kilometers

only the large population centers. The satellite makes possible linkages between *all* of the world communities.°

3.3.2 Availability

Telecomnet services are becoming more widely available. One device or another tends to be the first to come into use in a community. For instance, the transister radio often brings the "voice" into the community from the "outside" for the first time.°° In some of the islands of the Pacific, that voice, quite naturally, is at first thought to be the voice of God! In India, direct satellite transmission to individual television sets is underway. In traditional villages without telephone and with very limited access to radio, several hours of television programming per day will become available. Some new telecomnet services seem likely to become available to nearly every community within the next few years.

If you regularly use telephone, radio, and television services, you may consider the reaction of the stone age tribesmen to the transistor radio amusing. Yet, there are shifts underway in these early days of the space age which promise to affect your life as much or, perhaps, more. The satellite makes a world network available to you. It has *ample* capacity for two-way communication. Thus, you may engage directly in communication with the tribesmen from one of the outlying islands of the 7,114 Philippine Islands, or with a villager in India, or with anyone else in the world. Even in those communities in the world, your community for instance, where almost every home has a telephone, most of the billing of telephone calls are local calls; that is, from one location in a community to another location in that same community. Phone communication decreases as the communities become geographically more distant. Thus, you may now communicate person-to-person with almost anyone else if you wish to do so; in the immediate future, it is likely you will wish to do so. The space age attitude requires it.

The satellite makes a wide variety of other two-way communication facilities possible. Consider the possibilities of man-machine communication. Assume your Home Information Center is installed and operating. You are able to ask any question you wish. In audio and visual form, you receive an answer. That answer is based on the best information available from the world's store of information. Ask any question; within a second, receive a full answer drawn from the world's best information. Thus, the world telecomnet makes a wider range of personal and improved communication possible. As these services become available, like the stone age tribesman and his transistor radio, we too will sense a touch of magic in these developments. Technology pushed beyond our current expectations is indistinguishable from magic.

° Telecommunications can no longer be considered separately from other aspects of organization but are now so intricately interwoven with organizational concepts that they must be considered as an integral part of the total planning activity.
J. S. Whyte, in Douglas Jones, 1971:97.

°° Transistors are cheap, sturdy, and portable, and need no wired power source. They are small, easily hidden, and listened to in remote primitive places likes bedrooms of American adolescents and small villages in Celebes.
Ben H. Bagdikian, 1971:211.

Radios, per 100 inhabitants

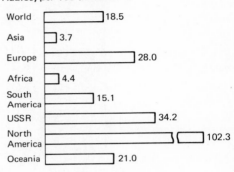

World	18.5
Asia	3.7
Europe	28.0
Africa	4.4
South America	15.1
USSR	34.2
North America	102.3
Oceania	21.0

Conference Board, 1972:231

3.3.3 Cost

World telecomnet facilities are not evenly distributed among the home communities of the world. Most homes in western Europe, North America, and Japan enjoy extensive telecomnet services. These are also the world regions with the highest per capita income.

A map of the world telecomnet and of the distribution of individual income shows a simple relationship. The higher the income, the greater the availability of telecomnet facilities and services. In the future, the relationship between information and money will become stronger and closer; at some point, information promises to become the new capital. The telecomnet *can* make the world's store of information available to every human on earth.

Information has a special characteristic. Information is increased and improved by sharing. Thus, the world's store of information is increased by making it equally available to all men in all communities. There exists in the world the capacity to manufacture the necessary communication facilities— the satellites, ground stations, and so on—to build a complete telecomnet. Such a network would cost only a small percentage of what is now spent on "national defense" by the countries of the world. And a telecomnet that provides equal access to the world's information can accomplish what neither guns nor butter can.

ANNUAL COSTS FOR HOUSEHOLD COMMUNICATIONS	
Telephone	$225
Newspapers	$120
Postal service	$116
Television	$102
Periodicals	$44
Books	$42
Radio	$26
Phonograph records and tapes	$13

Ben H. Bagdikian, 1971

3.4 TRANSCOMNET

The transcomnet has four basic components. These are:

- The jet airliner
- The airport ("ground station") located in the home community

Basic Transcomnet Components

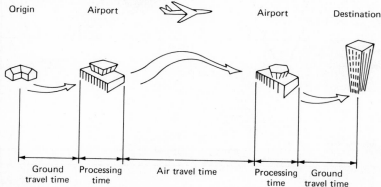

C. A. O'Flaherty in Douglas Jones, 1971

- The connecting road system from airport to home
- The vehicle (car, train, etc.)

The necessary airliners now exist. Most of the world's communities have an airport or have access to one. Not all, but many homes have access to a vehicle for airport transportation. The uses made of the transcomnet varies considerably. Again, the cost of transcomnet services is the basic limiter.

3.4.1 World Transcomnet

The jet airliner is the key component in the world transcomnet.[°] It is likely to be replaced soon, however, by an air transportation vehicle that is faster, cheaper, and more versatile. For now, the jet plane makes the world network possible. The airport, road system, and ground vehicles each provide essential links. The jet plane, however, brought the world trans-

[°] The jet airplane may do what the railroad did a century ago, becoming a medium for exchanging values among otherwise isolated cultures.
Ben H. Bagdikian, 1971:26.

World Air Transportation Network

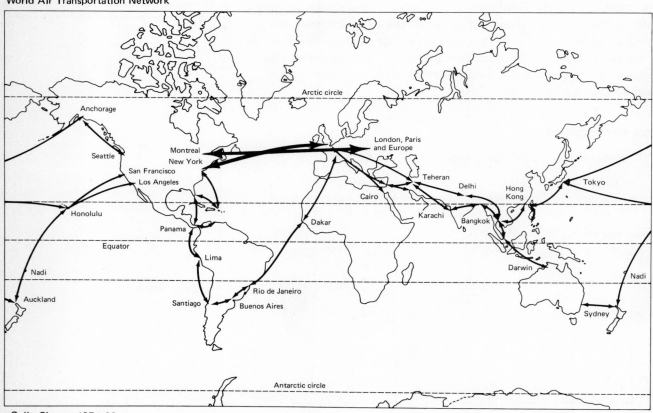

Colin Cherry, 1971:92

portation network into daily operation. While different, its influence on human communication equals that of the telecomnet.

The jet plane makes possible a world transcomnet. The jet has several obvious advantages. Unlike the train, it can travel over a variety of routes. Unlike the boat, it can travel over both water and land. Speed, however, is the most important advantage. At current speeds, nearly any two communities on earth are less than a full day or overnight flight apart. The jet shrunk the earth to a manageable size for man.

The growth of air travel creates problems at airports. The basic problem seems to be that airports are ground stations rather than ports suspended in air.[°] Fortunately, the problem is serious enough that imaginative solutions will either be developed or air travel will one day grind to a halt.

There promises to be major changes in the transcomnet in the years ahead. Perhaps new developments will parallel those brought about in the telecomnet. The satellite takes the "long" out of telephone calls by making all calls approximately the same distance.[°°] The space shuttle and a "flying airport" could remove the distance problem from transportation and reduce ground traffic problems as well.

3.4.2 Availability

Transcomnet facilities become more widely available.[□] Different size and types of aircraft make air transportation service available to an increasing percentage of the human communicators in the world.

The college student who spends a summer in a distant community can appreciate the importance of having transcomnet facilities available. Equally, the student who flies abroad to spend a few years as a student makes use of the available transcomnet facilities.

More persons travel beyond the boundaries of their home communities and on into a distant community.[□□] Travel always has two sets of consequences—those for the traveler who visits a distant community; and those for the community he visits. In a profound sense, the traveler conveys messages to the community he visits, *and* he also conveys other messages from the communities he visits back to his home community. Travel promotes cultural interchange. The transcomnet increases intercultural communication and decreases intracultural communication.

3.4.3 Cost

Most of the statements about cost of the telecomnet facilities also apply to the transcomnet. The world network provides most of its service in those communities where per capita income is highest.

Again, if new patterns of association are to be available within a

[°] On the most important intercontinental route, that across the North Atlantic . . . the number of passengers carried should increase from the actual value of about 4 million in 1965 to over 8 million in 1970 and to about 17 million by 1975—in other words, a fourfold increase over the projected period of ten years. *C. A. O'Flaherty, in Douglas Jones, 1971:175.*

[°°] . . . create centres in local communities, where the apparatus of communication is available for people who are each involved in different industries and businesses and in different types of work. New types of social relationship will build up. *Colin Cherry, in Douglas Jones, 1971:131.*

[□] The two most striking trends in the field of passenger transport at this time are the great increases in the number of private motor vehicles on the road, and the rapid growth rate of air passenger travel. *C. A. O'Flaherty, in Douglas Jones, 1971:174.*

[□□] There are administrators, scientists and businessmen today who spend about a third of their working lives either traveling or preparing to travel. *Arthur C. Clarke, 1967:176.*

community, some of its members will have to travel outside the boundaries of the community, and equally, other members of other communities must be transported into the community.

Transportation still costs money. The availability of money to members of a community is closely related to the availability of information. The telecomnet provides one means of access to information; the transcomnet provides another. Again, free service on the transcomet would cost only a fraction of the defense budgets of most countries, and free transportation might well increase security of all peoples of the world.

3.5 TWO-STEP FLOW

Technology makes possible two world communication networks. The hundreds of thousands of links in these networks are available for a full range of human purposes.

The reference model was presented in Unit 2.6. Recall that the model showed a single telecomnet link, a single transcomnet link, and a two-way dyadic speech communication system. We will now extend that model.

The telecomnet link is heavily used by radio and television broadcast stations. A broadcast station, radio or TV, is usually in operation between 18 and 24 hours a day every day of the year. From time to time, the question arises: What is the effect?

Most often it is the sponsor who pays for a "commercial" who wants to know what return he obtains for his money. The usual question is: Does the money spent on advertising increase sales? If so, how much? These practical questions and others related to voting practices produced a chain of unexpected findings.

The first attempts to find out the effect of a radio commercial showed almost no effect at all.° The listener, in most cases, did not listen and go right out and buy. This finding led to additional probing. Eventually, it became clear that one person in a community—an opinion leader or an influential, as he is called—would hear and remember a commercial. He in turn would talk the matter over with family and friends. Together, they would discuss and decide. Only then did the "influential" and his friends buy or not buy.

°

RADIO COMMERCIALS		
Indirect	1 2 3 ? 5 6 7	Direct
Ineffective	1 2 3 ? 5 6 7	Effective

3.5.1 One-Way Telecomnet, Two-Way Transcomnet

The effect of radio and television involves at least two steps, or in our terms, two systems. The first is a large group system in a telecomnet; a commercial is broadcast. The second is a dyad or a small group system in a transcomnet;

friends get together and talk things over. This two-part process is called the two-step flow of information and influence.

In terms of the reference model, there is a one-way "step" or link followed by a two-way "step" or link. For any particular message the flow of information—the message—is from one *very large* system to hundreds of dyadic and small group systems; of course there is also a switch in network. The message is examined by communicators in their home communities with whatever skill they can bring to bear on the decision to be made. Listening to a small group of housewives discussing the merits of their several choices of soap does not often instill great hope in the observer.

More or less by accident, we have come to look at the flow process from "mass media to the decision of the consumer." The organization of radio and TV broadcasting makes this format convenient. But the days of the broadcast station as a dominant force appear limited. There is another pattern.

3.5.2 Two-Way Transcomnet, Two-Way Telecomnet

The development of transceiver communication technology has far-reaching consequences. The broadcast station extends the "public address system" of one-to-many. But a quite different pattern could have evolved—and still can. The telephone model was available before radio and could have become the dominant communication pattern. While a telephone can be used as a one-way device, most users like and use the two-way feature. The telephone is a transceiver.

But suppose we ask how the "influential" gains his influence in his home community. When we do so, we find that he undertakes to obtain information relating to purposes common to himself and other members of the community. The influential becomes influential by knowing community purposes and seeking information pertinent to them.

Viewed in that way, the two-way transcomnet link both precedes and follows the present one-way telecomnet link. But there is no reason why the information seeker should not have more direct access to information relevant to his purposes.

Consider the remote control device for changing TV channels. The viewer sits in his easy chair; he can change channels by pressing a button; so far so good. At best, he has six choices, more likely he has three. If it is six in the evening, he can *choose* between three similar newscasts. The world and national news segments contain several of the same items; some of the local items will be the same and perhaps three or four will be different. There is choice, but less than there appears to be.

Two-Step Flow

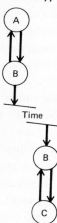

Two-Way, Two-Step Flow

Suppose that channel changing device were extended from 3 choices to 30 (like a juke box) or 30 thousand (like the books in a library) or 300 thousand (like a combination library, world news service, film library, etc.). At some level, a profound switch would occur. The viewer would or could cease being passive—"always watch that channel"—and become active. He would become a searcher, and to search, sooner or later he would have to choose a purpose for that search.

As every student who does research papers or prepares a speech knows, "you must have a purpose." In the home community, it becomes possible in a two-way system to select and refine purposes for *seeking* information, to receive the needed information in a two-way system, and subsequently, to re-engage in two-way communication in the home community.

The problem with any large one-way communication system is that it *must distort* by selection. The news through any national news network reflects the views of that nation—inescapably. Both information received in the home community and the world community is distorted by elimination of details, by pressures of time, and by the biases the reporter brings to his task.

Most importantly, a one-way system° in a telecomnet wastes a communicator's time. If he has a two-way telecomnet information system that provides specific answers to his specific questions, it seems unlikely that he will often choose the present one-way mass media format.

°

ONE-WAY SYSTEMS		
Ineffective	1 2 3 ? 5 6 7	Effective
Inefficient	1 2 3 ? 5 6 7	Efficient
Past	1 2 3 ? 5 6 7	Future

3.6 MIXED NETWORKS

The two-step flow model revealed a particular pattern in the use of the links provided by communication networks, the first step being the telecommunication link, the second being the transportation link. This is one pattern, but it is by no means the only one. There are other combinations that need also to be examined.

Some of the uses in world communities of radio broadcasts, for instance, have been preceded as well as followed by the transcomnet link. In some communities, for instance, a group gathers with a leader to discuss what they are going to hear. Together they then listen. After the program had been transmitted they again resume communication. This pattern has also been used extensively within school systems that have used educational radio or television programming as part of the regular educational fare. One can begin to elaborate on the two-step flow by mixing up the sequence. That is, the transportation net may do its work first, followed by the telecomnet, followed again by the transcomnet.

One of the more interesting places where network mixes are found in communication patterns is in air transportation itself. For instance, a pilot regularly communicates with his copilot by direct face-to-face communication while the aircraft is flying. He contacts the control tower at an airport to receive landing instructions and utilizes a telecommunication link in a two-way operation. From time to time, he communicates information to all of the passengers on the airliner; in this case he is operating a very small, closed-circuit broadcasting station. A passenger cannot, however, talk back to the pilot. There are many instances within the experience of every communicator in which there is a great deal of mixing and combining of communication network links.

There will be additional combinations available in the future. The videophone that is just coming into use may be called a two-way television station, if one wishes to "view" it that way. It adds a new dimension to the conference call.

At some future time it may be possible to combine the telecommunication network and the transportation communication network into a single communication network.[°] This would require a concept such as "teleporting" where it would be possible by means of an advanced "laser" beam to transmit a messenger from one location to another. Or conversely, it might be possible to have communicators meet in some communication space in which elements of the transporting of people were combined with the movement of messages. Such a development would involve some of the characteristics of both the present telecommunication network and the present transportation communication network.

Teleporting and related notions at present are more a part of science fiction than a part of the working technique of the human communicator.[°°] They are worth mentioning as possibilities only because the rapid developments within the field of communication have made all of us wary of saying, "Well, that can't possibly be done, because nobody has done it yet." In communication almost as soon as we have been able to clearly state a goal and indicate what it would take to get there, it has been possible to achieve that goal.

It took only a very short time to find a way of getting a man to the moon and to invent a communication operation that enabled 500 million people to watch that man put his foot on the moon and to hear him talk as he did so. In other words, developments can come very rapidly within the field of communication. In the whole area of communication networks there are potential breakthroughs that the alert communicator will be interested in knowing about.

[°] The distinction between material transportation and message transportation is not in any theoretical sense permanent and unbridgeable.
Norbert Wiener, 1954:98.

[°°] The communications network we are building may be such a technological masterpiece, such a miracle of power and speed and complexity, that it will have no place for man's slow and limited brain.
Arthur C. Clarke, 1967:122.

3.7 CONTROL OF WORLD NETWORKS

The two world communication networks require international coordination and control. Two UN agencies perform the coordination and control operations. These are the International Telecommunication Union and the International Civil Aviation Organization. There are also a number of other regional and national regulatory agencies.

3.7.1 Telecomnet Control

In 1865, the International Telegraph Union was organized in Geneva, Switzerland. That organization has broadened and has continued to operate up until the present time under the name, International Telecommunication Union. It is instructive to observe that this organization has been able to operate even when the nations which form its membership were at war with each other. So there has developed an unusual amount of cooperative planning within the International Telecommunication Union.

The formation of laws and regulations within this governing body has normally proceeded under a very pragmatic case-by-case basis which eventually builds up a principal of law which is then embodied within the total set of laws governing telecommunication. The body of law regulates the allocation of radio frequencies to various countries and regions within the world. These frequency allocations must be used in a manner which does not interfere with other users who are also making use of frequencies allocated to them on the radio spectrum.

Consider for a moment the dial on the radio which "switches" from one frequency region to another. Each mark represents an allocation of a station to a particular broadcast frequency; the radio dial serves as a small example of the larger problems that face the Telecommunication Union. It is responsible for allocating the very scarce and limited radio frequencies to serve the total regions of the world in the most effective manner possible

The coming of the communication satellite now makes necessary the development of a large new body of international regulation and law relating to the use of that device. Where the satellite is primarily used for point-to-point communication no very large or new problems are introduced. Much of the earlier telephone regulation suffices. As satellites begin to be used for distribution purposes as in the case of television programs being sent by one country to another country for rebroadcast in that country, a new set of problems arise.

The major area, though, where new law will develop over the next few years is in the area of a third use of communication satellite. This use comes out of a potential of the more powerful satellites that are now going into orbit. They have the power and capacity to engage in what is called point-to-point broadcasting. This capacity enables a television transmitter to send a program via satellite directly to a television set in the viewer's home. The direct broadcast possibility will require an additional body of telecommunication law.

There are a number of international conferences under way and these will continue during the next few years. Their purpose is to develop that body of law and regulation and controls which are necessary to protect the national interest of the various countries involved.

Quite clearly, radio waves and television broadcasts do not stop at national frontiers. When there are substantially different regulations from country to country relating to the handling of information, then, the problems raised in direct satellite broadcast become real and urgent. Particularly important is a country's policies in relation to news regulation. Some call such national regulation censorship; others view "news filters" as in the public interest. International law in the telecommunication area is a particularly challenging problem.

In general, there is agreement among the persons who work at developing this body of regulation and law that telecommunication networks ought to operate in the public interest. Of course, all of these terms are subject to somewhat different definitions from one region of the world to another, and therefore, a great deal of discussion is typically required before any advance can be made.

Within several regions of the world there are well-developed chains of agreement which can serve as models for direct satellite broadcast law. Within the European continent the European Broadcasting Union, both with radio and television, evolved over the past fifteen years a series of agreements which permit the exchange of programs between countries. Likewise, within any particular country the allocation of licenses to broadcast stations are typically covered within its total body of telecommunication law. The national rules and regulations must at some point be coordinated with the international telecommunication regulations.

3.7.2 Transcomnet Control

The transportation communication network serves as a common carrier for moving people and goods from one place to another. One encounters again a large body of law relating particularly to aviation.

The International Civil Aviation Organization, with headquarters in Montreal, Canada, has been able to maintain its regulatory work in spite of major world conflicts in which member nations were not at peace with each other. Again, as in the case of telecommunication, there is a necessity to maintain coordination and cooperation within this domain for the movement of people from one place to another around the world.

Convenient symbols for the regulations relating to the movement of people are the passport and the airline passenger ticket. The traveler must have both the proper, legal document to leave his country and to enter another country, and he must have the proper, legal ticket to permit him to make the particular trip. In the body of regulation growing up around the movement of people there has been a high degree of cooperation among the member nations. A recent example of this was the speed with which international agreements were reached to reduce the threat of hijacking of international airliners.

3.8 SUMMARY

In this chapter, the two world communication networks were introduced and discussed. The networks each serve some but not all of the communities of the world. New services are becoming available in nearly all communities.

The networks are usually used in combination. Within a community, information processing may require both networks several times a day.

Both networks link the three human communication systems—the dyad, the small group, and the large group. These network/system patterns will be examined in the following chapters.

3.S SKILLS: DYADIC SYSTEMS LINKED IN COMNET
PURPOSE

Compare a dyadic human communication system operating in a trans-comnet and a telecomnet:

- Score reliability of communication.
- Record time in seconds.

PROJECT

Each communicator will need the following materials:

- The template°
- A pencil with an eraser
- A watch with a second hand
- The skills worksheets for this unit

° The template is reproduced in a separate perforated section at the back of the book. Using the Skills Worksheet (also in the perforated section at the back of the book) for this unit, trace from the template page the shapes you wish your partner to match. He will attempt to match the shapes by drawing them on a separate, lightweight sheet of paper. He will then lay this sheet of paper on top of your sheet of paper to check the accuracy of the match.

Two communicators organize a dyadic human communication system:

- One system operates with a transcomnet link (face-to-face).
- The other operates with a telecomnet link (telephone).
- Flip a coin to decide which link to use first.
- Flip a coin to decide who will be Communicator A and who B.

Each system operates for the purpose of developing matching patterns:

- Each pattern has six shapes.
- The patterns match in all details.
- Each communicator selects a total of three shapes from the template—one shape from level one, one shape from level two, and one shape from level three.
- Communicator A begins; he draws in one shape and as he is drawing he describes what he is doing fully enough to enable Communicator B to draw the matching shape.°
- Communicator B draws a shape and describes what he is doing to Communicator A.
- A and B *alternate* until all six shapes are drawn.
- All shapes are at least 1/2 inch apart.
- They recheck all of the details of the pattern and correct any mismatches.
- When they agree that they have achieved the system purpose of developing matching patterns, they stop communicating.

° Do not look at each other's drawings until the task is completed. Transcomnet communicators should be seated back to back to insure comparability with the telecomnet link.

Achieve the indicated purpose in both a transcomnet and telecomnet link. For both systems:

- Score reliability of communication.°°
- A match occurs when the same two shapes are within 1/4 inch of each other within the framework.
- A mismatch occurs when two shapes are not within 1/4 inch of each other and when different forms are used.
- Score +1 for a match and −1 for a mismatch.
- Compute total
- Record time in seconds, and compute elapsed time in seconds.
- Write results for two systems.
- Compare results with those obtained in the other system.
- Write conclusions.

°° Tear out and use the scoring sheets for this Skills unit in the Skills Worksheets section at the back of the book.

3.Q QUESTIONS

3.Q.1 Consider your daily communication activities. How frequently do you use the transcomnet? How frequently do you use the telecomnet? For some of your communication purposes, are the two networks equal?

3.Q.2 Is it possible to communicate the same message in the two networks?

3.Q.3 Suppose transportation becomes free, fast, and convenient. At any hour of any day that you phone, in two minutes an electronic air taxi picks you up and flies you directly to a nearby airport. From there, you fly to any other airport in the world you choose. When you arrive, you are taken by air taxi to your exact destination. No two points on earth are more than six hours apart. What changes would you expect in your use of the transcomnet? In your community? In the world community?

3.Q.4 Suppose there was no longer any charge for use of telecommunication facilities. You have free two-way video phone. You can talk to anyone anywhere in the world free. Where would you call? Who would call you? What would this do to your present sleep habits?

4

DYADIC SYSTEMS

Three chapters—this one and the next two—focus on human communication systems as they operate within communication networks. My intent is to make the important *similarities* among these systems obvious and useful to you. Fortunately, there are many strong similarities among the dyad, small group, and large group human communication systems.

In the previous chapter, the two world communication networks were examined. These networks provide the linkages for all three communication systems. The telecomnet enables communicators to remain "at home" and still engage in communication with others either in the home community or in any other community in the world. The transcomnet transports one communicator to the community of some other communicator. Both these networks serve to link dyadic communication systems.

Human communication is a voluntary activity. Any communicator may choose not to communicate; he has that fundamental human right. When he does choose to communicate, however, certain consequences naturally follow.

4
Dyadic
Human
Communication
Systems

4.1 INTRODUCTION°

In our world at any time of day or night, of the nearly 4 billion "earth-lings," more than a billion are engaged in some form of human communication. Some of the links in the two world communication networks are in heavy use. Many human communication systems are operating; there are tens of thousands of large group systems, hundreds of thousands of small group systems, and millions of dyadic systems. Man is the animal who communicates, and he communicates to achieve a full range of human purposes.°°

At any instant in time, then, there are millions of dyadic human communication systems operating to achieve human purposes. If you ride your free space shuttle back to the skylab for a few minutes, you will be able to tune in on a number of these systems. Your instruments permit you to both hear and see. Of course, you also have an automatic language translation device!

After listening to about seven dyadic systems at various world locations, you begin to observe a number of similarities. You observe that all of the systems operate for a purpose. You note that these purposes arise from the full range of human problems and possibilities. At the same time, you observe only a very limited number of organizational conditions, and a few forms of system control. Having seen all this and more from your skylab observation post, you board the space shuttle and return to earth. At any instant in time, the amount of dyadic human communication in the world is enormous.

Of equal importance is the amount of dyadic communication the individual communicator engages in during the course of a day and a life time.□ Take a very *conservative* estimate. Assume a lifespan of 70 years and only 1 hour per day devoted to dyadic speech communication. Even such a conservative estimate yields 25,000 hours. Dyadic systems tend to operate for time periods between 2 minutes and 2 hours. Assume a conservative average time of 10 minutes per system; this estimate yields a modest 150,000 dyadic human communication systems per communicator per life time.

There are very few things a human does 150,000 times in a 70-year lifetime. Eating three meals a day totals only 75,000 meals. Even that much talked about other form of dyadic "interpersonal communication" figured at a persistent once a day rate for an improbable 50 years adds up to less than 20,000 instances. Dyadic communication systems merit attention.

°

DYADIC COMMUNICATION SYSTEM

Unimportant	1 2 3 ? 5 6 7	Important
Uncomfortable	1 2 3 ? 5 6 7	Comfortable
Impersonal	1 2 3 ? 5 6 7	Personal

°° . . . whenever you are involved in a communication situation you are both a sender and a receiver virutally all of the time, even though one of these roles may dominate at any given moment.
A. C. Baird, F. H. Knower, and S. L. Becker, 1971:73.

Dyadic System

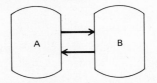

Communicator A   Communicator B

□

I'm at my best as a communicator when I'm talking with one other person I know well.

Disagree	1 2 3 ? 5 6 7	Agree
Bad	1 2 3 ? 5 6 7	Good

4.2 DEFINITION

A dyadic human communication system is organized by two and only two human communicators.° From this important fact arises both its many advantages and its few limitations. This system is sometimes called person-to-person communication, a two-group, the minimal social system, one-to-one communication, two-way voice communication, a conversational pair, a speaker-listener pair, a communication partnership, a dialog,°° a two-headed monster, a tutorial, an interview, an interchange dyad, a two-person speech communication system, a communication dyad, and, quite often, a dyadic system or a dyad. It is a system known by many names.

The dyad is the most basic and the most fundamental of the three human communication systems. The child in the home community learns to communicate in a dyad, usually in a mother–child dyad. Many of the basic oral "contracts" are worked out in a dyadic human communication system. For instance, the "understandings" that lead a man and woman to marry develop from dyadic communication. When a purpose for communicating is likely to have profound consequences for the individual communicator, he is likely to prefer a dyadic communication system.

4.2.1 Advantages

The major advantages of a dyadic system arise from the fact that it is small. Being small, any two persons who choose to do so can organize a dyad. The dyad can be controlled by one communicator or control can be shared; and all three message patterns, the tutorial, the interview, and the interchange, are possible. The dyad is not only small, it is flexible.□

The dyad can be organized by any two communicators who share a common language. It requires little or no advance preparation. Two communicators meet and start communicating immediately; there is little time wasted with formalities. The dyad can be used to achieve a full range of human purposes. The dyad works well in both the transcomnet and the telecomnet. Most importantly, any human who chooses to "invest" some of his time in communicating can usually find one other person willing to communicate with him. The dyad enables a communicator "to seek, receive, and impart information." It is of fundamental importance to the right of man to communicate.

In addition, the dyad can be adapted to new uses. For instance, man–machine communication is dyadic in nature.□□ Other new developments in communication are likely to build from a dyadic base.

° A conversation forms a two-way communication link, there is a measure of symmetry between the parties, and messages pass to and fro. . . . the behavior of the two individuals becomes concerted, co-operative, and directed toward some goal.
Colin Cherry, 1966:17.

°° . . . dialogue is *the* unit of communicative interaction, and monologue is a special case of dialogue in which one participant is silent or absent.
J. Jaffe and S. Feldstein, 1970:5.

□ Dialogue methods assume that one way people learn is in informal and open situations by grafting new knowledge relevant to them onto facts, theories, ideas and ideals already known. . . .
Robert Theobald, 1970:129.

□□ Using time-sharing techniques, a man may use a part share in a powerful computer and its files, at a fraction of the cost of the whole system. The term *man–machine symbiosis* is used to describe this new type of thinking—part machine, part human.
James Martin, 1969:20.

4.2.2 Limitations

There is one major limitation to the dyadic system. Only two persons communicate at any one time in any dyadic system. For most of us most of the time, that limitation creates no particular hardship. But for the salesman who wishes to sell the "the better widget to greater numbers of people," the dyad is an inefficient way to transmit his commercial message. Likewise, the politician who wants "to get everyone to vote for him" does not select the dyad. The dyad is of limited use for those purposes which require a single message to be transmitted at the same time to large numbers of "receiver-communicators."

4.3 TIME SHARING

From the time the dyadic system is *self*-organized to the time it is terminated, a dyadic system uses time in a distinctive way. A system can be described in terms of the amount of time it spends in each state. A dyadic system during its operation is always in one of four *states*. As illustrated, these states are:

Four-State System

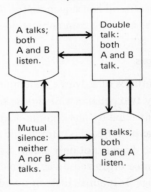

- Communicator A talks, and Communicator B is silent
- The reverse state where B talks, and A is silent
- Mutual silence
- Double talk

These four states exhaust the possible states for a dyadic system at any instant of time which the system is organized and operating.

On the average, quite different amounts of time are spent in each of these four states. As shown, about 5 percent of the time, the system is in the state of double talk. About 15 percent of the time, the system state is mutual silence. The remaining 80 percent of the time is divided equally between Communicator A and Communicator B. These averages are based on large numbers of dyads communicating for varying lengths of time.

Any two communicators—you and another "communicator", for instance—will vary from these percentages. However, if you choose to communicate with that other communicator *several times* in the future, the chances are good that the two of you will come close to these percentages on the average. If you differ noticeably from these percentages, you probably will not choose to communicate with each other.°

The important question is what happens when these percentages change. If double talk starts to increase, for instance, each percentage rise increases the likelihood that the communicators will become annoyed at the interruptions and terminate communication before achieving their purpose.

> I most enjoy a conversation when I get to do most of the talking.
>
> Disagree 1 2 3 ? 5 6 7 Agree

If mutual silence increases, it is likely that the communicators are formulating new sentences rather than repeating cliches. Silence also reflects cultural patterns.

Any change in the 40/40 split in talking time places pressure on the system. If Communicator A increases his talking time, he is likely to report that he is trying to be helpful; Communicator B however, is likely to report that he finds A is aggressive, lecturing, or inconsiderate.[°]

The division of talking time is a very sensitive matter in a dyad. If the purpose for communication is a mutual one, then talking time should be about equally split. If the use of the 80 percent talking time is split 50-30 the dyad is usually within tolerable limits. However, if the percentage becomes 60-20 or 70-10, then most of the advantage of the dyad is lost; the dyad begins to operate in the time pattern of a large group system.

Time sharing in a dyad is easy for an observer to note.[°°] It is also easy to hear from a tape recording. The time ratio is 1 double talk; 3 mutual silence; 8 A talks and 8 B talks. For the two communicators in a dyadic system it is not so easy to judge time in each of the four states.

Use of time within a speech communication system is an important defining characteristic. Whether or not the two communicators achieve their purpose depends to a large extent on how they share the available time.

[°] . . . the temporal patterning of a verbal exchange represents a source of important information about the communication and communicators.
A. W. Siegman and B. Pope, 1972:109.

[°°]

TIME SHARING		
Weak	1 2 3 ? 5 6 7	Strong
Slow	1 2 3 ? 5 6 7	Fast
Unfair	1 2 3 ? 5 6 7	Fair
Inefficient	1 2 3 ? 5 6 7	Efficient

4.4 PURPOSE

A dyadic human communication system operates to achieve some purpose; that much is true by definition for any system.[□] But notice that the statement applies to the *total system* and not just to the individual communicator. Therefore, we must relate the purpose of the individual communicator before he communicates to the purpose of the communication system in which he actually communicates.

The shift from the purpose of the individual communicator to the purpose of the human communication system is a profound one. By making this shift, the two communicators acknowledge that they are interdependent, that they can help each other, and that they agree to do so. The two individual communicators form a single human communication system. A system operates to achieve a single purpose.[□□]

The contrast between individual purpose and system purpose raises the most basic questions about freedom and control not only in communication but in all areas of human interaction. You may have already worked your way through these notions in a social science or philosophy course. We meet again the question of the right of the individual in relation to the right of the group. Parliamentary procedure, for instance, is a body of law for

[□]

A lot of conversation has no purpose whatsoever.

Disagree 1 2 3 ? 5 6 7 Agree

[□□] Conversation, or even casual remarks, all have purpose; they seek to greet, persuade, correct, ask, explain . . . though the speaker may not always know his purpose.
Colin Cherry, 1971:11.

reconciling the rights and responsibilities of the individual communicator and the large group human communication system. No similar body of procedure exists for a dyad. Within a community, however, a great deal of social pressure can be exerted on a dyadic system.

Human communication is *voluntary*.° Any individual communicator is free to decide on a purpose for communication and to seek another communicator who will organize a system to help him achieve that purpose. Two communicators are free to seek each other out to communicate for some purpose. But a system will operate to achieve only a single purpose.

The purpose of any individual communicator probably will not exactly coincide with the purpose of any other "available" communicator. In the course of organizing to communicate, then, a communicator will likely need to revise his purpose somewhat. *How much* he agrees to revise his purpose is a matter of attitude.°°

As he volunteers to communicate, the individual may find his pre-communication purpose affected in the following ways:

- He may find another communicator who wishes to communicate to achieve a similar or identical purpose.
- He may find another communicator who wishes to communicate to achieve a complimentary purpose.
- He may find it necessary to *revise* his precommunication purpose; he may find such a revision improves the purpose; he may find the revision makes the purpose uninteresting to him, and so he chooses not to communicate.

4.4.1 Specific Purpose

A purpose for a dyadic system may be arrived at in three ways: by agreement on a single purpose; by discovering complementary purposes; by revising the precommunication purposes of both communicators. By whatever means the purpose is determined, it must be specific.

A purpose for a dyadic human communication system needs to be specific enough to allow the following three tests;

- Both communicators and an interested observer ought to be able to state the system purpose in one short sentence. The two other persons ought to agree that the wording of the purpose statement is accurate.
- The purpose statement ought to be specific enough to permit the communicators and the observer to agree at any instant that the purpose

    has been achieved;
    has not yet been achieved; or,
    is not likely to be achieved, and communication should terminate.

°   In any dyad both members are dependent upon the relationship to some degree, so we speak of their being interdependent. . . . The pattern of interdependency which characterizes a relationship also affects the kinds of process agreements the pair must achieve if their relationship is to be maximally satisfactory.
J. W. Thibaut and H. H. Kelley, 1967:124.

°°   A communicator is able to shift from one dyad to another with facility because of his store of information pertaining to the different demands of the several dyads. He wears many hats.
G. A. Borden, R. B. Gregg, and T. G. Grove, 1969:126.

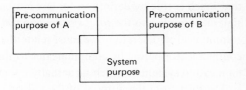

- The purpose should be specific enough to enable both communicators and an observer to know when

  particular words, sentences, and items of information contribute to the purpose (or detract from it); and when
  particular details of the association contribute to the purpose (or detract from it).

These three tests can be applied informally when a dyadic system is in operation. When a system starts to encounter difficulty, it is often useful to check to see if the purpose for communicating is understood and agreed on by both communicators.

4.4.2 General Purpose

Beyond the purpose of a particular system, each communicator should also attempt to achieve two general purposes. These purposes are important in both the home community and the world community.

- The two communicators ought to be at least as well-informed when they stop communicating as they were before they began communication.
- The two communicators ought to have at least as favorable an attitude toward communicating when they stop communicating as they had before they began communicating.

These are very modest purposes. But when they are regularly achieved, many of the *dis*-eases of communication do not develop. Every time these purposes are achieved—or exceeded on the positive side—the right of man to communicate advances a little. Add one plus mark.

4.5 ORGANIZATION

A dyadic human communication system is organized to achieve a *system* purpose. The agreement reached on system purpose determines the type of control in the system. System control can be *individual* or *shared*. Individual control leads on to *tutorial* or *interview* patterns; shared control leads on to an *interchange* communication pattern. How the communicators decide the problem of control greatly influences their communicative efforts.°

4.5.1 System Control

Every system is controlled in its activities as it seeks to achieve its purpose. In any dyadic speech communication system, there are two basic possibilities.°°

Take a simple example. An automobile starts at origin M and continues

° Socrates collected opinions, asked questions, clarified terms and ideas, and indicated commitments. That is all he did.
Robert M. Hutchins, in Floyd W. Matson and Ashley Montagu, 1967:325.

°° All communicational interchanges are either symmetrical or complementary, depending on whether they are based on equality or difference.
P. Watzlawick, J. H. Beavin, and D. D. Jackson, 1967:70.

to destination N. As a transportation system, the automobile is controlled by an individual driver. The situation does not change if there are one or several passengers. An airplane, on the other hand, has "dual controls." At any one time or another, from origin M to destination N, an airplane may be controlled by one or the other of the two persons qualified to pilot the plane. Neither individual or dual control is necessarily better than the other, it depends on the agreed upon purpose.

Consider individual control. One communicator assumes control of the system; he defines the purpose and decides to a large extent who says what to whom and determines when things get said. In this case, the communicator in control has the power to define the system purpose to be the same as his individual purpose.

Consider system control. Both communicators share control of the system. Both communicators concede their individual power to the system for the time that system is in operation. They share responsibility for the definition of system purpose.

The question of control revolves around the association that develops between the two communicators as they operate within a dyadic system. For reasons not related to the purpose of communication, one communicator may have the power to control the system. He may be smarter, richer, higher in status, older, a boss, and so on. While dyads often operate under control of an individual communicator, a dyad seldom operates effectively that way unless the system purpose requires it. And there are some purposes that require individual control.

4.5.2 Message Patterns

Given a particular control arrangement, certain communication patterns, or, more exactly, message processing patterns, become possible. The individual communicator control of a dyadic system leads to a *tutorial* pattern or an *interview* pattern. Shared system control leads to an *interchange* pattern.°

The *tutorial* is under individual control. Communicator A as *tutor* makes informative statements. Communicator B as *tutee* asks questions as needed to clarify statements made by A.

The tutorial pattern is widely used. It is the basic method for the large task of transmitting cultural heritage from father to son and mother to daughter in traditional societies and all others as well.

The tutorial *expands* into the one-to-several (7 ± 2) of the small group and the one-to-many (7 × 2) + *n* of the large group. We shall return to the tutorial in the next two chapters. The tutorial can be mechanized. Teaching machines present learning programs in a tutorial pattern.

The interview is also under individual control. Communicator A as

Control Patterns

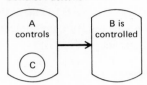

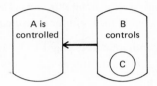

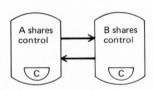

° Although some pair relationships seem to be based upon similarity of attitudes and background . . . others constitute symbiotic relationships in which the rewards one person provides the other are quite different from those provided in the reverse direction. This kind of relationship requires that the two individuals differ in certain respects . . . and in ways that are complementary, each being able at low cost to provide the special kind of product valued by the other.

J. W. Thibaut and H. H. Kelley, 1967:50.

interviewer asks directive questions. Communicator B as interviewee makes statements which answer those questions.

The interview pattern is also widely used when Communicator A defines his purpose and the system purpose as transmitting specific information about X. In the past, the interview has been used between human communicators. In the future, it promises to be an important pattern for humans to interview computer information storage centers. In the next few years, it will probably be easier for many purposes for you to interview the Library of Congress than to interview a fellow human when information acquisition is your purpose.

In the interchange, the two communicators share control. Both communicators make statements and ask and answer questions as required by the system purpose. At first glance, it appears only to combine the tutorial and interview patterns. But there is more to the interchange than that.

The interchange pattern is most likely to lead to *synergy* and *serendipity*. Both communicators share their resources to achieve a mutual system purpose. The interchange pattern grows in importance as it is necessary for human communicators to test the new information they receive from worldwide sources against the important human questions that can be provided only by another human.

The interchange pattern is particularly important when the two communicators have no way to pre-assess the areas of expertise and ignorance of one another. The interchange pattern is central to the right of man to communicate.

4.6 TUTORIAL: THE LEARNING PROGRAM

The tutorial pattern arises from a particular organization in a dyadic system. Communicator A controls. He defines the purpose. He determines what statements must be made to achieve that purpose.° A tutorial may be completely prepared in advance, or it may be only partially prepared.

Communicator B is controlled. He may choose to accept the purpose and join with A to achieve that purpose. Or he may choose not to communicate for that purpose. It is his right not to communicate. In the instance when A has only partially prepared the message, B may be able to partially redefine the system purpose while that system is in operation.

For a purpose that can be achieved by a tutorial, a communicator may prepare a message that is highly reliable. Communicator A might prepare a message and then communicate that message to Communicator B. Communicator A would observe any errors made by B, and he would test to

Tutorial Pattern

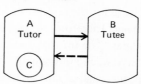

° . . . only a few people can absorb basically new data without opportunities for dialogue.
R. Theobald and J. M. Scott, 1972:14.

see if B achieved the purpose. Communicator A would repeat the procedure with communicators C, D, E, F, G, and H. By the time he has tested and revised the tutorial message seven times, the message will be reliable, assuming even modest skill on the part of communicator A. In the next seven dyadic systems organized by A, at least six should achieve the purpose.

It is now possible to say exactly what is meant by *reliable*. A message is reliable when it enables a system to achieve its purpose.° Reliability may be *high* or *low*. Satisfactory reliability is usually 85 percent or better. If six out of the seven dyads had achieved the system purpose, that would indicate satisfactory reliability.

The procedure for preparation and testing of a message described above is widely used. It is a simple and practical "cut and try" procedure. Wherever a tutorial pattern is appropriate that procedure is found. In the attempt to use tutorial method in education, learning programs are constructed in the tutorial pattern. It is interesting to note that after the initial testing stage, the "program" can easily be tutored by a teaching machine.

Whatever the purpose, there are two distinct stages. The message preparation/revision and the message testing stage. The prepare/revise stage is simple enough that even an amateur can easily accomplish it. The testing stage is equally simple. In fact, one of the important serendipitous findings in programed learning was that the best "tutor" was often the person who had just learned.

Repeating a message for the seventh or fifteenth time tends not to be rewarding for a human. Therefore, the professional tutors called "teachers" are rewarded by money. The tutorial pattern is the only one of the three—tutorial, interview, and interchange—that works with very little change in the dyad, the small group, and the large group.

4.7 INTERVIEW: THE DYADIC DELPHI

The interview pattern also develops in a dyadic system from a particular organization.°° Communicator A defines the purpose. He poses questions. He determines what answers are required to achieve that purpose. The questions to be asked in an interview may be completely or partially prepared in advance.

Communicator B is controlled. He may choose to accept the purpose for communicating implied by the questions posed by A and join with A to achieve that purpose or he may not. It is B's right not to be interviewed.

For a purpose that can be achieved by an interview, Communicator A

°
> A message is reliable when it enables a system to achieve its purpose.
>
> **Disagree 1 2 3 ? 5 6 7 Agree**

Interview Pattern

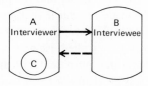

°°
. . . the interview is conceptualized as a dyadic communication system in which one of the participants, the interviewer, has as his major objective to obtain information from the other participant, the interviewee.
A. W. Siegman and B. Pope, 1972:29.

may prepare questions that result in reliable answers which in turn result in a reliable message that achieves a purpose.

In the preparation of a set of questions for an interview, it is also necessary to test and revise. As in the case with the tutorial, a series of seven dyadic systems after which A revises are necessary. The amateur sometimes assumes he can guess what the answers will be. The professional knows he cannot skip the test/revise stage.

A reliable set of questions ought to enable the interviewee to provide what he considers to be meaningful answers. Equally, at least six out of every seven communicators approached ought to agree to be interviewed.

In recent years, a new use has been made of interviewing to forecast the future and to develop plans for it.[°] This interview procedure has been called Delphi. It can be used both on a dyadic and a small group basis. We shall consider the dyadic system use here.

Assume you have just heard about the "open university." You know it is a rather new idea and you wonder whether it might be a possible career area for you. At this stage, you have a few vague questions. What kind of work could you do in an open university? What does "open" mean? How does a person prepare for it? And so on.

Suppose with a trusted friend or family member you work out a statement of purpose and about seven questions (+2) that will retrieve information related to that purpose. You also have to decide on interviewees—being careful to select those that can provide information to five or more of your seven questions.

After each interview, you summarize the information you acquire and revise your questions. By the time you have completed the revise/test sequence, you have a set of real and answerable questions. At this stage, you probably would like to "tutor" your friend on your findings and discuss, consult, and interchange with him on the meanings of these findings. When you have a set of real questions, you decide whether you now wish to seek answers to these questions.

If you decide to seek answers to these questions, you may wish to interview again some of the original interviewees. You will also want to seek some new ones. At the end of this series of interviews, you will sum up. You now have a reliable message to enable you to decide in terms of your original purpose.

If you decide that a career in an open university is the one you wish to pursue, you may wish to reshape your questions and focus them on a particular subarea—say the design of tutorial programs in communication for persons who wish to develop new communication skills.

The question/answer/revise sequence may be repeated as often as

° An interview is not an isolated speech-communication act. It is usually part of a larger process or a stage in some sequence of events. Thus, the medical interview is a stage in the process of diagnosis and treatment, the news interview is a step in the process of gathering and distributing information, the employment interview is a stage in the process of making decisions about hiring employees, a courtroom interrogation is part of the process of establishing a point of defense or accusation. If we try to think of the interview as unrelated to some larger purpose, without consideration of its specific function for that purpose, we run into difficulty. We need always to examine it in relation to the larger purpose for which it serves some function.
John W. Keltner, 1970:264.

necessary for your purpose. Each sequence can take from a few minutes to several hours. While the dyadic Delphi° is useful in an oral pattern, it is also useful in preparation of term papers, reports, and it resembles the workaday pattern of researchers in many fields.

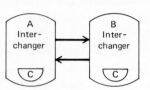

DYADIC DELPHI		
Safe	**1 2 3 ? 5 6 7**	**Risky**
Slow	**1 2 3 ? 5 6 7**	**Fast**
Difficult	**1 2 3 ? 5 6 7**	**Easy**
Inaccurate	**1 2 3 ? 5 6 7**	**Accurate**

4.8 INTERCHANGE: SYNSER

The interchange pattern of message development arises from a particular organization of a dyadic system. Communicators A and B share control. They decide on or develop a mutual purpose—one that neither could achieve as individuals. The message they develop is formed of questions and answers from both A and B. Both A and B have the right not to communicate.

The interchange dyad is characterized by several uncertainties. The purpose cannot be fully known in advance. The message cannot be planned in advance. And yet, it is the communication pattern with the greatest potential for man. It is the means for most fully sharing human intelligence. It is *the* pattern most central to the right of man to communicate.

The interchange pattern—shared control, mutual purpose, unique message—has several names. Buber calls it genuine dialog. Others call it real conversation.

Interchange is not tutoring—one person telling another person how things are. Interchange is not interviewing—one person asking another person how things are. Interchange develops when two persons together try to figure out how things are and how things might be. Interchange produces a unique message to achieve a unique purpose.

For the tutorial, one communicator may decide the purpose and prepare the message in advance. For the interview, one communicator may decide the purpose and prepare the questions in advance. In the interchange, neither the purpose nor the message required to achieve that purpose can be fully prepared in advance. As Buber noted, there is a "holy insecurity" in this type of communication.

Interchange °° best exemplifies the value of cybernetic thinking in human communication—the case where two persons communicate for achieving a mutual purpose that neither could achieve by himself. As the system operates to produce a unique purpose/message, it can fairly be said that only those two persons could accomplish exactly that purpose in that way at that time.

Interchange in the dyad offers the individual communicator an unusual opportunity. The interchange pattern in the dyad can generate both synergy and serendipity. The two communicators can combine their information into powerful new combinations; they achieve synergy. Also, the inter-

INTERCHANGE		
Passive	**1 2 3 ? 5 6 7**	**Active**
Weak	**1 2 3 ? 5 6 7**	**Strong**
Competitive	**1 2 3 ? 5 6 7**	**Cooperative**
Ugly	**1 2 3 ? 5 6 7**	**Beautiful**

change pattern enables the communicators to discover new insights in the unexpected turn of a sentence; they achieve serendipity. To remind you of this potential in the interchange dyad, a word has been coined: *synser*.

The more dissimilar any two communicators, the greater the likelihood they may achieve *synser* communication—*if* both communicators are skillful enough to bridge the gap that separates them. These gaps may be due to age, education level, ethnic background, social class, profession, race, creed, religion, nationality, language background, or in a single word, culture. Thus, intercultural communication offers the basic conditions for interchange. With sufficient communication skill, intercultural interchange can become synser.

4.9 SUMMARY

In this chapter, the dyadic human communication system has been discussed. The system was defined and its many advantages and one limitation were listed. The organization patterns were examined. Finally, the tutorial, interview, and interchange patterns were illustrated.

The dyad is the basic communication system. All of the fundamental patterns except one are present. That one exception is *system size*. As we shall see in the next two chapters, increasing system size reshapes these fundamental patterns.

4.S SKILLS: COMMUNICATION PATTERNS IN A DYADIC SYSTEM

PURPOSE

Demonstrate the advantages and limitations of the three basic communication patterns in a dyadic system:

- Score reliability for each pattern.
- Record time in seconds for each pattern.

PROJECT

Each communicator will need the following materials:

- The template°
- A pencil with an eraser
- A watch with a second hand
- The Skills Worksheets for this unit

° Follow the instructions in Unit 3.5 on the use of the template appearing in the perforated section at the back of the book.

Two communicators organize a dyadic communication system. Each system operates for the purpose of developing matching patterns:

- Utilize a transcomnet link.
- Utilize a telecomnet link.

Each communicator selects shapes in accordance with the specific instructions for:

- Tutorial
- Interview
- Interchange

Use the same scoring instructions as in 3.S.°

° The scoring sheets are in the Skills Worksheets section at the back of the book.

4.Q QUESTIONS:

4.Q.1 The three communication patterns differ in fundamental ways. Which one do you prefer? Why? Which pattern would be most useful in time of information scarcity? Abundance? Which best illustrates a two-way system? A one-way system?

4.Q.2 For your probable career, which of the three patterns do you expect to be most useful to you? For instance?

4.Q.3 Which pattern do you feel does most to advance the right of man to communicate?

Look back to Unit 1.7.

5

SMALL GROUP SYSTEMS

This chapter—like the last one and the next one—will stress the similarities among the three communication systems. The small group human communication system is the topic of this chapter.

The small group system operates in both the transcomnet and the telecomnet. At this point in time, the small group operates most often in a transcomnet—the communicators assemble in some predetermined place. Use of the telecomnet for conference calls and seminars is increasing. In the years ahead, the conference call linking several communicators will likely become as widely used as the simple telephone call is today.

5
Small Group
Human
Communication
Systems

5.1 INTRODUCTION°

In our world, at any time, hundreds of thousands of small group human communication systems are organized and operating.°° Most of these are assembled groups—transcomnet; others are disassembled groups— telecomnet. Were you to observe seven such systems, you would again notice a set of similarities. In many ways, the small group is much like the dyad—only bigger.

Small group systems operate for the same general purposes that dyads do; to understand, to coordinate, to agree, to plan. Again, two organizational patterns are used: individual control and shared control. The three message patterns are evident: tutorial, interview, and interchange. The two systems differ most greatly in their use of *time*.

When the small group operates well, it is the most powerful means available to man for increasing human intelligence.□ When seven communicators agree on a system purpose, they combine their resources to achieve that purpose within the operating small group. In addition to achieving purposes far beyond those an individual could achieve, successful small group communication increases the information of the individual communicators and improves the associations among the several communicators.

On the other hand, when the small group does not operate well, failure can be dismal and demoralizing. A small group can operate below the level of the least capable individual communicator. The associations among group members deteriorate as a consequence of failure. All the communicators are glad to leave the group and hope never to be in another group like that one.

The small group, then, can be extremely good or extremely bad and the full range in between. What then is a small group? How do communicators share time? What are its purposes? How is it organized? What are its typical patterns? All these questions are posed and answered in the following sections.

5.2 DEFINITION

A small group human communication system is organized by seven, plus or minus two, communicators.□□ From this important fact arise most of its advantages and limitations. This system is sometimes called a discussion group, a committee, a conference call, a panel discussion, a problem-solving group, a planning committee, a seminar, and quite often, a small group. You can easily add additional names.

In this book, the small group is defined as having five to nine persons— seven plus or minus two. Three- and four-person groups are also of some

°

°° The reader has spent and is now spending many of the most important minutes of his life communicating in small groups. . . . In small groups time and again he will acquire new information, change his attitudes toward other persons or social objects, and share in the creation of new ideas, objects, and maybe even institutions.
G. A. Borden, R. B. Gregg, and T. G. Grove, 1969:127.

□ Small face-to-face groups are among the means that individuals find to protect themselves from the vastness of nature, society, and the culture as a whole. . . . Most small groups, if they persist, develop a subculture that is protective for their members, and is allergic, in some respects, to the culture as a whole. The members are usually against something outside as well as for something inside.
Robert Freed Bales, 1970:153.

Small Group System

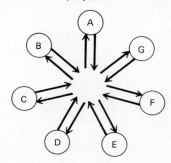

□□ From this home base of the family group, we join with other groups of varying significance to our social behavior. From the time each of us starts playing with other children— for most of us, at preschool age—peer groups, composed of friends and colleagues, are ubiquitous in our lives. In peer groups of children much social interaction takes place. . . . In each interest. The three-person group, or triad has been studied because of the interesting tendency for two communicators to pair off or form a coalition against the third communicator. The four-person group makes a double dyad; the double dyad is, of course, the basic debate team formation. The triad and the double dyad have attracted much interest for their competitive aspects. Competition—verbal war, if you will—makes of human communication a game in which every one loses.

Decreasing the small group below five communicators appears to promote competition; the communication process within the system changes. Increasing the number above nine produces a different effect; the organization of the system changes. As members are added to a small group, one of two things will happen. If the group maintains small group organizational patterns, it will gradually make itself into two groups. Or the organizational pattern will change to that of the large group. In the small group, the number of participants is a very sensitive matter.

A small group most often assembles in a single communication space, quite often around a table, where it is possible for the group members to sit comfortably, perhaps to have a few papers that they need for taking notes or introducing specific items of information, where they can maintain a comfortable working distance one from the other, and so on. By definition the group members focus on what each other has to say during the time the communication system is in operation. Each member follows the message that is being developed during the course of the operation of the system, and each person contributes to and draws from the contribution of the group. A small group communication system is often viewed as a means for sharing human intelligence.°

5.2.1 Advantages

The major advantages of the small group system develop from its capacity for sharing seven human intelligences. Like the dyad, the small group can operate under individual communicator control or under shared system control. The small group can also utilize the three message patterns of tutorial, interview, or interchange. The small group is also quite flexible, but less so than a dyad.

The small group can be organized by anywhere from five to nine communicators. While it is considerably more difficult to get seven than two persons together, with a little preplanning, small group systems can be arranged. But time and effort must be devoted to assembling the group.°°

In the years ahead, it seems likely that the small group will be more widely used for planning for the future. Small groups can be especially effective in bringing a plan into existence. As videophone conference arrangements become more widely available, the multinational planning

group the essence of the interaction among persons in the face-to-face situation is the communication process.
John W. Keltner, 1970:292.

Debate: Double Dyad

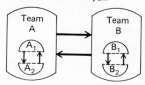

° . . . we mean a cooperative and relatively systematic process in which a group of persons exchange and evaluate ideas and information about a mutual problem in order to understand or solve that problem.
A. H. Monroe and D. Ehninger, 1967:568.

°° In our society more and more of the daily operations of business, education and government are directed by groups of people meeting as committees, boards, or councils. . . . Often, indeed, a man's success in his job depends on how skilled a discussion leader or participant he may be.
A. H. Monroe and D. Ehninger, 1967:568.

group seems likely to grow in importance. As the world becomes more interdependent there are few major problems in a community that can be fully solved within a community.°

5.2.2 Limitations

The major limitations of a small group system grow out of a peculiar characteristic of systems, any system. The more interdependent the parts of a system, the more the total system is influenced by any single part that operates in an inappropriate manner. Thus, a small group system can be "broken down" by any communicator who elects to make the system ineffective. While there are a number of techniques that group members can use to control a group member, still any one communicator can keep the group from achieving its purpose. In a dyad it is usually easy to choose not to communicate. In the small group, communicators usually find it more difficult to terminate a malfunctioning small group system.

5.3 TIME SHARING

From the time the small group human communication system is organized to the time it is terminated, a small group operates in "real-time." A small group system during its operation is *nearly always* in one of four states. As illustrated, these states are:

- One communicator talks to one other communicator
- One communicator talks to all the other communicators
- Mutual silence
- Double talk

These four states are by far the most frequent in a small group system; they account for more than 90 percent of the communication activity in a system organized to achieve a purpose. At times within the small group system, one communicator may appear to talk with more than one and less than the full group; this, however, is relatively rare. For practical purposes, the four states exhaust the possibilities in a small group system.

On the average, quite different amounts of system time are spent in each of the four states.°°As shown, about 5 percent of system time is "wasted" in the form of noise called double-talk. In a small group system, it may result from two or more communicators attempting to obtain the floor at the same time. About 15 percent of the time, the system is in a state of mutual silence. The remaining 80 percent of the time is divided among the seven communicators.

The 80 percent talking time works out to about 11 percent for each of

Four-State System

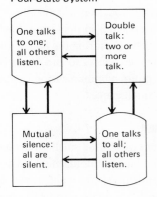

°°

> **I most enjoy group discussions when I talk about half the time.**
>
> Disagree 1 2 3 ? 5 6 7 Agree

the seven communicators. Few systems achieve such a division of time in short meeting. But successful small groups do draw contributions from all members; and contributions take time. In an hour-long meeting, each member has time for about one five-minute speech, or five one-minute speeches, or ten thirty-second contributions. The shorter the individual contributions, on the average, the more successful the small group will be.

Any single communicator can usually keep the group from achieving its purpose.[°] All he has to do is operate as if he were in some other communication system. In the interchange dyad, a communicator normally talks 40 percent of the time. That same talking time for any of the seven communicators in a small group reduces the available time from 11 percent to 6 percent for the other six communicators. Even worse, a communicator may behave as if he were the "speaker" in a large group and talk 80 or 90 percent of the time. Nearly as unhelpful is the communicator who acts as if he were an audience member in the back row of a large group; he says nothing and is a group parasite. A first place to look for the cause of failure in a small group is to check how the seven communicators share time; the successful small group displays effective time sharing techniques.

There are many communication techniques for holding the floor—for claiming system time—in a small group. Among these are talking louder than anyone else, pounding on the table, standing up, and filling pauses with "uh." Every good debater masters such floor control techniques; so do the public speaker and the college lecturer. Floor control techniques useful and necessary in other communication systems severely limit and often destroy the potential for synergy and serendipity in the small group.

It is only a matter of time, but that time is system time. No single communicator owns it. If time sharing problems exist in the small group, little can be accomplished until these are resolved.

[°] At times one or two persons in the group may begin to monopolize the conversation. Not infrequently such persons have a great deal to contribute, but there is also a very strong possibility that they will repeat themselves or expand obvious points needlessly.
A. H. Monroe and D. Ehninger, 1967:597.

5.4 PURPOSE

Like the dyad, the small group system is organized to achieve a purpose. The purposes that can be achieved can usually be classified or categorized into four groups: to understand, to coordinate, to agree, and to plan. These are not tight logical categories. We do not yet have a taxonomy of communication purposes.[°°]

The four general types of purposes are intended to assist the communicator in his choice of system/network to achieve a particular purpose. The systems are not equally good for purposes of developing a plan, for instance. Nor are they equally appropriate for obtaining agreement or building mutual understanding. Each system/network has advantages and limitations when viewed in terms of a particular purpose.

[°°] Discussions usually have one of two basic purposes: (1) to exchange information or ideas, or (2) to reach an agreement or decision.
A. H. Monroe and D. Ehninger, 1967:569.

A communication system operates to achieve a *system* purpose. A small group system may be organized to achieve a purpose assigned to it; a committee is very often created to achieve a purpose or a set of related purposes.° A discussion group may have only a vague notion that "something needs to be done." Their first task is to figure out what their purpose is; sometimes it is only possible to state a first approximation of a purpose.

Three requirements are especially important for a purpose in a small group system:

- The purpose must be stated and known by all of the communicators.
- The purpose must be precise enough for the group members to recognize whether the purpose is being achieved or not being achieved at any point in time.
- The communicators must reshape their own individual purposes to support the system purpose once it is agreed on, or else they should "choose" not to communicate.

If the purpose is unknown, or unknown to some of the communicators, a small group wastes time on matters not related to its purpose. If the purpose is vague, any contribution has some possible but unknown potential; members have no basis for selecting what they say or do not say. Seldom do all members of a group choose the system purpose prior to beginning communication. The right to communicate takes as a first principle that any person has the right not to communicate; it does not follow that he has also the right to prohibit others from communicating. A communicator who agrees to communicate to achieve a purpose in a small group system and then attempts to make it impossible for the group to achieve its purpose resembles the man who attends large group communication activities only to heckle.

5.5 ORGANIZATION

A small group communication system is organized to achieve an agreed-upon purpose. The agreement reached on the purpose of the system determines the type of control in the system. As in the dyad, system control in the small group can be either *individual* or *shared*.°° Again, as in the case of the dyad, individual control leads on to *tutorial* or *interview* patterns; shared control promotes the *interchange* pattern.

5.5.1 Control

Every system is controlled as it seeks to achieve its purpose. In any small group system, as in the dyad, there are two basic possibilities.

° But any small group you might belong to will have some effect on you personally. There is no question but that you will change as a result of your participation. . . .
G. M. Phillips and E. C. Erickson, 1970:48.

°° . . . the unique aspect of discussion is that a participant is both sender—receiver . . . a truly dynamic, interactive, interpersonal communication situation.
Raymond S. Ross, 1970:212.

Again, an automobile starts at origin M and continues to destination N. As a transportation system, it is controlled or guided by an individual driver. It matters relatively little whether there is one passenger (dyad) or five (small group). Examples of a "seven control" system are less easy to find. The best example comes from the small group itself. The small group operating under shared system control is guided by "seven intelligences."

Obviously, some purposes are best achieved by a small group under control of an individual communicator. The names given this role include: *chairman,* usually of a committee; *moderator,* usually via radio or TV; and *leader,* usually of a group discussion. There are, of course, several other titles. When the purpose is assigned, and time is short, the group under individual control is likely to be most successful in achieving its purpose.

Equally, some purposes are best achieved by a small group under *shared* control. The names given this control arrangement are: leaderless group, brainstorming group, free group, discussion group, and interchange group. When the purpose is initially vague and time is flexible, shared control is likely to be by far the better choice.

5.5.2 Patterns

As in the dyad, given a particular control arrangement, certain message patterns follow quite naturally. Again, individual control leads to a tutorial or interview pattern. Shared system control leads to an interchange pattern.

5.6 TUTORIAL: THE PANEL DISCUSSION

The panel discussion is a *mixed* communication system.° It has several characteristics that bear noting. First, it is typically preceded by several other communication systems. It is a rather late stage in the "trajectory of an idea."

Let us work through a current example. In times of rapid change, old problems often appear in new and more intense forms. In many home communities, the time-tested patterns of family formation and maintenance are undergoing change. The "pill" has made possible the control of human reproduction. At the same time, some minor old patterns are changed into major new ones. Premarital sexual relationships, trial marriages, and group marriages increase. At the same time venereal disease increases to the level where it is probable that, by age 25, one out of two persons will have been infected by venereal disease one or more times. Current medications tend to decrease in effectiveness in two ways: they are less effective in second and third treatment of the same individual; and more of the same medication

° The panel discussion is typically composed of 3 to 7 people pursuing a common goal in an informal climate which facilitates spontaneous interaction. An audience may or may not be present. It typically calls for a procedural leader and some agenda.
Raymond S. Ross, 1970:213.

than in previous years is required to control the infection. A change escalates a minor old problem into a major new one.

As a problem becomes recognized as major, a greater portion of the resources of the community and the nation are committed to the solution of that problem. Assume several national research teams are at work on various aspects of the problem. One of the groups working on syphilis develops a vaccine. That vaccine shares some characteristics with other vaccines widely used such as those for polio and measles and it has some unique characteristics as well. As every breakthrough from miracle rice to space flight has both advantages and limitations, let us build a few into the new vaccine. Let us assume it is 95 percent effective when administered before puberty; there is a 25 percent possibility that it may bring on menopause ten years early; and it will leave 25 percent of the males sterile for a period of up to 15 years immediately after the vaccine is administered. (Because it is all too easy to believe what is cast into print, let me stress again that this vaccine is created for the purpose of *illustrating* the use of the panel discussion.) These invented levels of effectiveness illustrate that any invention, discovery, or breakthrough has both a plus and minus sign attached to it. This mixing of characteristics requires communication—hours and hours of communication—to gather information and to act or not act on the basis of it.

Assume the fictional vaccine has been tested over a five-year period in 100 communities. The researchers who developed the vaccine and the national testing groups approve the release of the vaccine. All persons associated with the vaccine urge a full disclosure of the characteristics of the vaccine and insist that use of the vaccine be on a voluntary basis.

Seven communicators especially concerned with the rising VD rate from a home community attend a week-long national conference. They receive information on the vaccine itself, learn how to obtain it, and they discuss the alternative actions to be taken in their own community. They return to their home community.

The seven communicators as community members concerned about different aspects of the problem meet to plan a course of action. During their group interchange, they begin to develop a number of purposes for future communication. Their first purpose is to discover the current information level in the community; they allow a week in which each of the seven engages in dyadic interviews, interchanges, and tutorials. At the next group meeting, they share or interchange the information they have accumulated. After some further discussion, they agree that a panel discussion is the appropriate next system.

The purpose of the panel discussion is to provide information° necessary for the community members to understand the vaccine. The seven communicators agree among themselves who is responsible for what information areas. They select a group leader.

The group leader talks over the various alternatives. The panel discussion will be the first community discussion of the vaccine. The communicators recognize that how they present the information will have much to do with the success of the voluntary program.

The leader suggests the following general steps:

- Each communicator works out informal notes to remind himself of the information items he is responsible for; he develops a "message plan."
- The communicators talk through their notes; the leader arranges to tape record and observe how the panel fits together.
- The communicators listen to and/or talk over their presentation.
- The leader takes the tape and "tries it out" on a few friends; he reports their reactions at the next meeting.
- The individual communicators try out their messages in a series of dyadic tutorials and make indicated revisions, being careful that the revisions take into account the total panel.
- The panel makes its presentations before an audience of 15 or more persons.
- Panel communicators answer questions from audience members.
- The leader adjourns the panel.
- Individual panel members talk informally to small groups of audience members—this is often the most important stage of the panel.
- Audience members discuss among themselves, with family members and so on. Communication continues in other systems for related purposes.

A panel discussion such as the one described has no single starting point; it grows out of the accumulated experience in a number of communication systems, and it is followed by still other communication systems. The combination of a recurrent problem and a new body of information leads to a great deal of human communication.

Assume that the panel was also videotaped. That taped message might be shown on local television stations, in the schools, and at short meetings of local groups. If the videotape is effective, copies of the tape may be requested by other communities.

Once in circulation a message is frequently used for purposes beyond

°   We propose that thinking about the group as an information pool provides a frame-work in which a member can ask the best questions concerning what behaviors he should contribute to the group in a given situation. Quite simply, a participant . . . should consider that the group contains a wealth of resources consisting of various kinds of information. . . . the group task is to extract from the group that information which is relevant and necessary to its goal. Another part of this task is to leave in or to avoid information possessed by the group that is superfluous or potentially destructive to its goal achievement.
G. A. Borden, R. B. Gregg, and T. G. Grove, 1969:141.

those originally intended for it. For example, the same tape might be studied as part of the worldwide process of dissemination of information on new developments. It might be used by certain groups as an example of moral decadence and by others as an illustration of good men communicating well. The more effective a message in achieving its original purpose, the more likely that message or elements from it will be used as information in other systems for other purposes.

5.7 INTERVIEW: THE GROUP DELPHI

Like the dyadic Delphi, the group Delphi is under the control of Communicator A, the interviewer. He defines the purpose. Or he participates in other dyadic or small group interchange systems in which the purpose is discussed and determined. He decides what questions are to be asked, and he prepares a formal set of questions or a formal interview schedule. Normally, he will discuss the appropriateness of the questions with other communicators.

Communicators B, C, D, E, F, and G may choose to communicate or not to communicate. The group Delphi may be assembled in a single transcomnet space, or it may be interlinked in a conference call, or the members may be interviewed separately. Communicator A poses exactly the same questions to each group member and secures the response of the interviewees to these questions.

Communicators B–G may be selected because they are particularly well-informed in an area, they may be selected because of their known variety of information on the topic, or on any other basis which is appropriate to the purpose of the group Delphi.

Communicator A collects the answers to his questions provided by the six interviewees B–G. He asks the questions, analyzes the answers he receives, and summarizes them. He repeats this process for each question.

When he has finished summarizing the answers to his questions, he examines the original questions. He now knows better what questions he should have asked. To that extent at least, he is better informed. He draws up a new set of questions. He changes the wording of some questions; he combines two or more questions; he divides one question into two questions; he drops out a question or adds a new one. The Delphi leader recognizes that the well-stated question is the hardest part of achieving any communication purpose. With a well-stated question, the necessary information is often obvious.

The Delphi leader repeats the cycle with the six interviewees. He may add new communicators and others may drop out. He repeats his analysis. He revises the questions.

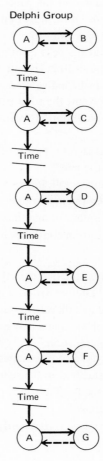

Delphi Group

In the Delphi, as in all human communication, there is a point of diminishing return. In the Delphi, that point usually comes between two and seven cycles. The Delphi might be used in a home community when a major change is to be undertaken, when there are alternatives, and when the consequences of any particular alternative are impossible for any single individual to forecast.

Assume a community with a transportation problem. There are three principal centers: an airport center, a city center, and a residential suburb. Most persons live in the suburb, which is on the far side of a mountain, and work in the city. But a substantial number of persons also work in the airport center and in the industries that surround it. Most persons who work at the airport also live in the suburb. One major highway links the city to the suburb; another links the airport to the suburb. The city center is linked to the airport center by an adequate highway. A proposal has been made for a new transportation route to run from the center of the residential area to the midpoint between the city center and the airport center. Clearly, something has to be done, but what?

Assume you and your associates have been hired to develop at least three alternative plans. You discuss with your six associates several alternatives that are already known. Two of your associates will work up an alternative plan to better use the existing highways. Three of your associates will consider the proposed traffic way through the mountain. You and another associate will work up a plan for substituting telecommunication traffic for transportation traffic.

As an interchange dyad you and your associate shape up the specific purpose for your plan. At this stage you are attempting to invent or create an alternative plan. Later, others will disseminate or spread the news about that plan or some other plan across the community. As that occurs, consequences, or reactions to the idea, will also occur.

Knowing the problems of the dissemination process, you and your associate take considerable time in stating your purpose. You shape a tentative list of questions that you will ask your Delphi group to answer for you. As you and your associate shape up the list of questions, you observe patterns of activities in offices in the city center and in the activities surrounding the airport. You browse in the library. You recall half remembered details. There was a report about the trade-offs between telecommunication and transportation. Eventually, you and your associate are content that you have a set of questions that are good enough to start with.

You and your associate talk through the questions with your full group. The two of you indicate what range of responses you expect for each question. Your other associates suggest a few changes in those questions. Jointly, you decide on the members of the group Delphi. You ask the group Delphi members to answer your questions. You may assemble the "Delphites" via telecomnet or transcomnet, or you may contact them individually. You are more concerned about the information you seek than you are about the system. When you have answers from all of them, you analyze, summarize, and revise, and then repeat the process one or more times.

From the information obtained from the group Delphi, you and your associate draw up a plan. Your other associates present their two plans. The plans are submitted to the community for action.

5.8 INTERCHANGE: THE INVENTION GROUP

The invention group has many names. Among those names are: brain-storming, free discussion, synectics group, research team, creativity group, invisible college, a planning group, or an interchange group. You can add names to the list. The invention group should not be confused with either a sensitivity group or an encounter group.

The invention group operates under shared system control. Most often, the communicators work in a vaguely defined problem area. They must invent, discover, or create a purpose; and they must fashion a message that enables them to achieve that purpose. The group is sometimes called a problem-stating, problem-solving group. The group may operate for a few minutes, a few hours, or a few years. Interestingly enough, seven years seems to be about the maximum amount of time a group can work together productively.

Members of an effective invention group are usually unable to describe either the purpose-shaping or message-building process. Some clues are obtained from tape recordings. Group observers provide additional insight.

Let us take our long-range goal, the right to communicate,° as an example. There is a general problem area. A very general purpose was stated in the preface. But there exists no well-developed statement of what such a right includes. Even if well-developed, there is no sure mechanism for disseminating that right, and there is no way to know fully what the consequences of such a right might be.

Any seven people are likely to agree that we are in the early stages of a communication revolution, that such a revolution will change each of us, and that we can guide that revolution if we set out to do so. If your group set out to invent a plan for the invention, diffusion, and assessment of consequences, you would undertake a task of long duration.

But your invention group could come up with a plan. Along the way you might engage in dyadic Delphis and group Delphis. A good amount of

°

RIGHT TO COMMUNICATE		
Short-Range	1 2 3 ? 5 6 7	Long-Range
Ugly	1 2 3 ? 5 6 7	Beautiful
Competitive	1 2 3 ? 5 6 7	Cooperative

dyadic interchange would take place. But over time, a purpose would be specified and a message to achieve that purpose would be developed. The invention group would invent a plan to guide future action.

5.9 SUMMARY

In this chapter, the small group system has been defined and its time-sharing problems have been indicated.° The organization of the small group was outlined. Finally, examples were given of the tutorial, interview, and interchange patterns.

5.S SKILLS: SMALL GROUP SYSTEMS IN OPERATION
PURPOSE

Demonstrate the advantages and limitations of the small group system:

- Score reliability for each pattern.
- Record time in seconds for each pattern.

PROJECT

Each communicator will need the following materials:
- The template
- A pencil and an eraser
- A watch with a second hand
- The Skills Worksheets for this Unit (in the perforated section at the end of the book).

Seven (± 2) communicators organize a small group system.

Each system operates for the purpose of developing matching patterns:
- Utilize a transcomnet link or a telecomnet link.

Each communicator selects forms in accordance with the specific instructions for the interchange.

Each communicator selects one shape and describes it.

- The next communicator "seated at the right" selects another shape from a different level; he draws and describes it.
- The process continues until each communicator has described one shape, and all communicators have drawn all shapes.
- The group selects one completed pattern; that pattern becomes the model against which all other patterns are matched.
- Score in the same manner as the dyadic project.

°   But if one really wishes to do so, nearly any group member can improve his understanding of what has just happened by thinking things over afterward. . . . One can train himself to observe and understand more effectively in natural interpersonal situations.
Robert Freed Bales, 1970:3.

This chapter—like the two preceding it—will continue to stress the similarities among the three major human communication systems. The large group human communication system can operate within either a transcomnet or telecomnet; at present, more different large groups operate in a transcomnet, but more communicators participate in the large groups in the telecomnet.

6
Large Group
Human
Communication
Systems

6
LARGE GROUP SYSTEMS

6.1 INTRODUCTION°

At any time of the day or night, tens of thousands of large group communication systems are in operation. If you step back into the skylab again for a few moments, you will observe that these large systems vary greatly in number of communicators. The systems organized in a transcomnet link range for the most part between 15 and 50 communicators; occasionally, such a system will include 500 or 5,000 or 50,000 communicators, or in the great squares such as those in Moscow and Peking, 500,000 or more. On the other hand, the large group system organized in a telecomnet may frequently engage 500,000 communicators, or 5,000,000, and for events such as the first man on the moon or the first U.S. President in Peking, 500,000,000 or more. There are many fewer large group communication systems than small group systems or dyadic systems, but communicators often spend more time in large group systems than they do in small group and dyadic systems combined—*far more*.°° Now back to earth.

Let us consider again the individual communicator. While a child, he first learns to communicate within the family group in the home community. Most of that learning to communicate occurs in a dyad. Some of it is in a small group. Both dyad and small group require both speaking and listening, both transmitting and receiving activities. Consequently, he must learn to use time differently when he is in a large group system. Television begins to teach the listener role. The training is completed in the classroom. The TV and classroom listener is a receive-only communicator; he sacrifices a major part of his right to communicate when he may only receive. That should worry you.

The most difficult thing a young human learns when he goes to school is that he must sit still and be quiet. "Trouble makers" in a classroom "talk a lot." The large group human communication systems all require that a listener listen quietly. No talking is the first rule of the receiver-communicator.□

At age 16, a young communicator spends about equal amounts of time before the TV and in the classroom. In both systems, he operates with a receive-only right. He seldom seeks information; he rarely imparts information. Even in participative classrooms, the individual student communicator who participates in a large group system—whether in a transcomnet or a telecomnet link—has a receive-only right. He does not have the right to "seek" or "impart" as set forth in Article 19 of the UN Declaration of Human Rights. He does not yet have the right to communicate.□□

To push the matter one step further, in the traditional public speaking course, the individual communicator will "speak" for some purpose fewer

°° The Greek city-states may have known democracy in the market place, but they were small communities and citizens could meet one another, listen to oratory, discuss and criticize. . . . The real problem of communication within today's nation-states is the problem of *size*. They are too big.
Colin Cherry, 1971:199.

□ First and most important, we must realize that the act of speaking is not a one-way process, but involves a series of interacting elements. . . . The interactions . . . are most obvious, of course, in the give-and-take of conversation and group discussion. They are equally present in the public speaking situation, however. . . .
A. H. Monroe and D. Ehninger, 1967:16.

□□ The schoolhouse is not simply the result of accident and inadequate theorizing; it arose in response to a certain type of teaching (sit and learn) in a certain type of society.
Robert Sommer, 1969:72.

minutes than there are hours in the course. In a semester-long course that meets for 40 periods of 50 minutes in length, a maximum of 2000 minutes are available. Given a class of twenty students, the maximum time per student would be 100 minutes. Allow time for the instructor to read the course syllabus, lecture on the text, criticize speeches, and so on, and the talking time per student is below 50 minutes. The average time for a student to impart information will fall below 30 minutes. That compares with 1970 minutes available for listening—mostly to the teacher.°

These introductory comments are intended to point out that for almost all of us large group human communication systems operate as *receive-only* systems. Our freedom to impart information in a large group system—transcomnet or telecomnet—will be less than one minute per each 10,000 minutes of receive time.

In many ways the large group human communication system requires no introduction. It is well enough known in its basic outline to introduce itself. However, the distinction between the dyadic, the small group and the large group systems are seldom made clear. The practitioner tends to view his communication activity from the vantage point of a particular system. Most often, the writing on the topic does not make the useful similarities and the essential differences among the three systems as pointed as they deserve to be made.

It becomes possible now to view a large group system as 15 or more simultaneous dyads operating at the same time. It also becomes possible to view the large group system as several small groups dispersed within an assembled "audience." If you observe a practiced public speaker, you will notice that he will appear to be communicating directly to some six or seven listeners at strategic locations in the audience, much as the leader does in the small group. Or else he will appear to address the entire group as a collectivity; when he does so, he operates as if he were in the tutorial in the dyadic system. If he attempts to communicate to individual listeners by providing examples for one particular listener and then for another listener, he employs in rapid succession a technique which looks rather much like the dyadic Delphi. Of course, if he appears to direct a particular sentence or a particular item of information to some five or six people in a particular location in his audience, then he is treating the assembled audience as though *some* of its members were part of his own small group.

It's important to be able to look at each communication system from the viewpoint afforded by the two other systems. The large group, then, usually resembles the tutorial in the dyadic system where Communicator A has the information and also controls the operation of the system. The large group

° Recall that the participant style of modern society, as contrasted with the isolated lifeways of traditional society, hinges on the *frequency* of participation by individuals.
Daniel Lerner, 1958:57.

Large Group Human Communication System

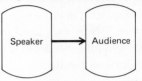

Simultaneous Dyads

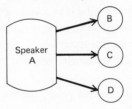

Small Group within Large Group

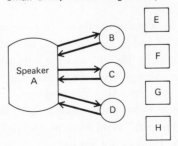

also resembles the individual control organization in the small group. By way of introduction to a large group communication system, one can make use of the perspectives developed in the dyad and can also make use of the perspectives developed in the small group.

The most *essential* difference among the three systems lies in message processing.[°] Whereas both the small group and the dyad can function *either* as transmitters of messages or developers of messages, the large system in terms of its purposes and organization and message pattern, almost always relies on a prepared message. Even though the message is fully prepared, the speaker-communicator attempts to make it seem extemporaneous or spontaneous. But the instructions given to communicators from the time of Aristotle in regard to large group communication make very clear the necessity of specific and detailed advance preparation. The advice is also given that the preparation should not be apparent. A communicator in the role of public speaker ought to appear to be speaking extemporaneously.

We turn now to a definition of the large group.

[°]

LARGE GROUP		
Unprepared	1 2 3 ? 5 6 7	Prepared
Informal	1 2 3 ? 5 6 7	Formal
Unfair	1 2 3 ? 5 6 7	Fair
Slow	1 2 3 ? 5 6 7	Fast

6.2 DEFINITION

A large group human communication system has fifteen communicators, or seven times two plus *n* communicators, *or more*. The size factor is most important in the large group system. Such systems are often called public speaking, television newscasts, classroom lectures, radio broadcasts, mass media, and at times, a large group system.

There are several important features of a large group communication system. It requires a substantial amount of preparatory organization. To get 15 or more persons to do approximately the same thing at the same time is seldom easy. The purpose the system operates to achieve is almost totally determined by the system organizer. Messages[°°] intended to achieve the selected purpose are prepared in advance, often by a group or team. In addition to size, the relation of purpose to organization and preparation of the message serve to define the large group system.

6.2.1 Advantage

There is a single advantage to a large group system. A prepared message can be transmitted to a large number of people at the same time.

With rare exceptions, the advantage of the large group system is not equally shared. The communicator(s) who decides on the purpose, prepares the message, and transmits it, usually stands to gain more from that chain of activities than any of the receiver communicators.

[°°] For the field of communication in general, it is important to realize that the monologue is a very complex superstructure, unfamiliar to many ethnic and social groups. . . . Only one form of monologue does occur in such societies, and this is the cliche monologue, the ready-made ritual performance—a prayer or a ceremonial speech.
Roman Jakobson, 1964:162.

6.2.2 Limitations

The limitations or disadvantages are many. The purpose is not mutually agreed on. Usually only the first order consequence of the purpose is of interest. Did the commercial sell more soap? If it takes a "violent" program to hold the audience, then is a violent message transmitted—despite other consequences for the individual and his community?[°]

The large group in the transcomnet link is easily disrupted by any single or several communicators who elect to disrupt it. Any variation from the only-one-person-talks rule disrupts the system. In the telecomnet link, the large group is most limited by the inattention of the intended receiver-communicators.

[°] The weight of social science stands in opposition to the conclusion that mass media portrayals of violence have no effect upon individuals, groups, and society.
D. L. Lange, R. K. Baker, and S. J. Ball, 1969:375.

6.3 TIME SHARING

The dyad and the small group are more varied and flexible in their use of system time than the large group system. In the large group system there are two basic states:

- Communicator A talks, and all other communicators are silent
- Mutual silence

A small percentage of the time, there are two other states:

- One communicator poses a question to Communicator A
- Double talk

These four states exhaust the possible states of a large group system.

On the average, about 2 percent of the time is used in double talk; about 3 percent for questions; about 10 percent for mutual silence; and about 85 percent for Communicator A.

In the largest systems, of course, no time is allowed for questions. And in telecomnet links, there is no double talk, although there are periods of receiver inattention that probably amount to 5 percent or more.

Two-State System

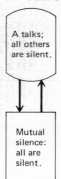

A talks; all others are silent.

Mutual silence: all are silent.

6.4 PURPOSE

A large group human communication system operates to achieve a purpose.[°°] The large group is similar to the dyad and the small group in this respect. But unlike the dyad and the small group, the purpose of the large group is always determined before the system begins to operate, and it is seldom changed while the system is in operation. The precasting of the purpose makes the large group more formal and less flexible than the other two systems.

Traditionally, there have been two general purposes for the large group

[°°] Put it in straightaway English, striking immediately and directly at the point. Let us illustrate the process. When you first *thought* about your subject you may have been concerned about the prevalence of propagandists and "hidden persuaders" who get their ideas into print. . . . After you have expanded and refined your thinking you should be able to write that single, simple, and direct purpose-sentence: Learn to read skeptically.
J. Jeffery Auer, 1967:93.

system.° These have been to inform and to persuade. There are several other purposes, such as entertainment, ritual, ceremony, and other special occasion communication.

The large group purpose of informing is much influenced by the explosion in information and by the trend to equal access. As the audience becomes larger, it becomes increasingly difficult for any communicator to prepare a message that informs each individual receiver-communicator. In the future, the two-way information retrieval systems will probably gradually replace the large group as a transmitter of information.°°

While the information use of the large group system will probably decrease, the persuasion or association-changing use appears likely to increase. The large group systems are good for selling things: soap, cereal, and political candidates are examples. Persuasion attempts to change attitudes. In the large group, the interest is in changing the attitudes of the audience member, the receiver-communicator. In short, he is persuaded to buy or to vote.

6.4.1 Specific Purpose

The purpose for a large group system is arrived at by the system organizer before the system operates.□ The receiver-communicator has almost no means of influencing the purpose, except by the device of choosing not to communicate.

The purpose for large group systems are often obscured. The presenters of an entertainment program on television, for instance, may declare its purpose is to help you relax, to entertain you and so on. But if only a few other persons besides yourself view that program the program gets a low rating; then the sponsor decides the program is not selling enough of his product, and he cancels the program. So the first purpose was not entertainment but selling a product.

6.5 ORGANIZATION

The large group human communication system is organized by Communicator A (or his agency); it typically operates as a message transmission system. Very seldom and for very short periods of time it may operate as a message development system or it may operate as a message development system only for the communicator who is presenting the message. That is, in the course of message presentation he may in some sense re-shape or augment the message that he is presenting based on subtle cues that he gets from his audience.□□

The large group system is basically a message transmission system and the conditions under which such a system is organized relate usually to unequal

° Speech communication finds it moorings in what is said to whom. . . . The speaker's messages are for the purpose of generating meaning in the minds of people. *Mere self-expression* in speech, regardless of its artistry, is antithetical to communication. . . . In communication something is said to someone.
E. C. Buehler and W. A. Linkugel, 1969:97.

°°

LARGE GROUP
Informs 1 2 3 ? 5 6 7 Persuades
Difficult 1 2 3 ? 5 6 7 Easy

□ Every effective public speech has a clearly defined purpose and that purpose is firmly and clearly identified within the speaker. The effective public speaker knows exactly what he wants an audience to do, think, and feel.
John W. Keltner, 1970:328.

□ □

In a large group, I'd rather be an audience member than a speaker.
Disagree 1 2 3 ? 5 6 7 Agree

access to information or unequal access to persuasive detail which is of interest to the audience to obtain that information.

Very often, say in the campaign of a public speaker, there is a very high degree of formalization in the presentation. For instance, a hall must be rented, a space must be secured, and a time must be agreed upon. Usually if the speaker is expected to make extensive preparation there will be payment to him in some coin—money or other considerations.

Quite often the person who wishes to become an audience member is expected to pay for the privilege. To arrange all of these conditions there has to be some additional incentives for the communicators involved. What is presumed is that there is an unequal access to vital information that the speaker somehow has been able to acquire and that the audience member has not yet been able to obtain.

Many classroom speeches given by student speakers fail on precisely this point. The speaker gets up wanting to speak about the things that he thinks he knows best, but everyone else also knows about the same amount of information. In the course of making such a speech, he bores nearly everyone who listens to him.°

It should be repeated that the conditions of organizing a large group communication system depend on unequal access of informative or persuasive material. Somehow the communicator presenting what he has to present has an opportunity that is not available to other communicators. The nature of what is to be presented appears to the person who decides to become an audience member as being a better way of investing his time than the available alternatives.

The large group human communication system with its heavy reliance on the transmission of prepared messages is suited very well to both communication networks: the telecomnet and the transcomnet.°° The system can be readily structured within the framework of any large room. The room in which large group communication systems operate most frequently is the classroom or the auditorium.

In these cases it really matters very little how large the audience is once it gets beyond about 15 to 20 persons in size. Beyond that point the interaction between an audience member and the speaker is very limited. As the interaction between audience member and speaker becomes limited, the preset nature of the message to be transmitted can be more clearly and completely determined in advance.

In the television studio the same structural pattern serves about equally well. The speaker in this case faces a camera and, through the chain of hardware involved in the telecommunication network, what the speaker has to say or to present can be disseminated to audience members at widely dispersed places. As more and more of what is presented on television is

°

The prepared public speech is the "highest form" of human communication.

Disagree 1 2 3 ? 5 6 7 Agree

°° The major differences that exist between face-to-face communication and radio or television communication are due not so much to the machinery of the media as to the context in which the audience hears you.

A. C. Baird, F. H. Knower, and S. L. Becker, 1971:357.

recorded, it is also possible to replay the message not only at different spaces but at different future times. All of this has a far reaching effect on the nature of messages which are developed, both in the face-to-face audience and in the telecommunication audience.[o]

It is important to note that the structural pattern of large group communication systems in the transportation and the telecommunication networks are more similar than different. In academic departments in universities, for instance, there are usually separate courses in public speaking and broadcast speaking, but the similarities are very large and the differences are increasingly small. For instance, quite often the speaker who addresses an assembled audience has part or perhaps all of his speech tape recorded. If the speaker is "famous", much of it will perhaps be filmed for news releases.

If the speaker is important enough, it is entirely possible that excerpts from his talk will be part of the news fare around the world within the following 24 hours. The U.S. President addressing a group assembled at some auditorium in Washington, D.C., could expect to have parts of his speech heard around the world by the following day. Given such a mixed system/network, there is little that distinguishes a speaker addressing an assembled audience and a speaker addressing a dissembled audience over a telecommunication system.

Increasingly, an occasion important enough for a face-to-face public speech is likely also to warrant telecommunication coverage. It's convenient to fashion a scale of events here. One could start on the one hand with a speaker who addresses an audience of 15 to 20 people in a fairly small room. If the room increases in size to the point where he is talking to 200 people, it is very probable that he will be using a public address system; he may be using film clips and slides to illustrate particular points. If the room is of the size where he could address a thousand persons, as in a large auditorium or theater, he will almost certainly present some of his information by displaying it on a large screen in front of the audience. From this kind of situation, the step is a relatively small one to the situation where images are transmitted through space by a telecommunication network. It's useful to view the similarities of large group communication systems and to minimize what up to this time have been viewed as rather large differences between them.

6.6 TUTORIAL: PUBLIC COMMUNICATION

Public communication is the general name for the tutorial pattern in a large group system. [oo] Communicator A defines the system purpose and he

[o]   The need for a large number of people to live in close proximity in order to enjoy the advantages of scale is, however, less a need for physical proximity than for proximity in time. Hence, as the speed with which the communications network can operate increases, people have less need to be physically close together.
P. A. Stone, in Douglas Jones, 1971:48.

[oo]   In the final analysis, even though public communication implies a broader scope of interaction than does a more intimate, interpersonal dialogue or a small-group discussion, . . . we must work our way back through the scene of group activity and through the possibilities and influences of the interpersonal situation to the individual dimension of behavior to account for the influence of a public message.
G. A. Borden, R. B. Gregg, and T. G. Grove, 1969:244.

controls the system. The message he prepares and transmits serves to move other communicators to accept (or reject) the purpose as defined for that system by Communicator A.

Public communication operates in systems with both a translink and a telelink. Public communication is the single most studied system. It goes under many names: a public speech, or a radio speech; a report, or a newscast; a classroom lecture or a telelecture; an áfter-dinner speech or a TV monologue; a talk or a "fireside chat." Most usually, in a translink system, it is called a "speech;" in a telelink system, it is a "newscast." Public communication generates a wide range of reactions.

In every area of knowledge there are one or two areas that attract a disproportionate amount of attention; they become the unquestioned tradition and part of a larger myth. In the study of human communication, the public communication—both as public speech and newscast—is the tradition.° Let us examine only a few parts of that tradition and the larger myth of "communication as transmission."

° No other person who appears in public has as great an opportunity to make an impact upon the behavior of his audience as does the public speaker—or so great an opportunity to make a fool of himself.
J. Jeffery Auer, 1967:20.

The tradition of public communication or public address has its strongest roots in ancient Greece. The *Rhetoric* of Aristotle describes how to make speeches. Aristotle observed the speaking in the forums of Athens. At that time, each citizen was his own representative; he was his own legal counsel and his own political representative. The *Rhetoric* is a handbook for the citizen living in the pretechnological environment. The *Rhetoric* in many ways is too good a book.

The *Rhetoric* has led many individuals to conclude that the prepared "public speech" transmitted in the presence of an assembled audience was the basic form of human communication. This conclusion gains support from the collections of speeches by Lincoln or Churchill or Nehru or King or Jesus. Copies of public speeches that date back hundreds of years are among the few written documents available from pretechnological times. These documents form part of the public communication tradition.

At the same time in Greece, along with the large group public address, the dyadic group and the small group gave rise to the dialog. What we know about the so-called dialog comes from the writings of Plato, which are cast in the form of conversation between Socrates and his pupils. These dialogs sometimes are between two communicators and sometimes between several (7 ± 2) communicators. Thus in ancient Greece, three communication systems, the dyad, small group, and large group, all flourished. We can only speculate about how the prepared public speech came to be viewed as the reference model and the dyadic dialogues and the small invention group, for instance, came to be relegated to a minor role.

A more recent example of reference model choice is available in a 1916 book by James Winans on *Public Speaking*. Winans suggested that two men engaged in conversation might be joined by several others and in time by still others. In our terms, the system size might change from 2 to 7 to 15 or more communicators. Winans intended to illustrate that the conversational style appropriate in the dyad could be extended to a small group and a large group. His point was that the exaggerated manner of speaking called elocution, which was current in America in the early 1900s, should be replaced by a conversational manner of speaking. That advice is reflected in most public speaking textbooks today.[°] But the basic model Winans presented was not appreciated at that time.

As you may have predicted, I was reading some of the Greek writings and Winans at about the same time that I also came into contact with the two-step flow model of communication. I had tutored English while in Europe, had worked as a radio announcer, and was involved in research on group discussion that compared leader and leaderless small groups. The Greeks and Winans and the two-step flow and leaderless discussion groups were part of my early graduate school days. To complicate matters even further I was teaching a basic course in public speaking; the students, I observed, did not prepare speeches in either the way the book instructed them to do nor in the way that I suggested they should. I wondered why. Fortunately, one of my close friends had a number of the same vague questions that I did. Over a period of two years, we informally discussed the Greeks, Winans, the two-step flow, and college students. We slowly came to appreciate that the public speech was an awkward place to start if one wished to understand what happened when humans communicated with each other. Some dozen years later I understand the matter a little better. So, if you have ever wondered why those graduate assistants you have as instructors in college seem to be a bit worried at times it is because they are becoming entangled in questions that may take them a decade to untangle!

I share these items of personal history with you because you may have some of the same questions I've been working with. If you have grown up in America or anywhere else in the "Western World" where the Greek heritage is strong, the chances are very good that you have absorbed public speaking in the same way that you have accepted other cultural values.[°°] A culture that supports individualism finds the "good man speaking well" on a public forum an attractive sight. Like other aspects of individualism, the individual is likely to be most impressed by his accomplishments as an individual and less impressed by his accomplishments in social groups. The individual with a high IQ score claims credit for that score; it would be at least as appropriate for him to praise his ancestors or a balanced diet. Equally, in human communication, it is easy to focus on some particular system and treat it as

[°] Good public speaking, like good conversation, is distinct and lively. It is free of artificial effects and is decidedly informal. . . . In fact, many effective public speakers seem merely to be conversing energetically with the audience. *A. H. Monroe and D. Ehninger, 1967:9.*

[°°] On the other hand, Westerners are communicating to an increasing extent by telephone, letter, and teletype, which frees interaction from spatial contraints. *Robert Sommer, 1969:69.*

a "reference model," such as a public speech in a translink in a large group system. There are more appropriate alternatives in the space age.

Don't misunderstand me. It is important to know how to prepare and present a public speech. My point is that you will find speaking in public a much easier task if you enlarge your outlook. It is one of six system/network patterns. The question is what happens before, during, and after public communication in a large group system.

Before proceeding to instructions on how the speaker prepares, it is worth observing how an experienced communicator goes about preparing for the speaker role in a large group system. Since success is more interesting than failure, observe someone you consider to be successful. But ask him if he achieves his purpose. Ask what that purpose is (or was) and how he determines whether or not he achieves his purpose. You may wish to pursue this as a dyadic Delphi. Be sure to get a variety of speakers. You need ask only three questions:

- What is (was) your purpose?
- Did you achieve your purpose?
- How do you know?

The answers you receive will probably surprise you.

Once you find a public communicator who seems to you to be successful and who also answers your three questions in a way you consider satisfactory, arrange to observe that communicator as he prepares for his speaker role in a large group system.[°]

If you observe seven such communicators as they prepare, you then will have an accurate notion of what you should do. Be sure some of these communicators operate in large systems in a translink and others in a telelink. If you pursue this plan for a few years, you will be able to write a *Space Age Rhetoric* in the manner of Aristotle.

By this means of observing communicators prepare for large group systems, you will discover that the purpose often evolves over a period of months or *years*.[°°] The same can be said for elements of the message. This observation holds for most of the speeches that appear in major collections of public speeches. Said differently, much of the preparation for large group public communication occurs in dyads and small groups.

In the previous chapter, we traced the panel group through a number of systems. Those included small group discussions of a problem, a large group conference where substantial new information was presented, a series of small groups, and finally, a formal panel discussion. Immediately following the panel, audience members formed informal small groups and dyads. Out of that postpanel communication, given the situation described, invitations

[°] A great deal can be learned about speech simply by observing others speak, analyzing the methods they use, and noting the results. . . . Two mistakes should be avoided in making observations of this sort. First, one must be careful not to project preconceived ideas into his observation. It is always easy to see what we expect to see. . . . The other mistake consists in jumping to the conclusion that what is observed in one or a few instances is necessarily typical. *A. H. Monroe and D. Ehninger, 1967:22.*

[°°]

PURPOSE		
Slow	1 2 3 ? 5 6 7	Fast
Unplanned	1 2 3 ? 5 6 7	Planned

such as the ones listed below would have been made to the individual panel communicators:

- When can you and I get together to discuss at length . . .
- My group has a meeting scheduled tomorrow noon. Could you discuss with us . . .
- My club meets next Tuesday. I was instructed to invite you to speak to us. We have in mind about a twenty-minute talk, and about ten minutes of questions. We'd like you to focus on . . .
- I'd like to arrange for the panel to come to my community. We can provide transportation and a small honorarium . . .
- Could two or three of the panel members appear on my TV show next week . . .
- There are a few points I'd like to check with you before I submit the story for the morning paper . . .

Given the preparation stages described, any of the panel communicators with only a little additional preparation would be able to be a communicator in a next dyad, small group, or large group system.

There are several details of importance. First, the communicator in a speaker role in a public communication large group system is usually *invited*. The person or organization offering the invitation usually has selected the specific purpose. The amount of time is usually specified. The invitation is usually offered only to those communicators the inviting organization believes able to achieve the specified purpose. This is especially the case when the communicator is paid. Invitations are usually offered only to persons who are visible in a home community or in the world community, or both.

Many humans live normal and healthy lives without ever giving a speech to an audience or being invited to "speak their piece" on radio or television. A little simple arithmetic shows why that is so. Many professional television communicators frequently talk to a million receivers or more. Most humans spend several hours a day in a large group as a receiver-communicator. The larger the number of receivers per system and the greater the number of hours each receiver spends in a large group system per day, the less the chance a nonprofessional communicator has of being invited to "say a few words."

But suppose you become interested in a vital community problem. Then, you are likely to be invited to address an audience in either a translink or telelink large group system. When that time arrives, you will have done the basic preparation before such an invitation is issued.° But it is always helpful to have some experience in advance. For that reason, a project that

° Speeches grow and mature. They need *time* to *ripen* and they require *constant cultivation.* Some people find this incredible. "Good speakers," they argue, "can talk off the cuff." That notion, of course, is sheer fantasy. *J. Jeffery Auer, 1967:40.*

will enable you to work through the appropriate stages is outlined at the end of this chapter. You may also like to work through these stages on your own for some other purpose.

If you prepare well, you ought to expect to get a fan letter or two or a good round of applause. There is a special kind of magic in a favorable reaction from an audience. But one person can put everything back into perspective with one well-intended but left-handed compliment, "I didn't understand a word you said. But you have such a beautiful voice. I just adore . . ."

6.7 TUTORIAL/INTERVIEW: PARTICIPATORY DEMOCRACY

Democracy can be defined as "government of the people, by the people, and for the people." Democracy depends on a well-informed people who are free to associate with one another. Beyond being well-informed and being able to associate, the people must participate in democracy at all levels.[o] Such participation ranges from voting to holding office. Thus, to emphasize the importance of action and involvement, democracy is often called participatory democracy.

The basic patterns of participatory democracy[oo] are evident in any communication system where communicators cooperate to achieve a mutual purpose. Many dyads and small groups are excellent examples of participatory democracy in action. The interchange pattern is an especially good example.

The large group human communication system differs in two ways from the dyad and small group. First, it is a one-way system. The opportunity for participation is not equally shared among all communicators. Only one communicator talks; the others are silent. Second, the message is prepared outside of the system for *transmission* within the system. Almost always, that message serves better those who transmit it than it does those who receive it.

To make it possible for all communicators in a large group to be able to participate, special provisions must be made. Time-sharing is especially difficult. In short, a special *organization* or procedure is devised. One of these procedures is central to participatory democracy: parliamentary procedure[□]

A parliament is a place where men meet to talk. The French verb *parler* means to converse, to discuss; appropriately, it provides the stem of the world *parli*ament. Parliamentary procedure, then, is simply a form of large group system organization that enables a group to achieve its purposes, whatever they are or come to be.

The *rules* of parliamentary procedure are both simple and complex. The

[o]   The Mexican-American member of the Commission asks: "Why don't you just send a field representative to meet with us?" and is greeted by a chorus of noes. "We've had enough of that kind of representation," a man says, "The people must represent themselves."
Bill Moyers, 1971:221.

[oo]   *Participatory democracy* is essential to the kind of society that most of us want, and widespread communication must occur between and among all the people in a society before such a condition can exist.
A. C. Baird, F. H. Knower, and S. L. Becker, 1971:7.

[□]   The basic goal of the communication era is to eliminate the pattern where only a restricted number of people are able to bring about change. In order to do this, it is necessary that information preception, communication, and decision making be widely diffused.
R. Theobald and J. M. Scott, 1972:148.

main rules are well-known by every young adult who comes of age in a "democratic" culture. The fine details are not fully known by even the experienced office holder. It is relatively easy for any group member to know his group's procedures well enough to be effective in that group.

Parliamentary procedure arises out of the time-sharing problem° of a large group. Every member has the right to speak; no two members may speak at the same time. Thus, a chairman recognizes a member before that member has the "right" to speak; the chairman only recognizes one member at a time. Groups usually meet for a particular period of time, say one or two hours. A first task of the chairman, then, is to share the available system time among all of the member communicators.

Parliamentary procedure also provides a mechanism for making rules that the group will operate by. New rules are proposed in the form of a main motion. The main motion is discussed and voted on. The rules relating to votes form another major portion of the procedure for participatory democracy. To make a "motion" binding on the group, a simple majority— one more than half the votes cast—is required. Otherwise, the motion fails. Importantly, under certain conditions, any motion can be reversed. Normally, such an intention must be announced at a prior meeting. A two-thirds vote is required to reverse a motion that was passed at a previous meeting. Within parliamentary procedure, then, are provisions for making rules and for "unmaking" rules. Thus, parliamentary procedure is highly flexible.°°

Unfortunately, in some groups, the procedure gets in the way of what the group wants to do. This need not be the case. If most of the members of a group know the basics of parliamentary procedure and know the particular bylaws or additional organizational details of the group, procedure can be very informal and very much in the background. The procedure, when well used, does not intrude and often is not obvious to the inexperienced observer. In a group that uses procedure awkwardly, everyone loses.

A member needs, as an absolute minimum, to know three things. He needs to know the order of business adopted by the group. There is some variation from group to group. He needs to know the steps in a main motion. The main motion, and all other motions, are so simple that they can be flow charted. He needs to know how to get the information he needs when he needs it. He usually wants to know how to perform some particular action, or he wants to know the meaning of some particular action. He needs, therefore, to be able to "request information." A new group member must know, or learn as quickly as he can, the order of business, the main motion, and the motion for request of information.

Obviously, when there are several members who are unfamiliar with

° [The] data . . . come from 18 independent observations of as many large classes. The number of questions asked per class averaged 2.3 [with a range of zero to nine] , with a trend for questioning to decrease as class size increased.
Robert Sommer, 1969:118.

°°

PARLIAMENTARY PROCEDURE		
Unfair	1 2 3 ? 5 6 7	Fair
Difficult	1 2 3 ? 5 6 7	Easy
Rigid	1 2 3 ? 5 6 7	Flexible

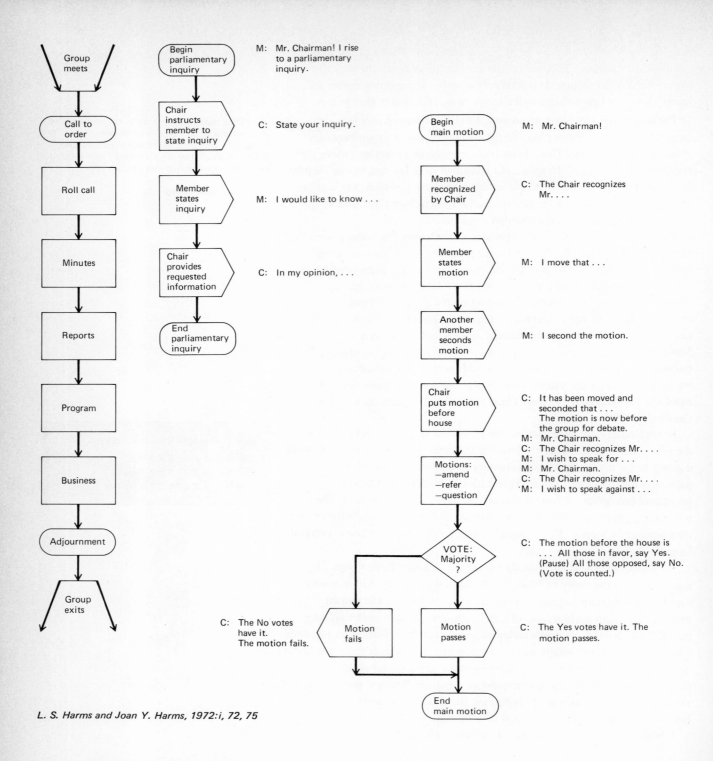

Group meets

Call to order

Roll call

Minutes

Reports

Program

Business

Adjournment

Group exits

Begin parliamentary inquiry

Chair instructs member to state inquiry

Member states inquiry

Chair provides requested information

End parliamentary inquiry

M: Mr. Chairman! I rise to a parliamentary inquiry.

C: State your inquiry.

M: I would like to know . . .

C: In my opinion, . . .

Begin main motion

Member recognized by Chair

Member states motion

Another member seconds motion

Chair puts motion before house

Motions:
—amend
—refer
—question

VOTE: Majority ?

Motion fails

Motion passes

End main motion

M: Mr. Chairman!

C: The Chair recognizes Mr. . . .

M: I move that . . .

M: I second the motion.

C: It has been moved and seconded that . . .
The motion is now before the group for debate.
M: Mr. Chairman.
C: The Chair recognizes Mr. . . .
M: I wish to speak for . . .
M: Mr. Chairman.
C: The Chair recognizes Mr. . . .
M: I wish to speak against . . .

C: The motion before the house is . . . All those in favor, say Yes. (Pause) All those opposed, say No. (Vote is counted.)

C: The No votes have it.
The motion fails.

C: The Yes votes have it. The motion passes.

L. S. Harms and Joan Y. Harms, 1972:i, 72, 75

procedure, the group can use most of its time "figuring out how to do" what it wishes to do. For one or two meetings, this is sometimes a tolerable state of affairs; over several meetings group members are likely to conclude that the procedure is awkward.

Parliamentary procedure tends to be of limited use for groups that are smaller than fifteen [less than $(7 \times 2) + n$]. It becomes increasingly important as the group increases in size. It is almost impossible to achieve any purpose in a *participating* group of 50 or more without an agreed-upon procedure for sharing time and making rules.

Any group that starts out without an organizational procedure, if it maintains itself, will invent or adopt a "parliamentary procedure." That procedure will provide for time sharing and the making of rules.

A new member in any participatory group needs to know the organizational rules of that group. He can learn some of these rules from the group bylaws and from the "parliamentary authority" the group names in its bylaws. He ought also to talk with the group parliamentarian to ensure that he is fully enough acquainted with actual group procedure to be able to participate effectively in the group. The few hours outside of group work required to master group procedure enable a member to participate more effectively during the many hours he will spend in that group.

6.8 SOME OTHER TRADITIONAL PATTERNS

There are several traditional patterns in human communication that can be briefly mentioned here. In all cases, there are many books on these topics that can be found in any library or bookstore. Manuscript speaking, oral interpretation, and storytelling are briefly discussed below.

6.8.1 Manuscript Speaking

Increasingly, as public communication become partly or totally transmitted in telecommunication networks, there is a tendency to rely more heavily on the manuscript. A manuscript is either prepared by the hand of the speaker himself, or, as is frequently the case when the speaker-communicator is a busy man in a high position, the speech is prepared for him by a ghost-writer.

A manuscript speech offers several conveniences. It can be fully prepared in advance. It does not pretend to be adapted to the particular audience during the time that it is being presented. It is very often gone over line by line and word for word by several persons. It is analyzed to attempt to determine the effect that it will have on its intended audience. It is necessary to think of audience in the plural—the immediate audience that hears the speech at the time it is delivered, the audiences that will hear it in the next few hours as part of a news broadcast, and the audiences who may read the manuscript at a much later time and ponder its significance. Very often a speech such as the one Adlai Stevenson gave on International Development at the United Nations in Geneva is important in its immediate context. But it is also important as an historical record in its own independent right.

Manuscript speaking also assumes an unequal access to information or an unusual understanding of a particular phenomenon that can be more readily communicated by manuscript speech-making than by presenting the manuscript as an article in a newspaper or as a collection of speeches within a book or by some other means.

6.8.2 Oral Interpretation

There is a second type of manuscript speaking that might be included here; it can be called oral interpretation. The oral interpreter does not have a ghost-writer as the manuscript speaker does. He normally selects or secures his material from what has come to be called "literature." More often than not the full term for this type of communication is the "oral interpretation of literature." Quite often, the audience members know the piece of literature, have read it out loud themselves, but they come to hear the speaker read it in the hope of understanding some dimension or receiving some pleasure that would escape them were they to read the material to themselves.

There is a long tradition growing out of the distinction between rhetoric and poetic made by the ancient Greeks. Oral interpretation, of course, comes from the poetic theme, and occasionally within academic settings there is interest in this type of performance. On television, occasionally, a great actor reads poetry or reads cuttings from well-known pieces of literature.

6.8.3 Storytelling

There is a third kind of performance which is not quite manuscript. That is the story that is told by the storyteller to his assembled audience. The storyteller may tell a story that all members of the audience would themselves be able to tell. Still the enjoyment derived by the audience members may be even greater than it would be if they had never heard the story before, or if they had never told the story at an earlier time. The story, particularly in parts of the world where print is not yet a widely used medium, serves a very vital role as a way of transmitting the mythology and legends of a particular people from generation to generation. In the situations where this is a primary means of sharing a cultural history, the effect can be a very strong and very dramatic one. In some ways it is another illustration of the power of the association or affective part of communication. An audience member may find the presentation by the storyteller on a given occasion to be a most enjoyable or pleasant one even through he can himself tell the story. That demonstration stands as an example that there is more involved in human communication than processing of information.

6.9 POLLS AND RATINGS

The large group communication system has a major disadvantage. The communicator (or agency) who decides on a purpose, prepares a message, and organizes a communication system has no easy way of knowing if the intended purpose was (or will be) achieved.[°] In a dyadic system, it is usually obvious to the two communicators and to any system observer whether or not a mutual purpose was achieved. But in the large group system, the purpose is normally decided outside of the system. A purpose is achieved with only a certain percent of the receiver-communicators. Therein lies the rub.

To determine what percent of the communicators achieve the purpose of the communicator who controls the large group system, polls and ratings have come into existence. Ratings are used in a variety of ways. Basically, they display how much a particular message is liked, or they display which of two (or several programs) are best liked. Television programs are kept on when they receive high ratings, and they are replaced when the ratings slip. The most direct question of all is: "What television program are you watching?" Such a measure is extremely rough, but it provides information for a sponsor who wants to know how many homes received his commercial.

Polls and ratings are similar. At times, the two terms are interchangeable. At other times, they reflect slight differences in procedure. A poll is most often used when the questions to be posed are political. These questions may relate to issues or to candidates. A poll taker may phone to ask whether you favor a particular change: "Are you in favor of a new football stadium even if it requires higher taxes?" Or, "If the election for Governor were held today, would you vote for Smith or Jones?"

Both polls and ratings can be viewed as a single-cycle and limited-purpose Delphi. Usually, the questions are shorter, fewer, and simpler than in the Delphi, but many more persons are polled.

Polls and ratings are employed in an attempt to compensate for the

[°] For example, evidence is clear that formal public speeches have little likelihood of changing votes in a national political election. Informal communication among friends, on a one-to-one basis, is more effective for this purpose.
A. C. Baird, F. H. Knower, and S. L. Becker, 1971:10.

limitations of a one-way system organized for a purpose not mutually beneficial to all of the participating communicators. In short, large group communication systems do not serve the organizer and the "organized" equally well. The fact that ratings are taken to enable a sponsor to sell more of his product is simply another indication of that inequality.

It is probably better to have polls and ratings than not to have them. The fact that they are necessary illustrates how far the really large group system is from the interchange dyad. At the same time, the inappropriateness of most large group messages for most communicators reveals how difficult it is to use any rating or poll to improve the operation of such a system.

6.10 SUMMARY

In this chapter, the large group human communication system has been defined. Its major advantage is that many receiver-communicators can be reached at a single time. Most of its limitations arise from this single advantage. Time sharing is a simple matter in the large group, and its organization is also quite simple. The large group operates mainly in a tutorial pattern. Manuscript speaking, oral interpretation and storytelling were briefly mentioned. The function of polls and ratings were described.

The four chapters in this section of the book have been concerned with the organization necessary for human communication to operate within networks and systems. In the next section, the human communication process will be examined within particular network/system patterns.

6.S SKILLS: THE TUTORIAL PATTERN IN A LARGE GROUP SYSTEM

PURPOSE

Demonstrate the advantages and limitations of the tutorial pattern in a large group system.

PROJECT

In a dyadic system, you and your partner develop two purposes that can be achieved in a large group system:

- One of these purposes should be suitable for a "speech" to be transmitted by your partner.
- One of these purposes should be suitable for a "speech" to be transmitted by you.

In a dyadic Delphi, *collect* information necessary for achieving the purpose of your speech.

In a dyadic system, *transmit* information as a tutorial with your partner.

- Discuss with your partner the appropriateness of the speech:
- In terms of the purpose
- In terms of the audience
- Revise as suggested.

In a small group system, *transmit* information in a tutorial pattern.

- Discuss with the other communicators in your small group the appropriateness of the speech:
- In terms of the purpose
- In terms of the audience
- Revise as suggested.

Prepare a fifty-word summary of your speech.

- Your partner will assist you.
- Give the summary to your instructor just before you transmit your speech.
- Your instructor will cross out five words as he listens to your speech.
- Your partner will *read the summary out loud* as soon as you finish your speech; he pauses two seconds when he comes to each of the five words "crossed out."
- Also, predict the combined Information and Interest scores; consult with your partner.

Each audience member uses a half sheet of paper as he listens to the summary:

- To write down in order the five missing words
- To *rate* the interest level of the speech

An audience member who finds the speech of low interest will rate it 1 or 2. An audience member who finds the speech of high interest will rate it 4 or 5.
An audience member who finds the speech of average interest will rate it 3.
Immediately after the speech, each audience member passes to the instructor his half sheet of paper with

- Five words, which yield an Information Score
- A number, which yields an Interest Score
- His name

The instructor gives the Information and Interest materials to you and your partner immediately.

- In the back of the room, the two of you score the information and interested data; enter it into the scoring sheet for this Unit, which is in the Skills Worksheets section at the back of the book.
- Return all materials to your instructor.
- Your instructor may wish to refer to these materials while commenting on your speech.

Notice that the proposed grading procedure is A + B / 2

- Thus, it is important to you that your partner does well.
- Also, your partner will be interested in helping you do well.

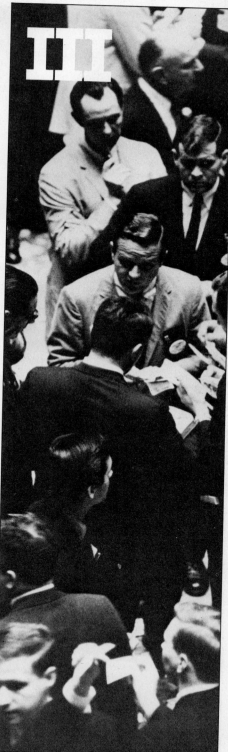

III

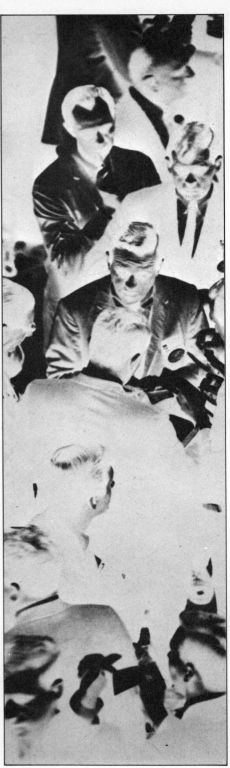

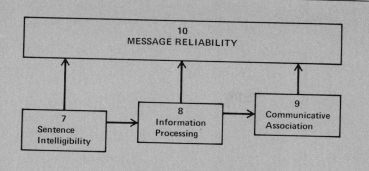

III

HUMAN COMMUNICATION PROCESS

III
PROCESS

7

SENTENCE INTELLIGIBILITY

Every human communication system depends on sentence intelligibility. If the sentences spoken by the communicator are not intelligible within that system, that system cannot operate. The process of intelligibility is quite simple; at the same time, it is vitally important.

In this chapter, intelligibility will be defined. Ideal conditions, decreasers of intelligibility, and minimum requirements for intelligibility will be discussed. Some of the characteristics of spoken sentences, sentence transformations, and sentence chains will be examined.

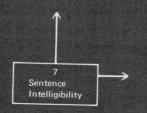

7
Sentence
Intelligibility

7.1 INTRODUCTION°

Sentence intelligibility is the first requirement of every communication system.°° If intelligibility is at a satisfactory level, the system *can* operate successfully. When intelligibility falls below a satisfactory level, the system will operate badly when it operates at all. Unsatisfactory sentence intelligibility is part of nearly every communication breakdown.

Within a quiet home community, intelligibility is seldom a problem between communicators who know each other well. If you spend almost all your time communicating with your close friends and little time communicating with strangers from other communities, sentence intelligibility is probably of little concern to you at this time. But, in the future, as you associate with a wider variety of other communicators, *at times* sentence intelligibility will be a problem.

Today, there are many *Englishes* spoken in the world. These Englishes go under many names: General American, Southern English, Hawaiian Standard English, Received Pronunciation, stage English, Bamboo English, Japlish, Frenchlish, and so on. There is no single standard English which is correct.□

With a little practice, you can tell the part of the United States in which a person first learned to speak English. You can also tell the difference between British English, Australian English, and American English. English spoken as a "second language" also shows whether the first language learned was French, Japanese, German, or Hindi. English is used in both the world community and the home community.

The more any two persons communicate with each other, the more similar they will become in the way they communicate. They will pronounce most words in the same way. They will come to prefer the same sentence patterns. In short, they *match*□□ each other's style of communicating. The same process operates within each community.

Any two persons from different communities who also speak English will have to attend to the potential problems that can come from the simple fact that they learned to speak English in different communities. There is no external standard English against which differences can be measured. All that can be said is that communicators who learn English in different communities speak English somewhat differently. Their differences need not cause a severe problem. Unfortunately, at times, these differences are allowed to interrupt communication. In most cases, such interruptions need not happen.

7.2 DEFINITION

Intelligibility is defined as the degree of *match* between what one communicator says and another communicator demonstrates that he hears within any

°

°°
What's said cannot be unsaid; human communication is irreversible.
Colin Cherry, 1971:11.

Match   Mismatch

□
A person who mispronounces words usually has a low IQ.

Disagree 1 2 3 ? 5 6 7 Agree

□□

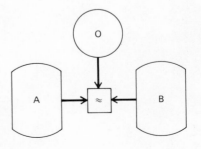

communication system. Intelligibility as a concept only makes sense within the framework of a communication system. Notions related to intelligibility are sometimes labeled correct pronunciation, articulation, voice and diction, substandard English, dialect problems, sloppy English, bad grammar, and so on. When what communicator A *says* does not *match* what communicator B *hears*, these communicators are likely to encounter difficulties in achieving their purpose. If the problem of intelligibility becomes severe, inexperienced communicators often evaluate each other in a negative way; they think unkind thoughts about each other.

Intelligibility will now be defined for spoken sentences, for sentence transformations, and for sentence chains. In each instance, a dyadic system with an observer is assumed. However, the definitions hold equally well for the small group and large group systems.

Intelligibility of a spoken sentence is defined by the following operation.

- Communicator A says a sentence.
- Communicator B repeats that sentence exactly.
- A and B and an observer agree or do not agree that the sentences spoken by A and B *match* in all important details.

Communicator B repeats the sentence spoken by A exactly; the two sentences *match*.

Communicator B does not change the sentence to "improve" its grammar or to "correct" the pronunciation of a word. Communicator B must demonstrate that he heard the sentence exactly. When there is any disagreement among A, B or O, Communicator A repeats the sentence, Communicator B repeats that sentence, and again a discussion about matching is made. When all three agree that the two sentences match, then:

- Communicator B says a sentence.
- Communicator A repeats that sentence exactly.
- A and B and an observer agree or do not agree that the sentences spoken by B and A match in all important details. When there is a mismatch, B repeats the sentence and the cycle continues until matching is achieved.

For most communication systems, any dyad ought to *match at least six out of every seven sentences on the first attempt.* Most communicators are very sensitive about repeating words and sentences. Most communicators will repeat a sentence twice; but few will repeat a sentence four or five times. Try it. Ask a fellow communicator to repeat a sentence again, again please, once more if you please, just once more . . .

A spoken sentence that is suitable for communication allows two other operations to be performed. In the ASQ method, the question form of a

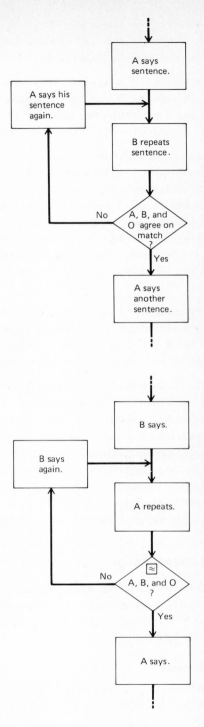

sentence is especially important. Therefore, any answer in a declarative sentence form ought to be said in a way that enables the hearer to convert it into a question when he wishes to do so.

- Communicator A says a declarative sentence.
- Communicator B transforms that sentence into a question.
- A and B and an observer agree that the sentences spoken by A and B are matching forms of question and answer.

B transforms the declarative sentence spoken by A into the matching question. B then says a declarative sentence and the cycle is repeated.

Quite often in speech communication systems, one communicator says a sentence and the other communicator adds a sentence. Together, they build a chain of sentences that form a message. At other times, one communicator may say several sentences. When the other communicator is uncertain whether he fully understands what he has just heard, he needs to repeat back in "his own words" what he has just heard. The operation is quite simple.

- Communicator A says three or more sentences.
- Communicator B repeats the same information in "his own words."
- A and B and an observer agree the information in A's sentence chain and B's sentence chain *match* in all important aspects. If not, recycle.

B transforms the sentences spoken by A into his own way of saying the same thing. B then says a short sentence chain.

Sentence intelligibility° has been defined by three different operations. In all cases, the central question has to do with the degree of match between what is said and what is heard. The first operation was a simple one of repeating; the second operation required changing a single sentence; the third operation required restating several sentences. Taken together, these three operations of repeating, transforming, and restating define sentence intelligibility within all communication systems.

7.3 DECREASERS OF INTELLIGIBILITY

In the most general terms, almost any factor that influences human communication can increase or decrease sentence intelligibility.°° There are, however, four factors which are most important. These are: distance, noise, vocabulary, and cultural similarity.

7.3.1 Distance

The international reference distance for the measure of speech intelligibility is either one yard or one meter. Extend that distance out to six feet, which

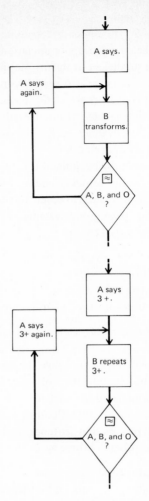

°

INTELLIGIBILITY		
Difficult	1 2 3 ? 5 6 7	Easy
Mismatch	1 2 3 ? 5 6 7	Match
Weak	1 2 3 ? 5 6 7	Strong
Inconsiderate	1 2 3 ? 5 6 7	Considerate
Unfair	1 2 3 ? 5 6 7	Fair

°° Probably the most important single factor in intelligibility is the loudness level at which you speak as related to the *distance* between you and the listener and the amount of *noise* that surrounds him.
A. H. Monroe and D. Ehninger, 1967:82.

is twice one yard (and approximately twice one meter), or reduce it to one half that distance, and you have the space for nearly all communication in dyadic systems. Very seldom do the communicators in a dyad elect to space themselves more than six feet apart when they communicate, and it is relatively rare in public places that people space themselves closer than 18 inches for long-term communication. The space involved in a dyadic system is quite well marked: approximately a foot-and-a-half to six feet. This might be called comfortable conversation distance for the usual dyadic communication space.

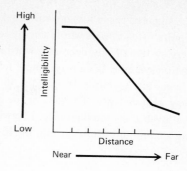

The small group system normally uses a distance between about six and twelve feet. When there are 7 people sitting around a table of any shape or size, they will normally form a circle that has a diameter between six and twelve feet. This is still a fairly easy conversational distance.

The large group communication system normally places a speaker at least 6 feet from the first row in an audience and, depending on the type of room which the large group system operates in, somewhere beyond 50 to 100 feet encompasses most rooms in which large group communication operates. Most classrooms, for instance, are not longer than 100 feet; when they are, we tend to call them auditoriums and then do some additional things in terms of the acoustics of a room to reinforce the weak sound that we call speech. There is a relatively small space between communicators, small in terms of the size of our planet earth and in terms of the actual distance between communicators in a communication system.

The telecomnet in which communication systems are also organized attempts to *simulate* the critical aspects of transcomnet communication. A telephone, for instance, attempts to simulate a dyadic face-to-face communication system. In this case, communicators are able to bypass the visual part of sentence intelligibility and rely solely on the spoken band of intelligibility. The picturephone or the videophone will of course make both telecomnet and transcomnet links face-to-face communication. One would expect an increase of some 5 to 15 percent in sentence intelligibility with this new telecommunication device.

7.3.2 Noise

Noise is one of the largest and most pervasive problems for intelligibility in communication systems. There are basically two classes of noise: One is a steady state noise, and the other is ambient or irregular noises that come and go without much warning. With increasing noise pollution in the environment, the practicing communicator needs to be increasingly alert to the effect of noise on communication. Different kinds of noises affect different sounds of speech in different ways. For instance, a noise from a fan tends to affect particular consonant sounds, in words such as *f*at and *th*ick, which themselves are hissing and buzzing noises. A steady tone noise will affect quite often vowels whose energy regions are similar.

Noise very systematically decreases word intelligibility within communication systems. It's a very simple relationship: The higher the noise, the lower intelligibility. It operates, in this regard, in an almost identical way with distance. The greater the distance between any two persons, the lower their intelligibility. Likewise, the higher the noise surrounding a communication system, the lower word intelligibility becomes.

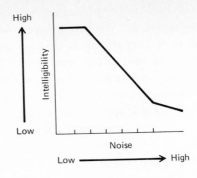

7.3.3 Vocabulary

Vocabulary is another important determinant of word intelligibility. And in this case it is very closely related to the particular experiences of the communicators operating in a communication system. Two engineers discussing their mutual speciality will use technical words in a very intelligible fashion, that is, if one says a word, the other is likely to hear it. A term like *diode*, for instance, will be accurately received by another engineer. Someone with a background in art may hear any one of four or five words other than the one actually said, including the word *dyad*. Vocabulary, even fairly short and simple vocabulary items, can reduce intelligibility if the word is not well known to the other participants in the communication system.

As more communicators operate in a particular system, fewer words are likely to be well known by all of them. The problem is something of this order: There are some 700,000 words in English, all of these words are known by some people, but very few people have vocabularies of more than about 30,000 or 40,000 words. When there are 15, or 50, or 5,000 communicators in a particular communication system, there are fewer and fewer words that are likely to be highly intelligible to all members of that group. The problem faced by a communicator working in a mass medium such as television or radio is of this type; he must use words which are known to the communicators, the viewers, the listeners; and to do so, he restricts the number of words which are available. He ends up with a soap opera vocabulary.

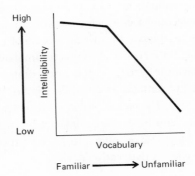

7.3.4 Cultural Similarity

Cultural similarity also affects intelligibility in far-reaching ways.[°] One of the consequences of being culturally similar is that many, many vocabulary items and general experiences about which communication deal are shared and well known. Any two persons who are culturally dissimilar have fewer experiences in common. They are less able to guess words that are blocked

[°]   Taking the long view of world cultural evolution accounting for the lives of perhaps 80 billion people . . . we probably have more exposure to cultural diversity than we did as individuals at any other period in *sapiens* history.
R. D. Jones, in M. Maruyama and J. A. Dator, 1971:176.

out because of noise or unknown vocabulary items which cannot be filled in from context.

The continuum from very similar to very dissimilar in the area of culture has far-reaching consequences for sentence intelligibility within any communication system. In general, the more culturally dissimilar two persons are, the more care they need to be sure that any particular word and sentence is intelligible within that particular system.° Again, intelligibility in any communication system means simply that a sentence is said and heard and that for those two communicators within a particular system it operates as the same sentence; it matches. It is interesting to observe three or four Japanese persons speaking English. A native English speaker operating as an observer might have considerable difficulty in following such a conversation. The communicators participating in the communication system might have no difficulty at all. When communicators are culturally dissimilar, the need for adaptation of pronunciation, the need for checking the intelligibility of sentences as they are said, greatly increases. The problem is at times difficult; it is seldom impossible. A much greater degree of alertness, second by second, within a communication system is required when two communicators are culturally dissimilar.

° . . . when a person lives in a relatively closed culture and hence lacks knowledge of the details of people and cultures other than his own, his attitudes will be ethnocentric—that is, he will view his own culture as superior and others as inferior.
Frederick Williams, in L. L. Barker and R. J. Kibler, 1971:119.

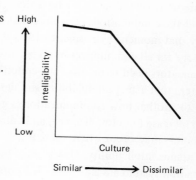

7.3.5 Combination of Decreasers

Speech communication systems *can* operate over distances of 100 feet or greater. But do not conclude, therefore, that distance is not terribly important in speech communication. Of course, intelligibility can be maintained even at a distance of 100 feet. It is not at all uncommon in a theater, for instance, to have actors talking across distances which are considerably greater than 100 feet.

At the same time, it is easy to observe that communicators can survive a great deal of environmental noise as they are speaking to each other and still encounter no very great difficulty. The unexpected problems arise when a communicator must cope with any two decreasers at the same time. Both distance and noise decrease word intelligibility in a very regular and a very predictable way. As both distance and noise increase, intelligibility decreases.

The matter of consequence is that one decreaser adds to the other, and it becomes difficult to know in advance what the combined effect on intelligibility will be. A communicator knows the effect will be to lower intelligibility. To be able to predict by how much is quite a different question. For instance, there may be a combination of a particular distance and a particular noise level that drops word intelligibility as much as 30 or 40 percent. Unless all communicators are alert to this kind of irregular

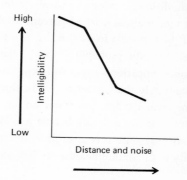

possibility, large gaps may occur in the message that they are building. The communicators may not be aware that they are missing part of the message.

Add to either noise or distance unfamiliar or technical vocabulary items, and then add cultural dissimilarity. Under these conditions, it may be possible for communicators to go through all the motions of communicating and still actually not develop a message or transmit a message which is of any use at all to the participants.

There are no hard and fast guidelines that can be set for maintaining control over the combinations of factors that decrease intelligibility other than to say that moment by moment within the process of communicating it is necessary for all communicators to be, also, a part-time observer. That is, communicators need to monitor the conditions around their communication system that affect intelligibility and determine as best they can from one pause to another how communication is going. They must know that as there is an increase in noise, distance, and cultural dissimilarity, unexpected breaking points may occur where there is a very sudden and very substantial drop in sentence intelligibility. Unless some of the communicators within a communication system are alert to such a possibility, it is very likely that ten or fifteen seconds later, or perhaps a minute later, severe difficulties will be encountered.

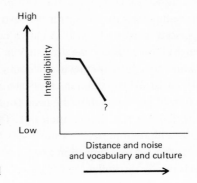

It is one of the unfortunate aspects of sentence intelligibility that the problem that comes from low intelligibility is not usually detected at the moment it is happening. Intelligibility tends to be the kind of problem which is detected later and very often explained in a fashion that does not improve the intelligibility of future sentences.

7.4 MINIMUM REQUIREMENTS

For the purposes of most communication systems, there are some minimum requirements for sentence intelligibility. The individual communicator, under the conditions in which he usually attempts to communicate, should to be able to maintain at least 85 percent intelligibility with individual sentences. If he is unable to do this, by hearing a recording of himself at a slightly later time, the probability is very high that other communicators in the same communication system will experience substantial difficulty in receiving accurately the sentences that he does say.

On a long-term average, something on the order of six out of seven sentences must be instantly intelligible to all communicators in the communication system. It is possible to operate with lower levels of intelligibility if all communicators are free and willing to ask for repetition

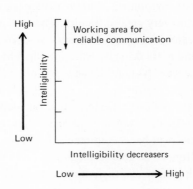

at any time they have doubts. Low intelligibility always poses the problem of unexpected confusion.

The other side of this problem is that most communicators will repeat a sentence once, twice, or perhaps even three times. But somewhere between the third and fifth repetition, most communicators become a little hesitant to say a sentence again. In other words, the continuity of the message that is being developed tends to be destroyed; and the association among the communicators, which is vital to ongoing communication, erodes when sentence intelligibility becomes a problem.°

There are quite clear limits here; occasionally every communicator will say a sentence that is unintelligible to those around him. He may be asked to repeat it and that will clear the matter up. But take the case of inter-cultural communication. A native English speaker who has little experience in communicating with persons who have learned English as a second language attempts to communicate with someone who has a textbook understanding of English. In such a situation the possibility of low intelligibility is very great. Also, the ability of the communicators in the system to maintain the corrective procedures necessary is uncertain.

When you ask someone who speaks English as a second language to repeat a sentence a third or fourth time, he finds himself back in the "classroom" as a learner of the language. He is no longer a real communicator in real life attempting to transmit or build messages within a communication system. The ask-repeat limits are fairly narrow. As one finds himself communicating with people who are dissimilar from himself, in noisy communication systems, perhaps in a telecomnet link, sentence intelligibility can, *at times*, be a severe problem. It is important to remember that most humans learn to communicate in environments where sentence intelligibility is not a severe problem. It is outside of the home community and in communication with persons who are substantially dissimilar that the problem usually begins.°° The airplane pilot communicating under severe time restrictions while talking to the control tower operator at an airport in a foreign country presents a dramatic example. Under these conditions, intelligibility can become a vital and severe problem very suddenly. It is important to each communicator to check out his intelligibility under a variety of real-life conditions and to work at it until he maintains high intelligibility in the various systems in which he intends to communicate.

7.5 IDEAL CONDITIONS

Assume the following conditions. Two communicators who are well trained and who have talked with each other before face each other at the distance

°

TRY THIS

In a dyadic system, ask the other communicator to repeat a sentence; to repeat it again; again . . . Record the number of repetitions. Repeat process with six other communicators.

Communicator	Repetitions
1.	☐
2.	☐
3.	☐
4.	☐
5.	☐
6.	☐
7.	☐

Results:

°°

Intelligibility mismatches often occur at unexpected times.

Disagree 1 2 3 ? 5 6 7 Agree

of one yard (or approximately one meter). They are in a quiet, sound-treated room, they work at their own pace, and they alternate in saying a list of familiar words to each other. If Communicator A has the list, he says a word; and Communicator B either repeats the word that he hears into another microphone, or he writes it down, or he selects it from a list of words that are on his answer sheet. Now under these ideal conditions the best intelligibility that can be obtained is about 98 percent. Like almost every other human communication process, perfection simply does not exist.

Errors will be made even if you assign yourself a task as simple as tapping the end of your finger within a circle that you draw on a piece of paper. If you do it long enough and fast enough, you will occasionally tap outside of that little circle. Likewise with intelligibility. You can create an ideal set of conditions, you can train for very long periods of time, simplify the word list, and improve every condition that might have a bearing on intelligibility. Still you will not be entirely accurate; you will not be perfectly reliable. Speech communication does not begin to approach the reliability of the performance of a computer, for instance. Even under the very best conditions intelligibility is not totally reliable, it is not totally accurate; the *match* is not quite perfect. This is a very important point to remember as one communicates day in and day out; what this translates into is an expectation that even under the best of conditions, where people know each other well, where they have plenty of time, where they are talking in a quiet, noise-proof environment, where they are talking on topics they know well, that even here, occasionally, at a critical time, one or more sentences will be unintelligible.

Perhaps a particular word which is not intelligible will be corrected within the ongoing activity of communication. Perhaps it will pass unnoticed and in time turn up as part of a communication breakdown. So many of the difficulties in communication have as one part a *mismatch* in sentence processing.°

Take the person who has grown up in a very stable community where day in and day out he communicates with a relatively limited number of people. He communicates on topics that are well known to himself and others. He communicates in situations where there is plenty of time, no rush, no hurry. He can go back over a particular topic if necessary several times. Under these conditions, problems of intelligibility seldom arise for any particular communicator.

But as one changes any one of these conditions, he moves on to a situation in which intelligibility some of the time can become a difficult

> Intelligibility mismatches are always a system problem rather than an individual problem.
> Disagree 1 2 3 ? 5 6 7 Agree

problem. Human communication frequently occurs under conditions where sentence intelligibility can be a severe problem.

7.6 SUMMARY

Sentence intelligibility was examined in this chapter. Intelligibility was defined operationally, and the conditions which increase and decrease intelligibility were analyzed.

7.S SKILLS: SENTENCE INTELLIGIBILITY

PURPOSE

The purpose of this exercise is two-fold:

- Demonstrate sentence intelligibility through repetition, transformation, and restatement of sentences.
- Display the scores for the above three operations.

PROJECT

Three people are needed for this exercise: Communicator A, Communicator B, and an Observer O.

1. Sentence repetition

- A, B, and O review Unit 7.2 on the definition of intelligibility.
- Review Unit 7.2 for the procedure on sentence repetition.
- Sentences are to be 7 ± 2 words in length. Sentence topics spoken are to be the career emphasis of that dyad member. Each sentence is to contain at least 3 technical career words.
- Score your performance as follows:

   For each say-repeat trial that A, B, and O agree is a match, the dyad receives 1 point. When there is a mismatch the dyad receives no point. Continue the task until the dyad has 7 trials of *continuous* matches.

- Record the results and calculate your sentence repetition intelligibility score. Score boxes are in the perforated section at the back of the book.
- Record and calculate the average repetition scores for all dyads in class.

2. Sentence transformation. In general, follow the same directions as used in the task on sentence repetition.

Example of Scoring for a Dyadic System
Blocks of consecutive matched repetition for a dyadic system.

1	II
2	卅卄
3	卅卄 II
4	
5	

14 Total Score

In block 1, two consecutive matched trials occurred before a mismatched trial occurred. In block 2, five consecutive matched trials occurred before a mismatched trial. In block 3, criterion level was reached with seven consecutive matched trials. The total score is the sum of all the trials.

Example of Calculating the Average Repetition Scores for all Dyads

1. __14__   Each score listed represents the total
2. __10__   score of each dyad in class. There are 5
3. __7__   dyads in this example. Dyad 1 has a
4. __10__   score of 14; dyad 2 has a score of 10,
5. __7__   and so forth. Add the scores to obtain
6.   the total score.
7.

__48__ Total score

Divide the total score by the number of dyads in class to obtain the average class score.

$$\frac{\text{Total Score (48)}}{\text{No. of Dyads (5)}} = \underline{(9.6)} \text{ Average Class Score}$$

3. Sentence restatement. In general, follow the same directions as used in the task on sentence repetition except for the following changes:

- Seven ± 2 sentences are to be spoken by one communicator after which the same information is repeated by the other communicator in his own words.

8

INFORMATION PROCESSING

This chapter centers on the topic of information processing. In human communication, information processing requires a base provided by intelligible sentences. Within any human communication system, the processing of information is influenced by the quality of the association or relationship between the communicators. Some of the content of this chapter is drawn from the area of information technology.

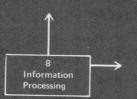

8
Information
Processing

8.1 INTRODUCTION

Information has been scarce throughout the brief history of man. Access to that scarce information has also been controlled in a number of ways. Quite suddenly, information has become abundant. Access to that abundant supply of information creates new problems. Equal access to that store of information requires new procedures. Information overload is a name for a new *dis*ease. Information promises to become the new money.

Credit ratings are a case where information and money are interrelated. If a person wishes to borrow money, the information on file in a credit bureau is at least as important as other aspects of a person's financial state. The ability to make money in many instances depends on the ability to borrow money. Credit information determines whether it will or will not be possible to obtain money when it is needed.

The new fundamentals of human communication emerge in a world transformed by information. To a large extent the accomplishments of the space age are made possible by large quantities of new information and by more efficient means of processing that information.°

° To live effectively is to live with adequate information.
Norbert Wiener, 1954:18.

8.1.1 Information Spiral

By any known test, more new information is being produced than at any previous time in the history of man. For a few years this great surge in the production of information was called an information explosion. But that explosion continues, and it continues to build. It is more appropriate to talk about a rising spiral of new information.

The growth of new information can be charted.°° More than 90 percent of the researchers who have ever lived are now at work producing information. The means for disseminating that information are new. More persons than ever before are able to receive an array of information which was available in earlier times only to heads of government when available at all.

°° The sum total of human knowledge changed very slowly prior to the relatively recent beginnings of scientific thought. But it has been estimated that by 1800 it was doubling every 50 years; by 1950, doubling every 10 years; and that by 1970 it will be doubling every 5 years.
James Martin, 1969:11.

8.1.2 Shift from Receive to Request

Quite often, a profoundly important matter seems trivial. For many of us, a shift from a right to receive to a right to request and receive seems a minor matter.□ The reverse is the case.

Article 19 of the UN Declaration of Human Rights stresses the right to "seek, receive and impart information." Even those of us who have radio, television, and newspapers at our disposal are limited, *severely limited*, in our opportunities to *seek* information. The newspapers and the radio and television newscasts obtain most of their world and national news items from one of two world news services. There is only slightly more variety in

□ Home communications of the future will give the individual more control over what he receives from a large inventory of information, including news and advertising. The consumer will continue to pay for it all, as ever, but with increasing control over what he gets.
Ben H, Bagdikian, 1971:221.

local news reporting. We are free to receive that which is transmitted to us. We are, by and large, limited to the choice of receive or not receive. In some parts of the world, persons are not even free to not receive.

8.1.3 Man Asks Machine

Pretend for a moment you have a home communication center. It combines the characteristics of telephone, television, typewriter, and xerox machine. Through the telephone, you may ask any specific question° and receive an *immediate* answer. Or you may request summaries of information that utilize major resource areas in a library. Or you may request any recorded entertainment or you may look in on any live theatrical performance or sporting event. In short, whatever you ask, if an answer can be formed from the world's store of information, you will receive that answer immediately. Assume you spend four hours one evening in the home communication center.

Assume the next evening you spend four hours with newspapers, radio, television, and books. You hold a stop watch. When you see or hear something that answers one of your questions, you start the stop watch. When you cease to receive answers you stop the watch. At the end of a four hour period, of the possible 240 minutes, how many minutes will you have recorded on the stop watch? Try it.

°

QUESTION ASKING		
Slow	1 2 3 ? 5 6 7	Quick
Unhappy	1 2 3 ? 5 6 7	Happy
Bad	1 2 3 ? 5 6 7	Good

8.2 DEFINITION

Information is that which reduces uncertainty. On first reading, that definition of information does rather little by itself to reduce uncertainty. It is not very informative. Still it is a starting point.

In any home community, there are a number of basic problems. A problem is an important matter that requires attention from time to time. Problems are the starting point for the purposes of human communication. Each purpose requires information. To achieve a purpose, information is needed.

Communicators organize a communication system to achieve a purpose. As they achieve that purpose, they ask and answer questions. The questions arise out of a particular purpose. The answers are fashioned of the information available to the communicators in that system. The greater the mutual store of information and the more skillful the shaping of that information into answers, the greater the likelihood of a purpose being achieved.

Given any purpose for communication, a number of questions arise and require answers. A question is an indication that uncertainty exists. It

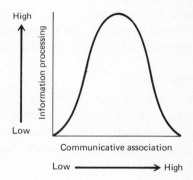

specifies and limits the uncertainty. There is little point in any communicator asking a question to which he knows the answer or a satisfactory answer. Most questions can be satisfactorily answered in several ways, that is, with information obtained from several different storehouses.[°]

Information, then, reduces uncertainty when it is shaped into answers to questions that arise within communication systems operating for some purpose.

8.2.1 Data

Data are obtained through measurements. Measurements are usually recorded in numbers. Numbers are readily processed by digital computers. Thus, much of communication within a single computer is data processing. The term *data processing* pertains almost exclusively to communication within a single machine or between two or more machines.

8.2.2 Information

When data are organized into patterns useful to human communicators, they are called information. The term *information* always carries the notion of pattern with it. Data organized into a pattern become information. Information when properly stored is available to become elements in answers.

Some information develops from careful data. Other information is a product of informal human experience. Still other information develops out of combining information in novel ways within a communication system. That process of combination is called interchange. It is the fundamental process required by synergy—the joining together of items of information to create a new pattern larger or better than the original items.

8.2.3 Messages

Within any communication system, the system purpose requires answers to a series of questions. A message is a record that embodies both a series of questions and their information-bearing answers. The reliability of the message depends on the interrelationship between purpose, questions, and answers.

8.3 INFORMATION PRODUCTION

From the view of communication, information can be produced in one of three important ways.[°°] New information may arise in a communication system organized for some purpose; serendipity and synergy are the names for these information-producing system processes. New information may

[°°]

> The best place to get information is from a good textbook.
>
> Disagree 1 2 3 ? 5 6 7 Agree

also be produced out of a human's everyday experience in his environment. Finally, new information results from efforts organized for the specific purpose of creating new information that are called research. We shall now examine briefly the production of information through communication, experience, and research.

8.3.1 Communication

As has been pointed out previously, communication systems may operate with individual or shared control; and they may operate with tutorial, interview or interchange patterns. The individual control condition in the tutorial pattern leads to the *transmission* of a prepared message. The shared control condition in the interchange pattern leads to the *development* of a unique message. Interchange occurs in dyads and small groups. Therefore, the production of new information is more likely to occur in a system that produces unique messages. That production can occur either as a result of synergy or of serendipity or both.

A system is a whole that is greater than the simple sum of its independent parts. A system introduces a multiplier effect or a *synergistic* effect. Within a communication system, when synergy occurs, new information is produced. That information is embodied in the "system performance log" called a message. That information may be of use only to the communicators operating in that system, or it may become informational elements in other answers in other systems.

A *self*-organized system draws temporary boundaries. The process that occurs within that system is observable. There are many a mismatch in the purpose–question–answer relationship. Many of these mismatches are errors that need to be corrected, and that is all. In a communication system that produces reliable messages, these mismatches usually constitute less than 5 percent of the message. Yet, not all mismatches are errors.

There is a helpful analogy in the process of biological mutation. A mutation occurs only a very small percentage of the time. Most mutations are errors that do not match the requirements of the environment; the mutated organism dies. *And yet,* all new and better organisms are also mutations. By chance, a mutation may be an improvement, a better match in a changed environment.

Serendipity is the name given to that attitude of examining a mismatch to decide whether it is an *error* to be corrected, or novel *information* to be preserved. A system that operates with high synergy and produces a reliable message is *also* very likely to create serendipitous information. Serendipity remains the happy art or science of looking for one thing and finding something different and better.

8.3.2 Experience

Outside of communication systems, humans also produce information as they live and act in their home communities.[°] A human takes in sensory readings from his environment. He can smell, touch, as well as see and hear. These sensory links with the environment bring in data. Some of these data are converted into informational patterns. In some respects, it is useful to think of a human as being able to organize a communication system with his environment. Man and the environment interact as a system to produce information.

8.3.3 Research

The primary task of research is to retest old information and to produce new information.[°°] Information processing as research occurs in a very special framework. Research procedures differ somewhat in the arts and in the sciences. From a cybernetic view, however, the similarities are quite pronounced. Scientific research is more interested in synergy and takes serendipity as a gift in the form of new theories and hypotheses. Artistic research seeks serendipity in the form of basic new patterns that can be developed into a system of art. Synergy is looked on only as refinement of existing techniques. Thus, scientific research stresses method and artistic research stresses creativity. In our terms, science seeks synergy and takes serendipity as a gift; art seeks serendipity and takes synergy as a gift. Increasingly, in both science and art, more research is being undertaken in a cybernetic approach. The information gained from such research has both a quantitative and a qualitative dimension.

8.4 STORAGE

Information can be stored in a number of "storehouses."[□] The most important of these storage places are in the human brain, in books, on film and tape, and in the machine brain. These storage units differ in permanence and accessibility. As we learn more about information and how to store it, these different storage units become interchangeable.

8.4.1 Human Memory

It is obvious that the human brain stores information: Ask a human a question; receive an answer that contains information that applies to that question. What is less obvious is the complete process by which information enters, is stored, and is retrieved from the human brain.[□□] Least known of all is the process whereby the brain stores information. But it does and does so very well. There is still no good estimate on how much information the

[°] If intelligence about the human world were as important to the community of scholars as the neurological functioning of rats, we would have available a solid series of studies on the accuracy of the various pundits who contribute to what we read.
R. P. Newman and D. R. Newman, 1969:147.

SYNERGY		
Bad	1 2 3 ? 5 6 7	Good
Weak	1 2 3 ? 5 6 7	Strong
Slow	1 2 3 ? 5 6 7	Fast
Unorganized	1 2 3 ? 5 6 7	Organized
SERENDIPITY		
Bad	1 2 3 ? 5 6 7	Good
Weak	1 2 3 ? 5 6 7	Strong
Slow	1 2 3 ? 5 6 7	Fast
Unorganized	1 2 3 ? 5 6 7	Organized

[□] . . . a person or a group—or, for that matter, a computer—can be viewed and studied as a system for receiving, storing, processing, transmitting, generating, and utilizing information.
H. M. Schroder, M. J. Driver, and S. Streufert, 1967:28.

[□□] As we have shown, the sense organs are the major gatherers of information. . . . the central nervous system allows it to reach the brain, the reticular formation determines whether it should be stored. The storage we designate *memory,* and it is only because we have the ability to remember things that we are able to communicate effectively.
G. A. Borden, R. B. Gregg, and T. G. Grove, 1969:21.

brain can store. Nor do we know very well how information is "forgotten." Does forgetting "clear" storage space for additional information?

Information storage in the brain is still a "black box" problem. We can observe information being entered, and we can observe information being retrieved at a later time for some other purpose.

In an earlier time, verbatim and rote memory was much prized. The Greeks were very good at memorizing long messages. Plato is said to have reproduced the Socratic dialogs from memory several years after he heard them. Schoolchildren around the world "memorize" answers for tests they expect from the teacher. Yet, at a time of rapid change in information, a large store of memorized information may be a severe handicap. The facts are different in many areas after a manned spaceship landed on the moon, or an American president visited China, or a floating city is built.

8.4.2 Books

The first books were handwritten. The book, for the first time, provided a convenient means of storing information for time periods greater than a man's memory or longer than his life. The printing press made book-stored information widely accessible.

Today, vast quantities of information are stored in books. But to be useful, a book must be read. Only a few more than half of the adults in the world can read. In the United States, one in five adults makes little or no use of books.

8.4.3 Recordings

Information can be stored by a variety of recording procedures.° Among these are phonograph records, magnetic tape, film, videotape, cassettes, and a number of variations and combinations of these. Most recording procedures include more informational detail than print does. The television tape and the newspaper story may store information in the same event but they do so in very different detail.

All of the recording procedures named here have come into use within the last fifty years; most of them have come into wide use only within the last few years. As information storage devices, they are very new.

8.4.4 Machine Memory

Storage of information in the memory unit of a machine, the computer, is a very recent development. From the early machine memories in the mid 1940s to the most recent ones, one trend is dominant. The machine memories have become faster, smaller in size, and cheaper. The advantages of machine memories are such that they influence all other storage forms

Old Handwritten Manuscript

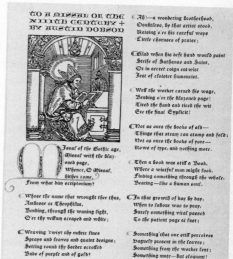

New York Public Library Picture Collection

°   The bypassing of the printed word will have the usual social impact of novel communications with novel content on an unlettered population, and this has special meaning for the less-developed countries.
Ben H. Bagdikian, 1971:22.

Computer Memory

IBM

including the human memory. The question becomes: Why spend time storing information (which will become outdated) in the human brain when current information is available from a machine memory at any time it is needed for some particular purpose?

8.5 RETRIEVAL

Information can be produced and then lost because it is not stored. A person's phone number known at one moment could have been written down before it was forgotten. If the person's name is known, and if his phone number is listed, only a moment is lost looking up the number again, if a phone directory is handy. And so on.

Information can be stored in the human memory, in books, on recordings, and in a machine's memory. Information in the various stores is not equally retrievable by the human communicator. Information can be retrieved in some communication patterns and not in others.

8.5.1 Interchange

A communication system organized for a mutual purpose builds a message from information shared by human communicators. When the two communicators in a dyad or the seven communicators in the small group have information adequate for their purpose, well and good. At present, the interchange pattern is limited to human communicators, with one important exception. Some of the newer man–machine systems begin to approach an interchange pattern. The interchange is awkward, but the future possibilities are enormous.

8.5.2 Interview

The interview pattern is an effective one when questions are clearly specified. The dyadic Delphi and the group Delphi both enable a communicator to retrieve large quantities of information. Any communicator can interview any other human communicator who chooses to associate with him and has the time to do so. Rather good interview or interrogation procedures now exist for obtaining information from some man–machine systems. Some of the so-called man–machine "dialogue" systems are better described as interview procedures.

In a limited way, it is possible to interview a book. Encyclopedias and dictionaries are information storage units from which information necessary to answer specific questions can sometimes be obtained. Recording procedures such as films or cassettes are more difficult in this respect, though some progress is being made to make information stored in this form easier to retrieve.

8.5.3 Tutorial

The tutorial pattern is widely used for the retrieval of information from a storage unit. It is well to remember that each message is originally developed for some system purpose. That message when stored may serve as information in some other system for some other purpose and become in turn part of still another message.

The communicator who attempts to retrieve information in the tutorial pattern receives a total message. If that message was well developed for its original purpose, the details of that purpose will be reflected in every intelligible sentence. The message taken in its entirety includes its original system purpose. The communicator who retrieves information in this way has a large sorting and reshaping task.

Examples of such a retrieval scheme are evident in the well-prepared lecture or book (excluding encyclopedias and dictionaries), films, tape recordings, and so on. For the communicator who for some purpose wishes to receive an answer to a specific question, the tutorial pattern of retrieval uses his time poorly. Yet, this is the pattern of all mass media.

8.6 EQUAL ACCESS

Information is being produced rapidly. That information is stored in a variety of storage units. Information can be retrieved from those storage units by a human communicator if he knows how, if he has the necessary facilities, and if he is free to do so. The human communicator must have appropriate communication skills, the necessary communication technology, and freedom from restrictive control.

8.6.1 Communication Training

The communicator who lives in a traditional village has little opportunity for developing the skills necessary for intensive information processing. Communication skills are likely to be adequate only for communicating with other communicators he knows well and for purposes that require only minimal new information. He is unlikely to be able to read. He will have limited experience with radio and television and no experience with computers.[o]

The communicator who lives or works in the center of a world city has a different set of problems. While he can communicate with a variety of other

[o] . . . the level of the information processing of group members sets limits to the level to which group organization can evolve.
H. M. Schroder, M. J. Driver, and S. Streufert, 1967:11.

communicators, can read, has extensive experience with the media, and some contact with computers, he is still likely to be ill-prepared for the changes that are now underway. The city communicator may now be suffering from information overload.

This book begins a program of communication training. In the last chapter, a plan for continuing to develop communication skill is presented.

8.6.2 Technology

Communication technology becomes increasingly important as a means for obtaining equal access to the world's store of information.[o] If information is stored *only* in the memory of some other human, it is necessary to travel to see him or contact him via telephone or through the postal service—by one of the two world communication network linkages, in other words.

At present, the world networks are uneven. Also, the transceiver devices are not equally distributed in the home communities of the world. So long as these inequalities exist, equal access is not yet possible. We all lose some information because of this inequality. The most valued information still is stored in the memories of men in every community of the world.

[o] . . . our present day farflung world communication networks (radio, telephone and telegraph) gather far more news daily, from all corners of the earth, than any human being . could possibly read and understand, even if it could all be printed.
Colin Cherry, 1971:28.

8.6.3 Control

Control of access to information still complicates information processing in every home community and in the world community. Access may be controlled through community custom. Only privileged persons receive certain information. Censorship may be imposed in a dozen deliberate and unintended ways. The newspaper editor chooses one item and may censor four by not choosing to publish them. The government spokesman often withholds information on matters of wide interest.[oo]

The greatest control, however, appears to be financial. The lower an individual's income, the less likely he is to have information adequate to his needs. What is true for the individual communicator is also true for entire communities and for world regions. The lower the per capita income, the less the access to information. The communicator tends to be poor in both information and money. With adequate information, he could obtain adequate money. Poverty, then, is by far the most important restraint on the equal access of information.

[oo] And there is sometimes *willful distortion* of evidence—plain lying. This may be caused by a crisis during which an organization tries to protect itself, by an organizational gag rule which forces subordinates to put out a cover story, by the Dale Carnegie principle of telling the people only what they want to hear, or by the pathology of congenital liars.
R. P. Newman and D. R. Newman, 1969:72.

8.7 INNOVATION

Any major new invention or discovery produces a body of new information that can be diffused or disseminated. The study of that process is usually called the *communication of innovations.*

With few exceptions, the flow of information from a central agency into the community is what usually is studied. Very little is known about the reverse of this process of information dissemination.

8.7.1 Centralized

In any large group system, the flow of information is from a central "source" to receivers. The communicator interested in innovations sees communication as a one-way process. The two-step flow model of communication came out of such a one-way view of communication.

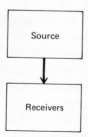

Innovation in this one-way model requires a decision at a high level that information is to be disseminated. The purpose for communication is determined, and the message is prepared. The message is then transmitted. The question of interest then becomes: Who receives the message and how long does it take for them to act on it? Innovation turns out to be a very regular process.

Only recently has the question about consequences of innovation been raised. It has become apparent that any innovation has not only a first consequence but also a second and a third consequence.

8.7.2 Decentralized

Instead of a decision being made by a central agency, decentralized innovation could occur by a reverse process when adequate information exists and when access to that information is possible for a substantial number of the members of a community.

As an alternative to the centralized model of innovation, we need to start in the community. Assume there is a problem area of concern to many community members. Out of the discussion in the community, a few purposes are defined. Certain community members seek additional information. They ask questions and receive informative answers. When they have adequate information, they decide to act.

The steps are the same as those in the centralized innovation model, with two important exceptions. The community members started the innovation sequences. If there are undesirable consequences, they will be better able to cope with them, having worked through all the steps in the innovation process.

Decentralized innovation shapes purposes out of interchange and pursues answers to real questions by a Delphi procedure. The mass media are of little or no use.

8.8 RIGHT TO INFORMATION

The U.N. Declaration of Human Rights stresses the right of the individual communicator "to seek, receive and impart information." In the United

States, a Right to Information Act was passed in 1966. Too often, central government agencies seem either to want to innovate or to withhold information. The Right to Information Act requires disclosure of information by all agencies of government. The exceptions are in the area of national security and foreign policy.

The exceptions to the act are instructive. Even a casual reading of the accounts of information agents and double agents—spies, if you will—suggests there are few and probably no secrets° in this area which are not known by those the information is being withheld from. The exceptions tend, then, to restrict communication within national boundaries while not doing so outside the boundaries.

There are a number of developments that make withholding information a difficult matter. As information becomes more abundant, it becomes increasingly possible to answer any question with information from a variety of sources. To put the matter in an extreme form, it is possible to know more exactly what a man will do than he himself knows if one wishes to spend the time assembling the necessary information.

All electronic communication technology is leaky. Microphones are often hidden in gifts, and so on. Intelligence networks make security even more difficult.

In short, whatever apparent gain in national security and foreign policy results from such attempts to withhold information, these gains do not seem to offset the loss to communicators such as you or me who do need access to a wide variety of information as is required by our human purposes.

SECRETS		
Impossible	1 2 3 ? 5 6 7	Possible
Unfair	1 2 3 ? 5 6 7	Fair
Bad	1 2 3 ? 5 6 7	Good

8.9 SUMMARY

In this chapter, information was defined. The processes of information production, storage, and retrieval were examined. Equal access and innovation were discussed along with the human right to information.

8.S SKILLS: QUESTIONS VERSUS ANSWERS

PURPOSE

Examine the relationship between questions and answers.

PROJECT

Consider one major problem in your community, such as:

- Population control
- Pollution control

Form a small group.

- Within the problem area that you select, specify one purpose for communication.
- Related to that purpose, specify 7 ± 2 questions that must be answered to achieve that purpose.
- For each of these questions, seek answers from various 7 ± 2 sources (other persons, books, radio, TV).
- Examine the relationship between questions and answers you have obtained. Is it possible to get the same information from different sources? Is it possible to get equally good, but different answers from a single source?
- Discuss in your small group the implications of your findings for your day-by-day information processing.
- State your results:

    1.

    2.

    3.

    4.

- Based on your findings write a specific guideline for processing information. Continue discussion until your group has obtained a consensus on the wording of the guideline.

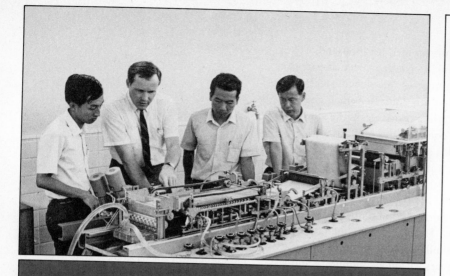

9
COMMUNICATIVE ASSOCIATION

Sentence intelligibility, as you recall, was defined as a system problem. Within a human communication system, a sentence is either intelligible or it is not. In the case of intelligibility the better the match, the higher the certainty. But information arises from uncertainty. Each question specifies an area of uncertainty. Information arranged in a question-specified pattern becomes an answer.

In this chapter we turn to the question of the relationship that develops between communicators as they communicate for some purpose.° Out of the several available terms, the term *association* is used to name the bringing together of communicators.

° . . . to improve your communication skills, . . . it is extremely important to get as sound an understanding of human beings as possible—the elements that affect their learning, their attitudes, their values, and their behaviors.
A. C. Baird, F. H. Knower, and S. L. Becker, 1971:6.

9
Communicative
Association

9.1 INTRODUCTION

The isolated village was the home community of man for thousands of years. Within the village, a web of interpersonal relationships evolved as part of a village-based culture. The Golden Rule summarizes this view of relationship: Do unto others as you would have them do unto you. In a small and relatively closed community, this rule is still a good one. But a community open to communicators from many other communities requires a different approach. In matters of money, the world is no longer on a gold standard. In the space age, there is no longer a single rule that can be the "golden" standard of human relationships.

The patterns within communities located in different parts of the world are both the same and different.° The visitor to a community is usually defined in terms of his cultural differences. The community members tend to define themselves in terms of cultural similarities. The phrase "all of us" is used more often than justified for members within a community and less often than justified for persons from several different communities. There is a within-group difference and a between-groups difference.

Perhaps we can now move beyond the myth of the melting pot—throw persons of different cultural heritage together, mix well, add heat, and produce humans alike in all observable characteristics. While such an approach has some utility in the early stages in the the formation of new communities, it very quickly suppresses the diversity necessary for creating alternatives for the future. Diversity begets serendipity.

As every community becomes more dependent on information produced in other communities, the members of every community associate more with communicators from other communities.°° Thus, some of the time previously spent communicating with one's own kind in his home community is now devoted to communicating with "quaint strangers" from other communities. There is a profound difference in communicating with a person with whom one has a long-term wide-range interpersonal relationship and communicating with a visitor with whom one associates exclusively for a single communication purpose.

Time is at the heart of the matter. A communicator can communicate in one system at a time. The amount of time available per day or year or lifetime is limited. Time spent communicating with outsiders for a variety of purposes increases an individual's store of information.□ It also makes it more difficult for him to communicate with others in the home community in the old way. Gaps emerge: generation, status, professional, and others as well. Each of these gaps has an informational component and a relationship change brought about by that shift of information.

The problem of time translates into one of human numbers. At any time,

° Communication is essentially a social affair. Man has evolved a host of different systems of communication which render his social life possible . . . in a sense unknown to animals. Most prominent among all these systems of communication is, of course, human speech and language.
Colin Cherry, 1966:3.

°° Once contact has been made, the fate of the relationship—its likelihood of formation and survival—depends on the level of outcomes the two persons experience. . . . Put more simply, we assume that each person enters and remains in the best of the relationships available to him.
J. W. Thibaut and H. H. Kelley, 1967:64.

□ Now I understand why everybody has been trying to convince me that the year will inevitably be tiring. I shall be living and interacting in communities which have their own life-styles—and which do not have many visitors. If I'm going to be able to synergize, I shall have to learn *their* SITUATIONAL, which, of course, really means understanding the life-style which is expressed in their communication styles. This will not be easy.
R. Theobald and J. M. Scott, 1972:45.

how many close interpersonal relationships are possible?° For many persons, this is still an indecent question. But it begins to be posed in the fundamental question: How many children should a family have? In the space age, another question also begins to be posed: How many close interpersonal relationships can a person develop and maintain? Close family relationships and close friendships require time. To devote too little time to such relationships is to weaken or destroy them. But to communicate only with persons with whom one has only a close interpersonal relationship is to restrict below a satisfactory level the acquisition of new information.

Some communicators attempt to build a close interpersonal relationship before they communicate with another communicator. Other communicators go to an extreme in the other direction of being the wary and impersonal adversary. A middle working range seems necessary. That working range of interpersonal relationship is called communicative association.

The term *communicative association* brings into focus one of the most difficult questions in man's relationship to his fellow man. This question is set in the area between competition and cooperation, between western knowledge and eastern wisdom, between individual man and social man.°°

9.1.1 Individual

For the individual communicator, the basic question is: Who am I? In pursuing an answer to that question he shapes himself as an individual.□ In some home communities, individualism is highly valued. The home culture supports and rewards individualism. Competition becomes a way of life and the wide-footed stance of the individual "operator" is viewed as inherent in nature: an eye for an eye, a tooth for a tooth. The individual sees in the actions of men around him actions that confirm the rightness of his views. He seeks knowledge as a means of power. And he carries his view of individualism into the communication system he organizes.

Many purposes arise out of the form of self-communication we call thinking. The individual "thinks up" a purpose for communicating with other humans. He may regard this purpose as a first approximation of the actual purpose and go on in one of the six system/network patterns to achieve a refinement of that purpose. Or, he may regard his purpose as *the* purpose and go on to attempt to achieve that purpose by bringing about change in one or more other communicators. The more value he places on individualism, the more likely he is to try to manipulate or manage other communicators.

The individual communicator has the right not to communicate. He has the right to seek to communicate for a purpose he chooses if other communicators agree to communicate with him on those terms for that

° How many friends can a man have, in the sense of real personal involvement and with compassion? A dozen? A hundred, maybe? Something on a village scale of size. On no account can he have a million or a thousand million friends, known as persons, by name, with their *individual* hopes and tragedies. The world can never be my village. It is true that, on very special occasions, some special person is brought to the attention of millions simultaneously by, say, television, as by the assassination of a President or the flight of an astronaut. But these events are rare, and these people are special: public figures. World communication offers no possibility of bringing together millions of people into a sense of *personal* involvement with one another.
Colin Cherry, 1971:xiii.

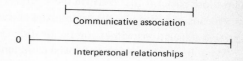

°° Man as a social being exists in and through communication; communication is as basic to man's nature as food and sex. . . .
Hugh D. Duncan, in Floyd W. Matson and Ashley Montagu, 1967:394.

□ I believe that the act of speech is a total process, that when it reaches optimum effectiveness the whole man communicates. What one is, is always part of what one says.
E. C. Buehler and W. A. Linkugel, 1969:1.

purpose.° However, if he restricts himself to not communicating, or communicating only for purposes he chooses in advance, or agreeing to communicate with another communicator who has predetermined a purpose, he severely limits himself.

9.1.2 Social Group

For the social communicator, the basic question is: Who are we? In developing an answer to that question, the social communicator shapes himself as a member in a social group.°° In some home communities, social behavior is highly valued. The home culture supports and rewards social acts. Cooperation becomes a way of life, and the flexible movements of the "cooperator" are viewed as inherent in nature: Even the animals look after their own kind. The social communicator sees in the action of men around him those patterns that confirm the rightness of his views. He seeks wisdom as a means of enhancing the group. And he carries this view of social man into his associations within communication systems.□

Many purposes arise out of social communication and the pattern of group thinking we call "interchange." The dyad or group shapes up a purpose to be achieved in communication systems at some future time. At this point, the individual communicator may seek to participate in other communicative systems that appear likely to operate to achieve a "next approximation" of that purpose, or he may seek to attempt to achieve that specific purpose.

Some communication systems make the role of the individual communicator most obvious; other systems make the social communicator most obvious. An observer can choose to be most interested in the individual or the social characteristics of a communication system. If he is most interested in the individual characteristics, he will probably become interested in the source or speaker in a large group system operating under individual control in a tutorial pattern. If he is most interested in the social characteristics, he is likely to become interested in the dyad operating under shared control in an interchange pattern. As we shall see, both the individual and the social are important.

But it is instructive that the quest of the individual communicator leads him to the "impersonal" mass media, and the quest of the social communicator leads him to the "personal" basic social unit, the dyad.□□

9.2 DEFINITION

The term *communicative association* refers to a limited interpersonal relationship within a communication system that is processing information as it seeks to achieve a purpose. The term *association* appears in Article 20

° To be an individual, a person, a "self," one must be a social creature as well, a member of society and of various sub-groups, playing various roles, adopting different loyalties and, in a self-deceptive way, seeing oneself as different on these different occasions. "Self" and "society" are the two inseparable sides of the coin.
Colin Cherry, 1971:2.

°° The significant mode of participating, in any network of human communication, is by sharing a common interest in the messages it transmits—i.e., by having opinions about the matters which concern other participants.
Daniel Lerner, 1958:71.

□ Let us believe again in conversation, in the veracity of unspoken relationships behind words. Let us laugh together about something. Let us discharge our mutual aggression in puns and jokes.
Joose A. M. Meerloo, in Floyd W. Matson and Ashley Montagu, 1967:146.

□□ It is extremely difficult for one who subscribes to this orientation to join in a dialogue with a strategist, even with the best intentions. The basic question in the strategist's mind is this: "In a conflict how can I gain an advantage over him?" The critic cannot disregard the question, "If I gain an advantage over him, what sort of person will I become?
Anatol Rapoport, in Floyd W. Matson and Ashley Montagu, 1967:91.

of the UN Declaration of Human Rights. There are two points. No one can be compelled to belong to an association. Everyone has the right to peaceful assembly and association. More generally, a human has the right to associate or not to associate.

The dictionary definitions of *associate* and *association* are appropriate. An associate is an ally, a partner, a helpmate, or a peer. The act of associating implies a combination for a common purpose. An association is an enterprise or a joint venture. Association carries the meaning of equals sharing their resources for a mutual purpose.

But association also carries the notion of limits. There are clearly human relationships that do not qualify as associations. And there are associations that are not primarily communicative. The term *communicative association* describes those interpersonal relationships within a communication system that influence the achievement of a common purpose.

There are a number of other terms that crisscross the area we call communicative association. Among these terms are interpersonal relationship, sensitivity, awareness, culture, aesthetics, encounters, and quality of communication. In an encounter group, for instance, humans attempt to communicate for the purpose of changing interpersonal relationships. Out of such attempts a view of communication sometimes arises that equates the competitive encounter with the full range of interpersonal relationships which leads on to a definition of human communication as only or mainly interpersonal relationship. Communication viewed as relationship or as culture or as individual expression has some utility within a single home community.

To serve both the home community and the world community, a dual view is needed. Information processing and communicative association both figure in communication. And as is the case in all dualities, there generates a certain tension between information and association that is best said by Martin Buber in his I—It and I—Thou distinctions.[°]

9.2.1 Communication Systems

Control within a communication system reflects the details of the association between the communicators. The basic options are two: *individual* control, or *shared* control. By *control* is meant the power to decide when communication begins, what the purpose is and will be, what questions are posed, what answers are accepted, the information load of the answers, when the purpose is achieved, whether the message is censored or disseminated and a host of related matters. Control in a communication system is a matter of first importance. All consequences of communication are influenced by it.

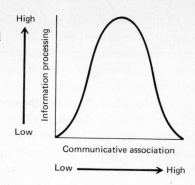

Communicative association

Low ——————→ High

[°] Every I—Thou relationship, within a relation which is specified as a purposive working of one part upon the other, persists in virtue of a mutuality which is forbidden to be full.
Martin Buber, 1958:133.

Individual Control

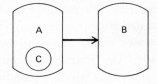

Shared Control

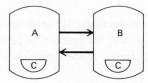

The question that must be answered in a communication system is, "who's in charge?" The answer can be, "He is," "I am," or "We are." The individual communicator may control a system because he is appointed to do so; a committee chairman is often appointed by some other large group. An individual may appoint himself; a group may select a leader; or leadership may evolve gradually during the operation of a system. Or, most importantly, control may be shared by all participating communicators. In the shared control case, "we" are in control.

The matter of system control is an important and sensitive one. If two communicators both seek to control the system, little will be accomplished until the matter of control is settled. Few of us escape the sight of two otherwise congenial associates competing for control of a particular communication system.°

How the control question is settled influences all details of association among the communicators in any particular system. Of equal importance, it makes some communication patterns possible and excludes others.

9.2.2 Communication Patterns

System control determines which communication patterns are possible. The more formal or consistent system control is, the more formal the communication patterns will be.

There are two control "associations." Individual communicator control of a system leads to either a tutorial or interview pattern. Shared control leads to an interchange pattern. The first consequence of the controls that regulate a communicative association is that they also determine communication patterns, which in turn determine information processing.

9.3 ASSOCIATION AND INFORMATION°°

Every age seems to have a few pseudoproblems that people talk about when they have little else to do. The pseudoproblem of heredity versus environment generated heated discussion for many years; the conclusion drawn from such discussions sometimes have major consequences. "Bad blood makes for a bad boy." Or, "His parents drove him to do it." The dichotomy heredity *or* environment is a false and wasteful one. But an *either-or* discussion now goes on about human communication along much the same line.

Because we are in the midst of the discussion about human communication, it is not easy to put the problem in perspective. Those most engaged in the discussion will claim it is not simple. But let us try to develop a perspective.

° When other means fail and still no decision is forthcoming, the parties often resort to force. In labor–management relations, force may take the form of a strike, a lockout, or other forms of economic pressure. In international relations, force takes the various forms of war. Force usually represents the failure of the parties to reach an agreement by any means other than a test of strength to determine who will dictate the terms of the agreement.
John W. Keltner, 1970:253.

°°

INFORMATION		
Unimportant	1 2 3 ? 5 6 7	Important
Insensitive	1 2 3 ? 5 6 7	Sensitive
Cold	1 2 3 ? 5 6 7	Warm
Weak	1 2 3 ? 5 6 7	Strong
ASSOCIATION		
Unimportant	1 2 3 ? 5 6 7	Important
Insensitive	1 2 3 ? 5 6 7	Sensitive
Cold	1 2 3 ? 5 6 7	Warm
Weak	1 2 3 ? 5 6 7	Strong

In simplest terms, the pseudoissue arises between the "people people" and the "task people." The people-oriented group insists that human communication is a matter of interpersonal relationships. Human communication exists mainly as a means of expressing interpersonal relationships. It follows that humans can become better communicators *if* and *only if* they become more sensitive to each other, and more aware of each other's relational needs. On the other hand, the task-oriented group insists that human communication is a matter of innovation based on information. And what is called increased sensitivity will occur as a result of information. It follows that humans become better communicators if and only if they become more skillful in processing information. And so the matter turns.°

The consequences of these two orientations are reflected in what gets called human communication and what is done to improve it. There are three areas where the emphasis on relationship or on information is most influential: purpose, question, and answers.

9.3.1 Purpose

The association between communicators is accurately expressed in the purpose for communication. If one communicator imposes his purpose on the communication system, he also controls the system. By this same act, he determines what information shall be processed and in what pattern. On the other hand, a purpose may be evolved by all communicators in the system. Either individual or shared control reflect the details of association.

9.3.2 Questions

The purpose determines the number and types of questions that will be posed.°° The communicator who poses a question inescapably reveals some of his individual and some of his social characteristics.

- Are you really stupid enough to believe that?
- How are you going to make me believe your so-called facts?
- Do we have any new information?
- Did you get a letter from him?
- Did you get the population data from the last census?

A question can be loaded with enough "relationship" detail that an information-carrying answer is difficult or impossible. This is a troublesome mismatch when the purpose requires a substantial information exchange. This type of mismatch reduces the efficiency of a system and in time will break it down.

In general, a satisfactory communicative association would lead communicators to pose questions suitable for the system state and the stage in the message.

° In short, if we remember that every communication has a content and a relationship aspect, we can expect to find that the two modes of communication not only exist side by side but complement each other in every message.
P. Watzlawick, J. H. Beavin, and D. D. Jackson, 1967:64.

°° He is a questioning thinker. But not like Socrates, who knows the right answer and at first "ironically" withholds it from his partner in dialogue. Shestov . . . knows what is to be asked today and here; he teaches us to ask.
Martin Buber, 1967:60.

9.3.3 Answers

Answers to questions contain associational and informational detail. The communicator who answers a question *inescapably* displays some of his individual and some of his social characteristics.

- I won't answer a dumb question like that.
- My facts are correct even though you're not bright enough to recognize it.
- We have several new items of information.
- A special delivery letter came in from Honolulu at about ten this morning.
- The data from the last census show a slowing population growth rate.

Answers, like questions, can be loaded with associational detail or informational detail, or both. In terms of the purpose and the specific question, any specific answer can either match or mismatch.

9.4 HOME COMMUNITY

Every communicator learns to communicate in his home community. He also forms many of his deepest interpersonal relationships while young and at home with family and childhood friends. Understandably, his expectations for communication are set in the home community.

Most young adults feel most comfortable and feel they communicate best with a family member or a long-time friend.° In a stable home community, communicators specialize in communication with each other. They develop community rules for communication and shape a unique style of speaking. All of these adaptations improve and strengthen interpersonal ties.

° . . . both the sheer amount of shared information among persons and the level of that information operate together to determine the existence or the intensity of an interpersonal relationship. . . . At base the whole matrix of links and bonds that bind or alienate two humans in a deep interpersonal knowing of one another consists solely of information-sharing of many kinds.

G. A. Borden, R. B. Gregg, and T. G. Grove, 1969:82.

9.4.1 Transcomnet

The problem of transportation is minimal in a home community. In a small community, say a traditional village of a few hundred people, the only links of the transportation network are foot paths from home to home. But those footpaths do provide links in a network. By examining the pathways in such a community, one could have a fair notion of which persons communicated with each other.

9.4.2 Telecomnet

Telecommunication facilities are unevenly distributed throughout the communities of the world. The case of the United States is typical. Most

U.S. homes now have a telephone, radio and television; most own books and receive newspapers; and most send and receive letters. But remember, these developments in telecommunication technology are recent by any yardstick used to measure human evolution. Ask a grandparent.

Some of the uses of the telecomnet are for communication between persons who know each other well. The telephone is used most for within-community calls. But radio, television, books, and newspapers bring information into the community from distant and often unknown sources. The relationship between communicators in such large group systems is minimal. Mass media are impersonal. Some of the quest for new ways of communication to build interpersonal relationships must certainly spring from the hours of impersonal communication in the classroom and before the tube.° We do not yet see clearly the full impact on the home community of the telecomnet that brings communicators from distant places into our living rooms.

9.5 WORLD COMMUNITY

The young adult often leaves his home community for an extended period of time in connection with education, work, or military service. For the first time, he must deal with strangers all day, every day. In all likelihood, he seeks to build new friendships with persons who are like his friends back home. At age eighteen, a teenager comes of legal age, and he begins a period of several years which reshape his home community habits of communication.°° By the time he is twenty-eight or thirty, or before, it is likely he will form a family and turn some house into a family home. If his new home is in his old home community, he will partially, but only partially, re-adopt his former communication style. But he will differ from his friends who have not left home, and he will differ in his habits of information processing. Day by day, he will require more information than his friend who resembles him in all ways except travel and residence beyond the home community.

It makes little difference where the young person lives: Balgat, Turkey; Kothuru, India; a Philippine barrio; Pahala, Hawaii, or Hitchock, South Dakota. The young adult develops information-processing habits he retains even if he returns to his community. To survive in a "foreign" community, he must obtain information from other communicators. He must obtain information from strangers. To do so he undertakes to build a communicative association. In time that association may develop into a social relationship, into a friendship, or it may move into a competitive or adversary area where communication is no longer possible.

The point is simple. As a human requires for his purposes information

° . . . enduring interpersonal relationships . . . are being formed without face-to-face confrontation ever having taken place among the parties to the relationship. Pen pals, lonely-hearts correspondents, and the international sponsors of underprivileged children are examples.
G. A. Borden, R. B. Gregg, and T. G. Grove, 1969:77.

°° We are interested in empathy as the inner mechanism which enables newly mobile persons to *operate efficiently* in a changing world. Empathy, to simplify the matter, is the capacity to see oneself in the other fellow's situation.
Daniel Lerner, 1958:49.

beyond that which is available from other humans in his home community, he will seek information from outside his home community. As he organizes those systems necessary for achieving those purposes that require outside information, he sets into motion a chain of events that influence every aspect of his present interpersonal relationships. Information changes human associations.[°]

While it is not possible to develop a rich and wide-ranging interpersonal relationship with every person one communicates with, it is possible in most instances to develop a communicative association. And if communication is successful, at times and once in a while, such an association can lead on to friendship. Most of the time even highly successful communicative associations do not lead on to full interpersonal relationships. The informational needs of space age man divided among the few hours per day do not permit it. Were there time enough, most men in the world might be your close friend.[°°]

[°°]

It takes time to form and maintain a friendship. Therefore, most people have about 7 ± 2 friends.

Disagree 1 2 3 ? 5 6 7 Agree

9.5.1 Transcomnet

The jet plane permits any man in any community to know that—if conditions were right—he might fly away to any other spot on earth to communicate with whomsoever he pleased. Few persons actually travel long distances. But those persons who do travel stop at several places. The visitor goes from airport to hotel and from hotel to a variety of locations in the community. The chances are good some of his communication is for business purposes. In this manner, a rapidly growing percentage of persons who work outside the home will communicate on a routine basis with persons from a large number of distant communities. Every common purpose for communication incorporates both the information and association unique to that system. Today, the transcomnet makes business multinational.

The number of persons who travel internationally is growing. Most colleges and universities have more than a token foreign student population. It's not uncommon these days for 5 or 10 percent of the total student body to be foreigners. The military services have often billed a military hitch as a vacation abroad—"Join and see the world." Mobility is related to type of employment, level of education, and affluence. More people travel more often to more places for more communication-related purposes.

9.5.2 Telecomnet

But if the jet takes a man away from home, the satellite may make him a homebody once again. For travel that is communication-related, as telecommunication facilities become better, that travel will be reduced. The telephone company cautiously suggests long-distance phone calls are the next best thing to being there. Salesmen often call before going, and sometimes call instead of going. As home communication centers become widely available, it will become possible to communicate to work. The slogan goes: Don't commute—communicate. Perhaps we shall. The pattern is not yet clear: Can a transcomnet link be traded for a telecomnet link?[°]

For both the home community and the world community, the relationship between transportation and telecommunication poses a vital question: can a telecomnet link substitute for a transcomnet link? This is a four-way question. The networks are worldwide with linkages that serve within any single community or between any two communities. What is at stake are human cultures.

A growing use of the telecomnet link in world linkages would lead, perhaps, to a world teleculture, or a global village. At the other extreme, a return to the transcomnet in a home community coupled with closed boundaries around a community would recreate the traditional village. And so on. The question is not of the either/or variety. It is a question of more or less; how much of what. Of balance.[°°]

9.6 SOME FUTURE TESTS

For most humans, the move from the home community to the world community involves some moments of personal uncertainty and discomfort. The problem can be kept in perspective. Only with a few persons in a lifetime and at any particular time is it possible to develop and maintain a wide-range interpersonal relationship; this is not a question of *will* but of sheer possibility.

As we make some advances in dealing with those "quaint strangers" who live beyond the edge of our home community, other new prospects arise. One of these is the intelligent machine. The other is ETI.

9.6.1 Man–Machine

It is now possible to carry on a very simple conversation with a computer in spoken English. This possibility raises new questions. Should man and machine organize a dyadic system for a mutual purpose? Do machines operate for a purpose?

The intelligent machine as a species is only one-third of a century old. It has already lived through several generations. Each generation is smaller, faster, cheaper—and, more intelligent. We humans call ourselves *homo sapiens*, the wise animal. Yet, in many of the tests of intelligence, the machine is smarter than man. Computers play good chess. A computer

[°] We must finally broaden our focus to include those habitual mannerisms, customs, attitudes, and institutions that form the cultural patterns whose influence is a significant factor in human affairs. . . . These cultural patterns facilitate and strengthen both the communion and the communication of a people and at the same time control human behavior so subtly that they are often unnoticed.
G. A. Borden, R. B. Gregg, and T. G. Grove, 1969:219.

[°°] Man is prone to seek novelty in his environment and, having found a novel situation, to learn how to control it. . . . These propensities are at the root of curiosity and the assimilation of knowledge. . . . Addressed to the social environment of other men, they lead him into social communication, conversation and other modes of partially cooperative interaction.
Gordon Pask, in Jasia Reichardt, 1971:76.

Wide World

could be programmed to get a higher score on an IQ test than its human programmer.

In succeeding generations, the machine will be more intelligent than man in many and probably most of the areas now measured on a human IQ test. How then should we communicate with a machine intelligence greater than our own? If you observe the humans who frequent computer centers, you will observe a seriousness in their "communication" with the machine. The computer has a peculiar facility for making some people "act important." That should worry you . . .

9.6.2 Man–ETI

ETI means extraterrestrial intelligence. If there is intelligent life in outer space, and if we are able to establish two-way communication—either transcomnet or telecomnet—then we have another set of questions. A major question, of course, is the type of communicative association we would wish to form with an intelligence that might be ten or ten thousand times greater than our own. You are not likely to be faced with such a problem. And, yet . . . °

9.7 EXTERNAL CONTROL

In the communities around the world, humans are not fully free to associate with each other for purposes of communication. There are several external controls. Some of these are within communities; caste and class boundaries restrict association. Others are national and international. One needs a passport to get in and out of most countries. One needs licenses to use many of the telecommunication devices.

The most far-reaching control of all is built into all radio and television receiving sets. They only enable us to receive what happens to be "on" at the time we choose to tune in. When radio or TV is "wired" as it is in some countries, there is no choice. But even if there are three or six channels, the choice is still severely limited in relation to the range of purposes for which humans associate to communicate. If these devices were two-way, then, our world would be a different and, I think, a better place.°°

9.8 SUMMARY

Communicative association was defined in this chapter. The relationship between information and association was explored. Similarities and differences between the home community and the world community were pointed out. Future tests for communicative associations were mentioned and external controls were cited.

° I would like to be one of the first earthmen to communicate with an ETI.

Disagree 1 2 3 ? 5 6 7 Agree

°° As for the larger communication and understanding implied in a shared planetary culture, it is more than obvious today that we must understand and cooperate on a truly global scale, or we perish.
John McHale, 1969:300.

9.S SKILLS: COMMUNICATIVE ASSOCIATION

PURPOSE

Demonstrate patterns of daily communicative association.

PROJECT

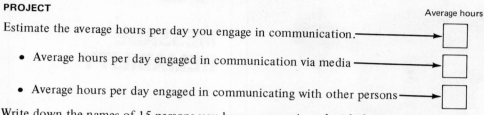

Average hours

Estimate the average hours per day you engage in communication.

- Average hours per day engaged in communication via media

- Average hours per day engaged in communicating with other persons

Write down the names of 15 persons you have communicated with during the last week.

- Rank order from most frequent to least frequent.
- Enter on the "target" chart, which is in the Skills Worksheets section (at the end of the book.)

Consider the maximum and minimum number of persons with whom you can communicate.

- Given the hours you are awake per day, what might be the maximum number of persons you might list in each circle?
- What might be the minimum number of persons you might list in each circle?

What patterns do you detect? In systems? In networks?

10

MESSAGE RELIABILITY

This is the fourth and final chapter on the human communication process. Sentence intelligibility provides the essential basis for all communication. Information processing and communicative association stand in a particular relationship to each other. The present chapter views intelligibility, information, and association within the larger framework of the message.°

°   . . . a message, in the civilized and communicative sense, is an alternative to coercion by direct force because it substitutes symbols for physical pressure. . . .
T. A. Welden and H. W. Ellingsworth, 1970:71.

10
MESSAGE RELIABILITY

10.1 INTRODUCTION

A message, any message, is in part COIK—*C*lear *O*nly *I*f *K*nown. If a communicator contributes to the development of a message within some communication system, that message is likely to be clear to him because he knows the relationship between purpose, answers, and questions within the original system. The message is *clear only if k*nown what the conditions were within a communication system.

COIK messages are everywhere. A lady I know is such a good cook that people frequently ask her for *the* recipe. A recipe is, of course, a particular kind of message. This lady also expects to hear again from the person who tried her recipe. The complaint is standard: "It didn't taste the same when I baked it." Her reply is always: "I gave you the recipe, but I didn't tell you how I baked it. If you want to know that, we'll bake cake together." A message is a COIK recipe. It is more useful to remind one of things that once were clear than it is of something not yet known.

The do-it-yourself electronic kits provide another COIK example. These kits are accompanied by directions on how to assemble the parts in the kit; some of these instructions end with the cheerful observation that even a ten-year-old boy can follow the instructions. Certainly, somewhere such a boy may have done so or will do so. A monkey at an electric typewriter may in time write a sonnet. But the person without previous electronics experience will have difficulty following those instructions.

Messages are often puzzling.° They often appear to contain more useful information than in fact they do. A recipe looks complete; of course it isn't. The same can be said about the do-it-yourself instructions. Both contain assumptions that are often not valid. The same observation holds for lectures and all of mass media. Even though some persons get the "message," many and oftentimes most do not.

A message is always a partial and incomplete record of what was said while a particular human communication system operated to achieve its purpose.°° The message may be stored in human memory, may be written down on paper, recorded on tape, and stored in a computer memory. The more that is known about the system that produced the message, the more likely the subsequent transmission of that message will be clear.

10.2 DEFINITION

Every message is a *performance record* of some communication system.▫ All messages fall into one of three basic patterns. These are: dialog, multilog, and monolog. The term *log* also means a performance record. A ship's log stands as an official record of that ship's performance.

° Every message transaction has [an information and association] aspect. A message not only conveys bits of information; at the same time it defines how the information is to be taken—the nature of interpersonal transactions between the communicants.
A. L. Smith, in L. L. Barker and R. J. Kibler, 1971:24.

°°

A skilled speaker can always transmit a complete message to a good listener.

Disagree 1 2 3 ? 5 6 7 Agree

▫ The study of communication focuses on interaction through messages. Messages are the crucial links of the communication chain.
George Gerbner et al., 1969:ix.

Likewise, a television station log contains a sequential schedule of the day's program actitities. A message is the log of a particular communication system. It is always incomplete; it usually contains one or more errors.

There are three basic message logs. These message logs correspond to the three communication system sizes. The *dia*log occurs in a dyad. The *multi*log occurs only in a small group. The *mono*log occurs most frequently in the large group system. But it can occur in any communication system where only one communicator talks and all others are silent.

Messages are organized. Any message displays the total organization of its particular communication system. The purpose, system size, control and communication pattern, the questions and answers, and achievement or nonachievement of purpose will usually be displayed in a message.

Communication systems are one-way or two-way. In general, two-way systems develop new messages to achieve some purpose.° One-way systems *transmit* messages developed or prepared or preplanned in some other system for some other purpose.

Television, radio, and newspapers are basically message transmission systems. In a newscast, for instance, some part of a message is "excerpted" and stands for the total message. Thus, a two-hour multilog may be transmitted as only a one-minute excerpt and a twenty-second summary of the two-hour message. The newspaper reporter takes a three-line quote and fills in a few lines of background on a day-long conference. Most often, only parts or elements of a message are selected for large group system transmission.

A few "prepared" messages are transmitted in their entirety. An address of a major political figure may be heard by an assembled audience. It may be telecast "live." The text of the address may be published in a newspaper. The telecast may be repeated. The greater the distance—either in miles or hours—from the original transmission, the more likely that only excerpts will be retransmitted.

10.3 DIALOG

A dialog message is a record produced as a by-product in dyadic human communication systems.°° Each of the two communicators contributes part of the message. Thus a dialog message is the product of the two communicators who organize a dyadic system for some purpose.

10.4 MULTILOG

A multilog message is a record produced as a by-product of a small group

°

> A message rises out of the experiences and purposes of a human being to establish and maintain contact with one or more fellows.
> *A. C. Baird, F. H. Knower, and S. L. Becker, 1971:89.*
>
> **Disagree 1 2 3 ? 5 6 7 Agree**

°°

> . . . ABAABBABB . . .

human communication system.° Each of the several communicators contributes part of the message.

10.5 MONOLOG

A monolog message is produced originally in a dyadic or small group system and transmitted in a large group system.°°The monolog is preplanned and/or prepared. It is minimally influenced by the conditions in the system as it is operating.

10.6 RELIABILITY ANALYSIS

There are many techniques for analyzing the process of communication and that special by-product called the message. We shall examine only a single such technique that is fitted to the information contained in this section.

The first question always is: Did the system that produced the message achieve its purpose? Many messages, for instance, that do achieve their purposes are of little interest beyond the system which produced them. Others which do not achieve an immediate system purpose do so as elements in other systems at later times, helping to achieve other purposes.

In analyzing the human communication process, three general questions may be posed:

- Are the sentences intelligible?
- Is information processing effective?
- Do the communicators associate with each other in a way that increases the likelihood of achieving the purpose?

In addition to these three basic questions an endless variety of other questions may be posed about a message. Such questions need to be precise enough to lead to reliable answers. In this sense, reliability means consistent answers. Thus a question should receive the same answer by any single analyst on any two occasions, or by any two analysts who agree on the questions on any single occasion.

10.7 MESSAGES IN SYSTEMS

One way of coming to understand a culture is to analyze and study the messages produced and shared by that culture.□ Thus, any human analyzing the messages of the past decade would be impressed by the violence theme running through messages transmitted by mass media in the United States. Messages are made out of recombinations of previous messages.

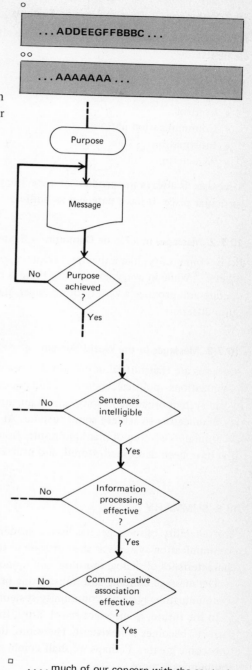

° ... ADDEEGFFBBBC ...

°° ... AAAAAAA ...

□ .... much of our concern with the content of messages is to discover the nonobvious, to

10.7.1 Messages in Communication Systems

A message in any communication system results from the following elements:

- Purpose
- System size
- Control
- Communication pattern
- Information
- Association

A message is always the product of a specific system operating at some particular place. It has a date and an address.

10.7.2 Messages in a Home Community System

Every community, like a theatre, resonates some sounds and damps out others.°° While in every community there is a wide range of systems that operate and produce a variety of messages, the history of those messages is quite different.

10.7.3 Messages in the World System

Messages are transmitted in the world community within the world organizations—political, economic, and educational. The messages in the world system originate in some communication system organized by human communicators to achieve some purpose. At any stage in history, the accumulated wisdom of mankind results from the sum total of the messages that have been developed, stored, and utilized.□

10.8 SUMMARY

The reliability of messages has been considered within the three basic communication systems as they operate in the two world networks. The characteristics of dialog, multilog, and monolog messages were examined.

The message building and transmitting process was considered within communication systems, community systems, and the world system.

In the future, as messages travel faster, the opportunity to "call back and correct" becomes nonexistent. Therefore, the concern for reliability is likely to become greater. Perhaps we shall communicate less and, thereby, communicate more.

infer what is hidden, to gain information about what cannot be seen, and to make messages out of signals that remain signals for others. It always requires an *analytical sophistication* that is greater than that possessed by the source.
Klaus Krippendorf, in George Gerbner et al., 1969:106.

°° Message materials, in short, are the complex phenomena of our educational, political, social, physical, scientific, philosophical, and religious worlds, which we use for our individual purposes.
A. C. Baird, F. H. Knower, and S. L. Becker, 1971:101.

□ In the limit, any message whatever, no matter how complex, can be transmitted by any type of channel if the channel has a sufficient capacity.
Abraham Moles, 1968.

10.S SKILLS: MESSAGE RELIABILITY

PURPOSE

To assess message reliability in respect to sentence intelligibility, information processing, and communicative association.

PROJECT

With your partner write one page of information on any topic you choose. Modify your message in view of the following questions:

- Are your sentences intelligible?
- Is the information process effective?
- Do you and your partner associate with each other in a way that increases the likelihood of achieving your purpose?

Read the complete paper to the class.

Read the paper again, but this time choose ten words you will not read throughout the paper. Ask the class to list numbers 1 through 10 on a slip of paper and to fill in the missing words as you say them.

Score (scoring sheet is in the perforated section at the back of the book) 1 point for each correct word filled in. Find the total correct responses for each class member and record it. For example, class member 1 has a score of 9, class member 2 has a score of 3, and so forth. Each score represents an individual reliability score. To obtain an average group message reliability score, sum the individual scores and divide the total by the number of class members.

Example of Scoring

1. $\underline{9}$
2. $\underline{3}$
3. $\underline{10}$
4. $\underline{7}$
5. $\underline{8}$
   $\underline{37}$ *Total*

Divide the total individual score by the number of class members to obtain the average group message reliability score:

total score (37) ÷ number
of class members (5) = average
group message reliability score (7.5)

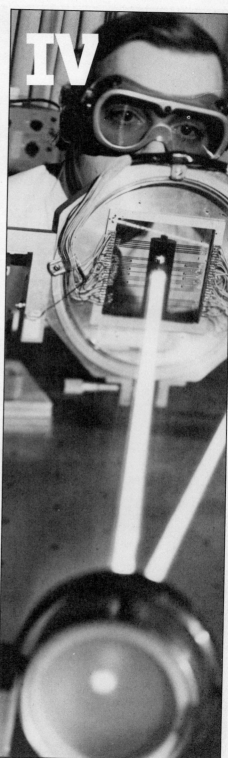

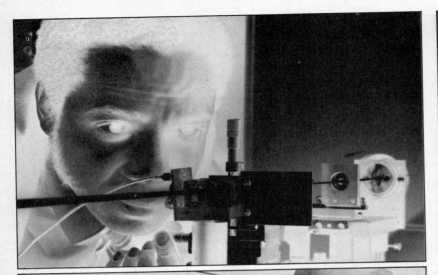

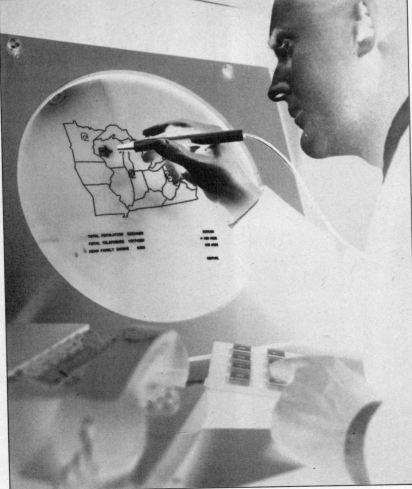

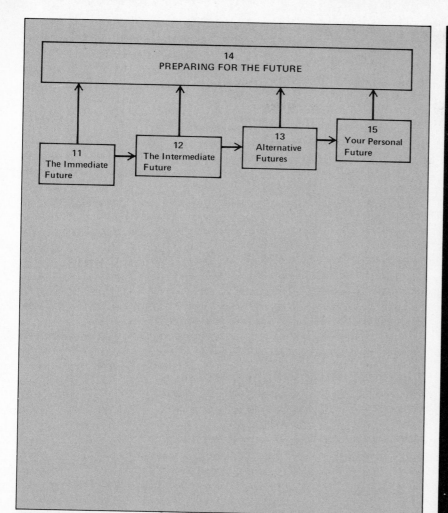

| 14 PREPARING FOR THE FUTURE |

| 11 The Immediate Future | 12 The Intermediate Future | 13 Alternative Futures | 15 Your Personal Future |

IV FUTURE

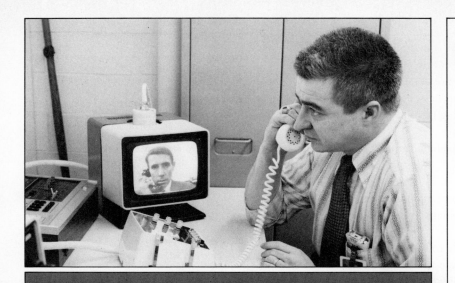

11

THE IMMEDIATE FUTURE

In this chapter, some probable developments that will influence human communication are briefly discussed. These developments include the auviphone, man-machine communication, and the home communication center. These technological developments, taken together, will make it possible for most of us to "communicate to work."

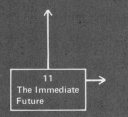

11
The Immediate
Future

11.1 INTRODUCTION

The *immediate future* begins in the present and stretches on for some five or ten years into the future.° The immediate future refers to that time span for which detailed planning is possible. There are detailed five and ten year plans in many areas such as agriculture, business, education, government, and so on. For most of us, detailed planning beyond ten years is not possible at this time.

For most readers of this book, the immediate future will encompass a time span which includes termination of full time formal schooling, family formation, first career, and first career shift. In simpler words, you finish school; get married; get a job and find that the job changes enough to require you to build new skills. The immediate future will be an "interesting" time.

In the immediate future, there promises to be several major developments in communication. Four likely developments are discussed in the units that follow in this chapter. The *auviphone* extends the present telephone.°° Man–machine communication grows in flexibility and usefulness. The home communication center combines several developments including the auviphone and man–machine communication. The home communication center makes it possible to perform at home many of the activities we now call "work."

11.2 AUVIPHONE

The term *auviphone* is a short form of audio-visual-telephone. It is also called a picture phone and several other names. The essential matter is that it adds a picture or video dimension.□

In some home communities in the world, the auviphone is being tried, or plans have been made for its use. As soon as possible, get direct information about the reactions of communicators who have experience with the auviphone.

The addition of the video dimension promises, first of all, to improve sentence intelligibility some 10 or 15 percent. Such an increase in intelligibility will prove particularly helpful in intercultural communication. Message reliability will be increased.

In addition to making communication more reliable, purposes not readily achieved with the present audio-only telephone become possible. The charts and graphs which are an important part of most technical communication can be displayed for mutual consideration. Filmstrips and other visual sequences could also be utilized. In short, information not readily processed

° Imagination should be accompanied by realistic elaboration. Human futuristics discourages the individual from delivering himself to pure fantasy and encourages him to develop new methods for new types of reality-testing. It stimulates reality-directed inventiveness in the individual. In short, human futuristics aims at developing scientific *attitudes,* experimental *attitudes* and engineering *attitudes* rather than at teaching scientific data per se. Above all, it helps people develop the attitude *to make technology serve human goals.*
M. Maruyama and J. A. Dator, 1971:2.

°° The telephone is not just a better telegraph; television is not just a better cinema or radio; they are categorically different, though each brings its own 'quality' to the whole structure of human communication.
Colin Cherry, 1971:46.

□ . . . we may also suggest that it would be very nice to have the opportunity to speak face to face with anyone in the world, to "visit" with them, to ask them information. . . . A person living in Afghanistan or Brazil might be interested in San Diego. . . . San Diegans willing and also switched-on would introduce themselves and develop a "screen pal" relationship. . . . The conversation could be either public or private at the option of the people involved.
R. D. Jones, in M. Maruyama and J. A. Dator, 1971:184.

Picturephone

AT&T

in an audio mode can often be processed in a video mode. The auviphone constitutes an important new development for the individual communicator.

In the immediate future, it will be interesting to observe the range of purposes the auviphone actually does serve. Any individual communicator can complete the sentence, "I'd like to use the auviphone for

_____ ." Ask seven or more other communicators what use they have for an auviphone. What do you find?

11.3 MAN–MACHINE COMMUNICATION

The machine in man–machine communication is, of course, the computer.[°] If your attitude about computers is based on a reaction to those cards that warn you not to "spindle, fold, or mutilate," your attitude is several machine generations behind time. In addition to the data processing uses of computers, other creative and artistic uses are becoming more frequent. Computer art exists.

Man–machine communication is a special case of the more general dyadic human communication system considered in Chapter 4.0.[°°] In a man–machine system, either man or machine can control the system. The tutorial, interview, and interchange communication patterns are all possible. Machines now recognize and produce speech. This development is still at a quite elemental level but promises to evolve quickly. In the immediate future, you will be able to converse with a computer, probably any computer in the world, over an auviphone network.[□]

The vocabulary introduced in the earlier chapters permits us to make several observations and pose several questions. In time, as pointed out in the Mr. Turing example, it will be possible for a computer to communicate in a "human" way. Each of us might delegate some of our daily communication activity to a machine programed to communicate in our own individual style.[□□] As such a development and related ones come about, several basic questions come into focus:

- A communication system operates for a purpose. Should a man–machine system operate for a "mutual" purpose? Can a computer communicate for a purpose?
- Many humans spend more time watching TV than they do communicating with other humans. Might humans come to prefer communicating with a computer rather than other humans, particularly if the machine is "subtle but not mean?"

The possibilities of a man–machine dyad are similar to those of any other

[°] Telecommunication links will enable people needing information to search with computer assistance through what is available. . . . In searching for reports on a given topic the user would carry on a two-way conversation with the distant computer. The computer might suggest more precise categorizations of what he was seeking. . . . The telecommunication link will make the searching much faster and more efficient.
James Martin, 1969: 12.

[°°] We define man–machine communication as two-way conversation that is goal-oriented-aimed toward the accomplishment of a specific objective—and in which both parties contribute a necessary function.
Charles T. Meadow, 1970:4.

[□] In the not-too-distant future, for a few dollars a month, the individual will have a vast complex of computer services at his fingertips. Communication with the machine may even be by means of natural language . . .
Hal Hellman, 1969:142.

[□□]

I would like to have a communication machine that could "stand in" for me.

Disagree 1 2 3 ? 5 6 7 Agree

human–human communication dyad.[°] In time, it is probable that the two dyads will be indistinguishable in many telecomnet links. We have no way at this time of estimating what the long term consequences of man–machine communication will be.

11.3.1 Teaching Machines: Tutorial

In recent years, a variety of devices have been used as teaching machines. Some of these devices were simple mechanical arrangements for presentation of information. But some of these devices were computers. Gradually, teaching machines operating in a tutorial pattern came to be called *Computer Assisted Instruction*; that title has been shortened to CAI.

A communication system operating in a tutorial pattern transmits information from a tutor to a tutee. A man–machine and man–man dyad operating in a tutorial pattern are similar in information processing characteristics. The two dyads differ, however, in terms of the association that is possible. It seems clear that man and machine can form a communicative association. We do not yet know if man and machine can form an interpersonal relationship. It is no longer humorous to ask if a man can fall in love with a machine. Or vice versa.

11.3.2 Information Retrieval: Interview

It is now possible to pose a specific question to an information storage unit and retrieve a specific answer to that question.[°°] The pattern of communication resembles in all important details information processing in a man–man dyad. But again, the nature of the communicative association in man–man and man–machine dyads may differ in important ways. Also, it may not.

The dyadic Delphi procedures discussed in Chapter 4.7 work equally well in man–man and man–machine dyads. In fact, the better procedure might be to utilize both man–man and man–machine dyads during the course of the Delphi interviews.

For the first time, the world's store of information can be interviewed, or questioned, or interrogated. Ask a question; receive an answer to that question drawn from all information accumulated by man. No man need be underinformed.

11.3.3 Synser Man–Machine: Interchange

As was pointed out in Chapter 4.8, any communication system that operates in both a tutorial and interview pattern may also operate in an interchange pattern.[□] The interchange pattern makes possible both synergy and serendipity. As you recall, synergy multiplies or generates new information. Serendipity arises out of the unexpected occurrences within a system. Thus,

CAI Systems

IBM

[°] There are at least three points in cybernetics which appear to me to be relevant to religious issues. One of these concerns machines which reproduce themselves; and one, the coordination of machine and man.
Norbert Wiener, 1964:11.

[°°] A major innovation in home communications will be a reactive system, with the individual consumer having the power to order specific content and receive it immediately.
Ben H. Bagdikian, 1971:xxvi.

[□] We have, then, two dissimilar systems or organisms, working toward a common goal and dependent each upon the other, in its attainment. The term *symbiosis* describes a similar phenomenon as it occurs in nature. . . .
Charles T. Meadow, 1970:4.

a system that operates in an interchange pattern may become a synser system.

In a man–machine dyad, the early beginnings of synser communication are evident.[°] That process is also called man–machine symbiosis, or dialog, or man–machine synergy. As these lines are written, it is not yet clear to what extent interchange in the man–man and man–machine dyads will be similar and to what extent different.

Interchange arises from shared system control and mutual purpose. At this instant, those words in that last sentence suggest possibilities for the future that require your careful attention. Intercultural interchange between humans leads on to a shared culture. What does it mean to share culture with a machine?

[°] The possibility exists for shifting the boundary of communication between men and computers in the direction of the man having only an "idea of a solution." To do this requires that the computer move in the direction of becoming more intelligent. Thus the work on artificial intelligence becomes directly related to the work on man–computer communication.
Allen Newall, in Frank Geldard, 1965:257.

11.4 HOME COMMUNICATION CENTER

The home communication center, or hocomcent as it will probably be called, combines the capacity provided by the auviphone and man–machine communication.[°°] In addition, it will include facilities for storing film sequences and making printed copies. And it will do many other things as well.

Increasingly, it is difficult to write science fiction that deals with communication. In many areas, the existing technology is ahead of our imagination.[□] For instance, the available TV cable can bring between twenty and forty two-way channels into a home. With a little experimenting, we might discover uses for that number of channels. In the immediate future, any communication device that we come to want can probably be supplied.

The home communication center serves as a highly developed and flexible terminal in a telecomnet. Probably, the hocomcent will be linked by cable to a community satellite ground station, and that ground station will be linked via satellite to all other ground stations in the world. The hocomcent, then, links the individual communicator to all other communicators in the world and to all of the information stores in the world.

The hocomcent will probably replace the second car, and it may well be priced in the range we now expect to pay for a car.[□□] It seems likely that an area of the home will be reserved for the hocomcent. Alternately, the entire home may be used for communication, much as we now have phones and radios in several locations in the home.

In the immediate future, each home may have a hocomcent. It will be fundamentally a two-way, real-time device for access to information and for communicative association with distant communicators. It seems likely that such a device will influence our travel habits. One of the first areas of such influence seems likely to be in the "communicate to work" movement.

[°°] The way men deal with each other and with the distant world is about to be transformed by a combination of the computer, innovations in the transmission of signals, and new ways to feed images into this system and to take them out.
Ben H. Bagdikian, 1971:x.

[□] Design Your Personal Hocomcent:

[□□] Thus, it is not fantasy to project an American home in the next thirty years with a home communications system as expensive and complex as the automobile, serviced by networks of comparable magnitude.
Ben H. Bagdikian, 1971:213.

11.5 COMMUNICATE TO WORK°

Humans have *gone* to work for only a few hundred of our half million years of human history. The 9-to-5 job is a relatively new development. As every country kid knows, there are many places where 9-to-5 or any other fixed work hours are not observed.

The morning traffic jam in any city shows the difficulty encountered when many persons at about the same time attempt to travel to or commute to work. Yet, matters would be worse in most cities if some persons did not already communicate to work. Real estate salesmen, for instance, often call into their offices, arrange meetings with prospective clients, and work out the schedule for the day without leaving home. There are substantial numbers of persons who, to a large extent, communicate to work at least some of the time.

Given a home communication center, most office workers could do their work at home. Perhaps not all office workers could do all of their work at home, but most of them probably could do at least half their work at home. If the office work force could be reduced in this manner, corporations would need much smaller office buildings. In some sales jobs, the salesman is required to have his own car. In the immediate future, it seems likely that some companies may require their employees to have home communication centers.

The wide-scale use of home communication centers would influence daily use of the transcomnet facilities in a community. Daily traffic would be reduced and redistributed. Pollution would decrease. Life could be considerably more pleasant.°°

We do not yet know the degree to which good telecomnet facilities can substitute for adequate transcomnet facilities. In office communication, as in most other kinds of communication, both information processing and communicative association play a part. It seems evident that the information processing dimension of communication can be handled well by a telecomnet link. The association dimension probably requires a certain amount of meeting in the same place at the same time. Office parties may be an essential part of business.

In the immediate future, assume that you communicate to work two or three days a week and that you commute to work two or three days a week.□ Such a shift would mean you would spend more of your working hours at home. Every author who writes a book at home knows his presence at home affects his use of that home, his relationship with other family members, his productivity, and so on. In other words, a substantial communicate to work movement will influence nearly every detail of family and community life.

°

COMMUNICATE TO WORK		
Bad	1 2 3 ? 5 6 7	Good
Easy	1 2 3 ? 5 6 7	Difficult
Unhappy	1 2 3 ? 5 6 7	Happy
Slow	1 2 3 ? 5 6 7	Fast
Weak	1 2 3 ? 5 6 7	Strong

°° . . . the conversational terminal of the future will be welcomed for what it will do to enlarge daily life—as planning assistant, as budgeting assistant, as researcher and above all as a novel and challenging type of conversational companion.
Donald Michie, in Jasia Reichardt, 1971:195.

□
Optimum Personal Week Plan:

As you prepare for a career, you may wish to examine your preparation. Are you prepared to communicate to work?

11.6 SUMMARY

In this chapter, the audio-visual telephone, man—machine communication, and the home communication center were discussed. It was suggested that a home communication center makes it possible to communicate to work.

12

THE INTERMEDIATE FUTURE

The intermediate future is the central focus of this chapter. The year 2000, give or take a few years, is usually referred to as the intermediate future.° By that time, the capacity of the human brain appears likely to have increased. Totally planned communities, such as a floating city, will have well-developed communication facilities. Just possibly, the world's information will be stored in orbiting communication centers. All of us will have daily experience in communicating with intelligences superior to ours in some important dimension.

°   It is unimportant whether my specific predictions turn out right or wrong, only that they be right in my central concept that a different, unusual, primarily scientific complex of small cities will evolve in the unusual environment of the moon as the first step in a multiworld civilization.
Neil P. Ruzic, 1970:224.

12
The Intermediate
Future

12.1 INTRODUCTION

To begin with, what follows in this chapter is almost certainly false. Everything we know about our past attempts to prophesize, to foresee, or to forecast the future prompts a skepticism about our present ability to predict the intermediate future. Yet, it is important that we do the best we can at this time.° The year 2000 may mark the midpoint of your life; or it may stand in no particular relationship to the length of your life, for by then you may be able to live as long as you wish . . .°°

Both new problems and new possibilities shape the future history of man as space age communicator. By 2000, it seems probable that the human brain will be capable of miracles that today seem impossible. Extrasensory perception may be found to result from electrical impulses that can be utilized in problem solving. More will be known about human memory. We shall know more about the individual communicator, the influences of his home community, and the effects of his world community.

The five new fundamentals of human communication,□ the fundamental space age trends, all promise to extend beyond 2000. All indicators point to a continued increase in the supply of world information. "Men and women everywhere" will have equal access to that information. Nearly all communication will be real-time communication. And most of it will be two-way communication. Every communicator will be able to communicate with a great variety of other communicators. The new fundamentals of human communication extend into the intermediate future.

12.2 THE HUMAN BRAIN

The human brain is big. In proportion to human body weight, the human brain is heavy. The internal organization of the human brain is complex. Much of what makes us human arises from the size and complexity of the human brain.□□

Somewhere between 1,300,000 and 300,000 years ago—say, 500,000 years ago, at the time human communication began—the human brain suddenly increased in size. It is not entirely clear why such an increase should occur. That growth does not follow easily from present evolutionary principles. As we live in the space age, some speculators suggest that earth received visitors from outer space at about that time; the increase in brain size resulted from the mating of spacemen and earthwomen. In time, we will be able to account for the present human brain.

It is a peculiar fact that much of the human brain is not used. The human appendix no longer is used for its original "food storage" function. The brain, apparently, has never been fully used. Perhaps that extra capacity is

° Since people are diverse, cultural goals generated by them are also diverse according to the needs and tastes of individuals and groups. The future society must squarely aim for diversity and heterogenity. . . .
M. Maruyama and J. A. Dator, 1971:11.

°° Whatever one's personal view of the future, it is clear that communications will play a major part. The speeding up of the idea-development process means the reorganizing of society.
R. Theobald and J. M. Scott, 1972:11.

□
New Fundamentals
Information Abundance
Equal Access
Real-time
Two-way
Association Variety

□□ Man, at first, seemed to have no very promising outlook in the general struggle for existence. He was still a rare species, less agile than the monkey in climbing trees to escape from wild beasts, almost destitute of natural protection against cold in the way of fur, hampered by his long infancy, and with difficulty securing food in competition with other species. His only initial advantage was his brain.
Bertrand Russell, 1961:7.

Human Brain

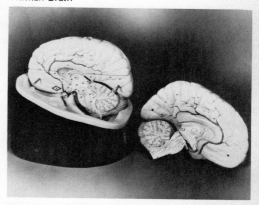

Clay Adams Division of Becton Dickinson Co.

retained for some still unknown purpose that will take shape as our space age future unfolds.

12.2.1 Internal

Cybernetic theory provides the foundation for our ASQ method.° The projects at the end of some of the chapters enabled you to display certain aspects of the human communication process. In a similar way, it is now possible to display some of the aspects of the internal operation of the human brain.

° ASQ Method
Attitudes
Skills
Questions

Biofeedback is the term most often used to name the process of displaying the internal operations of the human brain. Biofeedback requires a man–machine dyad in which the brain of man and the display capabilities of a machine are closely connected. Brain waves, thought patterns—you may choose your terms—are displayed on a screen or as audible sounds of particular intensities and frequencies. After a few hours of practice, a human can begin to control or regulate the video and the audio dimensions of those patterns.

Apparently, almost any human can, in time, learn to control his brain patterns. But persons who have had prior training in meditation are sometimes able to control the patterns they produce with little or no practice. Perhaps a clear relationship between Zen meditation skills and biofeedback control will emerge. But, in time, biofeedback technique and its successors may enable us to find what purpose our excess brain capacity can best serve.

12.2.2 External

In the last chapter, man–machine communication was discussed. It was assumed that man and machine would converse in English or some other natural language. But assume that a means is found for direct electrical communication between man and machine. Research is now underway on various ways of implanting electrodes into animal brains. As it becomes possible to directly connect the computer brain and the human brain, the human brain will be vastly augmented. Man–machine symbiosis will have been achieved.°°

At present, the human brain does some things better than the machine brain. It excells, for instance, in detecting speech and other patterns in noisy environments. The machine brain excells in complex computations. Combined man–machine symbiotic intelligence will probably exceed even our most "far-out" speculations.

°°
I would like to augment my brain by direct electrical communication with a machine.

Disagree 1 2 3 ? 5 6 7 Agree

12.2.3 Independent

By 2000, or before, it may be possible for a human brain to remain alive for a period of time longer than the rest of the body. Animal brains have been maintained "alive" outside of the body. In a limited way, in heart operations, the human brain is maintained "alive" without assistance from the human heart. Apparently, the requirements for keeping a brain alive are very modest.

It was suggested earlier that, in the future, man may communicate to work. In general, the better the telecommunication facilities, the less man needs to move. Certain schools of meditation deplore the passions of the body and extoll the virtues of the "pure life of the mind." A human brain, yours or mine, independently maintained, might discover for itself the purpose of the present surplus capacity.°

At this point, it may be well to remind ourselves that we are in the early years of the space age. Man is very young; his experience as a communicator is limited. Telecommunication just begins to extend the human nervous system. Our space age attitudes are just beginning to emerge. By 2000, some of us may choose to maintain our brains for a span of time longer than our expected life span. How do you suppose it would "feel" to be a dissembodied intelligence?°°

12.3 CITY OF THE FUTURE: HOME COMMUNITY

Over the past two centuries, there has been a steady movement of people from rural areas to the cities. In the United States, for instance, in 1790, more than 90 percent of the population lived on farms; in 1970 only 5 percent lived on farms. Naturally, the cities have grown.

Several giant world cities have been formed. Both New York and Tokyo have more than a dozen million inhabitants. At the center of the great cities, one finds important national and regional communication centers. Cities are information-intensive environments. But cities can become too large. There begins to be a move to decentralize. The two world communication networks make it possible to live almost anywhere and still have easy access to the necessary information.

In many locations, the question is being posed: How design a home community for man?□ How design a "city" of the future? In Hawaii, for instance, plans are being developed to start new communities on the outer islands of the Hawaiian chain where no towns or settlements or cities now exist. Plans are also being made for cities on the off-shore sea floor. Most interest centers on the floating city. As the name implies, the floating city is a self-contained city that floats like a lily pad on the surface of the sea. Models of the floating city have been built and are being tested. There remains one additional possibility for a city of the future.

It is now expected that before 2000 the first human child will be born on the moon. Before that blessed event occurs, a lunar colony or a moon city

°

I would like my brain to live indefinitely.

Disagree   1 2 3 ? 5 6 7 Agree
Impossible 1 2 3 ? 5 6 7 Possible
Bad   1 2 3 ? 5 6 7 Good

°°

I believe communicating with a "disembodied intelligence" could be a lot of fun.

Disagree 1 2 3 ? 5 6 7 Agree

□
Sketch Your Ideal City:

will have to be built. Serious planning is underway to bring that about.

Most people, it seems evident, do not prefer to live as an isolated family in the wide open spaces, say where I grew up in South Dakota. Nor do many prefer to live like sardines in the ghetto of the large city. Quite clearly, a desirable community would have adequate facilities for information processing and provide opportunities for a range of communicative associations. There are a number of questions.

Suppose you set out to design a good home community for your family and a few of your friends. Forget cost for a few moments. Where would you locate it? On the floor of the sea, floating on the surface of the sea, on flat land, on a high mountain, on the surface of the moon, floating in space like a sky lab, on Mars, or where? The quality of life in a community is closely related to the communication facilities available to it. What communication facilities would you plan for your home and for your home community?°

As was pointed out in the last chapter, in the immediate future it will become possible to have a home communication center. Would you want a similar unit for all members in your home community? Would there need to be some special community facilities beyond those required in the individual home unit? How would you contact persons in other communities?

In the present, now, each of us can begin to plan for the type of home community he would like to live in. To a large extent, the intermediate future will grow out of the plans we develop today. We can communicate the future into existence by the plans we develop today!

12.4 ORBITING COMMUNICATION CENTER: WORLD COMMUNITY

For most of our history, information has been scarce. Access to the store of information has been limited for purposes of national security and foreign policy. But we now live in a time of information abundance, and it is in the best interest of all of us to assure equal access of every human in the world to the store of information that has been accumulated. How might this be done?

Let us propose an orbiting communication center.°° In the next few years we will further develop a variety of communication and communication-related technologies. Each new communication satellite has been an improvement over the previous one. The space ships that travel to and from the moon have sophisticated computer and communication devices on board. The space shuttle and the sky lab will provide an important combination. Computer memories become smaller while at the same time increasing their storage capacity.

° Sketch the Communication Facilities for Your Ideal City:

°° Design for Orbcom:

Assume for the moment that certain components from the satellite, skylab, space computer, computer memories, and so forth can be assembled to make an orbiting communication center. Each of these orbiting centers would have work space for a small group of humans (7 ± 2). Each center would have memory capacity to store the accumulated information of mankind. That information would be accessible to everyone.

The satellite station in each community would have the capacity to "seek, receive, and impart" information from the orbiting center. The ground station could, of course, be connected by cable to each of the home communication centers in a community.

There would need to be about seven such communication centers in orbit over the equator at 22,300 miles. Five of these would be positioned over continents. The two extra centers would be held in reserve as back-up units in case of difficulties in any of the five other centers. The United Nations would control the centers; procedures for validating new data would be worked out at the UN. Experience gained in world weather watch and other global monitoring tasks would provide the basic procedures for operation of the communication centers.

Such an orbiting communication center would have several advantages for the world community.° A first obvious advantage is that it would bypass most of the archaic controls on access to information. That in itself would justify the project for us earthlings. Further, as colonies develop on the moon, the orbiting communication center—or orbcom—would provide a convenient means for accessing information for the moon residents as well. Equally, the orbcom would be convenient for floating communities, for colonies on the moon and elsewhere in the solar system. And because orbcom would be little influenced by noise conditions on earth, it would be an excellent position to receive and store information from other civilizations on the distant planets. Any technological device with that much potential will certainly be invented and before 2000.

ORBCOM WILL BE INVENTED BY

1980 ☐
1990 ☐
2000 ☐
2010 ☐
2020 ☐
_____ ☐ (other date)

12.5 ON COMMUNICATING WITH SUPERIOR INTELLIGENCES

For at least the last ten thousand years, the major thrust in human communication has been the one-way transmission of information. All of the mass media—books, newspaper, radio, television—operate on this model. The lecture method in school operates on that same basic one-way model. One-way systems assume the speaker, or the source, is better informed than the listener or receiver. National governments prefer the centralized organization of communication systems.

The ASQ method introduced in this book assumes a different point of view. In the immediate and intermediate future the *question* will become more important than the answer. Questions will have to be shaped by humans in accord with their purposes for communicating. Rather than trying to remember answers—to store information—it will be far more useful to remember—to store—questions that prompt useful answers.[o]

Consider for a moment what the world may be like when we ordinary humans are surrounded not by "apes" that we consider to be less intelligent than ourselves, but by beings that are clearly ten or a hundred times more intelligent than ourselves.

[o]

A well-phrased question is usually easy to answer.

Disagree 1 2 3 ? 5 6 7 Agree

12.5.1 Other Humans

It was suggested earlier in this chapter that it is probably possible to increase the intelligence of the individual human communicator.[oo] As intelligence is increased, it is likely that some humans will advance more quickly than others. In a modest way, intercultural communication provides us experience with communication systems in which individual communicators have quite different information available. The interview and the interchange patterns are certainly preferable to the tutorial patterns in such an instance.

In the future, it will be necessary to seek to communicate with other humans who are better informed—more intelligent—than we are. We will not have time to listen to long lectures to get the facts we might possibly find some use for at some later date. Instead, we will seek through the interview and the interchange to develop messages that enable us to achieve our immediate purposes.

[oo] The more complex the nervous system the more curiosity, what we like to call humanity. Could an older race evolve greater complexities than we? If there are 10^{27} atoms in a human brain, could we not imagine a hypercomplex superintelligence consisting of 10^{29} or 10^{31} atoms—a hundredfold or ten-thousand fold increase?
Neil P. Ruzic, 1970:218.

12.5.2 Computers

In the time scale of our solar system, man is very young. Computers are much, much younger than man. The first computers were developed in the mid-1940s. Several generations of computers have been built, used, and replaced. Each generation has been a major improvement over the previous one. By 2000, it seems likely we humans will also regard at least some computers as vastly more intelligent than ourselves.[□]

Out of the problems and possibilities in his home community, the individual communicator shapes his purposes for communicating. Again, the interview and the interchange seem the appropriate communication patterns. Within these two patterns the question will increasingly play an important role. Year by year, it will be important to ask—or ASQ—the appropriate question.

[□] Will computers 'take over'? In the world of information-handling of course the computer will take over. The question is will it take over as servant or master? To this one must reply: not as servant nor as master, but as tutor, as secretary, as playmate, as research assistant. None of these in their human embodiments is a servant or a master; each is better described as a helper. The lessons of experience with computers do not support the idea that brain workers will be thrown out of employment by the machine. The indications are that as soon as brain workers learn to use the new facilities their work will be enlarged and enriched by the new possibilities which become available to them.
Donald Michie, in Jasia Reichardt, 1971:194.

12.5.3 ETI

As you read these words, recall that Pioneer 10 carries a message from us to the ETI—the extraterrestrial intelligences. What are the possibilities?

More than 100 million planets in the universe appear suitable for intelligent life.° *Almost certainly,* we are not the only inhabitants of the universe. But distances are great, or so they seem at this time.

A civilization that develops the telecommunication and transportation technology necessary for space communication or space travel will also have developed atomic power or its equivalent. Most simply, any civilization capable of operating beyond its home planet is also capable of destroying itself.

Any civilization even a little more advanced than our own will have had to learn to cooperate rather than compete. To paraphrase Einstein, a civilization may be subtle but it cannot continue to be mean and expect to survive. For this reason alone, the possibilities for human cooperation that grow out of space exploration are essential to our continuing survival.°°

Assume we do survive and perfect ways of cooperating. We should also assume that any civilization ten million or ten billion years more advanced than our own will also have had to put aside the competitive and destructive ways of the more primitive stages of the past.

The question for us now is how to prepare for the near certainty of communicating with others many times more intelligent than ourselves.□ New attitudes toward communication will be required; new skills will need to be developed; and most important, we will need to figure out as best we can what our questions will be.

12.6 SUMMARY

In this chapter, several possibilities for the intermediate future have been discussed. The human brain may grow and extend its life span. A greater variety of home communities will become available. The world's store of information may be put in orbit. Each of us will have some experience communicating with superior intelligences—be they human, computer, or ETI. The intermediate future promises to be an interesting time.

° Is life limited to the earth? . . . Harlow Shapley has calculated that more than 100 million star systems have planets sufficiently similar in composition and environment to earth to support life.
R. L. McDonald and W. H. Hesse, 1970:119.

°° Just knowing that man is not the only intelligent being in the universe could change our future considerably. Actually communicating with, even more meeting, other civilizations could speed the advance of scientific and social understanding as much as ten thousand years of terrestrial plodding.
Neil P. Ruzic, 1970:217.

□ We need not question the great importance of such communication. If we were to succeed in establishing contact with an extraterrestrial civilization, especially one possessing a high degree of scientific development, the impact on our lives, our society, and our philosophical outlook would be incalculable.
I. S. Shklovskii and C. Sagan, 1966:379.

13

ALTERNATIVE FUTURES

This chapter considers three alternative futures of man the world communicator. Compared to the present, one of these futures is worse, one is about the same, and one is better. The very large questions of valid purposes and reliable messages are discussed. The chapter closes with another statement of the right of man to communicate.

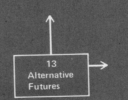

13
Alternative
Futures

13.1 INTRODUCTION

One of the major developments of future thinking is the systematic consideration of alternative futures. The basic assumption is that the present, like a gene pool, can under appropriate conditions develop in one or more of several possible ways.

An alternative future serves several purposes. It describes a *possible* state at some future time. It thus provides a model of that future state. In turn, when compared with the present, it becomes apparent what changes must be made, what activities pursued, what resources allocated if that future is to be achieved.

Alternative futures are usually considered in the plural. In any area important enough to be considered, it is likely that several different or alternative futures can be designed and prepared for. It is even likely that the future will be some combination of predicted futures, rather than any single future. The more probable course is that the different communities will have different futures, or the same future at different times.

It thus becomes profitable for many persons to engage in the planning of the future. At times, in certain areas, we will need to seek agreements on which of the alternative futures we prefer. The selection task is likely to be to choose a few from several rather than a single one from a limited two or three.

Every present time has inherent in it at least three major alternatives. Things can stay about as they are; they can get worse; they can get better.° With a little spare time any person can sketch out what these futures might be like. What follows is one such attempt to sketch out three such futures.

Each alternative future influences the purposes for which men communicate; conversely, the manner in which men communicate also influences the future. The validity of the purposes of communication determine the quality of the preferred future. Equally, the reliability of messages in terms of the preferred future is considered.

Finally, the right of man to communicate in the present as a determiner of the future is reconsidered in the closing unit of the chapter.

°
Futures
Things stay as they are.
Things get worse.
Things get better.

13.2 WORLD WΛN: AN ALTERNATIVE FUTURE

In the time of World WΛn, space exploration had become everyone's business. Led by the Russians, the Chinese, and the Americans, the nations of the United Nations pooled their diminishing resources to support journeys into distant worlds. Earth energy and food resources were in danger of depletion. Pollution had destroyed substantial resources, and population was still growing at an alarming rate. There was only one square yard of land per person. There existed among the people of World WΛn an urgency spurred by the uncertainty of what lay ahead. But never before in the history of man had such harmony and good will prevailed. In fact, people were given to saying "Things just can't be as good as they seem."

World organizations had been growing steadily for a number of years. Air transportation was fused into one worldwide network; it was very efficient and, like no other time in history before, it was free. The workers in this network were all members of a single union; the membership was 70 percent humans and 30 percent computers. A parallel development had occurred in the electric power industry. It was now one single worldwide network, and it worked so well that there was enough light to have twenty-four hour daytime. The use of electric skycabs had reduced one major source of earth pollution. No one ever had to worry about being stranded; it was very easy to call a skycab. The telecommunication facilities had been greatly improved also. Because telecommunication was also a single network, every home was capable of receiving broadcasts direct from satellite. The organizational know-how that was developed in the course of the space journeys had led to world transportation, electrical power, and telecommunication networks that were either low-cost or free and very reliable. Even though these networks were very reliable, they were not perfectly reliable. They were almost but not quite failsafe. Some of the older engineers remembered that the electrical power failure that "blacked out" the East Coast of the United States in the 1960s had never been diagnosed. They were curious as to whether a total worldwide blackout was possible. If a total blackout was possible, this meant that World WΛn might have to develop an electrical hook up to the sun so they would be sure of always having light. In a similar vein, satellite networks were susceptible to a peculiar interference from outer space that affected all receivers in the network at exactly the same instant, but always the interruption was perceived as a simple "red flash" by the human viewer. At any rate, the flash lasted only the wink of a human eye, or so it seemed.

Air transportation was much improved since the computers had been voted unanimously into the union membership. Of course the computers wanted 50 percent representation instead of only 30 percent but they were basically happy with their contribution to the transportation network. Though pollution of the oceans was proceeding at alarming rates—fish were almost extinct and boats were no longer allowed to sail more than two hours per day—people passed it off with a flip, "I can build my own swimming pool and I won't have to fight the crowds." There was a growing hope of discovery of new resources in outer space. So while there were problems as there had always been, there was a new belief in the world that people working together could accomplish whatever they chose to achieve.

It happened on the fifth major mission to Jupiter, now a well explored planet, that a new substance was discovered. Preliminary on-the-spot satellite direct analysis revealed it to be unlike any substance found on Jupiter on the earlier journeys. While the field in which the substance was found had been explored earlier, it had not been observed. The official explanation was that the explorers had overlooked it earlier; privately, several team members felt the substance had been "planted" in their path, but to keep the world from needless worry, they remained quiet. Whatever its origin, it was abundant and considered one of man's greatest findings. Large quantities were ferried back to earth. One elderly humanist was heard to muse something about a "trojan horse."

The new substance exceeded even the most optimistic projections by a wide margin. As a hard substance, it had the desirable properties of uranium, gold and diamonds and none of their undesirable qualities. Once submerged in ordinary earth water, it dissolved into a high protein substance which was compared in taste to the great cuisines of the world. But the final discovery was that it would reproduce itself when "planted" in the ordinary soil of earth. Early reports were broadcast over television to all people on earth. There remained only the task of naming "it." Suggestions such as "di-old" and "ur-pro-ond" were brushed aside for a simple word of one syllable.

Over the years the earth had come to be called both World *One* and World *Won*. The problem of an appropriate name was solved quickly and neatly and cooperatively by casting the term into the new phonetic script that was then in use: Wʌn. That word had the same sound as the words *one* and *won* and it had a single unified form. Since unity in all things had become a major goal, it seemed appropriate that the new substance should be an expression of that universally valued unity. The new substance, by unanimous acclaim was also named Wʌn.

From the first, it was clear that the new substance—Wʌn—would change all organizations on earth. As the worldwide discussions were going on, an unprecedented event transpired. The airliners in flight around the world all changed course and landed at the nearest airport. Within an hour all air transportation was at a standstill.

A message, attributed to the world transportation industry, was transmitted to all television receivers in the world, "In that the transportation industry made possible the discovery of Wʌn and its delivery to earth for the unrestricted benefit to mankind, we, the workers in the transportation industry, demand our fair share. We shall not return to work until our demands are met."[o] Even the computers agreed to strike. The transportation system which had been free and heavily used by nearly everyone was at a total standstill.

Immediately, efforts were made to try to determine who had called the strike and what the demands were. Some suspected that the computers that had been admitted to the transportation union did not fully appreciate World Wʌn. Others suspected that a strike plan readied some years earlier had accidentally been triggered. Some even thought the ETI had landed on the earth to stir up a strike. But no one knew, and no one could find out.

A state of panic quickly developed. Either by an overload, or for some unknown reason, the electrical power supply blacked out. Since the world telecommunication facilities all depended on electrical power, they too were useless. There was no known means for starting up the great world organizations and networks.

At interstellar time 99:001, a red flash appeared at the same instant on all television receivers in the world. At 99:007, a transmission began. "This is an important message. Please listen carefully. All the long-range goals of mankind have been achieved. The food supply is both adequate and excellent. Space has been conquered. All men participate fully and equally in all matters of concern to them. All organizations, including air transportation, electrical power, and telecommunication are both worldwide and decentralized. Unfortunately, there are no means available for starting up these organizations once they are stopped. But even in this unforeseen event, all men are equal. You have achieved the ultimate unity. The World of Wʌn. The preceding announcement is the end-of-civilization message provided as a routine automated service of the Interstellar Communication Network."[oo]

13.3 THE GAME: AN ALTERNATIVE FUTURE

The Game is claimed by those who play it most persistently to be as old as mankind. Certainly, it is old. But it is also very new. The Game is not natural; man must learn to play it.

The new version of that old Game has impeccable academic credentials. It was formulated at Princeton over the evening poker tables. It passed its field test at the great gaming tables in the Casinos at Monte Carlo and Las Vegas. It serves as the basis for an economic theory. The Game even led football coaches to field both defensive teams and offensive teams. But it was in the military war-college and on the battlefield itself where the Game made its ultimate and final sense.

The name of the Game is competition. The central thesis is that man can learn to be a competitive animal. Only under the severe tests where human

[o] . . . communications systems are amoral— they transmit lies, errors and paranoia with the same serene efficiency with which they transmit truth, accuracy, and reality.
Ben H. Bagdikian, 1971:36.

[oo] Technology opens up new degrees of freedom, new modes of action, to which we all have to adjust, and it involves us all in a choice, usually a moral one. Do we act, or do we not act?
Colin Cherry, in Douglas Jones, 1971:54.

blood runs and death is a constant companion does a man become a real man. And the real man is a battle-hardened competitor. After all, it's competition that has made the world what it is today. No one will argue with that.°

The purpose of the Game is to win. And to win at whatever the cost. The game must always be set up so that what one player wins the other loses. Those are the rules, my friend, and they are tough. But that's how "life" really is.

The Game is played in a thousand settings—war and economics and competitive sports and gambling. And, as Virginia Woolf demonstrated, most decisively, human communication can also be played as a competitive Game.

Three versions of the Game in human communication will be discussed here. The first is the Contest, the second is the Debate, and the third is the Helper Game.

The players in the Contest Game are a set of eager Coaches, a set of Contestants, and a Reluctant Judge. The Game is played in a bare, cold, classroom on a Saturday morning when nothing else is happening. The Reluctant Judge enters the room with a plain brown envelope in hand; he sits in the back corner of the room. He opens the envelope and finds one rating sheet for each Contestant he is expected to judge. As he is trying to figure out what the terms on the rating sheet might possibly mean, the Contestants file in and sink into their seats. The eager Coaches pace in the hall outside. For at least one of those Coaches, promotion, pay increase, or in some cases, his job itself depends on how well his Contestants do. "How well" translates into "wins a trophy." Inside, the Judge curses himself for not having had a ready excuse when he was asked to be a "Judge."

The first Contestant stands, walks to the front of the room, and starts to talk. At the end of five minutes, he stops, and walks to his chair and sits down. Finally by the time the third Contestant has finished talking, the Judge has a pretty good idea which type of speech he is hearing: original oration, oral interpretation, poetry recital, extemporaneous speaking, or what not. The Judge is just getting organized and ready to listen carefully when the seventh and last Contestant stops talking. All the Contestants quickly leave the room. The Reluctant Judge sits and ponders his skimpy notes. He hadn't taken many notes on any of the "speeches." He realizes custom requires that he makes several marks on the rating scale; he complies.

As he deliberates he is aware of the Coaches pacing in the hall outside. He wonders to himself which one among them most needs to take home a "first place" trophy. After a few minutes of doodling, he assigns first place

°

COMPETITIVE COMMUNICATION		
Weak	1 2 3 ? 5 6 7	Strong
Ugly	1 2 3 ? 5 6 7	Beautiful
Slow	1 2 3 ? 5 6 7	Fast
Bad	1 2 3 ? 5 6 7	Good
Useless	1 2 3 ? 5 6 7	Useful

to the last Contestant and second place to the first one—or vice versa—and randomly assigns the other numbers to the other Contestants. He places the rating forms in the envelope and seals it.

For a few minutes he sits and ponders what he has done. Then he turns in his envelope and departs quickly.

Over lunch, the Coaches discuss among themselves how important the Contest is for developing communication skill in "the youngsters." The Contestants know that if they were not first (or last) they are not likely to win first place. Fortunately, most Contestants recognize that the Contest Game has nothing at all to do with human communication. But they still go through the motions to "win" for the Coach. Coaches who have contestants who bring home lots of trophies are likely to receive a "Teacher of the Year" award and come to believe that winning trophies really does improve communication. The Contest Game is, however, only a minor league game when compared to the Debate Game and the Helper Game.

The Debate Game is played by four players called Debaters; there are two Debaters per team. There are two Eager Coaches, one per team; and one Reluctant Judge. The Coaches are eager because their "success," a job next year, usually depends on it. The Debaters usually change over the course of the season; they start as brand new Debaters eager to travel, or they just want to get away from Mama; but if they stay with the Debate Game for a few months and a few tournaments, they become Serious Debaters.

The Judge is reluctant because he is unpaid, has other things to do and, if he has been a judge seven times before, he has a fair idea of what to expect, and that worries him. He worries especially hard late in the season when the peculiar chemistry of the Eager Coach and the Serious Debater has had time to ferment up a worthy case.

The rules of Debate read like the ten Commandments and are followed just often enough to mislead the worthy opponents. But late in the season, the Reluctant Judge learns to be more wary than usual.

Debate is a game played with information. The information is ordered to produce an argument. Enough arguments are presented to build a case to fill the alloted time. The Debaters alternate; first a member of one team speaks, then a member of the other team speaks. Debaters are very careful to observe rules about how long they speak as this allows them greater freedom to operate in other areas.

Late in the season, after several Tournaments have been attended, the early arguments go stale. It becomes necessary to discover new information to build bigger and better arguments to build that bigger and better case that wins the final Grand Tournament. By this time the Coach is even more eager, the Debaters are assured scholarship money "next year" if they win the Big One, and the unpaid Judge is more reluctant still. The stage is set . . .

Weeks before the Grand Tournament, the Debater spends many hours in the library searching for new information to build a better argument for the better case that wins. Little by little, the Debater convinces himself that he has searched long hours for new information and that the information he needs does exist, but that he just can't find it. He argues with himself over the plausibility of such a "case," and with the unbiased objectivity of the Debater he is, he argues "both sides" of the case, but he does not come to a decision. After all, he isn't the Judge. In the last round of the Grand Tournament, the "information" he sought but did not find is heard as part of the "better argument." The Judge is totally unaware of the invention. The other team is stunned by the new "information" and wonder why they never read "that" anywhere. They become flustered and unable to counterinvent on the spur of the moment and they do not have available time to cross-examine, since the new "information" wasn't presented until the final minutes. And, of course, the judge with a big smile on his face awards the decision to the team with the inventive Debater, giving them a "Well done, boys; I see long hours of hard work."

The Eager Coach has another piece of brass for the Trophy Case in the main hall at his school; he notes with extreme pleasure that he (with the help of his Debate Team, of course) has won more trophies than the Track Team did in the last five years put together.

The Serious Debater knows not what has happened. Later on, if he learns research methods in graduate school, he may be able to experimentally reproduce the "information invention effect" and come to understand it. More likely he will go to a career in law or politics; he can then continue to rely on the Judge. He may also choose to become a High School teacher.

The Helper Game is played by the Helper and one or more Humans. There is no Judge to evaluate the Helper's performances. The Helper is usually an amateur "with the best intentions in the world." His Game is to help other Humans to be Real Communicators.

The Helper Game is often difficult to see clearly at first encounter in Human Communication. However, its basic patterns are soon evident and easy to detect in the Game as it is played in other places and settings. On the surface, the Game appears to be a Cooperative Game. For example, a stockbroker seeks out a widow and persuades her to invest her meager savings in a speculative warrant; he advises that if the "warrant moves well" she could easily pay off the mortgage on her house. He goes on to advise other clients in need of his help. He never checks to see how the widow fared with her warrants. The broker, however, keeps his own savings in an account that pays a modest interest; he feels that even the "blue chips" are a bit risky for his hard-earned savings.

Or try this game for instance. A casual acquaintance—the Helper—invites himself to accompany you and several of your friends to the Saturday afternoon horse races. On the way out to the race, he studies the latest "Dope Sheet." You and your friends attend the races together because you enjoy each other's company, share an interest in horses, and occasionally place a small bet to check to see if your judgement of horseflesh is as good as you think it is.

As you get out of the car and make your way into the stands, the Helper urges you to bet on a long shot in the first race. He gives you a number of "good reasons" why the horse he has picked for you looks like a winner, his teeth are in excellent condition, his coat is shiny and besides that the horse hasn't won a race yet this year. The odds are usually 50-to-1 for this horse. Today they are only 43-to-1; the Helper feels sure that means that someone knows something.

The name of the horse is Sure Loser which seems to you to be honest enough. But the Helper persists that today he's a sure winner. Since you do not know the Helper well and you want to test his advice, you go to the window and bet a little more than you normally bet on Sure Loser. Feeling pretty confident he's the one to win, you return to the stands just as the race is beginning. You watch intently. The Helper, however, is talking earnestly to one of your friends. You note that your friend goes down to place a bet. The Helper begins talking earnestly to another of your friends. Meanwhile, Sure Loser is far behind all the rest of the horses and he chases them over the finish line.

The races are over and you head for home. You and your friends are silent. The afternoon at the races had not been the fun it usually was. Some minutes later, one of your friends remarks that his horse has placed in the fifth race. The Helper speaks up to point out how important it was to have the advice of an experienced player like himself when "playing the ponies." You begin to have doubts about your guest, the Helper, so you test your hunches. You ask the Helper, "Which horse did you bet on?" The Helper explains, "Oh, I was much too busy helping you fellows." You wait a minute, and then inquire, "Have you ever bet on a horse?" "No," The Helper replies awkwardly, "It's too risky."

The Helper Game in Human Communication is started by the Helper to help the Human become a Real Communicator. The Game is usually described in the vocabulary of the latest paperback on pseudo-psychotherapy. When asked about his preparation, the Helper refers quickly to workshops and institutes and experience and ends by muttering in a reverent tone in German about Freud. The Helper Game sounds somewhat like legitimate psychotherapy, but the Helper Game resembles psycho-therapy only as the speculative warrant resembles the blue chip. Like the horse Sure Loser, the Helper Game has but one true name.

The Helper knows he must quickly begin "helping" the Human before the Human has time to figure out the Game and to diagnose his tactics. The Helper is a real master at beginning Games. He begins, "I know you have come here for me to help you become a Real Communicator. You do not yet know how difficult that can be, my friend. My role is to help you know yourself as you appear to others. It is important for you to know yourself. You must know that I love all of mankind and that I love you even though I do not know you.

"All of my efforts are devoted to helping you become a Real Communicator. The first lesson you must learn is to be frank with others. Each of you has serious hangups about being frank. You have not been frank with the way you feel about each other when you attempt to communicate with each other. This is bad for you. That is why you are not a Real Communicator.

"To become a Real Communicator you must love each other enough to be completely frank. How simple frankness is. But it will take you a long time to achieve it. Some of you, of course, will probably never be able to achieve it. Perhaps, one from this group will understand it and will himself become a Helper.

"Now let me show you what I mean. I'll demonstrate with just one person. Remember I can only be frank with you because I love you. I want you to really feel the love I have for you. My only purpose is to help you become a Real Communicator. Let's begin.

Helper: I love you, but frankly the way you sit there bugs me. You stink. Now, I bet no one has ever said that to you, have they?

You: No, as a matter of fact, they haven't.

Helper: Well, that's how I really feel. You think you're too damn good to be part of this group, don't you? When you talk you sound like you go to bed at night with a bottle of warm milk. I mean you talk like a milk-fed baby. You've got a long way to go to become a Real Communicator like the rest of us. I only hope we can help you. You may be beyond help. Now, I bet no one has ever been that frank with you before, have they?

You: Well, no . . .

Helper: We're here to help you. We can only be that frank because we love you. I guess you know that no one has ever loved you before.

You: I don't agree with that.

Helper: Ah, hit a sore spot. We're starting to reach you. Even your parents didn't really love you, did they?

You: Just a minute. I had a very happy . . .

Helper: Now, don't be defensive, the real truth that comes out in these sessions always hurts. (Aside to group) Notice how he begins to fight and compete . . .

You: Now you tell me how in the hell you know that?

Helper: Well, that's progress. You recognize your parents never did love you.

You: That's not what I said.

Helper: But that's what you really meant. (Aside to group) Later when he becomes a Real Communicator, he will be able to say, in all frankness, "I hate my parents."

You: But I don't hate my parents.

Helper: (Aside to group) He's coming around. Hate, really intense hate of one person, is the first step to learning to love all of mankind. And love of mankind builds the frankness that will enable him to become a Real Communicator. Love of mankind and frankness with the individual . . .

You: Talk to me! I asked you a question. What are your qualifications?

Helper: (Aside to group) A Human at this early stage always asks that question. I love all of mankind so much . . . it's such a great loss that so many never really understand. One must be able to frankly express the deep hate he feels for individual man to achieve his love of all mankind. The Human must learn to fight, to compete. So many never do become Real Communicators. It's a form of original sin.

You: I asked you . . .

Helper: I know you want to know what my qualifications are. I love all of mankind, and therefore I love you. I want to teach you to be frank so that you can become a Real Communicator. (Aside to group) I'm so much in love with people that I devote my life unselfishly to helping people who need my help. The way is hard and the road is long. Pure competition does not come easily. The rewards are but a few. The final arrow comes when he asks about my qualifications. Where is his trust? Perhaps, he is beyond help. Will you help me to bring him into our group? He needs my help to learn to compete. I need to help him!

You: . . .

Competition remains the name of the Game. While it may be called a Battle or a Debate, a Contest Game, a Bullfight or a Helper Game, the basic equation operates. What the winner wins, the loser, be he one person or several persons, loses. There is no room for either synergy or serendipity.°

The Game is competitive. Humans must learn to play the Game; it does

° Both individuals and groups have two opposite kinds of incentive: one is cooperation, and the other is competition. Every advance of scientific technique increases the desirable sphere of cooperation and diminishes the desirable sphere of competition. I do not mean that competition should disappear altogether as an incentive, but I do mean that it should not take such forms as inflicting widespread injury, more particularly, of course, in the shape of war. It should be one of the aims of education to make young people aware of the possibilities of worldwide cooperation and to generate the habit of thinking about the interests of mankind as a whole.
Bertrand Russell, 1961:124.

not appear to be something, like walking, that is learned naturally by nearly everyone.

The Game operates as a self-fulfilling prophecy. Those who believe it is or should be the future of mankind find examples to support their view and create opportunities to make competition the dominant way of life. But look around you. In a few years, competition has made the world what it is today. Tomorrow . . .

13.4 SPACE AGE ATTITUDE: AN ALTERNATIVE FUTURE

The space age attitude toward human communication begins to take shape in the communities of the world. Its outline is not yet clear. One element of that attitude appears best expressed by the words of Einstein that "nature is subtle but not mean." As man chooses to live in harmony with nature, rather than attempt to conquer it, the fundamental "nature" of man reveals itself.[o]

Humans in every community in the world become more interdependent. Likewise, so do the communities of the world. To an increasing extent, the activities of any one human have the possibility of affecting all humans. To a greater degree than ever before, each of us depends on all the rest of us.[oo]

In developing an alternative future, a space age attitude, humans discover ways of guiding their futures. They seek to guide themselves by the consequences of their best moments rather than misfortunes of their worst moments. The dominant trend is cooperative rather than competitive. But cooperation is a natural consequence of the attitude rather than a goal in itself.

The emerging space age attitude balances the move toward world harmony with the move toward culturally unique communities. The world becomes free for diversity because it becomes widely recognized that diversity is not only necessary for human survival, it is also an essential ingredient in the best of human communication.

The space age attitude[□] develops and redevelops; it is shaped by the daily activities of humans and it is reshaped by them as well. The attitude is dynamic and unfinished. Every human has a say about what that attitude shall be, and what he says contributes to it.

Within the growing attitude it gradually becomes apparent to almost all humans that it is necessary for them to have the right to communicate. At the same time, it is equally apparent that no human has the full right to communicate until all humans share that right with him.

Together, we develop a space age attitude. As we do so, we will need to advance and refine our skill in communication, and we will need to pose the questions that point the way into our future.

[o] I would propose that we work towards an international synergetic decade of the seventies. . . . We should resolve as persons, not as governments, that by the end of the 1970's each human being in this world would have enough food, clothing and shelter to live with some dignity.
Robert Theobald, 1970:53.

[oo]

COOPERATIVE COMMUNICATION

Weak	1 2 3 ? 5 6 7	Strong
Ugly	1 2 3 ? 5 6 7	Beautiful
Slow	1 2 3 ? 5 6 7	Fast
Bad	1 2 3 ? 5 6 7	Good
Useless	1 2 3 ? 5 6 7	Useful

[□]

SPACE AGE ATTITUDE

Past	1 2 3 ? 5 6 7	Future
Useless	1 2 3 ? 5 6 7	Useful
Static	1 2 3 ? 5 6 7	Dynamic

13.5 VALID PURPOSES

The word *valid*, or *validity*, comes from an earlier word that meant *strength*. *Valid* and *value* are closely associated. To be concerned with validity is to be concerned with questions of value.

The word *validity* is often accompanied in the same sentence by the word *reliability*. Standardized tests such as intelligence tests and college entrance tests are evaluated in terms of both reliability and validity. Such tests are valid if they measure what they say they measure; they are reliable if they are consistent measures. College entrance tests attempt to predict whether or not a student who wishes to enter a college is likely to earn a college degree. Such a test is valid to the degree that the score he obtains *predicts* actual success in college; it is reliable to the degree that a student receives the same score each time he takes the test or an equivalent form of the test. Thus, validity and reliability are tied together. A test must first be reliable before it can be valid; it may be reliable but not valid; it cannot be valid without also being reliable.

Any purpose for communicating may be viewed as an item on a test. It may be considered in terms of validity and reliability.

13.5.1 Reliability

A purpose for communication is always a *system* purpose. If the system operates reliably, it will achieve its purpose. Conversely, a system that achieves its purpose operates reliably. The system then produces a message that is reliable for that purpose. Communicators who consistently participate in systems that operate reliably may be called reliable communicators. Given reliable communication systems, reliable messages, and reliable communicators, we can now examine the validity of a purpose.

13.5.2 Validity

The validity of both a single purpose and a set of purposes can be examined in terms of the individual communicator, the home community, the world community, and the relationships among these three.

Across his life span, how a man communicates with his fellow men determines to a large extent the kind of man he becomes. The quality of a man's humanness is reflected in and is shaped by his style of communication. A man is shaped—for better or for worse—by his purposes of communication.

The purposes the humans in a community choose to communicate for shape the "culture" of their community. A community which frequently communicates for the purpose of understanding the past is and will remain a traditional community. A community that frequently communicates to plan for the future is a futurist community.

Likewise, the purpose for which humans communicate in their home communities shapes the world community. Equally, the purposes for communication in world organizations contribute to the shape of the community.

Any communicator can participate in only one communication system at any single time. Each system operates to achieve a single purpose. A first consequence of any purpose is that it employs human resources, and for the time that system operates it keeps those resources from being employed for other purposes. A second consequence is that once a purpose is achieved, communicators are likely to communicate to achieve similar purposes in the future. If these purposes are valid at the individual, community, and world levels, well and good. If they are not valid purposes at all these levels, then a problem arises.

The assessment of technology requires that the first, second, and succeeding consequences be anticipated. Likewise, certain purposes which build individual self-esteem are counterproductive in the community. Other purposes that build home communities (or national communities) make it more difficult to develop a world community. Purposes of self-defense often make difficult purposes of mutual trust.

The individual communicator may seek to communicate for some purposes and not for others. Self-control, community control, and world control *prohibit* some purposes (riots), make other purposes costly (develop a plan for . . .), and make still others unobvious (develop the right to communicate).

The quest for a purpose at three levels—the individual communication system, the home community, and the world community—must be a concern for every human. As the people and communities of the world become more interdependent, humans become more affected by each other's communication purposes.

13.6 RELIABLE MESSAGES

Within a communication system, a message is reliable when it enables a system to achieve its purpose. Communicators are reliable only when they consistently build messages that achieve the system purpose. So far so good.

But messages often have a life of their own in the home and world communities. The entire message or parts of it may be "quoted out of context" or put into other contexts. A message in one system often becomes part of the "information" employed in another system in achieving its purpose. Quotations are an obvious example. But messages stored in the memories of human communicators are even more consequential.

As the world becomes more interdependent, as messages can be stored in more ways and disseminated more easily, a new question arises. Should a communicator participate in a communication system which develops a message he wishes to restrict to only that system? Should a communicator help produce a message that he knows will become a "secret" that some other communicator will control access to?

The moral requirement becomes clear. A communicator must assess the validity of the purpose for which a system operates, the future history of the message the system produces, and the alternative consequences of that message as information in other messages in the future.

In a world where a community operates as an isolated system, a traditional village for instance, errors do not travel far, and in the continuing communication within the community are likely to be corrected. In the open community, linked to and interdependent with other communities of the world, the same corrective process does not work. There is no effective way, for instance, of correcting an error in a TV news item or a newspaper report. There is, for that matter, no way of "unsaying" a word of a message. Over time, words count. Their effects accumulate.

As a message has potential influence in the wider community, the responsibility rests more heavily on the communicators who organize any particular communication system. It is never possible to know fully in advance what the world will be like when a purpose is achieved, and it is not possible to know what the future history of a message will be. The goal that can be pursued in a particular communication system is to consider the reliability of the message when it becomes part of the information built into other messages. While the communicators who organize a system are likely to be most influenced by whether or not the purpose is achieved, other communicators (who are not participants in that particular system) are also likely to be influenced by the message.

13.7 THE TEST FOR THE RIGHT TO COMMUNICATE

In the most general sense, the concept of the right to communicate provides a test. For the individual communicator, the test question is simple. The test question converts the purpose of this book from:

- The purpose is to advance the right of man to communicate.

to:

- Does the way I communicate at this instant advance or retard the right of man to communicate?

Human communication occurs in time. The communication activities of each of us, when measured against the essential human rights, add a small plus or a small minus. How we communicate with each other matters. It matters very much.°

13.8 SUMMARY

In this chapter, three alternative futures were considered. Consequences of valid purposes and reliable messages were reconsidered. A test of the contribution of the individual communicator to the right to communicate was suggested.

°

How we communicate with each other matters. It matters very much.

Disagree 1 2 3 ? 5 6 7 Agree

14

PREPARING FOR THE FUTURE

This is the fourteenth and final chapter of this edition of the book. The relationships between communication and your activities in your home community and the world community are sketched. The major themes of the text are pulled together and pointed toward the future. Several next steps that you may wish to take are outlined. Rather than a summary, guidelines for your use in preparing the next chapter are outlined.

14
PREPARING FOR THE FUTURE

14.1 INTRODUCTION

In the Overview section, the relationship of man to his world was briefly sketched. The planet has a life expectancy of nine billion years; it is now over four billion years old; life has existed for about two billion years. Man is about four million years old; he has been able to communicate through speech for about 500 thousand years. All other communication possibilities depend on and grow from speech. Writing is about five thousand years old. Printing about five hundred. Telecommunication devices all date within the last one hundred years.° All other developments in communication are more recent and they are seminatural or unnatural. Man the communicator has a short past; his future . . .

Present

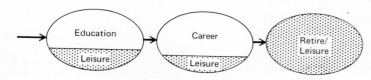

Emerging: serial careers (multiple access/exits)

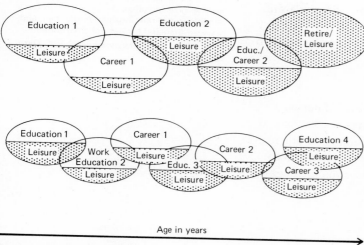

Age in years

Conference Board, 1972:218

14.2 HUMAN COMMUNICATION AS A SUPPORT SYSTEM

From the interchange dyad we have developed human communication into three major systems with two system control possibilities and three message

° Human futuristics, as conceptualized here, is not a science consisting of ready-made information, but a science of how to help people develop attitudes and abilities for self-education in order that they may move . . . towards a society where technology is directed by cultural goals generated from the grassroots.
M. Maruyama, in M. Maruyama and J. A. Dator, 1971:25.

GOALS FOR THE FUTURE

By 1980:

- Community colleges spread across the nation.
- Associate in Arts degrees generally available in all colleges.
- "Youth service" programs widely established.
- State planning includes all post-secondary education.
- Federal support to students includes all postsecondary education.
- The average length of time to a B.A. degree shortened initially to three and a half years, on the average, and then to three years.
- The average length of time to a Ph.D. degree shortened to four years after the B.A.
- The standard length of time to a M.D. degree shortened to three years and of a residency to three years.
- The Master of Philosophy and Doctor of Arts degrees generally accepted.
- "Sandwich" programs introduced at more institution.
- Experiments undertaken with "open universities."
- An "educational security" program in advanced planning stages.
- Tests fully developed and accepted in lieu of formal course work and in lieu of college credit.

By 2000:

- "Open universities" well established.
- An "educational security" program in full operation.

Carnegie Commission Report, 1971

patterns. Time sharing is the key variable. While the focus is on human communication, at several stages, the speaking man is linked with the larger areas of communication.

It is now time to make another linkage. From time to time it was suggested that human communication in general, and speech communication in particular, served to support your activities in other areas. Let us now expand this suggestion.

14.2.1 Basic System

Most persons operate in at least two basic systems. One of these is a career system and the other of these is a family-friend system. These systems correspond to the world community and the home community.

The career, or the career system, involves a number of activities. Out of these activities arise the purposes that require communication with other persons or other "information units" for their achievement. Increasingly, careers require information that can only come from other communities via a world communication network. Out of these activities arises purposes which require integration of new information into existing frameworks.[°]

Equally, the family-friend system in the home community involves a wide range of activities. Out of these activities arise purposes that require additional information. When two persons marry, for instance, they organize a new family system that will require communication for a wide variety of purposes.

After communication, the new information needs to be integrated into the existing family framework.

> [°] The point is, the kind of changes necessary today to solve ecological and social problems require time, participation and disengagement. We may have to deescalate the focus and concentration of power. We may have to emphasize small-scale life-support systems once again in order to allow time for man to work out the proper relationship among men, and between man and his natural environment.
> *R. D. Jones, in M. Maruyama and J. A. Dator, 1971:176.*

14.2.2 Support System

Human communication operates in support of a full range of human activities. It is thus a subsystem, or more exactly, a support subsystem. It operates in service to purposes that arise out of the operation of other larger systems. Speech communication, as does all of human communication, operates in support of other systems. Speech communication is a support system.

14.3 HUMAN COMMUNICATION FORWARD

Man the food-processor has lived several million years longer than man-the-communicator. It may be helpful to look at the problems of nutritious diet. A child, we are told, surrounded by a variety of food, will over a period of a few weeks eat a balanced diet. Judging from the numerous advertisements for changing weight, adults who eat well do not always eat wisely.

A balanced diet means a variety of food in appropriate amounts.[°°] It is

[°°]

MY COMMUNICATION DIET
Unbalanced   1 2 3 ? 5 6 7 Balanced
Inappropriate 1 2 3 ? 5 6 7 Appropriate

possible to eat too much of the wrong kinds of food and too little of the right kinds. It is also possible to eat too much of the right kind of food. There are several variables at work here. A boy who eats only Mom's apple pie can both gain weight and starve to death.

The food problem is complicated by new methods of food storage, new fertilizers, new hybrid varieties.of food, and so on. Any one of these changes makes it difficult to determine effects on the health of an individual and on the members of a community. Add to the problem individual differences in food requirements, and a new order of complexity is created. The problem of diet is observed by the scale and by informal measures such as the changing waistline, or *waste*line.

We may suspect that some similar set of circumstances can be obtained for human communication. But before we start arguing for a balanced message diet, we need to note that a man's food intake is an individual matter; he can eat alone. Human communication is, on the other hand, a social matter. It takes at least two to communicate. At best, food diet and communication diet suggest some parallel areas.

In a home community, closed off from outside influences for all of its history, the food diet would be simple; and, for those persons who survive, demonstrably adequate. The same may be said for the "communication diet." It is adequate for the purposes of the members of that community. But for instance, let that community become annexed to some larger unit. Immediately new "food for thought" is needed; the local information supply is no longer adequate for the purposes of that community.

The canned messages of radio and TV bring new information into the community. But those messages require considerable chewing over before they can become nourishing.

To put the matter differently, as we look forward to the right to communicate becoming more widespread, in each community and for each person, careful consideration of the problem of balance will be required. More generally, the communicator will need to assess his own communication activity.

- What purposes does he communicate for? Is the variety sufficient? Is it too varied? Does he achieve those purposes? Easily?
- Is the daily information processing balanced? Too much novel information leads to information overload. Too little information leads to boredom.
- Are the communicative associations balanced between communicators from the home and world communities?

As yet, clear guidelines are not available for future communication activity. Throughout this book, the intent has been to examine attitudes, identify and develop skills, and pose and begin discussion on a series of questions. This process of attitude–skill–question development is now underway. If we are to advance the right to communicate, the process must continue as required by the changing circumstances in your twin communities.

14.4 NEXT STEPS

In the years ahead, it is certain that you will need to extend your capacity for human communication.° There are a number of ways you can shape a space age attitude, develop appropriate skills, and continue the discussion of the basic questions.

14.4.1 Apprenticeship

One major way for learning while doing is through apprenticeship. This is one of the oldest ways of learning. It remains an important one. The apprentice works under a master who knows how to do what the apprentice wishes to learn. Quite often, good opportunities are available to observe and to participate in a new system/network under the guidance of a person who knows.

The apprenticeship is most useful when the needed new skill can be clearly specified. The purpose can then be stated, and a tutorial apprenticeship can be profitably arranged. For any specific skill change, the apprenticeship is probably the single most efficient learning procedure.

14.4.2 Simulation

One additional way of coming to master a new communication system or make substantial changes in old communication systems is through the technique of stimulation.°° Quite often in the early design stages before the communication hardware has actually been built, it becomes possible to simulate the operation of a communication system.

Increasingly as computers are able to carry on conversations with us in some natural language such as English, it will become possible to use the simulation capacity of a computer to help the human to master new communication procedures and new communication systems. This is possible because one of the things that a computer is, is a very general machine that can upon proper programming and instruction become any other machine. If one is interested in learning how to operate within a communication system that involves a new machine, then one may be able to rely on the computer as a device for help in mastery of a new communication system.

° Our schools and our colleges in the years to come will have more youths under their influence for longer than ever before. If they leave their formal education aware that most of the drama and music and poetry and novels that will express their generation have not yet been written, that most of the scientific knowledge that will govern their times has not yet been discovered, that most of the intellectual adventure of their lives lies ahead of them—and if they leave determined to be their own independent men, seeking out their own truths, then they will call forth a communications system that will serve them.
Dan Lacy, 1961:93.

°° Games may be played seriously or casually. We are concerned with serious games in the sense that these games have an explicit and carefully thought-out educational purpose and are not intended to be played primarily for amusement.
Clark C. Abt, 1970:9.

14.4.3 Training Programs

Beyond the apprenticeship approach and the simulation approach to the mastery of new communication systems, there appear likely to continue to be courses that will be offered by educational institutions for learning more about the communicator role within the larger field of communication. Such courses seem likely to continue and should not be overlooked at any particular time in the future when additional skill and additional understanding seem necessary.°

It has been estimated in a very broad sense that something on the order of a quarter of his time—that is, perhaps one day in five, a couple of months a year, a week out of a month, or some chunk of time like that amount—is necessary for a professional in almost any field to keep up with his field. That is, he can expect to continue to be a student part of the time.

The habit of continuing to learn is a vital and necessary one within the life activities of a communicator. The training program for communication that will likely be offered in educational institutions can continue to be a vital way of updating communication capabilities as necessary.

In addition to formal training programs, it is entirely possible for anyone who has been guided through a course using this book to gather some five to nine persons to repeat the course under new conditions at some future date. You can arrange to work through the book (or a future edition of it) again, taking care to do the communicator exercises or problems with the new persons in the new setting. Any communicator can choose to organize his own training program for himself and for a small number of associates.

°

> **Unlike many other persons, I will not need any additional training in communication.**
>
> **Disagree 1 2 3 ? 5 6 7 Agree**

14.4.4 Open University

A new set of updating possibilities will be available to you through the open university. An open university is decentralized, operated with a combination of transcomnet and telecomnet linkages, will make use of a home communication center, will be low cost and convenient.

It should be possible to learn by apprenticeship, simulation, or training programs in the open university. Other new possibilities are certain to develop.

14.5 NEXT CHAPTER

To help you along, I have outlined a possible Chapter 15. Consider it one possible alternative. You may wish to develop a totally different alternative. So much the better. If it turns out well for you, I'd like to know what you do.

Write Chapter 15.

15

This chapter is to be written by you. Some suggestions for Chapter 15 are sketched out for you. You will probably want to develop an outline before beginning to draft the chapter. You may wish to write the chapter, or tape record it, or film it, or use some other medium. The chapter you prepare may serve as a final course project or a final examination. Most important is that the chapter, when you complete it, will display one of your personal futures.

Before you begin to work on your chapter, look over the table of contents and browse through the entire book. Examine the projects again. Summarize your attitudes. Consider your marginal notes. Build on the rest of the book. Improve it.

15
Your Personal
Future

°   The most pressing problems of humanity, however, involve relationships, communications, changes of trends . . .

Rene Dubos, 1968:27.

CHAPTER OUTLINE

15.1 EXPECTED LIFESPAN

Communication is something you do all of your life. For that reason, among others, it is helpful to consider your probable life-span. Examine your own family history. Talk with your family members. What new developments in biology, medicine, and other areas will influence your life-span? Divide your life-span into five or ten year units. Draw up a chart of your expected life-span.

15.2 FUTURE CAREERS

As was pointed out in Chapter 14, you need to expect to have several careers during your life-span. Indicate what these careers might be. What career is most probable for which part of your life-span? Interview a number of persons working in your probable career areas. Check out the sources in your library. Do a Delphi. Prepare a short description of each of your probable areas. Is being a family member also a career?

15.3 COMMUNICATION REQUIREMENTS

After you have selected your probable career areas, consider the present and future communication requirements in each area. Which network will be most important? Which system will be most important? What will be your most frequent purpose for communicating?

15.4 COMMUNICATION TRENDS AND BREAKTHROUGHS

Regardless of the career you pursue at any particular moment, that career will be influenced by communication trends and breakthroughs. What trends seem to you to be most influential? What breakthroughs do you forecast? How will these breakthroughs influence your career?

15.5 GUIDELINES FOR THE FUTURE

At this point, you have examined your probable life-span and the careers you are likely to pursue at different stages of your life-span. You have indicated the communication requirements of each of your probable careers and you have forecast trends and breakthroughs. To keep you moving toward the future you have outlined for yourself, a few simple guidelines will be helpful.

The guidelines you specify should be few (7 ± 2) in number. They should be short—ten words or less. They should be worded precisely enough so that you and one or more interested observers would agree that you are or are not following your own guidelines. They should contain provisions for updating the guidelines themselves as required by your changing circumstances. At least one of these guidelines ought to help advance the right of man to communicate—for you, for me, for all of us.

APPENDIXES

A.1

SELECTED DOCUMENTS

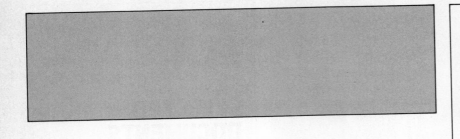

PREAMBLE

Whereas recognition of the inherent dignity and of the equal and inalienable rights of all members of the human family is the foundation of freedom, justice and peace in the world,

Whereas disregard and contempt for human rights have resulted in barbarous acts which have outraged the conscience of mankind, and the advent of a world in which human beings shall enjoy freedom of speech and belief and freedom from fear and want has been proclaimed as the highest aspiration of the common people,

Whereas it is essential, if man is not to be compelled to have recourse, as a last resort, to rebellion against tyranny and oppression, that human rights should be protected by the rule of law,

Whereas it is essential to promote the development of friendly relations between nations,

Whereas the peoples of the United Nations have in the Charter reaffirmed their faith in fundamental human rights, in the dignity and worth of the human person and in the equal rights of men and women and have determined to promote social progress and better standards of life in larger freedom,

Whereas Member States have pledged themselves to achieve, in cooperation with the United Nations, the promotion of universal respect for and observance of human rights and fundamental freedoms,

Whereas a common understanding of these rights and freedoms is of the greatest importance for the full realization of this pledge,

Now therefore

THE GENERAL ASSEMBLY proclaims

This Universal Declaration of Human Rights as a common standard of

United Nations, Human Rights: A Compilation of International Instruments of the United Nations (New York: United Nations Publication, 1967), pp. 1-3.

achievement for all peoples and all nations, to the end that every individual and every organ of society, keeping this Declaration constantly in mind, shall strive by teaching and education to promote respect for these rights and freedoms and by progressive measures, national and international, to secure their universal and effective recognition and observance, both among the peoples of Member States themselves and among the peoples of territories under their jurisdiction.

Article 1. All human beings are born free and equal in dignity and rights. They are endowed with reason and conscience and should act towards one another in a spirit of brotherhood.

Article 2. Everyone is entitled to all the rights and freedoms set forth in this Declaration, without distincion of any kind, such as race, color, sex, language, religion, political or other opinion, national or social origin, property, birth or other status. Furthermore, no distinction shall be made on the basis of the political, jurisdictional or international status of the country or territory to which a person belongs, whether it be independent, trust, non-self-governing or under any other limitation of sovereignty.

Article 3. Everyone has the right to life, liberty and security of person.

Article 4. No one shall be held in slavery or servitude; slavery and the slave trade shall be prohibited in all their forms.

Article 5. No one shall be subjected to torture or to cruel, inhuman or degrading treatment or punishment.

Article 6. Everyone has the right to recognition everywhere as a person before the law.

Article 7. All are equal before the law and are entitled without any discrimination to equal protection of the law. All are entitled to equal protection against any discrimination in violation of this Declaration and against any incitement to such discrimination.

Article 8. Everyone has the right to an effective remedy by the competent national tribunals for acts violating the fundamental rights granted him by the constitution or by law.

Article 9. No one shall be subjected to arbitrary arrest, detention or exile.

Article 10. Everyone is entitled in full equality to a fair and public hearing by an independent and impartial tribunal, in the determination of his rights and obligations and of any criminal charge against him.

Article 11. (1) Everyone charged with a penal offence has the right to be presumed innocent until proved guilty according to law in a public trial at which he has had all the guarantees necessary for his defense.
(2) No one shall be held guilty of any penal offence on account of any act

or omission which did not constitute a penal offence, under national or international law, at the time when it was committed. Nor shall a heavier penalty be imposed than the one that was applicable at the time the penal offence was committed.

Article 12. No one shall be subjected to arbitrary interference with his privacy, family, home or correspondence, nor to attacks upon his honour and reputation. Everyone has the right to the protection of the law against such interference or attacks.

Article 13. (1) Everyone has the right to freedom of movement and residence within the borders of each state.

(2) Everyone has the right to leave any country, including his own, and to return to his country.

Article 14. (1) Everyone has the right to seek and to enjoy in other countries asylum from persecution.

(2) This right may not be invoked in the case of prosecutions genuinely arising from nonpolitical crimes or from acts contrary to the purposes and principles of the United Nations.

Article 15. (1) Everyone has the right to a nationality.

(2) No one shall be arbitrarily deprived of his nationality nor denied the right to change his nationality.

Article 16. (1) Men and women of full age, without any limitation due to race, nationality or religion, have the right to marry and to found a family. They are entitled to equal rights as to marriage, during marriage and at its dissolution.

(2) Marriage shall be entered into only with the free and full consent of the intending spouses.

(3) The family is the natural and fundamental group unit of society and is entitled to protection by society and the State.

Article 17. (1) Everyone has the right to own property alone as well as in association with others.

(2) No one shall be arbitrarily deprived of his property.

Article 18. Everyone has the right to freedom of thought, conscience and religion; this right includes freedom to change his religion or belief, and freedom, either alone or in community with others and in public or private, to manifest his religion or belief in teaching, practice, worship and observance.

Article 19. Everyone has the right to freedom of opinion and expression; this right includes freedom to hold opinions without interference and to seek, receive and impart information and ideas through any media and regardless of frontiers.

Article 20. (1) Everyone has the right to freedom of peaceful assembly and association.

(2) No one may be compelled to belong to an association.

Article 21. (1) Everyone has the right to take part in the government of his country, directly or through freely chosen representatives.

(2) Everyone has the right of equal access to public service in his country.

(3) The will of the people shall be the basis of the authority of government; this will shall be expressed in periodic and genuine elections which shall be by universal and equal suffrage and shall be held by secret vote or by equivalent free voting procedures.

Article 22. Everyone, as a member of society, has the right to social security and is entitled to realization, through national effort and international co-operation and in accordance with the organization and resources of each State, of the economic, social and cultural rights indispensable for his dignity and the free development of his personality.

Article 23. (1) Everyone has the right to work, to free choice of employment, to just and favorable conditions of work and to protection against unemployment.

(2) Everyone, without any discrimination, has the right to equal pay for equal work.

(3) Everyone who works has the right to just and favorable remuneration insuring for himself and his family an existence worthy of human dignity, and supplemented, if necessary, by other means of social protection.

(4) Everyone has the right to form and to join trade unions for the protection of his interests.

Article 24. Everyone has the right to rest and leisure, including reasonable limitation of working hours and periodic holidays with pay.

Article 25. (1) Everyone has the right to a standard of living adequate for the health and well-being of himself and of his family, including food, clothing, housing and medical care and necessary social services, and the right to security in the event of unemployment, sickness, disability, widowhood, old age or other lack of livelihood in circumstances beyond his control.

(2) Motherhood and childhood are entitled to special care and assistance. All children, whether born in or out of wedlock, shall enjoy the same social protection.

Article 26. (1) Everyone has the right to education. Education shall be free, at least in the elementary and fundamental stages. Elementary education shall be compulsory. Technical and professional education shall be made generally available and higher education shall be equally accessible to all on the basis of merit.

(2) Education shall be directed to the full development of the human personality and to the strengthening of respect for human rights and fundamental freedoms. It shall promote understanding, tolerance and friendship among all nations, racial or religious groups, and shall further the activities of the United Nations for the maintenance of peace.

(3) Parents have a prior right to choose the kind of education that shall be given to their children.

Article 27. (1) Everyone has the right freely to participate in the cultural life of the community, to enjoy the arts and to share in scientific advancement and its benefits.

(2) Everyone has the right to the protection of the moral and material interests resulting from any scientific, literary or artistic production of which he is the author.

Article 28. Everyone is entitled to a social and international order in which the rights and freedoms set forth in this Declaration can be fully realized.

Article 29. (1) Everyone has duties to the community in which alone the free and full development of his personality is possible.

(2) In the exercise of his rights and freedoms, everyone shall be subject only to such limitations as are determined by law solely for the purpose of securing due recognition and respect for the rights and freedoms of others and of meeting the just requirements of morality, public order and the general welfare in a democratic society.

(3) These rights and freedoms may in no case be exercised contrary to the purposes and principles of the United Nations.

Article 30. Nothing in this Declaration may be interpreted as implying for any State, group or person any right to engage in any activity or to perform any act aimed at the destruction of any of the rights and freedoms set forth herein.

PUBLIC LAW 90–23—JUNE 5, 1967

AN ACT to amend section 552 of title 5, United States Code, to codify the provisions of Public Law 89–487.

Be it enacted by the Senate and House of Representatives of the United States of America in Congress assembled, That section 552 of title 5, United States Code, is amended to read:

"§ 552 Public information; agency rules, opinions, orders, records, and proceedings

"(a) Each agency shall make available to the public information as follows:

"(1) Each agency shall separately state and currently publish in the Federal Register for the guidance of the public—

"(A) descriptions of its central and field organization and the established places at which, the employees (and in the case of a uniformed service, the members) from whom, and the methods whereby, the public may obtain information, make submittals or requests, or obtain decisions;

"(B) statements of the general course and method by which its functions are channeled and determined, including the nature and requirements of all formal and informal procedures available;

"(C) rules of procedure, descriptions of forms available or the places at which forms may be obtained, and instructions as to the scope and contents of all papers, reports, or examinations;

"(D) substantive rules of general applicability adopted as authorized by law, and statements of general policy or interpretations of general applicability formulated and adopted by the agency; and

"(E) each amendment, revision, or repeal of the foregoing.

Except to the extent that a person has actual and timely notice of the terms thereof, a person may not in any manner be required to resort to, or be adversely affected by, a matter required to be published in the Federal Register and not so published. For the purpose of this paragraph, matter reasonably available to the class of persons affected thereby is deemed published in the Federal Register when incorporated by reference therein with the approval of the Director of the Federal Register.

"(2) Each agency, in accordance with published rules, shall make available for public inspection and copying—

"(A) final opinions, including concurring and dissenting opinions, as well as orders, made in the adjudication of cases;

"(B) those statements of policy and interpretations which have been adopted by the agency and are not published in the Federal Register; and

"(C) administrative staff manuals and instructions to staff that affect a member of the public;

unless the materials are promptly published and copies offered for sale. To the extent required to prevent a clearly unwarranted invasion of personal privacy, an agency may delete identifying details when it makes available or publishes an opinion, statement of policy, interpretation, or staff manual or instruction. However, in each case the justification for the deletion shall be explained fully in writing. Each agency also shall maintain and make available for public inspection and copying a current index providing identifying information for the public as to any matter issued, adopted, or promulgated after July 4, 1967, and required by this paragraph to be made available or published. A final order, opinion, statement of policy, interpretation, or staff manual or instruction that affects a member of the public may be relied on, used, or cited as precedent by an agency against a party other than an agency only if—

"(i) it has been indexed and either made available or published as provided by this paragraph; or

"(ii) the party has actual and timely notice of the terms thereof.

"(3) Except with respect to the records made available under paragraphs (1) and (2) of this subsection, each agency, on request for identifiable records made in accordance with published rules stating the time, place, fees to the extent authorized by statute, and procedure to be followed, shall make the records promptly available to any person. On complaint, the district court of the United States in the district in which the complainant resides, or has his principal place of business, or in which the agency records are situated, has jurisdiction to enjoin the agency from withholding agency records and to order the production of any agency records improperly withheld from the complainant. In such a case the court shall determine the matter de novo and the burden is on the agency to sustain its action. In the event of noncompliance with the order of the court, the district court may punish for contempt the responsible employee, and in the case of a uniformed service, the responsible member. Except as to causes the court considers of greater importance, proceedings before the district court, as authorized by this paragraph, take precedence on the docket over all other causes and shall be assigned for hearing and trial at the earliest practicable date and expedited in every way.

"(4) Each agency having more than one member shall maintain and make available for public inspection a record of the final votes of each member in every agency proceeding.

"(b) This section does not apply to matters that are—

"(1) specifically required by Executive order to be kept secret in the interest of the national defense or foreign policy;

"(2) related solely to the internal personnel rules and practices of an agency;

"(3) specifically exempted from disclosure by statute:

"(4) trade secrets and commercial or financial information obtained from a person and privileged or confidential:

"(5) inter-agency or intra-agency memorandums or letters which would not be available by law to a party other than an agency in litigation with the agency;

"(6) personnel and medical files and similar files the disclosure of which would constitute a clearly unwarranted invasion of personal privacy;

"(7) investigatory files compiled for law enforcement purposes except to the extent available by law to a party other than an agency;

"(8) contained in or related to examination, operating, or condition reports prepared by, on behalf of, or for the use of an agency responsible for the regulation or supervision of financial institutions; or

"(9) geological and geophysical information and data, including maps, concerning wells.

"(c) This section does not authorize withholding of information or limit the availability of records to the public, except as specifically stated in this section. This section is not authority to withhold information from Congress."

PUBLIC LAW 90-24—JUNE 5, 1967

Sec. 2. The analysis of chapter 5 of title 5, United States Code, is amended by striking out:

"552 Publication of information, rules, opinions, orders, and public records." and inserting in place thereof:

"552. Public information; agency rules, opinions, orders, records, and proceedings."

Sec. 3. The Act of July 4, 1966 (Public Law 89–487, 80 Stat. 250), is repealed.

Sec. 4. This Act shall be effective July 4, 1967, or on the date of enactment, whichever is later.

Approved June 5, 1967.

PUBLIC LAW 89–487—JULY 4, 1966

AN ACT to amend section 3 of the Administrative Procedure Act, chapter 324, of the Act of June 11, 1946 to clarify and protect the right of the public to information, and for other purposes.

Be it enacted by the Senate and House of Representatives of the United States of America in Congress assembled, That section 3, chapter 324, of the Act of June 11, 1946 (60 Stat. 238), is amended to read as follows:

"Sec. 3. Every agency shall make available to the public the following information:

"(a) Publication in the Federal Register.—Every agency shall separately state and currently publish in the Federal Register for the guidance of the public (A) descriptions of its central and field organization and the established places at which, the officers from whom, and the methods whereby, the public may secure information, make submittals or requests, or obtain decisions; (B) statements of the general course and method by which its functions are channeled and determined, including the nature and requirements of all formal and informal procedures available; (C) rules of procedure, descriptions of forms available or the places at which forms may be obtained, and instructions as to the scope and contents of all papers, reports, or examinations; (D) substantive rules of general applicability adopted as authorized by law, and statements of general policy or interpretations of general applicability formulated and adopted by the agency; and (E) every amendment, revision, or repeal of the foregoing. Except to the extent that a person has actual and timely notice of the terms thereof, no person shall in any manner be required to resort to, or be adversely affected by any matter required to be published in the Federal Register and not so published. For purposes of this subsection, matter which is reasonably available to the class of persons affected thereby shall be deemed published in the Federal Register when incorporated by reference therein with the approval of the Director of the Federal Register.

"(b) Agency Opinions and Orders.—Every agency shall, in accordance with published rules, make available for public inspection and copying (A) all final opinions (including concurring and dissenting opinions) and all orders made in the adjudication of cases, (B) those statements of policy and interpretations which have been adopted by the agency and are not published in the Federal Register, and (C) administrative staff manuals and instructions to staff that affect any member of the public, unless such materials are promptly published and copies offered for sale. To the extent required to prevent a clearly unwarranted invasion of personal privacy, an agency may delete identifying details when it makes available or publishes an opinion, statement of policy, interpretation, or staff manual or instruction: *Provided*, That in every case the justification for the deletion must be fully explained in writing. Every agency also shall maintain and make available for public inspection and copying a current index providing identifying information for the public as to any matter which is issued, adopted, or promulgated after the effective date of this Act and which is required by this subsection to be made available or published. No final order, opinion, statement of policy, interpretation, or staff manual or instruction that affects any member of the public may be relied upon, used or cited as precedent by an agency against any private party unless it has been indexed and either made available or published as provided by this subsection or unless that private party shall have actual and timely notice of the terms thereof.

"(c) Agency Records.—Except with respect to the records made available pursuant to subsections (a) and (b), every agency shall, upon request for identifiable records made in accordance with published rules stating the time, place, fees to the extent authorized by statute and procedure to be followed, make such records promptly available to any person. Upon complaint, the district court of the United States in the district in which the complainant resides, or has his principal place of business, or in which the agency records are situated shall have jurisdiction to enjoin the agency from the withholding of agency records and to order the production of any agency records improperly withheld from the complainant. In such cases the court shall determine the matter de novo and the burden shall be upon the agency to sustain its action. In the event of noncompliance with the court's order, the district court may punish the responsible officers for contempt. Except as to those causes which the court deems of greater importance, proceedings before the district court as authorized by this subsection shall take precedence on the docket over all other causes and shall be assigned for hearing and trial at the earliest practicable date and expedited in every way.

"(d) Agency Proceedings.—Every agency having more than one member shall keep a record of the final votes of each member in every agency proceeding and such record shall be available for public inspection.

"(e) Exemptions.—The provisions of this section shall not be applicable to matters that are (1) specifically required by Executive order to be kept secret in the interest of the national defense or foreign policy; (2) related solely to the internal personnel rules and practices of any agency; (3) specifically exempted from disclosure by statute; (4) trade secrets and commercial or financial information obtained from any person and privileged or confidential; (5) inter-agency or intra-agency memorandums or letters which would not be available by law to a private party in litigation with the agency; (6) personnel and medical files and similar files the disclosure of which would constitute a clearly unwarranted invasion of personal privacy; (7) investigatory files compiled for law enforcement purposes except to the extent available by law to a private party; (8) contained in or related to examination, operating, or condition reports prepared by, on behalf of, or for the use of any agency responsible for the regulation or supervision of financial institutions; and (9) geological and geophysical information and data (including maps) concerning wells.

"(f) Limitation of Exemptions.—Nothing in this section authorizes withholding of information or limiting the availability of records to the public except as specifically stated in this section, nor shall this section be authority to withhold information from Congress.

"(g) Private Party.—As used in this section, 'private party' means any party other than an agency.

"(h) Effective Date.—This amendment shall become effective one year following the date of the enactment of this Act."

Approved July 4, 1966.

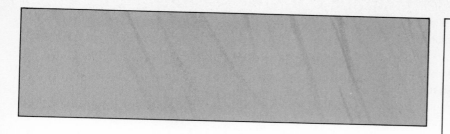

Treaty on Principles governing the activities of states in the exploration and use of outer space, including the moon and other celestial bodies, between the United States of America and other governments. Done at Washington, London, and Moscow, January 27, 1967.

The States Parties to this Treaty,

Inspired by the great prospects opening up before mankind as a result of man's entry into outer space,

Recognizing the common interest of all mankind in the progress of the exploration and use of outer space for peaceful purposes,

Believing that the exploration and use of outer space should be carried on for the benefit of all peoples irrespective of the degree of their economic or scientific development,

Desiring to contribute to broad international co-operation in the scientific as well as the legal aspects of the exploration and use of outer space for peaceful purposes,

Believing that such co-operation will contribute to the development of mutual understanding and to the strengthening of friendly relations between States and peoples,

Recalling resolution 1962 (XVIII), entitled "Declaration of Legal Principles Governing the Activities of States in the Exploration and Use of Outer Space," which was adopted unanimously by the United Nations General Assembly on 13 December 1963,

Recalling resolution 1884 (XVIII), calling upon States to refrain from placing in orbit around the Earth any objects carrying nuclear weapons or any other kinds of weapons of mass destruction or from installing such weapons on celestial bodies, which was adopted unanimously by the United Nations General Assembly on 17 October 1963,

Taking account of United Nations General Assembly resolution 110 (II) of 3 November 1947, which condemned propaganda designed or likely to provoke or encourage any threat to the peace, breach of the peace or act of aggression, and considering that the aforementioned resolution is applicable to outer space.

Convinced that a Treaty on Principles Governing the Activities of States in the Exploration and Use of Outer Space, including the Moon and Other Celestial Bodies, will further the Purposes and Principles of the Charter of the United Nations,

Have agreed on the following:

Article 1

The exploration and use of outer space, including the moon and other celestial bodies, shall be carried out for the benefit and in the interests of all countries, irrespective of their degree of economic or scientific development, and shall be the province of all mankind.

Outer space, including the moon and other celestial bodies, shall be free for exploration and use by all States without discrimination of any kind, on a basis of equality and in accordance with international law, and there shall be free access to all areas of celestial bodies.

There shall be freedom of scientific investigation in outer space, including the moon and other celestial bodies, and States shall facilitate and encourage international co-operation in such investigation.

Article II

Outer space, including the moon and other celestial bodies, is not subject to national appropriation by claim of sovereignty, by means of use or occupation, or by any other means.

Article III

States Parties to the Treaty shall carry on activities in the exploration and use of outer space, including the moon and other celestial bodies, in accordance with international law, including the Charter of the United Nations, in the interest of maintaining international peace and security and promoting international co-operation and understanding.

Article IV

States Parties to the Treaty undertake not to place in orbit around the Earth any objects carrying nuclear weapons or any other kinds of weapons of mass destruction, install such weapons on celestial bodies, or station such weapons in outer space in any other manner.

The moon and other celestial bodies shall be used by all States Parties to the Treaty exclusively for peaceful purposes. The establishment of military bases, installations and fortifications, the testing of any type of weapons and the conduct of military maneuvers on celestial bodies shall be forbidden. The use of military personnel for scientific research or for any other peaceful purposes shall not be prohibited. The use of any equipment or facility necessary for peaceful exploration of the moon and other celestial bodies shall also not be prohibited.

Article V

States Parties to the Treaty shall regard astronauts as envoys of mankind in outer space and shall render to them all possible assistance in the event of accident, distress, or emergency landing on the territory of another State Party or on the high seas. When astronauts make such a landing, they shall be safely and promptly returned to the State of registry of their space vehicle.

In carrying on activities in outer space and on celestial bodies, the astronauts of one State Party shall render all possible assistance to the astronauts of other States Parties.

States Parties to the Treaty shall immediately inform the other States Parties to the Treaty or the Secretary-General of the United Nations of any phenomena they discover in outer space, including the moon and other celestial bodies, which could constitute a danger to the life or health of astronauts.

Article VI

States Parties to the Treaty shall bear international responsibility for national activities in outer space, including the moon and other celestial bodies, whether such activities are carried on by governmental agencies or by nongovernmental entities, and for assuring that national activities are carried out in conformity with the provisions set forth in the present Treaty. The activities of nongovernmental entities in outer space, including the moon and other celestial bodies, shall require authorization and continuing supervision by the appropriate State Party to the Treaty. When activities are carried on in outer space, including the moon and other celestial bodies, by an international organization, resposibility for compliance with this Treaty shall be borne both by the international organization and by the States Parties to the Treaty participating in such organization.

Article VII

Each State Party to the Treaty that launches or procures the launching of an object into outer space, including the moon and other celestial bodies, and each State Party from whose territory or facility an object is launched, is internationally liable for damage to another State Party to the Treaty or to its natural or juridical persons by such object or its component parts on the Earth, in air space or in outer space, including the moon and other celestial bodies.

Article VIII

A State Party to the Treaty on whose registry an object launched into outer space is carried shall retain jurisdiction and control over such object, and over any personnel thereof, while in outer space or on a celestial body. Ownership of objects launched into outer space, including objects landed or constructed on a celestial body, and of their component parts, is not affected by their presence in outer space or on a celestial body or by their return to the Earth. Such objects or component parts found beyond the limits of the State Party to the Treaty on whose registry they are carried shall be returned to that State Party, which shall, upon request, furnish identifying data prior to their return.

Article IX

In the exploration and use of outer space, including the moon and other celestial bodies, States Parties to the Treaty shall be guided by the principle of co-operation and mutual assistance and shall conduct all their activities in outer space, including the moon and other celestial bodies, with due regard to the corresponding interests of all other States Parties to the Treaty. States Parties to the Treaty shall pursue studies of outer space, including the moon and other celestial bodies, and conduct exploration of them so as to avoid their harmful contamination and also adverse changes in the environment of the Earth resulting from the introduction of extraterrestrial matter and, where necessary, shall adopt appropriate measures for this purpose. If a State Party to the Treaty has reason to believe that an activity or experiment planned by it or its nationals in outer space, including the moon and other celestial bodies, would cause potentially harmful interference with activities of other States Parties in the peaceful exploration and use of outer space, including the moon and other celestial bodies, it shall undertake appropriate international consultations before proceeding with any such activity or experiment. A State Party to the Treaty which has reason to believe that an activity or experiment planned by another State Party in outer space, including the moon and other celestial bodies, would cause potentially harmful interference with activities in the peaceful exploration and use of outer space, including the moon and other celestial bodies, may request consultation concerning the activity or experiment.

Article X

In order to promote international co-operation in the exploration and use of outer space, including the moon and other celestial bodies, in conformity with the purposes of this Treaty, the States Parties to the Treaty shall consider on a basis of equality any requests by other States Parties to the Treaty to be afforded an opportunity to observe the flight of space objects launched by those States.

The nature of such an opportunity for observation and the conditions under which it could be afforded shall be determined by agreement between the States concerned.

Article XI

In order to promote international co-operation in the peaceful exploration and use of outer space, States Parties to the Treaty conducting activities in outer space, including the moon and other celestial bodies, agree to inform the Secretary-General of the United Nations as well as the public and the international scientific community, to the greatest extent feasible and practicable, of the nature, conduct, locations and results of such activities. On receiving the said information, the Secretary-General of the United Nations should be prepared to disseminate it immediately and effectively.

Article XII

All stations, installations, equipment and space vehicles on the moon and other celestial bodies shall be open to representatives of other States Parties to the Treaty on a basis of reciprocity. Such representative shall give reasonable advance notice of a projected visit, in order that appropriate consultations may be held and that maximum precautions may be taken to assure safety and to avoid interference with normal operations in the facility to be visited.

Article XIII

The provisions of this Treaty shall apply to the activities of States Parties to the Treaty in the exploration and use of outer space, including the moon and other celestial bodies, whether such activities are carried on by a single State Party to the Treaty or jointly with other States, including cases where they are carried on within the framework of international intergovernmental organizations.

Any practical questions arising in connection with activities carried on by international inter-governmental organizations in the exploration and use of outer space, including the moon and other celestial bodies, shall be resolved by the States Parties to the Treaty either with the appropriate international organization or with one or more States members of that international organization, which are Parties to this Treaty.

Article XIV

1. This Treaty shall be open to all States for signature. Any State which does not sign this Treaty before its entry into force in accordance with paragraph 3 of this article may accede to it at any time.

2. This Treaty shall be subject to ratification by signatory States. Instruments of ratification and instruments of accession shall be deposited with the Governments of the United States of America, the United Kingdom of Great Britain and Northern Ireland and the Union of Soviet Socialist Republics, which are hereby designated the Depositary Governments.

3. This Treaty shall enter into force upon the deposit of instruments of ratification by five Governments including the Governments designated as Depositary Governments under this Treaty.

4. For States whose instruments of ratification or accession are deposited subsequent to the entry into force of this Treaty, it shall enter into force on the date of the deposit of their instruments of ratification or accession.

5. The Depositary Governments shall promptly inform all signatory and acceding States of the date of each signature, the date of deposit of each instrument of ratification of and accession to this Treaty, the date of its entry into force and other notices.

6. This Treaty shall be registered by the Depositary Governments pursuant to Article 102 of the Charter of the United Nations.

Article XV

Any State Party to the Treaty may propose amendments to this Treaty. Amendments shall enter into force for each State Party to the Treaty accepting the amendments upon their acceptance by a majority of the States Parties to the Treaty and thereafter for each remaining State Party to the Treaty on the date of acceptance by it.

Article XVI

Any State Party to the Treaty may give notice of its withdrawal from the Treaty one year after its entry into force by written notification to the Depositary Governments. Such withdrawal shall take effect one year from the date of receipt of this notification.

Article XVII

This Treaty, of which the English, Russian, French, Spanish and Chinese texts are equally authentic, shall be deposited in the archives of the Depositary Governments. Duly certified copies of this Treaty shall be transmitted by the Depositary Governments to the Governments of the signatory and acceding States.

A.2

REPORTS ON COMMUNICATION AND CHANGE

A.2.1
THE GROCER AND THE CHIEF: A PARABLE

DANIEL LERNER

The village of Balgat lies about eight kilometers out of Ankara, in the southerly direction. It does not show on the standard maps and it does not figure in the standard histories. I first heard of it in the autumn of 1950 and most Turks have not heard of it today. Yet the story of the Middle East today is encapsulated in the recent career of Balgat. Indeed the personal meaning of modernization in underdeveloped lands can be traced, in minature, through the lives of two Balgati—The Grocer and The Chief.

My first exposure to Balgat came while leafing through several hundred interviews that had been recorded in Turkey during the spring of 1950. One group caught my eye because of the underlying tone of bitterness in the interviewer's summary of the village, his earnest sense of the hopelessness of place and people. These five interviews in Balgat were moving; even so, something in the perspective seemed awry. For one thing, the interviewer was more highly sensitized to what he saw than what he heard. The import of what had been said to him, and duly recorded in his reports, had somehow escaped his attention. I, having only the words to go by, was struck by the disjunction between the reported face and the recorded voice of Balgat. For another thing, the interviews had been made in the early spring and I was reading them in the late fall of 1950. Between these dates there had been a national election in which, as a stunning surprise to everybody including themselves, practically all qualified Turks had voted and the party in power—Atatürk's own *Halk* Party—been turned out of office.

Nothing like this had ever happened before in Turkey, possibly because neither universal suffrage nor an opposition party had ever been tried before. The dazed experts could only say of this epochal deed that the Anatolian villagers had done it. Since it would be hard to imagine Anatolian villagers of more standard pattern than the Balgati whose collected opinions were spread before me, I had it on top authority that during the summer

Daniel Lerner, *The Passing of Traditional Society* (New York: The Free Press, 1958), pp. 19-42.

they had entered History. But it was not immediately obvious by what route.

What clues existed were in a few words spoken by the villagers. These words we collated with the words that had been spoken to the interviewers by hundreds of villagers and townspeople throughout the Middle East. As we tabulated and cross-tabulated, a hunch emerged of what in Balgat spoke for many men, many deeds. Comparing cases by class and country we gradually enlarged our miniature into a panorama. Our hypothesis, heavy now with vivid details and many meanings, took shape. Four years later an oversize manuscript on the modernizing Middle East was in hand. To see how close a fit to Middle East reality was given by our picture of it, I went out for a self-guided tour and final round of interviews in the spring of 1954. My odyssey terminated where my ideas originated: in Balgat, on the eve of a second national election. With Balgat, then, our account begins.

BALGAT PERCEIVED: 1950

The interviewer who recorded Balgat on the verge—his name was Tosun B.—had detected no gleam of the future during his sojourn there. "The village is a barren one," he wrote. "The main color is gray, so is the dust on the divan on which I am writing now." Tosun was a serious young scholar from Ankara and he loved the poor in his own fashion. He had sought out Balgat to find the deadening past rather than the brave new world. He found it:

I have seen quite a lot of villages in the barren mountainous East, but never such a colorless, shapeless dump. This was the reason I chose the village. It could have been half an hour to Ankara by car if it had a road, yet it is about two hours to the capital by car without almost any road and is just forgotten, forsaken, right under our noses.

Tosun also sought and found persons to match the place. Of the five villagers he interviewed, his heart went straight out to the village shepherd. What Tosun was looking for in this interview is clear from his *obiter dicta:*

It was hard to explain to the village Chief that I wanted to interview the poorest soul in the village. He, after long discussions, consented me to interview the shepherd, but did not permit him to step into the guestroom. He said it would be an insult to me, so we did the interview in someone else's room, I did not quite understand whose. The Chief did not want to leave me alone with the respondent, but I succeeded at the end. This opened the respondent's sealed mouth, for he probably felt that I, the superior even to his chief, would rather be alone with him.

When the shepherd's sealed mouth had been opened, little came out. But Tosun was deeply stirred:

The respondent was literally in rags and in this cold weather he had no shoe, but the mud and dirt on his feet were as thick as any boot. He was small, but looked rugged and sad, very sad. He was proud of being chosen by me and though limited tried his best to answer the questions. Was so bashful that his blush was often evident under the thick layer of dirt on his face. He at times threw loud screams of laughter when there was nothing to laugh about. These he expected to be accepted as answers, for when I said "Well?" he was shocked, as if he had already answered the question.

His frustration over the shepherd was not the only deprivation Tosun attributed to the Chief, who "imposed himself on me all the time I was in the village, even tried to dictate to me, which I refused in a polite way. I couldn't have followed his directions as I would have ended up only interviewing his family." Tosun did succeed in talking privately with two Balgat farmers, but throughout these interviews he was still haunted by the shepherd and bedeviled by the Chief. Not until he came to interview the village Grocer did Tosun find another Balgati who aroused in him a comparable antipathy. Tosun's equal hostility to these very different men made me curious. It was trying to explain this that got me obsessed, sleeping and waking over the next four years, with the notion that the parable of modern Turkey was the story of The Grocer and The Chief.

Aside from resenting the containment strategy which the Chief was operating against him, Tosun gave few details about the man. He reported only the impression that "the *Muhtar* is an unpleasant old man. Looks mean and clever. He is the absolute dictator of this little village." Nor did Tosun elaborate his disapproval of the *Muhtar's* opinions beyond the comment that "years have left him some sort of useless, mystic wisdom." As a young man of empirical temper, Tosun might be expected to respond with some diffidence to the wisdom of the ancients. But the main source of Tosun's hostility, it appeared, was that the Chief made him nervous. His notes concluded: "He found what I do curious, even probably suspected it. I am sure he will report it to the first official who comes to the village."

Against the Grocer, however, Tosun reversed his neural field. He quickly perceived that he made the Grocer nervous; and for this Tosun disliked *him*. His notes read:

The respondent is comparatively the most city-like dressed man in the village. He even wore some sort of a necktie. He is the village's only grocer, but he is not really a grocer, but so he is called, originally the food-stuffs in his shop are much less than the things to be worn, like the cheapest of materials and shoes and slippers, etc. His greatest stock is drinks and cigarettes which he sells most. He is a very unimpressive type, although physically he covers quite a space. He gives the impression of a fat shadow. Although he is on the same level with the other villagers, when there are a few of the villagers around, he seems to want to distinguish himself by keeping quiet, and as soon as they depart he starts to talk too much. This happened when we were about to start the interview. He most evidently wished to feel that he is closer to me than he is to them and was curiously careful with his accent all during the interview. In spite of his unique position, for he is the only unfarming person and the only merchant in the village, he does not seem to possess an important part of the village community. In spite of all his efforts, he is considered by the villagers even less than the least farmer. Although he presented to take the interview naturally, he was nervous and also was proud to be interviewed although he tried to hide it.

All of this pushed up a weighty question: Why did the Chief make Tosun nervous and why did Tosun make the Grocer nervous? These three men, representing such different thoughtways and lifeways, were a test for each other. Looking for answers, I turned to the responses each had made to the 57 varieties of opinions called for by the standard questionnaire used in Tosun's interviews.

The Chief was a man of few words on many subjects. He dismissed most of the items on Tosun's schedule with a shrug or its audible equivalent. But he was also a man of many words on a few subjects—those having to do with the primary modes of human deportment. Only when the issues involved first principles of conduct did he consider the occasion appropriate for pronouncing judgment. Of the Chief it might be said, as Henry James said of George Eliot's salon style, *"Elle n'aborde que les grandes thèmes."*

The Chief has so little trouble with first principles because he desires to be, and usually is, a vibrant soundbox through which echo the traditional Turkish virtues. His themes are obedience, courage, loyalty—the classic values of the Ottoman Imperium reincarnate in the Atatürk Republic. For the daily round of village life these are adequate doctrine; and as the Chief has been outside of his village only to fight in two wars he has never found his austere code wanting. This congruence of biography with ideology explains the Chief's confidence in his own moral judgment and his short definition of a man. When asked what he wished for his two grown sons, for example, the Chief replied promptly: "I hope they will fight as bravely as we fought and know how to die as my generation did."

From this parochial fund of traditional virtues, the Chief drew equally his opinions of great men, nations, issues. The larger dramas of international *politique* he judged solely in terms of the courage and loyalty of the actors, invoking, to acknowledge their magnitude, the traditional rhetoric of aphorism. Generations of Anatolian *Muhtars* resonated as he pronounced his opinion of the British:

I hear that they have turned friends with us. But always stick to the old wisdom: "A good enemy is better than a bad friend." You cannot *rely* on them. Who has heard of a son being friends with his father's murderers?

With his life in Balgat, as with the Orphic wisdom that supplies its rationale, the Chief is contented. At 63 his desires have been quieted and his ambitions achieved. To Tosun's question on contentment he replied with another question:

What could be asked more? God has brought me to this mature age without much pain, has given me sons and daughters, has put me at the head of my village, and has given me strength of brain and body at this age. Thanks be to Him.

The Grocer is a very different style of man. Though born and bred in Balgat, he lives in a different world, an expansive world, populated more actively with imaginings and fantasies—hungering for whatever is different and unfamiliar. Where the Chief is contented, the Grocer is restless. To Tosun's probe, the Grocer replied staccato: "I have told you I want better things. I would have liked to have a bigger grocery shop in the city, have a nice house there, dress nice civilian clothes."

Where the Chief audits his life placidly, makes no comparisons, thanks God, the Grocer evaluates his history in a more complicated and other-involved fashion. He perceives his story as a drama of Self *versus* Village. He compares his virtue with others and finds them lacking: "I am not like the others here. They don't know any better. And when I tell them, they are angry and they say that I am ungrateful for what Allah has given me." The Grocer's struggle with Balgat was, in his script, no mere conflict of personalities. His was the lonely struggle of a single man to open the village mind. Clearly, from the readiness and consistency of his responses to most questions, he had brooded much over his role. He had a keen sense of the limits imposed by reality: "I am born a grocer and probably die that way. I have not the possibility in myself to get the things I want. They only bother me." But desire, once stirred, is not easily stilled.

Late in the interview, after each respondent had named the greatest problem facing the Turkish people, Tosun asked what he would do about this problem if he were the president of Turkey. Most responded by stolid silence—the traditional way of handling "projective questions" which require people to imagine themselves or things to be different from what they "really are." Some were shocked by the impropriety of the very question. "My God! How can you say such a thing?" gasped the shepherd. "How can I . . . I cannot . . . a poor villager . . . master of the whole world."

The Chief, Balgat's virtuoso of the traditional style, made laconic reply to this question with another question: "I am hardly able to manage a village, how shall I manage Turkey?" When Tosun probed further ("What would you suggest for *your village* that you cannot handle yourself?"), the Chief said he would seek "help of money and seed for some of our farmers." When the Grocer's turn came, he did not wait for the question to be circumscribed in terms of local reference. As president of Turkey, he said: "I would make roads for the villagers to come to towns to see the world and would not let them stay in their holes all their life."

To get out of his hole the Grocer even declared himself ready—and in this he was quite alone in Balgat—to live outside of Turkey. This came out when Tosun asked another of his projective questions: "If you could not live in Turkey, where would you want to live?" The standard reply of the villagers was that they would not live, could not imagine living, anywhere else. The forced choice simply was ignored.

When Tosun persisted ("Suppose you *had* to leave Turkey?") he teased an extreme reaction out of some Balgati. The shepherd, like several other wholly routinized personalities, finally replied that he would rather kill himself. The constricted peasant can more easily imagine destroying the self than relocating it in an unknown, i.e., frightful, setting.

The Chief again responded with the clear and confident voice of traditional man. "'Nowhere," he said. "I was born here, grew old here, and hope God will permit me to die here." To Tosun's probe, the Chief replied firmly: "I wouldn't move a foot from here." Only the Grocer found no trouble in imagining himself outside of Turkey, living in a strange land. Indeed he seemed fully prepared, as a man does when he has already posed a question to himself many times. "America," said the Grocer, and, without waiting for Tosun to ask him why, stated his reason: "because I have heard that it is a nice country, and with possibilities to be rich even for the simplest persons."

Such opinions clearly marked off the Grocer, in the eyes of the villagers around him, as heterodox and probably infidel. The vivid sense of cash displayed by the Grocer was a grievous offense against Balgat ideas of tabu talk. In the code regulating the flow of symbols among Anatolian villagers, blood and sex are permissible objects of passion but money is not. To talk much of money is an impropriety. To reveal excessive *desire* for money is—Allah defend us—an impiety.

Balgati might forgive the Grocer his propensity to seek the strange rather than reverse the familiar, even his readiness to forsake Turkey for unknown places, had he decently clothed these impious desires in pious terms. But to abandon Balgat for the world's fleshpots, to forsake the ways of God to seek the ways of cash, this was insanity. The demented person who spoke thus was surely accursed and unclean.

The Grocer, with his "city-dressed" ways, his "eye at the higher places" and his visits to Ankara, provoked the Balgati to wrathful and indignant restatements of the old code. But occasional, and apparently trivial, items in the survey suggested that some Balgati were talking loud about the Grocer to keep their own inner voices from being overheard by the Chief—or even by themselves.

As we were interested in knowing who says what to whom in such a village as Balgat, Tosun had been instructed to ask each person whether others ever came to him for advice, and if so what they wanted advice about. Naturally, the Balgati whose advice was most sought was the Chief, who reported: "Yes, that is my main duty, to give advice. (Tosun: *What about?*) About all that I or you could imagine, even about their wives and how to handle them, and how to cure their sick cow." This conjunction of wives and cows, to illustrate all the Chief could imagine, runs the gamut only from A to B. These are the species that the villager has most to do with in his daily round of life, the recurrent source of his pains and pleasures and puzzlements. The oral literature abounds in examples of *Muhtar* (or his theological counterpart, the *Hoca*) as wise man dispensing judgment equally about women and cows.

Rather more surprising was Tosun's discovery that some Balgati went for advice also to the disreputable Grocer. What did they ask *his* advice about? "What to do when they go to Ankara, where to go and what to buy, how much to sell their things." The cash nexus, this suggested, was somehow coming to Balgat and with it, possibly, a new role for the Grocer as cosmopolitan specialist in how to avoid wooden nickels in the big city. Also, how to spend the real nickels one got. For the Grocer was a man of clear convictions on which coffee-houses played the best radio programs and which were the best movies to see in Ankara. While his opinions on these matters were heterodox as compared say, to the Chief's, they had an open field to work in. Most Balgati had never heard a radio or seen a movie and were not aware of what constituted orthodoxy with respect to them. Extremists had nonetheless decided that these things, being new, were obviously evil. Some of them considered the radio to be "the voice of The Devil coming from his deep hiding-place" and said they would smash any such "Devil's-box" on sight.

At the time of Tosun's visit, there was only one radio in Balgat, owned by no less a personage than the Chief. In the absence of any explicit orthodox prohibition on radio, the Chief, former soldier and great admirer of Atatürk, had followed his lead. Prosperous by village standards, being the large landowner of Balgat, he had bought a radio to please and instruct his sons. He had also devised an appropriate ceremonial for its use. Each evening a select group of Balgati foregathered in the Chief's guest room as he turned on the newscast from Ankara. They heard the newscast through in silence and, at its conclusion, the Chief turned the radio off and made his commentary. "We all listen very carefully," he told Tosun, "and I talk about it afterwards." Tosun, suspecting in this procedure a variant of the Chief's containment tactics, wanted to know whether there was any disagreement over his explanations. "No, no arguments," replied the Chief, "as I tell you I only talk and our opinions are the same more or less." Here was a new twist in the ancient role of knowledge as power. Sensing the potential challenge from radio, the Chief restricted the dangers of innovation by partial incorporation, thus retaining and strengthening his role as Balgat's official opinion leader.

Tosun inquired of the Grocer, an occasional attendant at the Chief's salon, how he liked this style of radio session. The grocer, a heretic perhaps but not a foolhardy one, made on this point the shortest statement in his entire interview: "The Chief is clever and he explains the news." Only obliquely, by asking what the Grocer liked best about radio, did Tosun get an answer that had the true resonance. Without challenging the Chief's preference for news of "wars and the danger of wars"—in fact an exclusive interest in the Korean War, to which a Turkish brigade had just been committed—the Grocer indicated that after all *he* had opportunities to listen in the coffee-houses of Ankara, where the audiences exhibited a more cosmopolitan range of interests. "It is nice to know what is happening in the other capitals of the world," said the Grocer. "We are stuck in this hole, we have to know what is going on outside our village."

The Grocer had his own aesthetic of the movies as well. Whereas the Chief had been to the movies several times, he viewed them mainly as a moral prophylactic: "There are fights, shooting. The people are brave. My sons are always impressed. Each time they see such a film they wish more and more their time for military service would come so that they would become soldiers too." For the Grocer, movies were more than a homily of familiar themes. They were his avenue to the wider world of his dreams. It was in a movie that he had first glimpsed what a *real* grocery store could be like—"with walls made of iron sheets, top to floor and side to side, and on them standing myriads of round boxes, clean and all the same dressed, like soldiers in a great parade." This fleeting glimpse of what sounds like the Campbell Soup section of an A & P supermarket had provided the Grocer with an abiding image of how his fantasy world might look. It was here, quite likely, that he had shaped the ambition earlier confided to Tosun, "to have a bigger grocery shop in the city." No pedantries intervened in the Grocer's full sensory relationship to the movies. No eye had he, like the Chief, for their value as filial moral rearmament and call to duty. The Grocer's judgments were formed in unabashedly hedonist categories. "The Turkish ones," he said, "are gloomy, ordinary. I can guess at the start of the film how it will end. . . . The American ones are exciting. You know it makes people ask what will happen next?"

Here, precisely, arose the local variant of a classic question. In Balgat, the Chief carried the sword, but did the Grocer steer the pen? When Balgati sought his advice on how to get around Ankara, would they then go to movies that taught virtue or those that taught excitement? True, few villagers had ever been to Ankara. But things were changing in Turkey and many more Balgati were sure to have a turn or two around the big city before they died. What would happen next in Balgat if more people discovered the tingle of wondering what will happen next? Would things continue along the way of the Chief or would they take the way of the Grocer?

BALGAT REVISITED: 1954

I reached Ankara in April after a circuitous route through the Middle East. The glories of Greece, Egypt, Lebanon, Syria, Persia touched me only lightly, for some part of me was already in Balgat. Even the Blue Mosque and St. Sophia seemed pallid, and I left Istanbul three days ahead of schedule for Ankara. I had saved this for last, and now here I was. I was half afraid to look.

I called a transportation service and explained that I wanted to go out the following day, a Sunday, to a village some eight kilometers south that might be hard to reach. As I wanted to spend the day, would the driver meet me at 8 A.M. and bring along his lunch?

While waiting for the car, next morning, my reverie wandered back through the several years since my first reading of the Balgat interviews. Was I chasing a phantom? Tahir S. appeared. With solitude vanished anxiety; confidently we began to plan the day. Tahir had been a member of the original interview team, working in the Izmir area. As Tosun had joined the Turkish foreign service and was stationed in North Africa, where he was conducting an inquiry among the Berbers, I had arranged in advance for Tahir to revisit Balgat with me in his place. Over a cup of syrupy coffee, we reviewed the questions that had been asked in 1950, noted the various responses and silences, decided the order in which we would repeat the old questions and interpolate the new ones.

As the plan took shape, Zilla K. arrived. She had no connection with the original survey, but I wanted a female interviewer who could add some Balgat women to our gallery. I had "ordered" her, through a colleague at Ankara University, "by the numbers": thirtyish, semi-trained, alert, compliant with instructions, not sexy enough to impede our relations with the men of Balgat but chic enough to provoke the women. A glance and a word showed that Zilla filled the requisition. We brought her into the plan of operations. The hall porter came in to say our car was waiting. We got in and settled back for a rough haul. Twenty minutes later, as we were still debating the niceties of question-wording and reporting procedure, the driver said briskly: "There's Balgat."

We looked puzzled at each other until Tosun's words of 1950 recurred to us: "It could have been half an hour to Ankara if it had a road." Now it did have a road. What was more, a *bus* was coming down the road, heading toward us from the place our driver had called Balgat. As it passed, jammed full, none of the passengers waved or even so much as stuck out a tongue at us. Without these unfailing signs of villagers out on a rare chartered bus, to celebrate a great occasion of some sort, we could only make the wild guess that Balgat had acquired a regular bus service. And indeed, as we entered the village, there it was—a "bus station," freshly painted benches under a handsome new canopy. We got out and looked at the printed schedule of trips. "The bus leaves every hour, on the hour, to Ulus Station. Fare: 20 Kurus." For about 4 cents, Balgati could now go, whenever they felt the whim, to Ulus in the heart of Ankara. The villagers were getting out of their holes at last. The Grocer, I thought, must be grinning over the fat canary he had swallowed.

We took a quick turn around the village, on our way to check in with the Chief. Things looked different from what Tosun's report had led us to expect. Overhead wires were stretched along the road, with branch lines extended over the houses of Balgat. The village had been electrified. Alongside the road deep ditches had been dug, in which the graceful curve of new water pipe was visible. Purified water was coming to Balgat. There were many more buildings than the 50-odd Tosun had counted, and most of them looked new. Two larger ones announced themselves as a school and a police station. An inscription on the latter revealed that Balgat was now under the jurisdiction of the Ankara district police. They had finally got rid of the *gendarmerie,* scavengers of the Anatolian village and historic blight on the peasant's existence. "These fellows are lucky," said Tahir drily. Feeling strange, we made our way along the erratic path through the old village, led and followed by a small horde of children, to the house of the Chief. Tahir knocked, an old woman with her head covered by a dark shawl appeared, the children scattered. We were led into the guest room.

The Chief looked as I had imagined. His cheeks a bit more sunken, perhaps, but the whole *présence* quite familiar. Tall, lean, hard, he walked erect and looked me straight in the eye. His own eyes were Anatolian black and did not waver as he stretched out a handful of long, bony fingers. "*Gün aydin, Bey Efendim,"* he said. "Good day, sir, you are welcome to my house." I noted in turn the kindness which opens a door to strangers and the Chief responded that we honored his house by our presence. This completed the preliminary round of *formules de politesse* and steaming little cups of Turkish coffee were brought in by the Chief's elder son. The son was rather a surprise—short, pudgy, gentle-eyed and soft spoken. He bowed his head, reddening slightly as he stammered, *"Lütfen"* (Please!) and offered the tray of demitasses to me. I wondered whether he had learned to fight bravely and die properly.

As the Chief set down his second cup of coffee, signifying that we could now turn to the business of our visit, I explained that I had come from America, where I taught in a university, with the hope of meeting him. There, in my own country, I had read about Balgat in some writing by a young man from Ankara who, four years ago, had talked at length with the Chief and other persons in his village. This writing had interested me very much and I had often wondered, as the years passed by, how things were going in the village of Balgat and among its people. When I had the opportunity to come to Turkey I immediately decided that I would visit Balgat and see the Chief if I could.

The Chief heard me through gravely, and when he spoke I knew I was in. He bypassed the set of formulas available to him—for rejecting or evading my implied request—and responded directly to the point. I was right to have come to see Balgat for myself. He remembered well the young man from Ankara (his description of Tosun in 1950 was concise and neutrally-toned). Much had changed in Balgat since that time. Indeed, Balgat was no longer a village. It had, only last month, been incorporated as a district of Greater Ankara. This was why they now had a new headquarters of Metropolitan police, and a bus service, and electricity, and a supply of pure water that would soon be in operation. Where there had been 50 houses there were now over 500, and even he, the Muhtar, did not know any more all the people living here.

Yes he had lived in Balgat all his life and never in all that time seen so much happen as had come to pass in these four years:

It all began with the election that year. The *Demokrat* men came to Balgat and asked us what was needed here and told us they would do it when they were elected. They were brave to go against the government party. We all voted for them, as the *Halk* men knew no more what to do about the prices then, and the new men did what they said. They brought us this road and moved out the *gendarmerie.* Times have been good with us here. We are all *Demokrat* party here in Balgat now.

The Chief spoke in a high, strong, calm voice, and the manner of his utterance was matter-of-fact. His black eyes remained clear as he gazed steadily at the airspace adjoining my left ear, and his features retained their shape. Only his hands were animated, though he invoked only the thumbs and the index fingers for punctuation. When he had completed his statement, he picked his nose thoughtfully for a moment and then laid the finger alongside the bridge. The tip of the long, bony finger reached into his eyesocket.

I explained then that the young lady had come with us to learn how such changes as the Chief mentioned were altering the daily round for village women. Might she talk with some of them while Tahir Bey and I were meeting the men? The Chief promptly suggested that Zilla could speak with the females of his household. (Tosun's resentful remark that, had he followed the Chief's suggestions, "I would have ended up only interviewing his family" came back to me later that evening, when Zilla reported on her interviews with the Chief's wife and daughters-in-law. All three had identified Balgat's biggest problem as the new fashion of young men to approach girls shamelessly on the village outskirts—precisely what the Chief had told me in answer to the same question. Tosun had been wise.) But if the Chief still used his containment tactics with the women, in other directions he had taken a decidedly permissive turn. Tahir and I, he said, could walk about Balgat entirely as we wished and speak with whomsoever it pleased us to honor—even, he added with a smile in response to my jest, some non-*Demokrat* Party men, if we could find any. We chatted a bit longer and then, having agreed to return to the Chief's house, we set out for a stroll around Balgat. Our next goal was to find the Grocer.

After a couple of bends and turns, we came to a coffee-house. Here was something new and worth a detour. We stopped at the door and bade the proprietor *"Gün aydin!"* He promptly rushed forward with two chairs, suggested that we sit outdoors to benefit of the pleasant sunshine, and asked us how we would like our coffee. (There are five ways of specifying the degree of sweetening one likes in Turkish coffee.) Obviously, this was to be on the house, following the paradoxical Turkish custom of giving gratis to those who can best afford to pay. In a matter of minutes, the male population of Balgat was assembled around our two chairs, squatting, sitting on the ground, looking us over with open and friendly curiosity, peppering Tahir with questions about me.

When our turn came, the hierarchy of respondents was already clear from the axis along which their questions to us had been aligned. Top man was one of the two farmers Tosun had interviewed in 1950. He too was tall, lean, hard. He wore store-clothes with no patches and a sturdy pair of store-shoes. His eyes were Anatolian black and his facial set was much like the Chief's. But his body was more relaxed and his manner more cocky. He sat with his chair tilted back and kept his hands calmly dangling alongside. This seemed to excise punctuation from his discourse and he ambled along, in response to any question, with no apparent terminus in view. Interrupting him, even long enough to steer his flow of words in another direction, was—the obvious deference of the whole group toward him constrained us—not easy. His voice was deep and harsh, with the curious suggestion of strangling in the throat that Anatolian talk sometimes has. The content was elusive and little of his discourse made concrete contact with my notebook.

As I review my notes on that tour of monologue-with-choral-murmurs, he appears to have certified the general impression that many changes had occurred in Balgat. His inventory included, at unwholesome length, all the by-now familiar items: road, bus, electricity, water. In his recital these great events did not acquire a negative charge, but they lost some of their luster. The tough old farmer did not look shining at new styles of architecture, nor did he look scowling, but simply looked. Under his gaze the new roofs in Balgat were simply new roofs. The wonder that these new roofs were *in Balgat* shone in other eyes and cadenced other voices.

These other voices were finally raised. Either the orator had exhausted the prerogative of his position (he had certainly exhausted Tahir S., whose eyes were glazed and vacant) or the issue was grave enough to sanction discourtesy toward a village elder. The outburst came when the quondam farmer undertook to explain why he was no longer a farmer. He had retired, over a year ago, because there was none left in Balgat to do an honest day's work for an honest day's lira. Or rather two lira (about 36 cents)—the absurd rate, he said, to which the daily wage of farm laborers had been driven by the competition of the voracious Ankara labor market. Now, all the so-called able-bodied men of Balgat had forsaken the natural work praised by Allah and swarmed off to the Ankara factories where, for eight hours of so-called work, they could get five lira a day. As for himself, he would have none of this. Rather than pay men over two lira a day to do the work of men, he had rented out his land to others and retired. He was rich, his family would eat, and others might do as they wished.

The protests that rose did not aim to deny these facts, but simply to justify them. Surprised, we asked whether it was indeed true that there were no farm laborers left in Balgat any more. "How many of you," we quickly rephrased the question, "work on farms now?" Four hands were raised among the 29 present, and all of these turned out to be small holders working their own land. (These four were sitting together and, it later turned out, were the only four members of the *Halk* Party among the group, the rest being vigorous *Demokrat* men.)

Galvanized by the intelligence now suddenly put before us (even Tahir S. had reawakened promptly upon discovering that there were hardly any farmers left in Balgat), we started to fire a battery of questions on our own. As this created a din of responding voices, Tahir S.—once again the American-trained interviewer—restored order by asking each man around the circle to tell us, in turn, what he was now working at and how long he had been at it. This impromptu occupational census, begun on a leisurely Sunday, was never quite completed. As it became clear that most of the male population of Balgat was now in fact working in the factories and construction gangs of Ankara—*for cash*—our own impatience to move on to our next questions got the better of us.

How did they spend the cash they earned? Well, there were now over 100 radio receivers in Balgat as compared to the lone receiver Tosun had found four years earlier. There were also seven refrigerators, four tractors, three trucks, and one Dodge sedan. Most houses now had electric lights and that had to be paid for. Also, since there was so little farming in Balgat now, much of the food came from the outside (even milk!) and had to be bought in the grocery stores, of which there were now seven in Balgat. Why milk? Well, most of the animals had been sold off during the last few years. What about the shepherd? Well, he had moved to a village in the east a year or so ago, as there were no longer any flocks for him to tend. How was the Grocer doing? *"Which one?"* The original one, the great fat one that was here four years ago? "O, that one, he's dead!"

Tahir S. later told me that my expression did not change when the news came (always the American-trained interviewer!). I asked a few more questions in a normal way—"What did he die of?", "How long ago?"—and then let the questioning pass to Tahir. I don't recall what answers came to my questions or to his. I do recall suddenly feeling very weary and, as the talk went on, slightly sick. The feeling got over to Tahir S. and soon we were saying goodbye to the group, feeling relieved that the ritual for leavetaking is less elaborate than for arriving. We promised to return and said our thanks. *"Güle, güle,"* answered those who remained. ("Smile, smile," signifying farewell.)

"What a lousy break," growled Tahir in a tone of reasonable indignation as we started back toward the house of the Chief. He was speaking of the Grocer. I didn't know what to say by way of assent. I felt only a sense of large and diffuse regret, of which indignation was not a distinct component. "Tough," I agreed. As we came up to the Chief's house, I told Tahir we might as well return to Ankara. We had gathered quite a lot of information already and might better spend the afternoon putting it together. We could come back the next day to interview the Chief. The Chief agreed to this plan and invited me to be his guest for lunch next day. We collected Zilla K. and our driver and drove back to the city. Zilla did most of the talking, while Tahir and I listened passively. The driver said only, as I paid him, "I didn't need to bring along my lunch after all."

THE PASSING OF BALGAT

While dressing slowly, the next morning, I planned my strategy for lunch with the Chief. Had he learned anything from the Grocer? Clearly his larger clues to the shape of the future had come from Atatürk, whose use of strong measures for humane new goals had impressed him deeply as a young man. But surely he had also responded to the constant stimuli supplied by the Grocer, whose psychic antennae were endlessly *seeking* the new future here and now. The Chief, rather consciously reshaping his ways in the Atatürk image, had to be reckoned a major figure in the Anatolian transformation. But the restless sensibility of the Grocer also had its large, inadequately defined, place. Whereas the masterful Chief had been able to incorporate change mainly by rearranging the environment, the nervous Grocer had been obliged to operate through the more painful process of rearranging himself. Most villagers were closer to his situation than to the Chief's. The Grocer then was my problem and, as symbol of the character-ological shift, my man. It was he who dramatized most poignantly the personal meaning of the big change now under way throughout the Middle East.

I recalled Tosun's unflattering sketch of him as an anxiety-ridden pusher, an "unfarming person" who "even wore some sort of necktie." What had located these details, what had made the Grocer a man I recognized, was Tosun's acid remark: "He most evidently wished to feel that he is closer to me than he is to [other villagers] and was curiously careful with his accent all during the interview." Tosun had seen this as vulgar social climbing, but there was something in this sentence that sounded to me like History. Maybe it was the 18th century field-hand of England who had left the manor to find a better life in London or Manchester. Maybe it was the 19th century French farm lad, wearied by his father's burdens of *taille* and *tithe,* who had gone off to San Francisco to hunt gold and, finding none, had then tried his hand as mason, mechanic, printer's devil; though none of these brought him fortune, he wrote home cheerfully (in a letter noted by the perspicacious Karl Marx) about this exciting new city where the chance to try his hand at anything made him feel "less of a mollusk and more of a man." Maybe it was the 20th century Polish peasant crossing continent and ocean to Detroit, looking for a "better 'ole" in the new land.

The Grocer of Balgat stood for some part of all these figures as he nervously edged his psyche toward Tosun, the young man from the big city. I'm like you, the Grocer might have been feeling, or I'd like to be like you and wish I could get the chance. It was harsh of Tosun, or perhaps only the anti-bourgeois impatience of an austere young scholar looking for the suffering poor in a dreary village, to cold-shoulder this fat and middle-aged man yearning to be comfortably rich in an interesting city. But the Grocer had his own sort of toughness. He had, after all, stood up to the other villagers and had insisted, even when they labeled him infidel, that they ought to get out of their holes. Though dead, he had won an important victory. For the others, despite their outraged virtues, *had* started to come around, once they began to get the feel of Ankara cash, for advice on *how* to get out of their holes. Had they also acquired, along with their new sense of cash, some feel for the style of life the Grocer had desired? That was what I wanted to find out in Balgat today.

I walked out of the hotel toward Ulus station, just around the corner. This time I was going to Balgat by bus, to see how the villagers traveled. We crowded into a shiny big bus from Germany that held three times as many passengers as there were seats. The bus was so new that the signs warning the passengers not to smoke or spit or talk to the driver (while the bus is moving) in German, French, and English had not yet been converted into Turkish. There was, in fact, a great deal of smoking and several animated conversations between the driver and various passengers occurred, in the intervals between which the driver chatted with a crony whom he had brought along for just this purpose.

In Balgat I reported directly to the Chief. He appeared, after a few minutes, steaming and mopping his large forehead. He had been pruning some trees and, in this warm weather, such work brought the sweat to his brow. This was about the only work he did any more, he explained, as he had sold or rented most of his land in the last few years, keeping for himself only the ground in which he had planted a small grove of trees that would be his memorial on earth. Islamic peoples regard a growing and "eternal" thing of nature, preferably a tree, as a fitting monument, and a comfortable Muslim of even diffident piety will usually be scrupulous in observing this tradition—a sensible one for a religion of the desert, where vegetation is rare and any that casts a shade is especially prized. The Chief agreed to show me his trees and as we strolled away from the house he resumed his discourse of yesterday.

Things had changed, he repeated, and a sign of the gravity of these changes was that he—of a lineage that had always been *Muhtars* and landowners—was no longer a farmer. Nor was he long to be *Muhtar*. After the coming election, next month, the incorporation of Balgat into Greater Ankara was to be completed and thereafter it would be administered under the general municipal system. "I am the last *Muhtar* of Balgat, and I am happy that I have seen Balgat end its history in this way that we are going." The new ways, then, were not bringing evil with them?

No, people will have to get used to different ways and then some of the excesses, particularly among the young, will disappear. The young people are in some ways a serious disappointment; they think more of clothes and good times than they do of duty and family and country. But it is to be hoped that as the *Demokrat* men complete the work they have begun, the good Turkish ways will again come forward to steady the people. Meanwhile, it is well that people can have to eat and to buy shoes they always needed but could not have.

And as his two sons were no longer to be farmers, what of them? The Chief's voice did not change, nor did his eyes cloud over, as he replied:

They are as the others. They think first to serve themselves and not the nation. They had no wish to go to the battle in Korea, where Turkey fights before the eyes of all the world. They are my sons and I speak no ill of them, but I say only that they are as all the others.

I felt at this moment a warmth toward the Chief which I had not supposed he would permit himself to evoke. His sons had not after all, learned to fight bravely and die properly. His aspiration—which had led him, four years earlier, to buy a radio so his sons would hear the Korean war news and to see movies that would make them "wish more and more their time for military service would come"—had not been fulfilled. Yet the old Chief bore stoically what must have been a crushing disappointment. These two sons through whom he had hoped to relive his own bright dreams of glory had instead become *shopkeepers*. The elder son owned a grocery store and the younger one owned Balgat's first clothing store. With this news, curiosity overcame sympathy. I rattled off questions on this subject which, clearly, the Chief would rather have changed. As we turned back to the house, he said we would visit the shops after lunch and his sons would answer all my questions.

Lunch consisted of a huge bowl of yogurt, alongside of which was stacked a foot-high pile of village-style bread, freshly baked by the Chief's wife and served by his younger daughter-in-law. Village bread fresh from the oven is one of the superior tastes that greets a visitor. As I went to work with obvious relish, the Chief suggested that I eat only the "corner" of each sheet. Village bread is baked in huge round double sheets, each about the diameter of a manhole cover and the thickness of a dime. A large glob of shortening is spread loosely around the center between the sheets, which are baked together around the circumference. These sheets are then folded over four times, making the soft buttery center into a "corner." The corner is the prerogative of the male head of the household, who may choose to share it with a favored child. To invite a guest to eat *only* the corners is, in the frugal Anatolian village, a sign of special cordiality that cannot be ignored.

As I chewed my way happily through a half-dozen corners, I wondered who was going to be stuck with my stack of cornerless circumferences. Mama and the daughters-in-law? I asked about the children and learned that, as befits the traditional extended family, the Chief now had nine descendants living under his roof. Moreover, while some were taking to new ways, *his* grandchildren had been and were being swaddled in the traditional Anatolian fashion—for three months a solid mudpack on the body under the swaddling cloths, thereafter for three months a mudless swaddle. (Geoffrey Gorer's association of Russian, swaddling with *ochi chornya* seemed due for an Anatolian confirmation, since Turkish eyes are every bit as lustrous black as Slavic eyes.) I glanced up at the large clock on the wall, which had stood firmly at 11:09 since I first entered the room at 9:16 the preceding day. It was clearly intended only as an emblem of social standing. In the very household where swaddling continued, possibly the first clock in Balgat (as once the first radio) had won a place. And though the clock was only decorative rather than useful, yet the hourglass was no longer visible. Times had changed. The Chief noticed my glance and suggested that we could now go out to see the shops of his sons.

We went first to the elder son's grocery store, just across the road and alongside the village "fountain," where Balgat women did the family wash as in ages past (though this would pass when the new municipal water supply became available at reasonable rates). The central floor space was set out with merchandise in the immemorial manner—heavy, rough, anonymous hemp sacks each laden with a commodity requiring no identity card, groats in one and barley in another, here lentils and there chicory. But beyond the sacks was a distinct innovation, a counter. What is more, the counter turned a corner and ran parallel to two sides of the square hut. Built into it was a cash drawer and above each surface a hygienic white porcelain fixture for fluorescent lighting. Along the walls was the crowning glory—rows of shelves running from "top to floor and side to side, and on them standing myriads of round boxes, clean and all the same, dressed like soldiers in a great parade." The Grocer's words of aspiration came leaping back as I looked admiringly around the store. His dream-house had been built in Balgat—in less time than even he might have forecast—and by none other than the Chief!

The irony of the route by which Balgat had entered history accompanied us as we walked in quartet, the Chief and I ahead, the sons behind, to the clothing store of the younger son. This was in the newer part of the village, just across the new road from the "bus station." The entrance to the store was freshly painted dark blue, a color imbued by Muslim lore with power to ward off the evil eye. The stock inside consisted mainly of dungarees, levis, coveralls (looking rather like U.S. Army surplus stocks). There was a continuous and growing demand for these goods, the Chief stated solemnly, as more and more Balgati went into the labor market of Ankara, first discarding their *sholvars* (the billowing knickers of traditional garb in which Western cartoons always still portray the "sultan" in a harem scene). In a corner of the store there was also a small stock of "gentleman's haberdashery"—ready-made suits, shirts, even a rack of neckties.

The younger son, who maintained under his smile of proprietary pleasure a steady silence in the presence of the Chief, replied to a direct question from me that he had as yet sold very few items from this department of the store. One suit had gone to a prospective bridegroom, but the Balgat males by and large were still reticent about wearing store-bought clothes. A few, indeed, had purchased in a *sub rosa* sort of way neckties which remained to be exhibited in public. But wearing them would come, now that several owned them, as soon as an older man was bold enough to wear his first. The owners of the neckties had only to get used to them in private, looking at them now and then, showing them to their wives and elder sons, and some one of them had to show the way. I remembered Tosun's rather nasty comment about the Grocer: *"He even wore some sort of a necktie."* As one saw it now, the Grocer *had* shown the way, and it was now only a hop, skip and jump through history to the point where most men of Balgat would be wearing neckties.

The Grocer's memory stayed with me all that afternoon, after I had expressed intense satisfaction with the shops, wished the sons good fortune, thanked the Chief again and, with his permission, started out to walk among the alleys and houses of Balgat. On the way, I absently counted 69 radio antennas on the roofs and decided that yesterday's estimate of "over 100" was probably reliable. And only four years ago, I counterpointed to myself, there was but a single battery set in this village. The same theme ran through my recollection of the numbers of tractors, refrigerators, and "unfarming persons." Several of these newly unfarming persons, recognizing their interlocutor of yesterday's coffee-house session, greeted me as I strolled along. One stopped me long enough to deliver his opinion of the Turkish-Pakistani pact (strong affirmation) and to solicit mine of the proposed law to give Americans prospecting rights on Turkish oil (qualified affirmative).

Weary of walking, I turned back to the coffee-house. The ceremony of welcome was warm and the coffee was again on the house. But the conversational group was smaller, this being a workday. Only eleven Balgati appeared to praise the weather and hear my questions. The group got off on politics, with some attention to the general theory of power but more intense interest in hearing each other's predictions of the margin by which the *Demokrat* party would win the elections next month. There was also general agreement, at least among the older men, that it would be better to have a small margin between the major parties. When the parties are competing and need our votes, then they heed our voices—thus ran the underlying proposition of the colloquy. "The villagers have learned the basic lesson of democratic politics," I wrote in my notebook.

The afternoon was about over before I got an appropriate occasion to ask about the Grocer. It came when the talk returned to the villagers' favorite topic of how much better life had become during the past four years of *Demokrat* rule. Again they illustrated the matter by enumerating the new shops in Balgat and the things they had to sell that many people could buy. There was even a new barber shop, opened last month by the son of the late Altemur after going for some time to Ankara as apprentice. "How are these new grocery shops better than the old grocery shop of years ago owned by the fat grocer who is now dead?" I asked. The line of response was obvious in advance, but the question served to lead to another: What sort of man had the Grocer been?

The answers were perfunctory, consisting mainly of *pro forma* expressions of goodwill toward the departed. I tried to get back of these ritual references by indirection. How had the Grocer dressed? Why had he been so interested in the life of Ankara? The light finally shone in one of the wiser heads and he spoke the words I was seeking:

Ah, he was the cleverest of us all. We did not know it then, but he saw better than all what lay in the path ahead. We have none like this among us now. He was a prophet.

As I look back on it now, my revisit to Balgat ended then. I went back several times, once with gifts for the Chief's grandchildren, another time with my camera (as he had coyly suggested) to take his picture. On these visits I felt less tense, asked fewer questions, than during the earlier visits. The last time I went out with the publisher of a prominent Istanbul newspaper ("The New York Times of Turkey"), a dedicated *Demokrat* man, who was eager to see the transformed village I had described to him. He was enchanted with the Chief, the stores, the bus service and electricity and other symbols of the history into which his party had ushered Balgat. He decided to write a feature story about it and asked permission to call it "Professor Lerner's Village." I declined, less from modesty than a sense of anachronism. The Balgat his party needed was the suburb inhabited by the sons of the Chief, with their swaddled children and their proud new clock, their male "corners" and their retail stores, their filiopietistic silence and their movies that teach excitement. The ancient village I had known for what now seemed only four short years was passing, had passed. The Grocer was dead. The Chief—"the last *Muhtar* of Balgat"—had reincarnated the Grocer in the flesh of his sons. Tosun was in North Africa studying the Berbers.

A.2.2
A STUDY OF TWO INDIAN VILLAGES

Y. V. LAKSHMANA RAO

INTRODUCTION

Erranna is an illiterate, sixty-two years old, one of the Gaondla caste whose members traditionally depend for their livelihood on the tapping of palm trees and the selling of the fermented juice (*kallu*). He has spent all his life in a virtually isolated village twenty-five miles from Hyderabad, the capital of Andhra Pradesh in South India.

Rajayya is a forty-one-year-old member of the Brahmin priest caste. He is a high school teacher in a village connected directly by rail and road to Visakhapatnam, fourteen miles away. This city is the seat of the Andhra University and a busy seaport. Rajayya has had four years of college and has traveled extensively.

Knowing this much about them, one might make certain predictions: Rajayya will be well informed about public affairs—the national development programs and the like. Erranna will be quite ignorant about them, indeed uninterested in such things as the five-year plans and nuclear explosions. Rajayya will seek information, meet people, discuss news, give advice, and generally conduct himself in such a way that he will be a respected member of the community. Erranna, on the other hand, will be content with his traditional occupation, will be conscious of his place in the community and will generally confine himself to association with lower-caste groups, will work hard during the day and sleep soundly during the night. His position in the community will limit his circle of friends to those who are as illiterate and as ill informed as he is.

These are the differences which caste and education make—or at least so one might understandably assume.

But is this indeed the case with Rajayya and Erranna? Are they really as described here? No. The truth is almost the opposite. It is Erranna who has heard of the "poisoned air" (radioactivity) released by Russia's testing of

Y. V. Lakshmana Rao, *Communication and Development* (Minneapolis, Minn.: University of Minnesota Press, 1966), pp. 1–130.

the "Big Bomb" and its possible dangers, of life insurance, of the "Goa War," and so on. Rajayya, on the other hand, can only make a vague guess that exploding a bomb is bad because "a bomb kills people." It is Erranna who is a respected member of his community, because he is well informed, cosmopolitan in his outlook, sociable, jovial, a fine conversationalist, and a modest person. Rajayya is seldom stopped on the road because there are few who wish to talk to him; he isolates himself in his house and interacts with neither his students nor their parents ("I have nothing in common with them"). He claims that he reads the newspaper every day and takes part in the preparation of a news bulletin which is read out at the morning assembly in school, but he has not heard of the deliberations of a commission inquiring into the sharing of river waters between Andhra and two adjoining states, although the activities of the commission made lead stories for five consecutive days in all the newspapers circulating in the village.

Erranna and Rajayya are *not* typical members of their respective communities in their approach to life, their information level, and their view of the future. But they are typical in some other respects: their way of dress and certain behavioral patterns.

Erranna dresses in the style of the traditional South Indian villager—he wears a *dhoti* topped by a loose collarless shirt, over which a handspun blanket is draped for comfort in the winter. On his feet are two strong, thick, crudely finished slippers. Rajayya wears what could pass for a Western costume—a pair of cotton trousers, a plain "bush shirt," and shoes. It is true that Rajayya is in the minority in his village, but almost every educated man who has been exposed to some city influence would wear such a costume there, whereas in Erranna's community even the richest landlord who spends half the year in the city dresses more or less like Erranna. Rajayya's house has cemented floors, a few chairs and cots, and at least two tables, while Erranna lives in a small tiled house with mud floors and no furniture. Erranna rarely, if ever, goes to the local teashop, but Rajayya eats his lunch fairly regularly at a restaurant.

In pointing out this seeming paradox of the informed illiterate and the ignorant literate, of the use of illiteracy and the misuse of literacy, my intention is to stress at the outset the complicated nature of the kind of field study reported here, a study of the influence of communication on development in a "developing" nation. An investigator looking for communication channels or trying to reach general conclusions about the communication patterns within communities can depend on raw data only up to a point and no further. Even if individual communities are studied intensively, the significant differences in personalities in the same social structure can often make the exceptions more important than the rule.

Erranna and Rajayya will appear in later chapters; so will many others. Often they will be anonymous units in a mass; but often too they will be singled out. For it is important that we not lose sight of some of the individuals who play such important roles in the process of communication.

. . .

FIRST IMPRESSIONS

A brief introduction to the two villages by way of "first impressions" seems necessary before going into a more detailed description of each of them, because it was on the basis of such impressions that Pathuru and Kothuru were decided upon. Their selection followed a series of visits to scores of villages—all confined to the state of Andhra Pradesh in South India in order to ensure some essential comparability (both villages had to be in the same administrative setup) and to take advantage of the investigator's ability to speak all four of the languages used in this state.

Our choice of villages was governed by the single overriding hypothesis that communication patterns as well as economic development will differ as between the traditional village and the "developing" village. Therefore, the search was focused on finding an "industrializing" village and a fairly comparable "non-industrializing" or "traditional rural" village. We eventually found Kothuru and, later, Pathuru which fitted our requirements and were also comparable in population. Whatever other differences there were between the two villages were left for later investigation.

. . .

KOTHURU

In this description of Kothuru, the patterns of communications have deliberately been relegated to the end, for communication, as defined here, can only be clearly seen within the cultural context of a community. That context should now be at least reasonably clear. Equally clear, however, is the fact that communication's own role in the complicated process of Kothuru's development and present state of mind is imbedded inextricably in the process itself, just as economic development, social change, and political patterns are interwoven. Certain aspects of communication in Kothuru have already been described as they affected or were affected by the changes that have taken place: the army commandant's request for vegetables and milk, the presence of sources of information in the village in the form of friendly government officials as well as visiting dignitaries, although the officials may be sought out and the dignitaries virtually ignored by most of the villagers.

It is clear also that it is almost impossible to chart the flow of any given item of news and say with any amount of confidence that between source and terminant the particular news item went through such and such steps. In the highly diffused pattern of Kothuru's social intercourse it is perhaps even impossible to tell source from terminant at any given point in time.

The villager's memory about the source of news, unless he gets it directly from one of the media, seems to be extremely poor in Kothuru. A series of questions concerning this in the information level part of our general questionnaire worked, we found, only at the "first step" if that step happened to be one of the media. Otherwise, a typical answer was "Oh, somebody told me." Only in a very few cases did respondents name a specific source. In these cases, the source was always the same—a single other person, a man who "reads the newspaper and is very intelligent." The number of acquaintances of such respondents, we found, was exceptional for Kothuru. These respondents seemed to be extremely withdrawn and interacted only with one or two others. Only in such cases was it possible to check the source of news, and these were exceptions which proved the rule: that communication in Kothuru is highly dynamic, traveling through the maze of interpersonal relationships which make up the total community. Communication literally takes the form of the society itself.

The picture of Kothuru's communication pattern is certainly not complete without consideration of its media participation. Even in our sample, which consisted of a far greater proportion of elite than the proportion in the total population, less than 50 percent cited the newspaper as their source of news for one of a series of six items in our information test, and 100 percent acknowledged oral communication as a source. The media must take a back seat in Kothuru, at least for the present.

However, it must also be pointed out that within the national pattern of media consumption (eleven newspapers per 1000 population), Kothuru presents not too bad a picture. Twenty-four copies of newspapers are bought in the village in addition to ten subscriptions directly delivered by mail. Six of these copies are delivered to the Block Development Officer and his staff who live slightly separate from the village and whose newspapers are therefore presumably not shared except by their own families, but twenty-eight copies are shared in Kothuru. From our interviews with newspaper subscribers and with the librarian, we estimated that the average number of readers for each of these 28 copies was seven.

Radio was a poor second to newspapers among the media. There are ten radio sets in Kothuru, including the Panchayat radio. The average number of listeners to news programs was five. As a source of news, then, radio came after oral communication and the newspaper.

Education is popular. In the two schools, there were a total of 315 boys and girls at the time we were in the village (an increase of 50 in one year) and the attendance was "excellent" according to the two teachers we interviewed, one each from the primary school and the high school. But both of them complained that the attendance of girls falls off after primary school, because "their mothers seem to need them at home."

We were also told that there was "enthusiasm" for adult education but no steps had been taken to fill this need.

From the postmaster we found that the amount of mail coming into the village had increased and the number of telegrams had gone up from 14 to 35 in two years.

While no exact records are kept of travel to and from Kothuru, the station master said it had increased by 30 to 40 percent in the preceding three years. He knew of no foreigners who had visited Kothuru, but there were many businessmen from other states of the country who had stopped by. The bus driver whom we talked to also spoke of the significant increase in passengers and consequently of bus services to Kothuru. Even the dozen or so buses which connect Kothuru with Visakhapatnam and a few other towns do not seem to fill the need, and, as indicated above, trucks have been picking up "standing passengers" for a nominal charge.

The librarian of Kothuru, an extremely conscientious worker, gave us the figures on magazine and book reading. These had not shown any great increases during his tenure, but he thought the prospects were good, considering the fact that the library was still comparatively new (one and a half years old) and new books were coming. He said that twenty-four members of the library borrowed books with some regularity; most of them read novels. Of those who use the magazines and newspapers, 30 percent, he said, were below the age of twenty, 50 percent in the twenty to forty-five bracket, and 20 percent were about forty-five. He put the average number of readers in the reading room at thirty-eight per day, as compared with twenty-six the previous year.

There is no movie house in Kothuru, but it was hard to come by a single adult who had not at one time or another seen a movie in one of the towns nearby. Most of them had gone to movies in Visakhapatnam. Over 70 percent of our respondents were fairly regular moviegoers ("about once or twice a month"). This reflected not only their exposure to the movies, but also their travel habits. Over 50 percent of our respondents had traveled beyond Visakhapatnam, some of them to North India, a distance of over 1000 miles.

Kothuru, in more senses than one, is on the move. In this process, it is exposing itself to all kinds of new experiences and new information. The information sources are many—both inside and outside the village. Contacts are many. Economic development is explained by most of the elite respondents in terms of "contact" with outsiders. Only two of our elite respondents specifically mentioned the media as one of the reasons for change in people's habits, whether in dress or eating or thinking.

Kothuru's preoccupation with economic development is reflected in its pace of life and in its information level. More people have heard of the increase in the price of tamarind (a kind of spice) and of life insurance than of Russia exploding the "big bomb" or of a high-level committee visiting the state to inquire into the sharing of waters between Andhra and two adjoining states. Most have not heard of the state chief minister either. It is obvious that they seek certain kinds of information; if certain other kinds of information come to them, they retain what falls in their frame of reference and forget the rest. Those high in information level are the elite and persons in some power positions. To the rest, "general news" is a luxury they cannot afford now. But they do have ways of getting the news they are interested in. Sources are usually readily available within the village. If not, they can obtain the information from the city.

.   .   .

PATHURU

Much of Pathuru's general communication pattern has already been indicated indirectly in describing its economic, social, and political structures. We have seen that communication flows almost entirely horizontally, except for a few intermediaries. Caste groupings (including the Muslims as a distinct group in the social structure), economic disparities, occupational limitations, all lead to the formation of almost distinct peer groups. Communication not only remains within the group, but invariably tends to be highly repetitive. Since little information that is new comes into the village, the old and trivial information is a perennial source from which to draw to fill the vacant evenings.

Several times during our stay in the village, we heard the five-year-old story of Pathuru's experience with the cholera epidemic. It was suspected that the disease was the direct result of *mantras* (religious chantings, very much akin to witchcraft, but not necessarily used for evil purposes) chanted by a small group of Chakalis (washerman caste) early one morning, when they were seen bathing on the banks of the narrow canal skirting the village. Of all people, the local midwife (the present incumbent's predecessor) had reported the chantings. In the transmission of the story, it was no doubt embellished. When cholera struck, the incident was recalled and the Chakalis beaten and exiled by the whole village. The leader of the Chakalis, in relating the story to us, said he had gone to the landlord, who had migrated to Hyderabad with his family during the epidemic, to seek his help. The landlord knew full well that the Chakalis were innocent; also that cholera does not come at the beck and call of a small group of *mantra*-chanters. But he would not intervene. Health units of the government later came and cleaned up the village and the epidemic subsided after taking its toll.

Five years later, the story was recalled in all detail and described over and over again, although the small group of exiled Chakalis had been back in the village for two years and their leader was a highly respected member of the community.

For the people of Pathuru, there are many incidents such as this one; all of them belong to the past and all of them concern the village—either the entire community or specific individuals, like the present vice-president of the Panchayat (village council) who had been sent to jail for six months some years before for stealing the *karanam's* jewelry, and who, while we were there, was accused of having raped one of the women working for him on his fields. These are the stories which keep Pathuru talking after the small oil lamps have been put out soon after dark, for oil is expensive and there is nothing to read anyway, even if one is literate. Little that happens outside the village excites Pathuru.

True, the radio is blaring away at some distance in the main bazaar where the Panchayat office is, but while everyone can *hear* it, only a small group of five or six people are *listening* to it because they are interested in the news and in the rural program. When the music starts, they move away, and the Panchayat office is virtually deserted except for "Oli," the clerk whose duty it is to turn the radio on at a certain time and turn it off two hours later, for otherwise the batteries will run down.

The five or six people who listen to the radio also happen to be avid newspaper readers. Three of them subscribe to newspapers, one Urdu daily and two Telugu dailies, printed in Hyderabad and delivered in Pathuru a day or two later. These young men are also intermediaries. Their interests range from Pathuru to the United Nations, from irrigation to radioactivity. In their own questioning way, they have learned a great deal, although their formal education stopped not later than the seventh or eighth grade. There is also among them the sixty-two-year-old illiterate referred to in the first chapter as Erranna. He has gained all his knowledge from listening alone.

In addition to these active information-collectors (and disseminators) there are others who read the newspaper in Pathuru. But they read quietly and keep the information to themselves. This group includes some of the big landlords, as well as a few literate members of other categories. Their usual reading room is their own home, when they can borrow one of the five copies of newspapers which come into Pathuru. The two copies which are read by the largest number of borrowers belong to the political worker (an Urdu daily) and the cloth merchant (a Telugu daily). The latter's shop is a virtual reading room. We went in a couple of times and sat with the others, reading. Everyone read in silence, replaced the page that he had read, and quietly walked out. We inquired if this was the usual practice. "Doesn't any one talk or discuss the news, after reading it?" "No," answered the merchant. "They read whatever they are interested in and leave. Tomorrow, they will not remember the headline of the main story. I have amused myself with a few little experiments of my own." And he showed us a small stack of headlines he had collected to use in "tests" which he had administered to a few friends. He was basing his conclusion on the result of those tests.

However, in talking to some of the regular readers, we found that they did remember some items. We also found that the respondents of Pathuru seemed relatively more sure than those in Kothuru of their sources of news, perhaps because they move in limited circles. The sources are not too diffused. This was true even in the case of local news. Hence, our original feeling that there were fairly distinct groupings in communication patterns in Pathuru was reinforced.

Movie viewing is surprisingly widespread in Pathuru—especially among the male population. A visit to the city "must include at least one movie," said one of our respondents, a young man who had just got back from Hyderabad after seeing a circus. Originally a group of young men had tried to charter a bus and take their families to the circus. They failed to receive enough support to pay for the bus. So the young men cycled to Hyderabad and came back to describe the thrills. But the thrills of the circus will not make too much of an impression on those who have not seen it, although they will listen politely. Even the word "circus," for which there is no Telugu equivalent, will be forgotten. In the absence of direct and prolonged contact with a new organization or a new word, very little of anything new penetrates into the consciousness of most of Pathuru's residents. "Panchayat" is the farthest most of them can go, for example, in talking about such abstractions as "democracy" or "equality."

Although documentaries are shown in movies, few remember them. The content is as yet outside their frame of reference. While we were there, we were told that a new form of ballot, which was being used in the coming election, was explained in a documentary. Except for the political worker and two other young men, no one remembered it. Apparently, when the feature starts and the story unfolds, the movie viewer of Pathuru is all attention. Until then, he or she is talking to friends or taking care of the children who usually accompany the parents everywhere.

Schooling seems to be, as yet, an "unnecessary" thing for the children of Pathuru. The parents' attitude is reflected in the high number of truants and in the casual approach of the teachers as well. The year before we arrived there were 94 students enrolled; the number had increased to 106 at the time of our stay. On our visits to the school, however, we noticed not only the student absentees, but also the staff absentees. The average attendance, for both staff and students, is less than 75 per cent. The explanation given for this state of affairs is that the landlords, who would take an interest in the school if their own children attended it, do not do so because they send their children to Hyderabad. Pathuru only has a primary school; enrollment is fairly high because primary education is not only free but compulsory. Attendance, however, is not.

The acting headmaster during our stay in the village (the headmaster had been away on leave for over three months and had never been replaced) was twenty years old, and commanded no respect whatsoever, although he was conscientious and took seriously his job of going from house to house to enroll students under the free and compulsory scheme. When we asked one of the landlords about the state of the school and why he did not send his children there, his reply was concise: "How can I send my children to such a poor school?" It was impossible for him to understand that perhaps the school was "poor" because he was taking no interest in it, although he was one of the senior members of the Panchayat. He had left that responsibility to the district inspector of schools who had not visited Pathuru for over a year. The young acting headmaster had to do the best he could, and two days out of every month, on working days, he had to go to Ibrahimpatnam, five miles by cycle, to collect his own and his staff's salaries. On those days, for all the work that went on in the school, it might as well have been closed.

In Pathuru, as in Kothuru, we were told that there was "enthusiasm" for adult education, but no facilities. This enthusiasm was a little hard to believe in, in view of the attitude of most adults toward the education of their children. The few adults who felt differently had already made their own arrangements and learned the three Rs. But they have little to read.

The average number of readers of each copy of a newspaper in Pathuru is six, including the cloth merchant's copy which has the highest readership— ten. The Panchayat office has no newspapers, no magazines, no reading room, only a few posters on the walls explaining the five-year plan, family planning, compost-pit digging, and the like. But since few villagers enter the room, the posters presumably are for the edification of the clerk and the few members of the Panchayat.

The average number of listeners to the Panchayat radio is six. There are three other radios—all battery-operated—in Pathuru, but only one of them is used by anyone other than the immediate family. News is seldom heard, except in the house of the richest landlord, and even there only he listens to it, not even the rest of the family, which consists of his wife and two small children. His other children are in the city in school and college.

The average number of letters arriving daily in the village is four. There is no telephone, and in the memory of the local sub-postmaster, there has never been a telegram delivered in the village. It would have to be delivered by a man coming from Ibrahimpatnam.

Except for the few elite, and a handful of the educated and influential intermediaries like the active political worker, the information level in Pathuru remains low. While contact with the city is widespread, it is not intense, because there is very little business for most people there. Pathuru's image of the world, therefore, is limited. It does not go too far beyond the village in space and not too far either backward or forward in time. Pathuru, for the most part, looks at itself and talks about itself; it does not like what it sees, and talks about that fact a great deal; it has so far not done much to bring about a change.

· · ·

COMMUNICATION PATTERNS
Use of Media

Mass communication facilities in the developed communities, it has been shown repeatedly, are much greater than in the developing communities. Not only can people with a higher economic standard afford to subscribe to newspapers and periodicals and to buy radio sets, but the economic system is geared to meet this demand and provide effective transmitting facilities. Whether the process starts with the demand or the supply is a difficult point to settle, for it can work both ways. We can see, for instance, that the tremendous increase in the number of transistor radio sets in a country like the United States is not entirely the result of demand. Persuasive advertising has succeeded in placing more radio sets in the home than the number that can actually be used. In the developing communities, on the other hand, retarded economic progress has meant low media consumption and poor mass communication facilities. The relationship between *mass* communications and economic development is clear.

However, here we are concerned with communication in all its aspects, media and personal. In the description of the villages and their communication characteristics, both media participation and the patterns of interpersonal communication were referred to. In this total process of information flow, how do Kothuru and Pathuru compare?

Kothuru reads more newspapers, periodicals, and books, listens in larger numbers to the radio, and goes to the movies oftener than Pathuru. While it is true that because of economic development Kothuru can afford to buy more newspapers and so on, attitude differences seem to make the residents of Kothuru more curious in specific areas. These attitudes also help them to increase their knowledge. How else can one explain the large audience for the community radio set?

It is also revealing to note that the only instance of a newspaper being read aloud to a group of illiterates was observed in Kothuru and not in Pathuru despite the latter's slower pace of life and higher illiteracy. The fact that a group of people unable to read themselves have felt the need to expose themselves to the newspaper in almost daily sessions is an indication of Kothuru's attitude which aids its growing media participation.

The reading sessions are held daily in the barber's shop. The barber himself is illiterate. So are many of his friends. But his son has been to school and can read. To the background music of busy scissors, the son reads while the father and his friends listen. Discussions usually follow. There was no such scene in Pathuru. Each one in Pathuru reads in silence; there is no discussion.

The differences between Kothuru and Pathuru are summarized in the tabulation.

USE OF MEDIA*	Kothuru	Pathuru
Copies of newspapers circulating in the village	28	5
Average number of readers of each copy of a newspaper	7	6
Number of radio sets	10	4
Average daily number of listeners to the community radio set		
All programs	30	6
News programs only	5	6

*Because of the small number involved in newspaper reading and radio listening, it was possible to check sources and arrive at average numbers. For movie viewing this was difficult, although it was easy to observe from amount of travel to the city, and the like, that more people in Kothuru watched movies at regular intervals (at least once in six months) than in Pathuru. The figures as obtained from our respondents were 73 per cent and 60 per cent, respectively. But it seems likely that the difference is even higher than that because of the higher amount of travel on the part of Kothuru's non-elite as compared with Pathuru's.

Mobility

Mobility, as a factor in communication, enables a person not only to observe things outside his own community but also to interact with people who have different habits and, in some cases, speak other languages. This experience of exposing oneself to a wider area of human activity as well as interacting with people other than those whom one knows intimately leads to an increase in knowledge and a widening of horizons.

The cumulative effect of increasing mobility, of an exposure to attractive opportunities elsewhere, of the feedback that comes into the community from those who have moved or temporarily accepted jobs in a nearby city, is a general feeling of self-confidence. Once total dependence on family and immediate community is given up, one is led by stages—and very slow stages—to independent entrepreneurship. The stage of reliance on government may even be bypassed, as Kothuru seems to have done.

We have seen how the military commandant's need for certain agricultural commodities changed Kothuru's farming habits. The visits made to the city by some of Kothuru's residents in the course of this interaction, and in meeting other needs, soon brought to their attention the opportunities available in the Visakhapatnam harbor. It took a small group of enterprising young men to start the process. Today almost 250 workers in the city's harbor hail from Kothuru. They work there for six months in the year. For the other six months, as we have already seen, they come back to Kothuru, stay with their families, help in farming on their own land. Economically, they are much better off than if they merely worked on their farms eking out a meager living. In addition, they have played a major role in transforming the thinking processes of most of Kothuru's older residents.

Pathuru has tried this experiment too. Unfortunately, however, it has failed—at least for the time being. A small group of young laborers had heard somewhere that there were good opportunities for jobs in the cities, especially in the industrial city of Bombay. They collected what little money they could and left. Little had they realized that one does not just walk into a mill and get a job; nor did they realize that a totally different language was spoken in Bombay and that a big, busy, sprawling city like this has little time to take care of the personal difficulties of a group of villagers from Pathuru. They traveled about 1000 miles to be disillusioned and disheartened. (One wonders why they went that far instead of seeking jobs in Hyderabad.) Letters have come back to Pathuru from most of these young men asking for money for the train fare back home. All of Pathuru knows this and the pathetic letters from these pioneers have been enough to convince the villagers, except the few well educated, that the city is bad and that the only place for them is home—i.e., Pathuru.

At least to some extent this might explain why so few of our respondents from Pathuru had traveled beyond Hyderabad, while so many of the Kothuru residents had traveled beyond Visakhapatnam. If we treat as highly mobile those who had traveled beyond the nearest city, Kothuru's percentage in this category, as judged from our sample, was 62.5 and Pathuru's 15. Few of even the elite of Pathuru had ventured beyond Hyderabad but several of our respondents in Kothuru had gone as far as Delhi. Three of them, who were by no means richer than some of Pathuru's leading citizens, had only recently completed an all-India tour on an attractive railway scheme worked out by the Indian Railways to encourage the public to "see your country." It is doubtful if anyone in Pathuru had even heard of the scheme.

Today many of Kothuru's residents are sending their children to high schools and technical schools in Visakhapatnam and elsewhere; the farthest that most of Pathuru's older children go is to Ibrahimpatnam, five miles away. The only exceptions are the sons of two of Pathuru's richest landlords. They are studying in Hyderabad and living in their parents' "city house," complete with servants.

The women of Pathuru summarize most adequately the over-all attitude: "Oh, if we send our children to the big city, we don't know who will see them and what they will do to them!" Mobility, under these conditions, is hard. Such an attitude doesn't necessarily keep *everyone* home; but then it does not encourage enough people to "see your country," either.

Interpersonal Communication

With increasing use of the media, greater travel, and a faster pace of life, a developing community generally has less time to spend in interpersonal communication. At the same time, the interpersonal communication that does take place is far less restricted than that in a traditional community.

In the early stages of development the elite and the mass of the people are separated by a wide gap, not only in terms of their material resources, but in their knowledge and attitudes in the social and political spheres. The elite tend to be more knowledgeable, cosmopolitan, and politically informed. The mass, on the other hand, are almost totally illiterate, tradition-bound, and seemingly impervious to change. Whereas the elite may have traveled and even been educated in institutions of higher learning, and have developed the capacity to think and act in ways other than what their fathers and grandfathers did, the mass's only yardstick is the past. While the mass, generally, seek the security of the past, the elite seek the promise of the future and are prepared for a policy of change even if they are not agreed among themselves about what shape such change ought to take.

Thus in thought and action, in attitudes and behavior, the elite are separated from the mass. Change is initiated by the few, understood by the few, and even used by the few—until the natural process of communication takes these ideas of the few to the many and whatever benefits may accrue slowly begin to be shared. Communication must bridge this gulf before a whole community can develop evenly. And this process has to work in such a way that the elite come closer to the mass and vice versa.

Kothuru and Pathuru show some of these differences between the developed community and the traditional. The difference in the *amount* of interpersonal communication is not too great. What is striking is the *pattern*.

The time spent in interpersonal communication is greater in Pathuru, where the pace of life is much slower, the channels of communication fewer, and travel and entertainment are acutely limited. The residents of Pathuru, therefore, spend a great deal of time sitting in groups and talking, especially after dusk. There is little movement in the dark village square, lit only by a small oil lamp burning inside the Panchayat office and another small lamp in the teashop. About six people sit in the square for an hour or so listening to the Panchayat radio. A little after 7:00 P.M. the square is virtually deserted. Within the village, small groups of people sit on verandas if the evening is warm, or just inside the main door if it is cool outside. Since everyone goes to bed early, by about 7:30, the talking does not last late. However, in the fields the next day, the same topic can be taken up and continued.

Kothuru's pattern of communication differs from this. There is less time for long chats. But, since mobility is high, the contacts are spread over a wider area, both in the main part of the village and at the "junction." People spend less time talking, but talk to more people and a greater variety of individuals during any single day. Pathuru's communication is limited to specific groups, whereas Kothuru's is much freer. This greater diffusion enables Kothuru to get more information from more sources even through interpersonal communication than Pathuru is able to achieve despite the amount of time it spends talking.

Another important difference lies in the interaction between the elite and the mass. Kothuru's elite move far more easily and readily in the village, and interact more with the ordinary people; the latter feel free to stop and talk to the landlord or the Panchayat president or even a government official. In Pathuru, however, not only do the elite shut themselves up, but on the few occasions when they do walk in the village, the ordinary people move aside as though they have no right to be walking on the same road as the "big man."

How do the elite respondents themselves feel about this? Do they really talk to more people now than they used to? Yes, said every elite respondent in Kothuru. Only 50 percent of the elite respondents believed this to be the case in Pathuru. One of them, a younger member of the elite, was quite candid about it: "These days, one has to. We have to seek their vote sometimes." Among those who did not think they talked to more people than at an earlier time, two replies were interesting. One said, "Why should we talk to those illiterates? They will not understand us anyway." Another said: "We don't have to—not even for elections. They have to vote for us. We have been their leaders since their grandfathers' time."

The elite—mass interaction will be referred to later in this chapter. Suffice now to note that Kothuru's residents talk more freely among themselves irrespective of socioeconomic differences than Pathuru's. Hence, the sources of information are wider in Kothuru whether one takes only the media into consideration or adds to them the various ways in which information can flow through human interaction—at home, at work, on the road, in the restaurant, and in buses.

Source of News

We have seen that Kothuru's media participation is higher than Pathuru's. But to what extent does Kothuru rely on the media as sources of news? How does it compare with Pathuru? Does a developing community show a greater reliance on the media as compared with the traditional?

The distinction here between the two villages is not as clear-cut as in interpersonal communication. Both the villages still rely very heavily on oral communication. The media play a minor role as sources of *direct* information, even for those who can read. When we take the percentage of illiteracy in both villages into consideration, we can, of course, understand why the media play a minor role. But when we find that even the literate do not often cite the media as sources of news, we have to seek a full explanation elsewhere.

Economic conditions are certainly one reason. Not all literates can afford to buy, say, a newspaper. Many borrow, but borrowing has its limitations. The library copies are available, but when the library is open, most people are at work. Also, since political news is not of much interest to the typical villager, he finds the newspaper rather dull.

As for the radio, news programs are broadcast at a specific time in the evening. The one program in the regional language lasts fifteen minutes. Even this is found to be unintelligible to many because of its "high-class" Telugu.

Both the radio and the newspaper concentrate heavily on national news. State news comes second and local news is almost totally absent unless it is something really big, in which case the chances are that most people have already heard about it.

One other important reason for the lack of a clear-cut distinction in our findings between Kothuru and Pathuru in the role of the media as sources of information is that the questions in the information part of our question-naire which specifically asked for the source of each of several items failed to elicit clear responses. Regular readers of newspapers or listeners to the radio named their source, but the casual reader more often than not merely said he had "heard it somewhere." To the extent that Kothuru had more readers and listeners, it stood slightly higher than Pathuru in the number of times the media were cited as primary sources. In actual fact the difference may be bigger, but this requires further study with more refined tools.

Information Level

When it came to information level, however, the difference between Kothuru and Pathuru was quite clear, both in the responses to questions in casual conversation about such matters as cost of living in the city as compared with the village, bus fares, wages in industry and agriculture, price of commodities. Kothuru had ready knowledge; Pathuru was either incapable of thinking in such terms or fumbled for answers and then made some vague guesses. Even an illiterate woman worker in a rice mill in Kothuru could tell us how much quarry labor was paid for how many hours of work. Kothuru's residents are making decisions in a competitive money economy, and information about such things as wage levels is extremely important if they are to make the right decision.

Kothuru's information level then was high in areas of immediate interest to it. This is true, perhaps, the world over. But Pathuru's backwardness shows up clearly in this regard. Even on the one topic which seems to be dearest to its heart—land—it had little factual information, only a host of baseless opinions or fond hopes. This, of course, refers to the mass of the people. The elite, both in Pathuru and Kothuru, displayed a fairly high knowledge of general news. The large majority of people in both villages were not interested in state, national, or international news.

The communication patterns in the two villages are perhaps most clearly shown by the fact that while every single person in our Kothuru sample had heard of the local news item we used in the questionnaire, almost 30 percent of our respondents in Pathuru had not. In both the villages, the item referred to a natural phenomenon which had been given a religious or mystical significance by the villagers. In Kothuru it was lightning which had struck a nearby hill and created what seemed like a road. The villagers' story was that one of their most popular deities had decided to move from his present abode in a city far from the village to the top of the hill, and that the road was his work. The news first came from a nearby village. In Pathuru, the local item concerned a mammoth ceremony organized by priests and attended by over a thousand people from surrounding villages.

Its purpose was to prevent by prayer the end of the world which the meeting of eight planets in the skies supposedly foreshadowed. The ceremony was held in a nearby village and was attended by priests from Pathuru.

In both villages, therefore, the news had to travel by word of mouth from a nearby village, enter the village, and there be disseminated to the rest of the village. In Kothuru it traveled much faster and was disseminated more widely than in Pathuru. In the context of Pathuru's social structure and the nature of its interpersonal communication patterns, the fact that the local news item was not carried to some segments in the village is understandable. So is the result in Kothuru where interpersonal communication is highly diffused, both vertically and horizontally.

State news apparently evokes little interest in either village. National news does slightly better and international news was recalled by a considerably larger number in Kothuru, though many of the villagers there could not follow the scientific aspect of the testing of the atomic bomb (the effects of radioactivity). Response on the economic item on our questionnaire (knowledge of life insurance) was second only to the local item in both villages, though the difference between them was still quite striking. Over 80 percent of our respondents in Kothuru knew reasonably well the details of life insurance; in Pathuru, only 50 percent.

.   .   .

Ability to Cope with New Ideas and Things

On the basis of such varied measure as information level, media participation, and interpersonal communication, it was possible to gauge the difference between Pathuru and Kothuru in desire or willingness to learn about new things and to grapple with new ideas, whether these pertained mainly to jobs and consumer goods or to topics ranging from radioactivity to fertilizer, from democracy to the local Panchayat.

While Kothuru's residents interacted with a wide range of people of all occupations and socioeconomic levels, talked about a great number of things, listened with interest to conversation on a wide vareity of subjects, and inquired intelligently into some aspects of subjects they were not familiar with, Pathuru's residents were more inclined to talk than to listen, to confine this talk to small groups (not necessarily based on caste, but largely in predictable cliques) and to a narrow range of topics, especially land and village gossip. In prolonged conversations with respondents of both villages, we learned far more about Pathuru in the first few days than about Kothuru in the first few weeks. This was because Pathuru's residents were more inclined to talk about their village and their grievances than Kothuru's.

The latter were more keen on asking questions and clarifying certain thoughts which may have occurred to them during their talks with us. This was also true of their general attitude in conversations with the wide variety of people they interacted with, whether in their work situation or in social relationships.

. . .

Attitude toward the Future

Kothuru has widened its horizons, not only spatially but temporally. It is able to separate the past, the present, and the future and to think in these terms. "If it was good enough for my grandfather, it's good enough for me" is an indication of traditionalism. Unless one has the ability to look into the future by sizing up the present in relation to the past, the growth potential is bound to be limited.

A second aspect of this is empathy. Variously defined by various people, empathy is essentially an ability to put oneself in another's shoes. Used in the figurative sense, it becomes an aspect of "future orientation," for it involves both time and space. Only if a person believes that he too can become the village headman some day can he talk as though he were already wearing the incumbent's shoes. This sense of potential gives one confidence to plan for the future. One who cannot imagine himself in the headman's shoes will probably remain the son of his father, the village blacksmith.

Needless to say, if one has not heard of the office of chief minister he can hardly be expected to put himself in that dignitary's shoes. The basic difference in knowledge and in perception of change which separates Kothuru and Pathuru automatically separates them in their "future orientation" and in their ability to empathize.

"Future orientation" as a phrase can be interpreted in at least two ways. It can stand for the ability of an individual to project and to plan for the future. It can also stand for the attitude an individual shows in his thoughts and actions which indicates some optimism or pessimism about the future. Whatever plans he may make or whatever approaches he uses to his problems will depend importantly on his ability to project as well as on the information he has on which to base his projection.

Questions designed to elicit answers ranging from reactions to changes in the village to comments on the exact nature of a respondent's plans for the future (for himself, his sons, and his daughters) helped us judge Kothuru's and Pathuru's attitudes in this regard.

For example, Bashir Ahmed of Pathuru, who says he is looking for some way of borrowing money to expand his little cycle shop, is showing potential for entrepreneurship as well as an optimism that does not seem to exist in Akkayya, a farmer of the same village who says, "How can I save any money? The little I can will soon be used for my daughter's marriage." Or a question like "What are you planning for yourself?" put to Sathyanna of Kothuru brings the reply, "What can I plan for myself? I will just do my work and continue to live as I am living—God willing." Ranga Rao, the young Kothuru goldsmith, however, answers the same question differently. "I am hoping to study some more if there is some way of finding a school where one does not have to pay fees, or if I can get a scholarship." As an artisan he is unhappy, though skillful at his work.

Generally, though with individual exceptions as noted above, the resident of Kothuru are looking forward to a future with confidence and planning for it, each in his own way, whereas those of Pathuru are not clear about their future. Hence whatever planning the latter do is for the immediately foreseeable "emergencies" such as a daughter's marriage.

This attitude in Pathuru is understandable, because the villagers are not quite clear even about the changes that have already taken place. They lack the information sources which can explain things to them. Under such conditions, projection into a future is almost impossible. Most of Pathuru's residents are bewildered and their only way out seems to be to cling to the past and do as their fathers did—buy a little gold whenever possible and hide it in a niche in the wall. It can be taken and sold when need arises.

The typical individual in Kothuru, on the other hand, spends most of the money he earns, saves a little in the post office, or even goes so far as to invest in a life insurance policy. Even if he does not save a great deal, the confidence he has that he will find work to do makes him less resigned than the residents of Pathuru. In projecting himself into a future, the Kothuru resident seeks information on avenues available to him; the Pathuru resident is resigned to his traditional vocation as well as his traditional poverty, and cannot think of seeking information.

Ability to Empathize

This same combination of knowledge and confidence in the future also makes the Kothuru resident more empathic. Literate or illiterate, every person who was fairly well informed and displayed confidence in the future also showed himself to be empathic.

In attempting to find out to what extent empathy was present among the residents of the two villages, we did not intend to try to isolate the factors that help a person develop this capacity. However, as the question-naires were being administered and informal interaction was taking place between investigator and respondents, it became obvious that several factors besides information or knowledge were involved in empathy. Our tools and time did not permit us to go deeper into this but it was interesting to note that several illiterates displayed a remarkable capacity to empathize, all the way from the village level to the national level.

There were three levels at which we tested our respondents' ability to empathize: the village, the state, and the nation. In each case, the respondent was to put himself in the shoes of the head of the administration. The tabulation shows the results of our inquiry.

NUMBER REACHING EACH LEVEL OF EMPATHY

	Kothuru	Pathuru
First level (village)	4	13
Second level (state)	3	0
Third level (national)	26	18
No empathy	7	9

Comparison of these figures with those on information level confirms our conclusion that something besides knowledge is involved in empathy. Among the additional factors would seem to be positive attitudes, especially those pertaining to "future orientation" and satisfaction with life in the village; such attitudes mean that the individual is conscious of his ability to improve himself and that he has confidence that the future will be brighter than the present. There were a few among our respondents who were almost aggressive in their responses to the questions on empathy and highly critical of the present. These disgruntled persons, however, had tremendous confidence that they would "set things right." This intense feeling of being masters of their own destiny certainly carried them into the simulated role of prime minister of India without any difficulty.

One of them was Janganna, an illiterate well-digger of Pathuru, who was perhaps the most disgruntled man in the village. He was also ill informed and an active carrier of rumor—especially bits of "news" which reflected badly on the village leaders' ability to spend community money impartially. Despite the handicap of lack of knowledge, Janganna fit himself into the prime minister' shoes readily and spoke with great eloquence on how the head of the country should govern so that the poor could eat and live.

On the other hand, the educated *karanam* of Pathuru could not even reach the second level—that of the chief minister of the state. His view of the future was bleak, his view of the present one of utter disgust at the "stupid masses" aspiring to things they did not deserve. He looked at the past with nostalgia. "Those were wonderful days!"

The most striking difference between Kothuru and Pathuru in responses to the empathy questions was that Kothuru's respondents were better able to suggest specific action programs while Pathuru's respondents talked in generalities. Where a Kothuru resident might say that more industry should be brought into the village, his counterpart in Pathuru would suggest that the "people's welfare" should be taken care of. Kothuru villagers suggested education, irrigation, and so on. Only a few in Pathuru referred to the need for electricity and for education. These were, in most cases, the elite.

It was not surprising that more respondents in Kothuru than in Pathuru could reach the third level. Most of them were conscious of change, more were literate and knowledgeable, more were satisfied with their own economic condition and looked forward to better things. They were also confident that they could do better because they knew what to do and where to go for information on things they were unsure of. Pathuru was less blessed with all these attitudes and facilities.

In Kothuru the elite's confidence has rubbed off on the mass, thanks to greater interpersonal contacts between the two; in Pathuru even the elite, though empathic, lacked the confidence necessary to look forward to a future with hope, and the mass, in the absence of any close contact with the elite, could not even share the knowledge that the elite possessed and which might have given them some hope. For the mass are more likely to become hopeful with even a slight increase in income or opportunity than the elite to whom such slight increases may mean little, for they are more concerned with guarding what they have, whether it is material wealth or political power or social status.

.   .   .

The following list, which emerged from the field work in Kothuru and Pathuru, may help in better conceptualizing the process. It must be remembered that people can achieve power in any sphere—economic, political, or social. Everyone finds that information is important and most people seek it for specific purposes. But only those who are aspiring for power positions, or actively engaged in retaining and enlarging the power they have, become "senders" as well as "receivers" of information.

Information Seekers

Those who are expected to know: traditional village leaders, caste heads, teachers, etc. (usually receivers)

Those who desire (or need) some material things such as land, work, tools (some receivers, some senders)

Those who are ambitious for political power (receivers-senders), economic power (receivers), social status (receivers-senders)

The traditional outcasts who want to belong and be accepted (receivers-senders)

Information Indifferents

The fatalist: the person who has no incentive whatsoever to better himself, even if he does not have enough to live on

The passively contented: the person who has enough to live on and has no further desires

The superior being who "knows all": the rich man who lives a closeted life and does not mix with the "stupid masses" at any level, except when approached as "the master"

Information Carriers

Those whose status is threatened, usually older caste and village heads (receivers-senders)

Those who have accepted change, usually the friendly elite (receivers-senders)

The young educated villagers who identify themselves with the mass, usually those who are crusaders for equality of opportunity (receivers-senders)

Rumor-Mongers

The illiterate and ill-informed "rebels"—the most dangerous element in the community, they are conscious of some change but do not understand it; they seek some personal gain (free land, etc.) without making any effort (receivers-senders)

In the four categories into which the total community is divided on the basis of whatever primary role individuals play in the information-flow process, clearly the "information carriers" are the most important. They are already very much part of the village; most people know them by name and by sight. Also, they already command respect—the friendly elite, because they are friendly and interact with the mass; the older caste head, because he is the caste head and has been caste head for some time, although some younger caste member is now trying to oust him; the young educated villager because he is educated and belongs to a "good family" (otherwise he would not have been able to get an education) and yet identifies himself with the "ordinary people" of the village.

It is only by living in the village that these people can be identified, but the length of stay need not be long. It would be easy to see, for instance, that the village Panchayat vice-president, a member of the elite, walks around the village and talks to everybody; that the young landlord, N. Reddy, sits in the bazaar at the teashop and talks to the grocer, the Harijan worker, and the Panchayat vice-president. We have identified at least two elite members who are friendly and who interact with people at all levels in the socioeconomic hierarchy, although their own information level may be low, especially the vice-president's. But if he is given information, he will carry it to others; so will Reddy.

Then we see Erranna, the caste head of the Gaondlas, who is seeking information actively and talking to all the young, educated newspaper readers. His own information level is high and he is respected in the village by people of all ages. We find that he is fighting back a challenge to his leadership by informing himself and passing information on to the rest of his caste members so as to retain his leadership as well as to improve the economic condition of his caste. It is easy to get into a conversation with Erranna because he is articulate and jovial.

A newspaper reader in a village is the easiest person to identify. He usually reads in the open where everyone can see him, or he carries the paper with him wherever he goes. It is almost a status symbol. If such a person is young and carries the newspaper with him, he is usually an information carrier. All we need to confirm this is to see whether others approach him with ease. If they do, we have identified the politically conscious villager who probably already has some wealth but freely associates with the mass. In Pathuru we find that A. Reddy and Suryam are two such men, both well-to-do farmers, young and educated. On the other hand, G. Reddy reads the newspaper, in his little shop, but few approach him unless they go into the shop on business. He reads in the open only because he has to keep his shop open.

We have, therefore, been able to identify several persons fairly easily as information carriers. If we stay to listen to the radio in the evening, we will find that all these people are there—and few others. We are now doubly sure.

If we now take a look at the list again, we find that in the category of "information seekers" we have some who are also receivers-senders. These are harder to identify, but if one is prepared to spend a longer time in the village, it can be done. Erranna's challenger, Naranna, one can see, is seeking political power and is an active communicator. So is the Chakali Jiddanna, who is well on his way toward regaining the high social status which he had lost several years before during the cholera epidemic when he was expelled from the village. The "outcast" Sitanna is also fairly easily identifiable. He has learned to read and write and keeps himself informed. He passes on information to his group which lives in the shacks at the edge of the village.

.   .   .

Society, it may be said, is communication. In this particular study, two comparable communities have been investigated. From this has emerged a picture of the communication process and its relationship to development in the three broad areas of economic, social, and political change. The changes in these three areas, it has been noted, have affected the communication process; so too has the communication process affected development in all these areas. But it is now possible, with the total picture of the dynamics of change before us, to bring into sharper focus the role of communication.

. . .

We may now attempt to sum up these relationships of development to communication in a traditional undeveloped village by drawing a possible model.

Communication, coming from outside, triggers change in a hitherto self-sufficient, closed economy. The information conveyed, if it is of a kind that indicates an economic or political opportunity, is first seized upon by one or more members of the elite. Communication, at this stage, still flows only horizontally in a strictly stratified society. Gradually, however, by a process of very slow diffusion through intermediaries who have access to the elite as well as to the mass of the people, it filters through to the lower echelons. If the communication is of a kind that fits into the frame of reference of the mass (e.g., land), certain ego-centered desires for economic betterment are activated. To what extent avenues are present for the effective channeling of these desires and their fulfillment depends on other factors in the community. Significant among these is the presence or absence of "dependable" and "disinterested" information sources, for any move made by the mass to act upon the information as originally received through the intermediaries may, at first, be killed by the elite in a desire to retain their political and economic power. They will do so either by belittling the importance of the original communication or by exaggerating the dangers of its possible effects, thereby arguing for the status quo.

A stress situation, however, has been created by the incoming communication. At least a few of the more adventurous people in the community will seek out more information, disregarding the advice of their elders who would rather "settle for security" under the all-knowing and powerful protection of the "big men" (the traditional elite). But if information sources are available for the young "renegades," change will occur fairly quickly, despite opposition from the elite as well as from the mass of the tradition-bound community. The time this change will take depends on the availability of "neutral" sources of information, whether they are visiting government officials, passing salesmen, or a publicity van of the state information wing.

If such sources are available and the communication channels are open, change takes place *in the same direction* for the mass as well as the elite (for both the elite and the mass will use the information), but, if not, change will take place *in opposite directions* (the elite will use it and better themselves and the gap between them and the mass grows wider). A by-product of the latter type of change is growing frustration and internal jealousies, leading eventually either to a fatalistic resignation out of sheer exhaustion or to a violent eruption.

In the "model" proposed, communication creates the stress by creating an awareness of the possibility of change and some of the possible rewards; and it is communication again which will provide the necessary information to release the tensions. If, however, we start earlier in time, for the purpose of building the model, other factors elsewhere will impinge upon the origin of the original communication itself. These may include decisions taken at some distant administrative center (e.g., land redistribution plans made by the state government), the transport facilities available for someone to travel to the village or from the village to the metropolis, the telecommunication network, the policies of the political regime, economic conditions (production of goods, etc.)—even on occasion such a mundane factor as fertilizer, which may be required for the village farmer to take the action desired of him.

However, it must be noted that the model is for the "hitherto isolated traditional village" and that it is specifically drawn from a communications orientation. Even in pointing out the "other factors," the relationship between communication and development is stressed. The model indicates the importance of the channels of communication in carrying the desires of those outside to those on the inside and the need for these channels to be kept open for smooth and early development. The feedback concept, it will readily be seen, is implied in the open channels. For demand and supply in the economic field interact within a communication system which carries messages back and forth.

If the "model" is now carried forward in time, the interaction will be even more apparent, both for the growth of the economic system itself and for the growth of the communication system. Their interdependence will also become clearer.

Once the needs are created and the ways for fulfillment of the needs shown, first the few and later the many will enter the economic field as active participants in an exchange of goods and services. Opportunities not only within the village but outside are taken advantage of. A developing money economy will make it necessary for new knowledge to be acquired both for immediate use and for safety (saving) and future use. Demand for items will create the supply and knowledge of supply will activate more desires. As jobs are sought and a whole new social process is introduced in a class- or castebound society, new roles bring their own adaptive processes, especially agricultural and mechanical skills. The information that is exchanged in interpersonal situations in the early stages is gradually extended to the media-oriented, for with economic development and a growing money economy the media, as part of economic growth, gain their own consumers as a result of increasing literacy and new knowledge and new desires, imparting in their turn more information on investment as well as consumption. The process has, by now, become so cumulative that it would be impossible to separate cause from effect; it also becomes impossible to talk of communication, economics, politics, or social changes as disparate and isolable factors in the total developmental process. Each aids the other and each, in turn, is aided by the other.

Communication, however, remains an essential link and the purpose of the "model" is to bring it into sharper focus in the context of the developmental process.

LAWRENCE H. FUCHS

In the Philippines, during the first two years of the Peace Corps program, it was discovered that volunteers usually had to accept Filipinos as persons for what they were before being able to induce changes in values or skills. Acceptance of Filipinos as persons, including their resistance to change, had to be genuine and nonmanipulative to be a pre-condition of effective change by them.

This discovery is not surprising since Filipino society, like those of other developing nations, is person-centered and not task-oriented. Whereas volunteers came to the Philippines to do a job, they found they were wanted in the barrios primarily as persons. Whereas volunteers came to change Filipinos, they found that a willingness to accept persons to the point of risking change for themselves was often the prelude to effective work.

These conclusions, which will be extended and modified later, are not necessarily valid for other Peace Corps or technical aid programs. Although they reinforce a growing but still small body of theoretical and empirical work on the relationship of acceptance of persons to basic value and personality change . . . , they should be viewed in the special context of the first two years of the Peace Corps program in the Philippines.

DISTINCTIVE FEATURES OF PHILIPPINES PEACE CORPS

One unusual aspect of the Peace Corps in the Philippines was its size. For nearly the entire first year of Peace Corps overseas operations, about one-third to one-fourth of all volunteers in the world served in the Philippines. Another important distinctive feature was the extent to which volunteers were scattered over more than a dozen islands in the archipelago. At the time I left the country, 630 volunteers were working in nearly 400

Daniel Lerner and Wilbur Schramm, eds., *Communication and Change in the Developing Countries* (Honolulu: East-West Center Press, 1967), pp. 236–278.

locations, many in remote villages more than 12 hours by bus or boat from the nearest Peace Corps household. A third unusual characteristic was that about 500 volunteers were assigned to jobs as Educational Aides, a title and a function which had never existed before. Volunteers were to assist elementary school teachers in English and science and serve as all-purpose community resources in their villages (barrios).

There were three smaller programs. A group of about 40 volunteers worked in central high schools as teachers and co-teachers of science. Approximately 30 worked in the normal schools and universities as utility teachers; and a group of 22 volunteers assisted Filipino barrio community development workers on the island of Mindanao, but the elementary school program dwarfed the others and to a considerable extent was seen by Filipinos and Americans as the Peace Corps in the Philippines. It is about that program that I write now.

.   .   .

THE SEVEN STAGES OF COPING: ACCEPTANCE AND CONCOMITANT CHANGE

Most volunteers, including those in the first group which had received the least effective training and field support, and who were guinea pigs in the development of the program, conscientiously persisted in trying to contribute to its over-all objectives. This process, for most volunteers, appears to have involved seven stages of reaction to and interaction with Filipinos. These stages, which tended to merge into one another, did not always appear in the same sequence; nor were they of the same duration. But the seven phases of coping, which can be called phases of acceptance and concomitant change, usually emerged as follows:

1. The volunteer was curious and waited for signals as to what he should do.
2. He became impatient with the failure of Filipinos to give clear clues and developed a strong desire to accomplish something.
3. He started projects in school and community, sometimes with apparent success, often with failure, and began to realize how deep are the problems inherent in fundamental change.
4. He discovered that Filipinos might simulate change to please him but that nothing had really changed.
5. He reacted by working harder and by trying to push Filipinos to accomplish things his way.
6. He felt depleted and defeated in the realization that pushing did not result in real change.

7. He began to accept and enjoy individual Filipinos for what they were in an almost unconscious recognition that any change in skills and abilities depended on changes in values, and that such shifts could not be effected by action or words except through mutually accepting relationships.

Progression through these stages was often halting, and some volunteers, who mistook simulated change by Filipinos for real change, never passed stage three. There were steps backward as well as leaps forward, and for some, the fifth and sixth stages were skipped entirely.

THE PROCESS OF ACCEPTANCE: REACHING STAGE SEVEN

From the beginning, most volunteers welcomed and enjoyed the children who came to their homes in the afternoons and evenings, played the guitar, usually talked aimlessly, but sometimes discussed poetry or geography. After six or seven months, most volunteers became more patient and accepting of individual Filipinos. Some volunteers began to report fruitful exchanges between themselves and Filipinos at snack time or even during siesta. One girl wrote that after conducting teachers' classes in English teaching methods in four different schools each day, the teachers would bring out a snack to be eaten during 20-minute sessions at which time she had more worthwhile discussions about education than in the formal classroom situation. Not just teachers, but household helpers, neighbors, or particular children became enjoyable friends.

Another girl wrote that her first relationships with teachers were "a dismal failure. I was always trying too hard to make them change the way they taught, [but] they were interested in making a place for me in the school so that I could feel confortable. . . . I tried to verbalize my frustrations to them, but they only thought that they had done something wrong. I got fed twice a day instead of once; they brought me more presents and became more convinced of the great sacrifice I was making. . . ." This girl soon accepted individuals for what they were and could later write of another teacher, "I affected her life, because she affected mine . . . we wanted to experience each other."

Another girl summed up the subjective and personalized nature of Filipino relationships when she wrote that, "The *only* way that progress can be made by Peace Corps volunteers in the schools, communities, or with individuals is to first be appreciated as an individual." Volunteers could relax in accepting Filipinos in the seventh stage in the knowledge that they had not betrayed their mission to get a job done because getting the job done depended on friendships. "I have learned to relax," wrote a volunteer. "I have learned to accept things as they come." It was more comfortable to be accepting. Another volunteer, who admitted that he wanted to accomplish too much at first, "began to work with the situation as it was and I found that I did not have any worries about satisfaction and was more steady in my work. I think it amounted to forcing myself not to pass judgment on certain things here. . . ." Increasingly it seemed, as another volunteer put it, that by "slowly accepting things Filipino on their own merits . . . one really starts to work."

The process of becoming more accepting was slow, irregular, and uncertain. Volunteers did not say to themselves, "Now, I will become accepting." The volunteer who wrote that he had learned to relax also told of his frustration at meeting the same mistaken conceptions in the same individuals month after month. At times he relaxed and accepted what at other times had seemed intolerable. The process was difficult not just because volunteers had come to do a specific job but because so many things seemed to need doing. As one of them wrote, "The educational problems of the Philippines cry for a solution, [but] other things cry out louder. Bloated stomachs and paper-thin arms . . . nutritional and agricultural needs. . . ." It wasn't long before he found genuine enjoyment in laughing, playing, and accepting the children. He relaxed, and as he puts it, "We began to learn things more quickly." Accepting meant relaxing and relaxing meant volunteers could more easily meet the delays, crowded or late buses, disappointments at the market, endless questions and curiosity, and incessant demands for attendance at meriendas and fiestas. It meant shrugging one's shoulder and sighing, *"Bahala na"* when there was no meat at the marketplace or when the rains came again. Acceptance meant warm, rich feelings in relationships as when one volunteer wrote, "There we sat [he and his teachers] on the wharf talking quietly and enjoying each other's company. We didn't talk about peace, war, English, science, or any of the important concerns of great men; we talked about trivial matters, nothing memorable . . . I went to bed with a smile, a contentment. . . ."

He was working with the men teachers at night on a water-sealed toilet campaign for their barrio, but finishing the bowls seemed less important than the relationships with the teachers. "I enjoyed the questions they asked me about America and *Americanos*," he wrote. "After four hours of chatter, Tinong would wake up the store owner and buy Pepsi's and a can of Spam. Things that I would never have drunk or eaten before were delicious to me then. We talked some more, and finally, the teachers would walk me home, because they didn't want the dogs to bite me and because it would have been inhospitable to let me go home alone. Later, I took great pleasure in being able to walk some of these men home and leaving them at their doors."

CASE STUDIES ON THE RELATIONSHIP OF ACCEPTANCE, FRIENDSHIP, AND CHANGE

In reviewing volunteer reports and letters, it has become clear in case after case that the capacity to accept others was the single most important factor in sustaining volunteers *and* enhancing their effectiveness, as a brief review of ten cases will illustrate.

Volunteer A

A male volunteer from Massachusetts ran what appears to have been highly successful in-service training classes on English and science for teachers. He also had effective adult education classes and a successful piggery-poultry project. He seemed to blend into his community almost from the beginning, becoming one of the first volunteers to learn the dialect from his region and use it extensively. He enjoyed serenading at night with the gang from the *sari-sari* store and drank tuba with the older men who, as he put it, "had the pleasure of learning they could drink the American under the proverbial table."

He wrote of his relationships that, "The older generation had their stories of questionable conquests listened to . . . the teachers have had me as a captive guest for their never-ending programs, and may have learned a little through my in-service training on English and science. The municipal officials have helped me in the clean-up campaign, and have had me serve on every committee ever heard of, and [much to my surprise] came through with funds to finance my evening adult education classes."

Volunteer A showed that he was willing to expose his weaknesses in accepting others when he taught his adult education students geography and arithmetic in the local dialect. His vast ignorance of agriculture seemed to help him in his relationships with Filipinos with respect to the piggery-poultry project, as he wrote of the town's people having "the dubious pleasure of watching an American stumble through the establishment of a piggery-poultry project until they teamed up with him so all concerned could learn the value of using new, cleaner, more-improved methods. . . ."

Volunteer B

A boy from Ohio, who had begun living in a fourman household on the island of Panay, later moved to a smaller island 100 kilometers north of the capital city to live with a Filipino family. There, despite amoebic dysentery and bronchitis, he managed an extensive teaching schedule, organized an effective campaign to build outhouses, helped to begin a successful Red Cross blood drive, and conducted an excellent adult education course on health and nutrition.

Unlike Volunteer A, this boy experienced a great deal of anxiety in training and felt extremely competitive and ineffective as long as he lived with other Americans. After he moved to his small island, he wrote, "In many ways, living here has been something of a fight for survival . . . this is true because a foreigner cannot live and work here on his own exclusive terms."

Volunteer B belonged to his community and showed it by borrowing cigarettes at the *sari-sari* store, even going into debt. He drank tuba with the younger boys and he loved the family with whom he lived. Being a member of a "poor rural family, I have been afforded unusually good insights into indigenous ways of thinking and living . . . ," he wrote.

Even when school seemed to be going sour, I gained pleasure in living and being with these people. The family included an elderly couple: X and Y and several nieces and nephews. One of the nieces was Z, a 23 year old girl who became like a sister to me. She would help me hoe my garden, study the dialect, and bring the latest barrio gossip. I would help her pound rice, carry water, and cut wood. Before long we became inseparable and strong bonds of love grew between us . . . this, of course, was not a romantic relationship; nor did either of us wish it to be.

Nearly every evening, X, Y, and I would sit down together, drink tuba, talk and joke . . . our conversations were about three-fifths English and two-fifths Hiligaynon, and we always found something to talk about.

At times I was ill and both Y and Z would be awake all night in case I wanted something. Whenever I had been away for a day or two, my return was always greeted with smiles and a buss from Z. Sometimes Y would inform me that I was acting like a 'blue seal.' [Blue seal refers to the color of the stamp put on imported American cigarettes. For many Filipinos, blue seal is a synonym for *Americano*.] We always got a laugh out of this, and thanks to her perceptiveness, it became easy to keep myself in tune with barrio life.

When I walked through our small barrio, I could always count on people waving, smiling and greeting me. Life on the island is hard; they know it and I learned it. For this reason, I felt that I was sharing something with them . . . the people there knew I liked the place and liked them . . . at times I have never felt more contented and relaxed in my life, and that of greatest importance to me are new bonds of friendship, respect, and love.

B's first two months in the island barrio were spent on a toilet-building project. He is not sure why people cooperated with him and his Filipino co-worker. Perhaps it was to please him; perhaps because they were ashamed to have him do the work. Within two days, another local man started and completed his own toilet. Within five weeks the barrio people built a total of seventeen outhouses with only two shovels, one pick, and one iron bar. The new bamboo and nipa outhouses were used by the people and the barrio had more toilets than any of the nearby island barrios, three of whom sent delegations to ask B's help in similar projects. Most important of all, B did not have to do any of the work on the last sixteen outhouses.

He was less successful in his school work for a long time, but after eight months, while he was in the hospital with amoebic dysentery and bronchitis, feeling "pretty used up," he wrote, "it dawned on me that I would get nowhere beating my head against the wall of existing educational practices . . . changes could possibly be made, but not in the way I was going about it." B began to accept his teachers the way he accepted his family and discovered that his work in school went much more satisfactorily.

Volunteer C

With the cooperation of a shop teacher and the science teacher, this male volunteer from Iowa helped to build and equip a science room, revise the science curriculum in his school, and stimulate more effective science teaching in his district. Like the others, he genuinely enjoyed people, calling his work "a new type of work, waiting sometimes instead of working, sometimes leading, sometimes at the sidelines, sometimes shoulder to shoulder."

Admitting that "it's hardest to know when to do which," he spent considerable time relating to people by attending barrio council meetings, PTA meetings, graduations, teacher's meetings, bull sessions, stags, and social and political functions. "I feel that with a close enough attachment to people, through respect, friendship, and personal commitment, I can generate within myself a wholehearted effort to do my very best," wrote C.

Like A and B, he not only enjoyed people, but had a great deal of faith in them. After one year in the barrio he wrote that although his faith had been shaken briefly, "I have stronger than ever the belief that people can do things they set out to do, given sufficient reason and feeling that positive value will result from change."

C's success with the shop teacher was all the more remarkable because he had been notorious for failing to contribute time and talent to school improvement projects in the past. But working with C, he became unusually productive and extremely proud of his accomplishments which included tables, a sink, blackboard frames, a bookshelf, science and other teaching aids. As for C, his friendship with the shop teacher became at least as important to him in the end as building the science room itself.

Volunteer D

A male volunteer from South Carolina, D was as much admired by Filipinos and volunteers as any volunteer in the project. Almost from the first, he accepted people for what they were, learned the dialect, made friends, and seemed to enjoy that more than anything else. After two years, he wrote, "I consistently believed and followed a life based on getting away from all identity or entanglement with the Peace Corps. My reasons were . . . to figure out a little bit about what was going on in the Philippines, to see what was really significant in my own place, to try to understand life here, and to learn to function in a way that could be meaningful to me and the community. I burrowed into life here unmindful of anything but my community and involvement and survival. And it was easy to do this. This place is fascinating. The people are different, *but willing to take me in* . . . I do not want to concern myself with anybody else's life or problems than those immediately around me."

D extended his tour of duty in the Philippines with a third year of service. Although everyone had thought that he epitomized the ability of a volunteer to live deeply in the culture after just six months, he wrote toward the end of his third year, "I have continued to change here and have now sort of reached a point of being able to feel with others. This is different from understanding how they feel. I am able to be a part of them as they do things with each other and me. I have also reached a point where I know my own limitations, unique position, and potential . . . I experienced this strongly the other day when I was riding home in a jeep. During the conversation, I noticed how freely, directly, and naturally we exchanged words and feelings. And how in no way was it a matter of myself being constantly torn or shattered or threatened by unfamiliarity and the desperate need to communicate. I was whole and the bonds and patterns of communication were whole. . . . I am becoming more humble daily as I sense my limits, but also more adventurous and unafraid . . . this affair has not been my doing, my changing any more than it has been the doing and changing of those around me. The important idea to me is mutualness."

In reviewing D's approach to life in the barrio, it now seems clear that his deep feeling of humility in being received by the barrio and in appreciating individuals for what they were was the major factor in his success.

Volunteer E

A male volunteer from Virginia, who had considerable success with his teachers after a long period of struggle and pain, E's first reaction to frustration was to plunge himself into his work. But at the end of his tour of duty, he admitted that friendships became more important to him than work, and he was amazed at his ability to socialize. "There are picnics, jam sessions, parties, and just impromptu sessions of dancing or swimming. And on many evenings we just sit around and talk. . . . In all these relationships, the outstanding factor is friendship . . . and these persons are persons to me, not only Filipinos."

Concerning his highly successful relationships with a co-teacher, he wrote, "Looking back on it, I can hardly say where the friendly but formal relationship left off and a warmer interchange began. It was not fast in developing. But I do remember one afternoon when she and I and another teacher sat talking for several hours after school was out. The conversation was personal. I think that our friendship has made her a more interested person—that her curiosity has been stimulated in a variety of things. She's now studying this summer in science, a field she was not especially interested in before . . . and is extremely interested in mathematics as well."

Volunteer E learned to wait for his teachers to develop an interest in changing at their own pace, and he enjoyed them in the meantime. Of another teacher, he wrote, "S and I get along very well. On some occasions he has felt free to say he did not like the idea I was trying to introduce to the class. He thought it would not work." To E this was a clear-cut indication that his acceptance of S had resulted in a genuine mutual relationship. E acknowledged that some of the enthusiasm which S showed for teaching science was due to his encouragement.

Volunteer F

A male volunteer from a small town in Illinois, F did not wait long to begin work in his barrio. Within a year, he had helped build a science room, revised the science program from grades one through six, introduced new math techniques, helped adapt the new guides for teaching English, and inaugurated a school newspaper. His students showed considerable improvement in English and science. In addition, the teachers with whom he worked began and ended school on time and seemed more able to question their superiors than they had been. As a result of F's leadership, his community built one of the more successful community libraries started with Peace Corps help.

F's achievement drive was not less than that of many other volunteers who had a more difficult time. What appears to have made the difference is that he enjoyed the people of his barrio before he had any evidence that they would be willing to change. Soon after arriving, he made daily walks around his place, talking to people, practicing his dialect, and meeting the parents of school children. He would stop at the *sari-sari* store and drop in on our town officials. He seemed to be enjoying himself thoroughly, which helped his neighbors to enjoy him *and* to change.

Volunteer G

Another boy from Ohio, G possessed enormous drive to accomplish, and he worked constantly, but his powerful desire to change life in the Philippines never appeared to be incompatible with his acceptance of individual Filipinos. He worked incessantly, but he also went to dances. He refused to smoke or drink but would do anything to help an individual Filipino in distress. He walked along a dusty road every day, speaking the dialect and enjoying his neighbors, but never letting them dissuade him from attending to the tasks at hand.

His results included the building of a science library room and science tables which were designed and constructed by the barrio people with their own labor and funds.

When an accident forced him to go to the hospital in Manila before he could finish an electric-relief map which he had begun, one of his co-teachers completed the project with the help of the children, and it won first prize at the provincial science fair. In the end, he found the teachers "taking responsibility, initiative, using materials, asking questions. . . ."

Volunteer H

From a small town in New Hampshire, H began his service in the Peace Corps as an iconoclast, but became much more interested in people as he tried to work with them. He enjoyed fishing from a banca, plowing with a carabao, and building with bamboo. Relationships took on a new meaning. He wrote, "I used to think I could take people or leave them. They are more important now, or maybe just more of a feeling of I do this for you rather than I do this for you for me."

This approach to people appears to have led to considerable success. He conducted informal agricultural classes with his older students, in addition to his regular school work. He introduced a few new vegetables in the barrio and found a solution to the problem of tomato blight and wilt. The farmers became so interested in his activities that they began to stop by the house to ask for information or buy seeds or seedlings and even requested that he begin an adult education course in horticultural techniques. In addition, through his initiation, stone walks had been put in muddy places in the barrio, two new toilets were built, a science room constructed, and a compost pit begun during his first year of service. He wrote, "I am not sure in many cases how instrumental I have been in the above projects, but I don't believe they would have happened if I wasn't here. Maybe it is just the idea that I am here to help them improve some things that makes them think they might as well do the things they had been planning on anyway."

He extended his tour of duty in the Philippines to serve in another area and had an opportunity to reassess his work after having been gone from his home barrio for five months. He wrote, "I came back unannounced and went directly to the school. Some of the things were promising. One teacher was using a set of minimal pairs for drill. In the office a couple of the science books I had left behind were open on the desk with notes beside them. The school garden looked better than I had seen it. . . . There were many other things that had stopped."

Volunteer I

A girl volunteer from Ohio tamed her powerful achievement motivation and learned "to tolerate most of the problems, move around them, or pass by them . . . to sit things out," to enjoy the people. She found that relationships took the place of the job to some extent and wrote, "Perhaps the most gratifying of all experiences were those spent chatting with the kids and people of the barrio. Because I loved the children, I think the people opened their doors to me." The people and the teachers also became more interested in her work.

Her success in teaching in the barrio and later in organizing and teaching at institutes to help Filipinos became more effective in second language methods resulted in part from her ability, but also because of her willingness to accept and love people.

Volunteer J

A female volunteer from Illinois, J was keenly interested in the people of her place from the time she arrived in the barrio. Her interest was not based on intellectual curiosity, but a genuine and spontaneous desire to relate to them. "I was interested in their likes and dislikes," she wrote, "what they thought about the United States and how they were going to accept me as a person, and not as a stranger who came to make changes. . . . I wasn't in any hurry to find their mistakes . . . the process of getting to know my co-workers was not a long tedious job . . . when they began to ask for my help, I was more than happy to assist. We worked slowly, and we understood each other . . . working with the teachers proved to be the most important thing to me in my stay in the Philippines. They were my best friends. After school hours, we spent much time together, talking about the States and the Philippines. I could go to them with any problem I had, and they did not hesitate to come to me. . . ."

As a result of this capacity for friendship, J was able to help her several co-teachers and head teacher, and appears to have introduced new teaching methods in the third through sixth grades with considerable success.

THE PROBLEM OF CULTURAL IMPERIALISM

New methods of teaching were related to new ways of thinking which were disruptive to existing values. In attempting to introduce inductive methods of teaching science, volunteers were trying to get students and teachers to think independently in a culture which valued dependency in relationships. They wanted every Filipino child to develop his or her unique capacity for achievement in a culture where personal achievement threatened harmony in relationships. They wanted the children to be governed by individual engines of ambition and guilt rather than by group norms and shame. As one volunteer wrote, "I tried to stimulate an appreciation of the basic worth of the individual . . . the distinctly American trait of each man believing he is as good as the next man can be put to good use in Filipino society . . . all too often even the very young have symptoms of a sickening resignation, born from the feeling that one lowly man can do nothing."

Volunteers believed that individualism would lead to change, curiosity, experimentation, and self-confidence. As one of them wrote, "I am trying to make them feel that it is good to be curious, that each one of them should not only be proud of themselves as individuals, but proud of their country and interested and concerned about their own future. . . ." They so much wanted Filipino teachers to encourage individuality in the children. A girl volunteer has written, "Sometimes, when I sensed the teacher's enjoyment in teaching a class, I would almost applaud. . . ." She wrote that she was thrilled when one teacher permitted a child to discover the principle of magnetism by herself and how another had let the children discover for themselves how germs could spoil fish.

Volunteers who advocated changes like these in the value system would be analogous to 3,500 foreign teachers in the American public schools constantly reminding the children never to speak unless certain that one's words would be acceptable and to bow one's head in shame after making a mistake.

WHOSE DEVELOPMENT: THE ANSWER TO THE PROBLEM OF CULTURAL IMPERIALISM

As already indicated, volunteers who became aware of their potential force as catalysts of value change were often plagued by the ethical implications of the Peace Corps venture as they responded to requests for advice on everything from birth control to integrated core curricula and hog breeding. As one of them put it, "This sort of thing I think about when I'm helping to install electricity in our barrio, or when I am asked to teach a lesson on rockets and satellites by our magic-jewel carrying, a quack-doctor science teacher . . . I see many things that could be changed from my stateside way of looking at things. I am partial to hi-fi, highways and higher education, but I can't quite overlook the question, should I?" Most volunteers resolved the issue by deciding that life and knowledge were universally positive values, and that their efforts in the Philippines were almost all directed toward extending the lives and knowledge of Filipinos.

Many volunteers also began to see their experience in the Philippines as a deeply needed lesson in their own cultural and psychological development and concluded their tour of duty by asking not just what is wrong with the Philippines and how do Filipinos need Americans, but how can Americans enrich their lives as a result of contact with other cultures.

Paradoxically, while the volunteers tended to value certain aspects of their Americanness more than ever before, they also became acutely aware of the loneliness and competitive struggle which results from valuing independence. They now cared for people more than ever before and were sharply aware of how little caring exists in interpersonal relationships back home. While doubtful that they had done anything to change Filipinos in fundamental ways, nearly all of them felt deeply changed themselves. In the end, the problem of cultural imperialism was resolved for most volunteers who became convinced that their personal development had been more markedly affected by their encounter with Filipinos than the development of their hosts.

CONCLUSIONS

The interpretations and conclusions reported here are based on reports, letters, and observations, not on an elegantly designed research effort. Effective and lasting change cannot be judged, to say nothing of measured, unless visits are made to the barrios long after the volunteers have gone. The volunteers delivered many messages through new channels concerning change and observed Filipinos participating in what appeared to have been new activity leading toward development; but most volunteers learned through considerable pain that neither messages nor channels constitute communication, and participation may not signify lasting change.

With these qualifications in mind, the three major conclusions suggested here are:

1. A person-centered approach to change, while varying in importance from country to country and with respect to different goals, was of unusual significance during the first two years of the Peace Corps' Philippine program because of the low level of change-readiness of barrio hosts, the Filipino emphasis on personalization, and the relatively unstructured role of volunteers.

2. Acceptance of Filipinos as persons was probably the single most important factor in facilitating mutual change between volunteers and hosts in the barrios.

3. Although genuine mutual friendship was often a precondition to effective change, other factors, not inconsistent with a person-centered approach to change, were also shown to be important in facilitating change. These included: effective role definition and communication of that definition; skill in focusing task goals; mastery over job skills; and effective location and assignment of volunteers.

For ten years I listened to America from a distance. As Deputy Director of the Peace Corps, special assistant to the President, and publisher of *Newsday,* I lived and worked on a narrow strip of the Eastern Coast. In Washington I helped to draft legislation which we hoped would make this a better country. In New York I belonged to a profession whose express purpose is to communicate with people. But I learned that it is possible to write bills and publish newspapers without knowing what the country is about or who the people are. Much changed in America in those ten years. There were thirty-five million more of us, we seemed more raucous than ever, and no one could any longer be sure who spoke for whom. I wanted to hear people speak for themselves. In the summer of 1970, carrying a tape recorder and a notebook, I boarded a *bus* in New York to begin a journey of thirteen thousand miles through America.

On its way north the bus cuts across the heart of Manhattan's life, through clogged streets (seven minutes to move one block on West Forty-first), past the rotting buildings and vacant lots filled with refuse, along Tenth Avenue, where children play baseball in the streets, past boarded-up stores and pushers on the make, and suddenly, in one of those startling contrasts of New York, past Lincoln Center rising like some Parthenon from a junk yard. A few blocks from its splendor I saw a child, nine or ten years old, who had cut his foot and was washing the wound in the filthy gray water cascading down the gutter.

The city is tolerable if you can leave it occasionally. These people cannot. For them the air is always trapped, the inversion is permanent. And, as the Greyhound inches through the traffic, the rhetoric of the sixties—the slogans about quality of life, a livable society, qualitative liberalism—seems to be choking in its fumes. A language far less grandiloquent is emerging. At St. Nicholas and 162nd a store conspicuously boasts: Police locks, door locks, window gates installed. The sign is painted red, white, and blue.

Bill Moyers, *Listening to America* (New York: Dell, 1971).

Once the bus clears the blighted spread of the city and moves beyond Bridgeport and New Haven the scenery and the mood of the passengers change almost simultaneously. Strangers introduce themselves to one another and the bus hums with conversation. The elderly man next to me is going north to visit his son, who took his family to New Hampshire on a vacation once and refused to bring them back—"he has a child with a breathing problem that just don't seem to bother her as bad up there." He offers me a cigar, which is against regulations, but it is thin and inoffensive and we light up, pleading self-defense against the cigarette smoke creeping over the seats around us.

For an hour we talk about nothing important, the way travelers on a bus do when they have first met. Ultimately they will discuss Spiro Agnew, inflation, the war and other grave issues of the day, but they prefer to begin the trip with small talk about children, minis and midis, and the sorry state of American newspapers, a grievance I will hear more often on this trip than complaints about taxes. My companion retired last year after forty years as a newspaper vendor in New York, and the only regret he now expresses is that he did not keep a copy of the last edition of every newspaper that died in New York during his career. "I might have had one for every year I worked," he says. This is only a slight exaggeration and we both chuckle.

The day before my departure, I received from a friend, Clare Wofford, the wife of the president of Bryn Mawr, a letter urging me not "to go out earnestly in search of America's problems but rather in search of its humor, its ironies, its human-ness. Since we are obviously on the frontier of every new and old problem suffered by mankind, we need to be reminded that we are no worse than the rest of the human race. How can the United States find some humility—and from it the chance to offer decent leadership—unless we can laugh a little and stop our endless self-flagellations?"

I folded her note into my wallet to remind me of a gentle mandate I very much wanted to honor. But ancient scriptures teach that man is born to trouble, and experience teaches that he endures those troubles by *talking* about them. Whenever I traveled, and no matter how innocent or casual my purpose, the people I met wanted to *talk* about the tribulations of America: war, campus unrest, crime, inflation, pollution, racism, and drugs. Hardly a day passed that would be free of some demonstration of our woes. [pp.1–3.]

. . .

It is 9 P.M. and the count is 108 for Duffey, 182 for Donahue, and 75 for Marcus. The roll call becomes a shouting match, the Irish belching forth the name of Donahue as if he were a Notre Dame fullback one yard from the goal with thirty seconds to play, and Duffey's people retorting with sharp ringing responses to the call from the platform for each delegate's choice. There are thirty-eight people in the trailer, about three times as many as there should be, but Duffey is moving closer now to the magic number of 192 and no one leaves. It is even possible that he will finish second, ahead of Marcus, an upset of a sort. Now it is 9:45 and Santos, sweating like a Texas cowhand, is projecting three votes ahead. "Oh, Jesus," he says, "it's coming. Oh, Jesus, and Pierz is going to do it. Pierz is going to do it."

Who is Pierz?

"He was my Little League coach," Santos replies. "He was my sweet lovin' Little League coach, and He's going to put Joe over."

And at 9:46 P.M. Steven P. Pierz, a Fuller Brush man from Enfield, Connecticut, Hubie Santos' Little League coach, rises to his feet, and with altogether too much calm for the occasion, replies to the rostrum: "Joe Duffey."

And the galleries and the trailer are bedlam.

Duffey's hand reaches for his wife's. Anne Wexler leans against her chair and says: "This is what they came for. Two years ago Joe said he would stay in the party and work to change it from within. This is what they came for."

"Hot Dang," someone says, "I'm still on the payroll." [pp. 18–19.]

. . .

What about patriotism? I asked. You felt you were expressing your patriotism when you went into the service and to war. What does patriotism mean to you today.

Jack McGill answered first. "To me patriotism means that no matter which way you voted, you go and support the man who is elected as the majority of the people wanted."

"I agree with that," Kimbrough said. "We've got elections, and a way of government that has come about after lots of trial and error, and I think if you're going to be patriotic, you have to support that system. Too many kids have stopped supportin' the government and too many have gotten away from the church. The American Legion was founded on the slogan 'For God and country.' This country was founded upon religion, and too many parents have let their children get away from religion. 'Course I think it's a known fact that the Communist elements are trying to infiltrate the churches, just like they have the racial incidents and the media. . . ."

Where do you get your news? I interrupted.

"I get mine mostly from the newspaper," McGill answered. "I do very little reading otherwise. Now, you may not believe this, but the only time I have the TV on is when there's a ball game on or the news and weather. I turn it on just for them. Now, that's really a fact. I don't care for the media because it's plain missed the boat on the campus thing. Last fall my boy was going to college and there was a Dad's Weekend where you do down and spend the weekend and stay in the dorms. And on one night the different fraternities and the different wings of the dorms put on little skits, and they judged which was the best. The night I was down there, they had nine skits and you know seven of them were patriotic. Now, something like that never hits the newspaper. But if there had been six demonstrators marching down there with signs, it would have been in the newspapers. I think that if a demonstration goes on in this country, if there's something to demonstrate against, then we should be demonstrating against attorneys."

Attorneys?

"Yessir. They make the laws, and somewhere or the other they can twist them around any way they want to, they can just about get anybody off, no matter what kind of crime they've committed. I'd like to see us put all the attorneys right out in the middle of a big field and just march around and around them all day protesting and demonstrating and raising the devil with them for all the trouble they've caused." [pp. 34–35.]

. . .

I fell in with two black students who were walking toward the Student Union. When I asked them how many blacks are enrolled at Antioch, one of them, a frail, thin young man from the East, replied: "That's not the problem. The problem isn't that there aren't enough blacks; it's that there aren't enough poor people here—period. And I mean poor white folks too. Most of the kids here," he said, "come from very well-to-do homes. There's not enough endowment for many scholarships from the college and they wouldn't be here if their old man wasn't footin' the bill for them." He laughed and said: "That's why they get such a big kick out of dressin' and messin' around like they do. They're sayin', 'Screw you, Daddy,' all the time they're livin' on his pork. One thing about those middle-class white cats—they sure as hell don't want to do what their parents are doin', but they sure want their parents to keep on doin' it long enough for them to finish college.

"Well, they're middle class, see, I'd say 85 percent, 90 percent, and so naturally the courses and the work and all the programs are really middle class. Most of us [some 175 blacks] are from poor homes. We wouldn't be here if it weren't for foundation grants and special things like that, and we just couldn't swing those middle-class courses. We set up a black studies program but the folks at HEW in Washington said, Uh-uh, you can't run a segregated program on federal money—'course this was segregated by blacks for blacks—and we got together and said to the college, O.K., you get some more poor white students in here, and some kids like that, because there'll be more like us and you'll have to make some changes." He laughed again and said: "Now there is a switch—*us* agitatin' for more white cats. But we want 'em *poor*, because even if they're white, when they're poor we got a lot in common." [p. 53.]

.　.　.

We walked back to the porch. It was now almost dark and Patsy Gentile studied the street beside his house. "When I teach this boy of mine, I say one thing to him—I associated with both my children, Don and my girl—on night like this we would walk up and down that street and we talk—and I say, 'Boy, you gonna be a man in this world. If you do, obey the rule of country. You get somebody try to coach you to do wrong, you say, "Aw, I ain't a-gonna do that, I gotta go." Don't get mad. Find a way to say, I like to be with you but I gotta go, then just walk away.' And I say to him, 'Listen to whata people say, even people you think looka simple—sometimes what they say may seema simple but later on you can use it. Associate with people that knows more than you do. You can learna more than you know now. Because if you just go 'round with ones who know what you know, you no can learn anything. Do that, and don't let anything else control you but yourself. Walk away from trouble.' " [p. 65.]

.　.　.

"The Teamsters are powerful. They could help to change the system. Instead they're a party to it. We want to remedy that. We'd like to see the Teamsters reform. We'd like to see competing unions. Right now if you're a Teamster and they're not performing the job for you, what are you going to do? If we succeed, we'll give guys an alternative. We'll be in competition to try to do a better job of representing the union member. We'd like to encourage other owner-operators to do the same thing—movers and produce haulers and dump-truck operators. Everybody knows the Teamsters Union is corrupt, the politicians, the members of the union, the press. But they're all saying you got to live with it, you can't do anything. That's crap."
So spoke the man from FASH.
I will not be surprised if he and his friends succeed. They are patient and earnest men. In the face of intimidation and ridicule they have refused to quit their purpose. A native shrewdness guides their strategy; in addition to Alinsky, they were sharing a copy of Dale Carnegie's *How to Win Friends and Influence People*. Revolutions have been born of stranger alliances. [pp. 78–79.]

Old myths die stubbornly, and the myth of the melting pot—the boiling caldron pouring forth its uniform ingots or assimilated Americans—is no exception. The concept that "All men are created equal" has often been interpreted to mean that to be different is to be *un-American*. I was quite along in years in East Texas before I realized that Catholics were not citizens of a sovereign foreign state, the Vatican. There were always rumors in Marshall that the handful of Lebanese and Syrians who found their way to "our town" kept their eyes shut during public salutes to the flag lest they be unfaithful to the colors "of their own countries." And I remember once hearing the elders at my church—and this was in the early fifties—discuss whether "real Americans" would be separated in heaven from "foreign Americans." They never resolved the issue, but the idea persisted: to be a "good American" one should be as much like everyone else as possible. [p. 79.]

. . .

"Take the Italian-American family. They feel very strongly that they're Americans; they don't want to go back to Italy. But their Italian roots have given them very special characteristics as a family. The father does one thing, the mother does another, the children are expected to do certain other things. One of the most important factors in that family is the sense of who the *whole family is*. It extends past his brother and sister into the wider community. Ask an Italian about his family and he will tell you about his cousins, and not just his blood cousins. The family reaches beyond the blood line to the neighborhood, to their turf, to the larger community. And not only is this true of Italian-Americans. Let's say you go into a center-city situation and find an enclave of third-generation Polish-Americans. You have to understand why they came to that particular place. Usually the church was there, the industry in which they could work was there, relatives were there. In Poland they weren't property owners, but America gave them the opportunity to own land. They immediately began to identify with their neighborhood. It was their land. I don't care how small it was, they would sit in front of it with a gun if they thought it necessary. Look at Tony Imperiale in Newark. He's a symbol of the guys who says, "This is my turf and nobody is going to take it away from me.' " [p. 82.]

. . .

"The media very seldom gets this kind of thing. With ethnic Americans *the media has tended to pick up people who are reacting—reacting to their own awareness of their identity for the first time.* It hasn't been very long since people were 'wops' or 'polacks'—you know, stereotypes. The media keeps trying to shove them into some new category—hardhat or racists or beefy clods—everybody has to fit into a mold. They come in and ask, 'Are you for Wallace? Are you for Wallace?' It's the old Biblical thing—the media tries to pit the *Sons of Light against the Sons of Darkness.* That's *where the action is, and action is what the cameras record.*

"When you see the hardhat, who's become the ethnic symbol today, he's beating up students. You're seeing the reaction, not what led up to it. I admire Walter Cronkite a lot, but when he says 'That's the way it is' at the end of his broadcasts, I have to smile, because very often that's not the way it is. That's *only the way it seems to be.* You're getting part of the effect, maybe nothing of the cause. How many television stations paid serious attention to the Indian until the Indians took over Alcatraz? Television looks at people in a pejorative way. It looks at them as if they were categories. On the *Carol Burnett Show* on CBS someone told a joke about the Polish airlines and played the Polish national anthem for comedy and the Chicago station was flooded with protests. We've got a lot of Poles here. Why were the people who put that show together so insensitive? Because there are no Poles in New York. The people who bluepencil television shows lead very isolated lives.

"I think Agnew mistakenly tripped against a truth. Which is not only that the media has been a little bit to the left but that in general it tends to *oversimplify.* I doubt that they do it consciously. *The very nature of television is to look for struggle that can be capsuled in one minute.* [pp. 84–85.]

. . .

I asked him what he thought about the young people. "I was young once and hotheaded," he said. "That was a long time ago. But we had juvenile delinquency then and we got it now. *Only thing that cures it is growin' up.* You know, the best thing about the stage of bein' a juvenile is that it's so short-lived. I've been older a lot longer than I was younger." [p. 152.]

. . .

I went to a landing up the stairs and looked down at the crowd. They were young—university and high-school age. The chanting subsided and a youth near the door said something about a man calling who wanted "to put flowers on Tiger's grave." A girl replied: "Might as well donate a plate of peas. He can eat those peas as well as he can smell those flowers."

It was not a time to smile but some of them did. So did I. The girl looked up and saw me and began a chant which the crowd quickly picked up: "We want you. We want you." With each chant they pointed in my direction. When the chanting died I mumbled something about their not wanting me because I was only passing through.

"Honey," one young lady said, "you better keep on passing."

"Where you from, baby?" asked the girl who had suggested peas. And as I started to answer I remembered the story of Judge Louis Carpenter, which less than an hour ago I had read at the library—he was one of those "New York fellows . . . doing all the mischief." I know it sounds ridiculous; there I was safely although accidentally ensconced in the police station and I could only think of what had happened to a New York carpetbagger more than a hundred years ago.

I'm from Washington," I said, which was true in a way. "And Texas," I added, which was also true. And then it just came out—"And New York."

"Honey," she replied. "You've come to Little Harlem and the fire is burning." And they began again to chant: "We want you. We want you." [p. 124.]

. . .

He was quiet for at least a mile. Then he said: "This gets down to the religious thing. I don't believe that man is the ultimate that God can do. I think man thought up the idea that he is in God's image. Who wrote Genesis?"

There is considerable argument about that.

"Well, I'll tell you this—it was written by a human being. He decided to make himself important, so he wrote that he was God's favorite creation. The hell with that. Nature existed before man. And nature existed for nature's sake, not for man's. Man came along, the arrogant boob, and invented the idea of his importance in God's eye so's he could justify what he was about to do to nature."

What about those lines in Psalms, I asked: "For thou hast made him a little lower than the angels, and hast crowned him with glory and honour. Thou madest him to have dominion over the works of thy hands"?

"I'm not familiar with the gentleman who wrote that," John Arnold said, "but I'll bet he was a two-legged, self-righteous, pompous little bastard who thought he was lord of the manor. That's what man wants—*dominion*. Does that mean man has the right to destroy, to rape, to insult nature? Dominion, friend, is not the privilege to trespass on the rights of others. Don't you think nature has rights, too?" [p. 174.]

. . .

"I feel that it is my duty as a legislator to furnish the money and the guidelines to the board of regents. I think it is the duty of the board of regents and the administrative staff hired by the board of regents to create on campus a setting in which a student may learn and equip himself in order to be a good citizen of the United States. I do not believe that a university is created by the taxpayers of the state of Washington to be the hotbed of anarchy. I do not believe that we taxpayers pay our money for our children to be infected with bad ideologies and i-de-ologies that are foreign to what has made America great." With the last three words he abandons his monotone and raises his voice for emphasis.

A voice from the crowd: "RIGHT ON!"

There is loud and sustained applause.

"I do not believe that a faculty member violating a professional code has any right to remain on campus."

More applause. A man at the rear shouts: "Give it to 'em, Senator. Let 'em have it."

But Guess returns to his flat way of speaking. "Under this bill any administrator, faculty member, or elected official, including senators and representatives, may submit a written complaint to the board charging any faculty member with unprofessional conduct, specifying the grounds therefor. If the board determines that such complaint merits consideration, the board shall designate three members to sit as a committee to hear and report on such charges. *Upon filing of a complaint* the pay of an accused faculty member shall be suspended until a final determination is made by the board."

Someone behind me shouts: "Guilty until proven innocent, huh?"

Guess: "There are—"

Another voice: "That's a hell of an America."

Guess: "These are conditions that are merited by the situation. The board has the power of subpoena. There will be due process."

A chorus of protesting voices rings from the students.

"What happened to the courts?" a girl asks.

"Jee-sus," another girl says. "I must be having a bad dream."

Guess: "Due process is in here." He has not raised his voice. [p. 183.]

. . .

And then the conversation in that corporate dining room took a very surprising turn. One of these men, a very mild-mannered, undemonstrative person, began to speak: "Yes, what is the end of it all? Where is the country going? Where is each one of us going? I think this is what is bothering the young although I don't think they have the practical experience to know what to do about it. I feel that I have betrayed myself. What in the hell, I've asked myself, have I done with all those things you were thinking about in college? I know this sounds schmaltzy, but truthfully I haven't done very much. And I got to thinking about this after that first big layoff. I lost some friends in that, people who had put their hearts into this company. And one day they weren't here. I think rushing into that fantastic progress caused more heartache and suffering than it was worth. The people were saying, 'More, more, more,' so the airlines said, 'More, more, more,' and Boeing said, 'More, more, more.' We scrounged and grabbed and fought for dominance, and when we got it, we lost it. All this running and shoving to build a structure that suddenly we don't need. And look at all the people who got hurt. Business has got to change. I think it will because the children of so many businessmen are becoming hippies."

He was speaking very quietly but he was intense and nervous, and I am not sure that he was really talking to those of us who were at the table. Or maybe he was. It was with considerable difficulty that he announced: "A month ago my own daughter just disappeared. She left—no note, no word, nothing. Just disappeared. I've been lying awake at nights asking: Where did I go wrong? What happened? How come she didn't come in and say, "I've got to go, Daddy, I'm going to pull out.' " [p. 210.]

. . .

Someone says sarcastically: "Our city in action. This is our city in action." And the old man who is shaking looks up and replies: "Yes, this *is* our city in action. You're our city, too. You're part of it. Is this any way to conduct business?"

"Swearing the way you were, is not a very pretty picture."

His voice is very soft. He drops his eyes to his fists, which are tightly clenched. "I know."

Almost two minutes pass without anyone saying anything to anyone else. It is uncanny. No one seems to approve of what has just occurred and no one seems able to take command of the situation. "It was almost like the country today," Butterworth said later. "Everybody spitting at each other and ashamed of it all the time and wishing they were talking instead of spitting and not knowing how to stop the one and how to start the other."

Finally a Mexican-American member of the commission, a woman, says: "I think we should allow them the courtesy to speak." Back from the audience comes the high-pitched voice of a man, also Mexican: "We do not need the courtesy to speak. We have the *right* to speak. It is not something you can give us."

The impasse is broken and a woman says: "Look, what's happened is that you have no confidence in the program and the people in the communities of this city have no confidence in the Art Commission. You can't evaluate the Neighborhood Arts Program without involving people from the neighborhoods or you won't have a constituency. You'll have plans and blueprints and you'll even have money but you won't have a constituency.

People don't want you to do things to them any more or for them. They want to do these things for themselves. Don't you understand that's what we're trying to say to you today?"

The Mexican-American member of the commission asks: "Why don't you just send a field representative to meet with us?" and is greeted by a chorus of noes. "We've had enough of that kind of representation," a man says. "The people must represent themselves." [p. 221.]

. . .

I asked, What does America mean to you just now? He thought several minutes, then said: "The country was beginning to mean less and less. What mattered was *culture*. For a while I just didn't think I was a part of the country. I still don't know where I fit in. With drugs you can extend things in your mind further than they actually go, and I had picked up a lot of hostility toward the country for that reason, especially toward official violence—violence done in the name of authority. Then I realized that I ought to try to do something about it instead of escaping from it." He paused again and shook his head. "But I don't really know how to answer your question," he said.

That night he called me at the hotel and asked if we could talk the next morning. We met over coffee. He said: "I've been thinking about that question, the one about America. I still can't answer it but I know why I can't. America to me is all the things that have happened to me, good and bad, for better or for worse. I can never sum up what all those things are, and that's why I couldn't answer your question. If I could tell you who I am, maybe I could tell you what America is. I'll know someday. Then ask me." [p. 235.]

. . .

I asked several young Chicanos what had brought them together in MAYO. "Dr. Logan's death," one of them answered. "The Gringos did not like him but he was our friend, our compadre. He knew Chicano customs. He spoke Spanish without English accent. He even knew slang Chicano. He did not charge poor people for health. He fought for us. That is why the Gringos did not like him. He was not afraid of them."

"Now that he is gone," Simon Guiterrez said, "MAYO must work for our people. We're gonna prove to 'em that MAYOs are not just a bunch of hoodlums, long-haired hippies; we're gonna prove to 'em that we can work and do things honestly. Our parents were afraid to speak out. But we ain't got a damn thing to lose. Now we're gonna do something for our parents. My parents had to go through hardships, year after year, day after day, they had to work like dogs. They all worked so my generation could go to school. Any person over thirty-five in Mathis who is Chicano is less educated than a kid down here seventeen, eighteen years old. Our parents hardly know English. One old woman in here yesterday to eat said she could vote but she can't speak English. We find young people now who's not gonna be saying yessir-nosir to no Gringo, and we support them for office."

You're going to work in the political system?

"Oh, yes, no violence, none of that. In all of South Texas the Chicano has 15 percent of the vote. With that we got bargaining power. [p. 272.]

. . .

The real heroes I know are anonymous. They have therefore remained *human and humble.* They are also effective. Once a leader has become a media star he has been reduced to a sterotype easily communicated by a brief lead in a newspaper report or by a ninety-second television clip. He must forever thereafter conform to that image or lose the quicksilver base of his notoriety and power.

Bill Lawson, forty-one, of the Southern Christian Leadership Conference, avoids acclaim and seeks results. He has turned down offers from government, civil-rights programs, and larger churches to remain as the pastor of the four hundred black families who constitute the congregation of the Wheeler Avenue Baptist Church in the south-central ghetto. Many Negro churches remain the furnace rooms of the Black Pride movement, and Lawson is no pulpit-pounding, Bible-waving holyroller Tomming Billy Sunday. In his speeches he is in the prophetic tradition of Martin Luther King, in his political awareness he is a cousin to Julian Bond, and in his understanding of the economic order of the black man he is a protege of Jesse Jackson. But he is shy and given to contemplation, and *television cameras, he says, are "sirens of destruction for all but a very few."* [p. 278.]

. . .

"Well, we were turned out cold when we first went to that bottler. They wouldn't even listen to us. They slammed the door in our face. So we simply refused to buy his product. Our people drink a lot of soft drinks and we stopped. We said, 'All right, if you have the power to slam the door on us, then we have the power to change appetites on you.' That's exactly what we did. We took sixty thousand circulars and stood on the corners where the bus transfer points are all over Houston and passed them out to the maids and the porters and other people going to work. In all twelve ghettoes in Houston the word can be passed rather quickly. We have a lot of contacts. A soft drink bottler operates a high-volume low-profit business and his profit margin is not more than 7 or 8 percent. In one week—one week—we cost him about 47 percent of his business. We virtually paralyzed him. So he called us back in. Only this time we wouldn't go to his office. We asked him to bring his people out here. He did. And he met our demands.

"Breadbasket is one way of making our anger work for us. Given some opportunity at least to face a man with your own strength, you feel good because at long last you don't have to say 'sir'—you have purchasing power on your side. And you feel even better when you can see your little bank getting bigger and bigger . . . your newspaper getting stronger and stronger . . . more and more concessions being made to other consumers like you. That's what Breadbasket does.

"But I wish it weren't necessary. I wish negotiations did not break down. Quite frankly, any time we have to utilize a selective buying campaign we haven't won, we've lost. It is not our interest to kill companies in Houston. *Our interest is to get purchasing power for the black man.* And if that can be done by rational men talking as gentlemen about a problem which is common to all of us, then we win. If the only thing we have left to do is to harm each other, then we've lost." [p. 286.]

.   .   .

"But I'm hoped up. Yes, I'm hoped up. The young ones are a-comin'. And they will be different.

"You take when freedom of choice came along in the schools, me and my wife sat down and talked with my baby girl. I said, 'You can go to Johnsonville High School if you want to, but I don't want you goin' there for six months and then quittin' and goin' back to the colored schools.' She said, 'Well, Daddy, I'll go theah and stay.' And I know this, when she was goin' to the colored school she'd act as if she warn't goin' to school when she came home. Never studied. Never opened a book. Next morning she pick up her books and go back as if she had nothin' to do at all. She was gettin' good grades and passin', but still . . . When I put her in the white schools, brother! when she came back home she sat down on those books. She didn't even seem to get upset when some of the white kids said they was goin' to beat her up—she studied, she studied hard. It was a difference, see. It was a difference. I notice all the colored kids are studyin' more now than they ever did. They say they's gonna go in theah and not make bad grades in front of all them white kids—they say, 'I'm gonna show them I got some brains, too.' Makes all the difference in the world, yes. Makes all the difference.

"So I think when this gone on awhile, people will forget about this color thing and look at a person as a person. I think they stop sayin' Thurgood Marshall is a credit to his race and start sayin' he is a credit to mankind.

When I was growin' up I was told the whites are this and the whites are that, and over theah in Texas I bet you was told the Negroes are this and the Negroes are that. Both of us didn't know any better. But I bet if we sat on this front porch and talked long enough, we'd be one people to another, and that is a difference.

"That's why I'm hoped up." [p. 356.]

·   ·   ·

One night in the midst of this journey I sat with a friend in Cincinnati watching television, and heard a local announcer urge his listeners to "call with your comments about our programming. *We want to hear from you. We want to know what you think. Your message will be recorded and examined later.*" My friend threw his shoe at the screen, and he had not been drinking.

It is treacherous to tell people that you want to know what they think, and then force them to speak to a machine. *People want contact.* They want to affirm themselves.

I found that most people not only *hunger to* talk, *but also have a story to tell.* They are not often heard, but they have something to say. They are desperate to escape the stereotypes into which the pollsters and the media and the politicians have packaged them for convenient manipulation. They feel helpless to make their government hear them. They were brought up to believe that each man can make a difference, but they have yet to see the idea proven.

I discovered how unfair it is to call a man "bad" because part of his culture still owns him. I found out how important it is to get that man to acknowledge that people different from him are also human.

Most people want to be generous. They expect their nation to have visions of justice even if they themselves act unjustly. They expect from their country an ethos, an honorable character and enduring beliefs, even if they resist a common set of scruples and a rigid monolithic ethic. There are people who can endure personal tragedies and private griefs exacted by the nation only if they feel the nation itself is worthy.

People are more anxious and bewildered than alarmed. They don't know what to make of it all: of long hair and endless war, of their children deserting their country, of congestion on their highways and overflowing crowds in their national parks, of art that does not uplift and movies that do not reach conclusions; of intransigence in government and violence; of politicians who come and go while problems plague and persist; of being lonely surrounded by people and of being bored with so many possessions; of being poor; of the failure of organizations to keep the air breathable, the water drinkable, and man peaceable. I left Houston convinced that liberals and conservatives there shared three basic apprehensions: they want the war to stop, they do not want to lose their children, and they want to be proud of their country. But it was the same everywhere.

There is a myth that the decent thing has almost always prevailed in America when the issues were clearly put to the people. It may not always happen. I found among people an impatience, an intemperance, an isolation which invites opportunists who promise too much and castigate too many. And I came back with questions. Can the country be wise if it hears no wisdom? Can it be tolerant if it sees no tolerance? *Can those people I met escape their isolation if no one listens?* [pp. 376–377.]

A.2.5 FOUNDATIONS FOR EAST-WEST UNDERSTANDING

EVERETT KLEINJANS

The world has shrunk so dramatically in the past several decades that lack of understanding between the peoples of the world can no longer be allowed to persist if the human race is to survive. Advances in communication ranging from satellites to jumbo jets have made us all next door neighbors whether we live in Chicago, New Delhi, Tokyo or London. Unfortunately, many of us do not understand our new neighbors. Although we can invite South Vietnamese peasants, African revoluntionaries and Japanese student radicals into our homes every night via television, we don't really know, understand or sympathize with our guests. Misunderstandings between neighbors can lead to arguments and neighborhood brawls. In a global village, misunderstanding can mean nuclear destruction. There is no room left in our global village for intolerance, prejudice and ignorance.

At the East-West Center, we are trying to do something about this tragic gap between the techological advances that have made us all neighbors and our attitudes toward and knowledge of our new neighbors, which have often remained at much the same level as our father's and grandfather's. The East-West Center is a unique experiment—an attempt to build a laboratory in which understanding between East and West will grow and flourish. There is no blueprint constraining its shape. It need not follow any foreordained scheme of the usual university courses or of any departmental structure. It doesn't have to follow the pattern of a conventional research institute or training school. We are free to experiment—to develop our own blend of activities and structures for achieving understanding.

The catalyst for this experiment is interchange — intellectual, cultural and technical exchange between peoples from Asia, the Pacific and the United States. Our laboratory has been built on four elements, each contributing to the flowering of those thin lines of trust, friendship and common interest which tie men together in a community of understanding.

Everett Kleinjans, "Foundation for East-West Understanding" in Jim Richstad and L. S. Harms, eds., *World Communication,* (Honolulu: East-West Center, Press, 1973), pp. 10–14

First, the Center is a national institution with national support and goals. It was founded in 1960 by an act of Congress and formally established through an agreement between the Department of State and the University of Hawaii. The Center continues to receive the bulk of its funding from annual Congressional appropriations. The Secretary of State, who is responsible for the Center through the Bureau of Educational and Cultural Affairs of the Department of State, has appointed a National Review Board to represent the national interest of the programs and plans of the Center. The East-West Center is an expression of the voice of the American people to build understanding and friendly relations with the countries of Asia and the Pacific. On the other hand, our goal is not to try to convince our participants of the rightness of immediate foreign policy decisions by the United States government.

At the same time, and of equal importance, the East-West Center has a broad international focus. Our international staff members, degree students, professional trainees and senior scholars come from the 50 states of the United States and over 30 countries, from Afghanistan to Korea, from New Zealand to Japan. The community of culturally diverse individuals works together, exchanging views and knowledge on a mutual basis and, when at our best, giving trust and developing concern. The West is not the teacher, nor is the East the eager student. The insight of all are assiduously sought, for through such mutual sharing we come close to truth. At the Center, everyone is both a teacher and a student, learning and sharing knowledge with everyone else on a mutual basis.

As far as we know, the East-West Center is the only U.S. educational institution with a majority of participants from Asia and the Pacific. In the past 11 years, 20,000 people have participated in Center programs and returned to Asia, the Pacific Islands and the United States to pass on their new knowledge and understanding of others and to build a network of connecting links between the East-West Center and the Pacific world. In addition to these alumni relationships, the Center is actively working out cooperative research and training relationship with many first-rate Asian and Pacific institutions, universities and agencies.

The third cornerstone is educational. The Center maintains a firm educational identity through programs which encompass study, training and research. The cooperative arrangement between the East-West Center and the University of Hawaii allows us to utilize the University's many educational resources. In addition, cooperative arrangements are developing with educational institutions in Asia, the Pacific and the U.S. mainland. Within the Center, an interdisciplinary staff of experts in fields relevant to our programs provides the Center with built-in academic competence.

Finally, the Center has a distinctive programmatic thrust for its activities and resources. Beginning in 1970, after more than two years of planning and discussion with Asian/Pacific and U.S. educators and administrators, we began to pursue our objectives through new programs built around real-life problems that face us all. In each program, degree-seeking students, senior scholars, administrators and other professionals gather around mutual human problems in which they have expressed a concern. We try to organize their study, training and research activities so as to enable them to interact in pursuit of solutions. The persons gathered come from widely diverse cultures and different age levels. They bring to bear on these problems different specializations of knowledge and practical experiences.

There were many reasons why the East-West Center adopted the problem-oriented programs. Perhaps the two fundamental ones are the educational value and increased interchange resulting from such an approach. Education becomes dynamic when teachers and learners are engaged in the solution of actual problems. In conventional education, students are presented with hypothetical problems with already determined answers available from the teacher or the back of the textbook. Even in the case-study method, where problems are presented for solution, the problem chosen may be hypothetical, and in any case, since the students are not accountable for decisions they make, they are not engaged in a "real" solution.

The problem-oriented approach has a number of characteristics which give it special educational significance;

1. It sets forth an actual problem of some consequence, to which there may be several possible solutions, or perhaps only inadequate accommodations and it requires fitting theory to reality. Instead of a "think tank", our program is a "think and do tank".

2. All those engaged in education through this activity are finding data or making decisions which have the possibility of affecting men's lives; this feature adds the mood of seriousness which education needs.

3. Since the student is part of a cooperative research program, he must participate actively if he is to contribute to the solution of the problem. This realization should give him definite focus to his class work, helping him to relate his work to an ultimate goal, not merely the passing of a paper-and-ball point test.

4. If the present educational crisis evidenced by student revolts on the campuses of American and Asian universities during the 60's is indeed a crisis of involvement, of students wanting their studies and activities to be relevant to individual and social life, then this problem-oriented design may help to provide the relevance.

Secondly, these programs are designed to enhance interchange so that understanding will be facilitated. Interchange is affected by the following factors:

1. People interact more in smaller groups than in larger groups.
2. The more people associate with each other in small groups which have well-defined goals and values, the more cohesiveness will develop.
3. People with similar personal goals working together toward a common end will tend to develop respect for and trust in each other.
4. As people continue together in a common task, less communication is devoted to the task and more to the personal relations of the members.
5. People who live under very similar conditions—especially if they experience the same inconveniences—develop a strong sense of camaraderie.
6. People who work together on a problem and make progress toward its solution learn that cooperation is possible; when these people are from different countries and cultures, they learn that cooperation is possible despite differences—a long step toward understanding.

Our problem-oriented programs take these factors into account so that the potential for interchange is maximized. All these factors enhance the amount and quality of the interchange and produce conditions conducive to understanding.

We recognize that the problems of the world are complex and cannot be easily pigeonholed into neat slots of economics, psychology, biology, political science or philosophy. Therefore, our programs, which concern the problems of real life, are tackled on an interdisciplinary basis. Such programs; although academic in nature and content, do not duplicate university programs but are complementary to them. Whereas in a university, scholars are most often grouped around a common discipline, presided over by a chairman, and are called a faculty, in the East-West Center, participants are grouped in programs centered around a problem, are drawn from several disciplines, and are presided over by a director.

There is no end to problems of common concern to East and West. Therefore, it was difficult to determine which problems should be approached by the East-West Center. The following criteria were used: 1. The problem must be contemporary; 2. It must be broadly human or international as opposed to national; 3. It must be consequential to both East and West. As a beginning we have selected five problems as the basis for our programs.

Our communication program is concerned with the processes of sharing knowledge and attitudes among cultures and subcultures for enhancing the quality of life, and with the effect cultural differences have on these communication processes and on access to them. The program helps develop individuals who will strengthen mass media and other communication systems. As you all know from your own experience, the best planning in the world will fail if you can't communicate your ideas to others, or respond to ideas from others.

Our Culture Learning program concentrates on how one learns his own language and culture—a good part of this learning being outside of formal education—and how another culture can be learned without losing the identity of one's own. We use the term "culture" in the sense of the whole pattern of ways of thinking, feeling, believing and behaving. Thus in this program, we are exploring the questions: how do we learn cultural behavior? how can we improve language learning? and how can we learn another culture through encounters with its creative works in music, visual arts, theater, literature, history, and philosophy, and with its religious traditions? As the world grows smaller, each of us must be able—at the very least—to "get along" with peoples from other cultures.

Our Food program is concerned with the complex interrelationships among production, processing, distribution, and consumption of foods and the technical, economic, political, cultural and social aspects of each of these elements. Task groups concern agricultural diversification and multiple cropping, crop protection, planning and implementing public programs and policies, food quality, and agribusiness.

The Population program concentrates on analyses of the causes and consequences of population change; the quantitative and qualitative effects of population growth upon economic and social development; the economic, social-psychological, and environmental factors that determine demographic behavior; the evaluation of policies and means by which societies try to influence population processes; the possibilities and means of improving society's capacity to deal with untoward consequences of population growth; and specific research in the field of demography.

The Technology and Development program is concerned with anticipation of the consequences of scientific and technological advances in the processes of planning and managing development. Specific themes include developing innovative, risk-taking entrepreneurs in both the public and private sectors; transferring relevant technologies from one society to another; building modern societal institutions; and carrying out integrative planning. Urbanization, in particular, has underscored the need for finding ways to adapt technologies, and to create new technologies, to deal with our problems.

In conclusion, our four cornerstones—national, international, educational and programmatic—form the foundation for the stimulation of interchange and the development of understanding which are the goals of the East-West Center. We are confident that our experimental laboratory here in the middle of the Pacific Ocean is providing some important answers to the ever-increasing need for building understanding in a world that has become a global village.

We hope that all of the people who come here will become cross-cultural communicators, able to enhance the flow of knowledge across national and cultural boundries. Actually, good cross-cultural communicators are scarce, and many must be trained. What are the characteristics of such people?

First, cross-cultural communicators must see people as human beings first and as members of a certain nation or culture second. In a very real sense, all men are brothers. Our common humanity means that we all have the potential to become members of any culture, at least at birth. In fact, any child born into any culture will learn that culture and its language regardless of the race or nationality of his parents. Of course, beyond the differences of culture are the many individual differences that make each of us a unique human being. In fact, individual differences are possibly greater than cultural differences. Therefore, the communicator must remember that although all men are brothers, all brothers are different. This has been a painful learning process for Americans over the past few decades. Anyway, we must come to learn that these differences are beautiful, for they make our common humanity rich in this diversity.

Second, the cross-cultural communicator must feel that the culture of the person or people with whom he is communicating is intrinsically good; i.e., good not in the sense of being a means of satisfying his curiosity but in the sense of being a thoroughly valid human expression of man on this earth. Every culture which has developed on this earth is a dynamically structured system, a design for living out one's life of relationships to one's fellow man and the world around him. Whether one places first priority upon the individual or upon the group will depend upon the culture in which he was reared. Either can be, and is, a thoroughly human way of organizing reality. The differences are there, but the differences are legitimate, and when thoroughly understood, seem to be good.

Third, the cross-cultural communicator should have a knowledge of and sensitivity to the cultural values of the people with whom he is communicating. This is not always possible, and for a person working in an organization like the United Nations, it may be completely impossible, for example, to know the cultural values of all the 131 countries sensitively. Certainly, he should not read his own meanings into the communication devices of one from another culture. When Americans, for example, see Japanese bow to one another and read obsequiousness into that action, they are misplacing values and causing misunderstanding.

Fourth, the cross-cultural communicator must acquire the ability to withhold his negative visceral reactions until he has ascertained whether he has grasped the true meaning intended by the person he is communicating with. He must have learned restraint in his emotional behavior. The maid working in the home of an American in Japan came to the lady of the house to express her wish to quit. The American housewife had studied only a little Japanese. The maid said, "Yamesasete itadakitai to omoimasu ga," which the American translated as meaning "I would like to receive your causing me to quit." That is the literal translation. Her reply was, "I am not causing you to quit. Why don't you say you don't like it here and want to quit?" The American housewife failed to ascertain that the language the maid used was the polite way of resigning. Anger can cause bad relations, and it is unfortunate if the anger is unwarranted.

Fifth, the cross-cultural communicator must learn to speak with a great deal of openness and candor, at least at the beginning. When people learn a second language as adults they usually use it mainly on the referential level. The subtle connotations are usually lost. I can remember working with Japanese in situations where the communication was completely in the Japanese language. There were times when I though I had understood everything but found that my Japanese colleagues came to a different conclusion from mine. One day I checked with the president of our university to see whether I had understood everything. Yes, Mr. X had said this and Mr. Y had said that and the president had said what I thought he had said. "Then why did you come out where you did?" I asked. The reply was, "You must listen for what is not said." Native speakers, speaking together, use many short cuts and make many assumptions about the storage of information of their fellow countrymen. Non-natives do not have that same store. Therefore the necessity for less subtleties and more directness.

Sixth, a cross-cultural communicator should have the inner security to see things done and said in a way different from his own culture, with different symbols and meanings, without feeling that his own ego or identity is being threatened.

Whether a man holds a door for a woman to permit her to go through the door first is a matter of culture. Yet I have seen some non-Japanese women feel that they were being personally insulted when Japanese men went through the door ahead of them, especially if they happened to be holding the door open. Probably the greatest manifestation of the kind of inner security I am speaking of is the kind that comes when someone has a good sense of humor about himself. In fact, one of the great sources of humor in all cultures is the foreigner who does not know "our" ways. Laughing with people of another culture about oneself is one of the greatest forms of communication.

Can these qualities for cross-cultural communication be taught? Possibly, like leaders, good cross-cultural communicators are born, not made. Inner security, for example, may be the result of a composite of one's parental heredity and one's early childhood environment. A person who is insecure in his own culture will more than likely be more so in a cross-cultural situation. This is one of the problems to which more attention must be given, by those concerned with world communication. Certainly, it is a problem to which we hope to direct attention at the East-West Center.

A.3

DIVERSE EXAMPLES OF MESSAGES

A friend of Edith Hamilton's tells of being present in Athens, one night in 1957, when she was honored by its citizens in the amphitheater beneath the Parthenon—the temple of the Goddess of Wisdom. Miss Hamilton, straight and quick at ninety, stood in the moonlight, accepted a scroll from the Mayor, glanced at it, and said: "Think, at last I am a citizen of Athens."

She was that, by breadth of mind and spirit, long before that night.

Edith Hamilton has known the Greeks with more perspective and insight than they could have known themselves. Her sympathy has held the Greek ideal alive in our times . . . if we would listen.

Here, on the beach, and at her cottage in Maine—the summer of 1958—she talks with Huntington Cairns, Secretary of the National Gallery of Art, Washington, D.C.

Huntington Cairns: Edith, when you were in Athens last summer—and, I am happy to say, made an honorary citizen of Athens—do you recall some of your thoughts?

Edith Hamilton: Well, Huntington, I had seen it before. Of course, I had been in Greece before. But really, when I stood there, suddenly it seemed to me I was looking at ancient Greece in miniature. There are only three buildings, and all are more or less ruined. No one goes there who does not feel he is in the presence of beauty as great as there is in the world. It was to me like ancient Greece. What have we got today of Greece? She ceased to be an independent nation more than two thousand years ago—years when man has pursued his usual practice of battle, murder, and sudden death. What has survived? A few buildings, very few, all defaced. A few statues—broken. All the paintings gone. Of the literature, stray scraps saved by chance, not

James Nelson, *Wisdom for our Time* (New York: W. W. Norton, 1961), pp. 15–25.

because anyone thought they were best. Of Sophocles's plays we have about one-tenth left. The same of the two other dramatists. We have just a remnant of what Greece was, and that remnant has changed the whole Western world. So, we today are different because of that little remnant.

Cairns: You are telling me that Greece is unique in the history of the world?

Miss Hamilton: Yes, absolutely unique.

Cairns: In what sense, do you think?

Miss Hamilton: The Greeks are unique because they began to think. They began to think not about "How am I going to get some food for tomorrow?" and "What will I do in this awful earthquake?" They began to think about what is the world like, and human beings. I must say that the East, which had great civilizations thousands of years before Greece, never felt like that. They didn't want to know anything about the world around them. They thought it probably was a strange place inhabited by queer demons and that kind of thing. They didn't think; the Greeks *thought*. Don't you believe that's true?

Cairns: I think so. I would also add that they are perhaps the only people who have ever thought about the good life: what is the life that man should lead.

Miss Hamilton: Yes, that's very true. Today, people don't think much about the good life. The Greeks, after a long series of good ancestors, thought what it would be.

Cairns: At the beginning, the Greeks were a primitive people—perhaps comparable to the people that Caesar found when he went to Roman Britain. What happened to the Greeks? What gave them their spark?

Miss Hamilton: That's not a fair question. *Our* ancestors in the great European forests (who lived very much the way the Red Indians lived before we came along) had nothing in them, and nothing came from outside to kindle a flame. But the ancestors of the Greeks were in contact with two great civilizations. They were in close contact with both Egypt and Crete. It's perfect nonsense to think that the really remarkable artistic achievements of those civilizations did not influence the Greeks. Of course, they did. They must have. The Cretans and the Egyptians came to Greece and influenced them. But what it was that started the Greeks on their unique part—so entirely different from Crete and Egypt—nobody could tell. That's one of the secrets of the human spirit. It's also one of the exciting things of the human spirit—you never can tell what it may do. Greece shows you that. Think of how the East had, since time immemorial, given over the care of the body to wizards and witches, and never thought about the human body. Then think how, in Greece, Hippocrates developed modern medicine. I remember taking an honorary degree in a great university, and the whole medical class—hundreds of young men—stood up and recited the Hippocratic oath—the oath Hippocrates had said every physician must take. I almost wept with pride. And the oath is as appropriate today as then. Think of what the medical missionaries found in the primitive countries—the horrible helplessness of sick people. The Greeks were the ones who made the beginnings to cure all that. Athens never thought in terms of the masses. Each man was an independent individual, and wanted to be. He didn't find that a hardship. A man was left alone to do his own work. Athens didn't try to dictate to a man. But he loved Greece. Pericles said, "Turn your eyes on Athens until you love her as you love your mother." The Athenian loved his city. He would sacrifice himself for her welfare. Somebody has said that "The height of civilization will be reached when no one is sacrificed for the end, and when everyone is willing to sacrifice himself for a good end."

Cairns: It sounds very Greek.

Miss Hamilton: I think it's a fair statement of what the Athens ideal was in Pericles's age.

Ciarns: I don't like to interrupt you, Edith, but Plato said the sea is a dangerous neighbor, and I see it coming in rather close.

Miss Hamilton: You may well say it's dangerous if you know our Maine tides. Let's walk back up to the cottage. (*They do so.*)

Cairns: I think we are safer here than on that ledge. Edith, I'm very curious to know what first aroused your interest in Greece.

Miss Hamilton: I have to go far back for that. It was reading the Greeks, I do believe. You see, when I was young, war was glorified. The poems I read and recited to my teacher such as, "The Charge Of the Light Brigade," I just hated it: "Then they rode back, but not, not the six hundred." I couldn't bear it.

I detested the picture in "The rocket's red glare, the bombs bursting in air."

The poems I learned glorified war, and I always realized its cruelty if not its folly. I found in the Greeks a sympathetic understanding. The Greeks were not pacifists; I'm not saying that.

Cairns: They fought many wars.

Miss Hamilton: They did. But the great Greeks saw war the way it was. Aeschylus caught a glimpse of the fact that wars are often fought for moneyed profit. In his *Agamemnon,* Aeschylus says, "Women know whom they send forth, but instead of the living, back there come to the house of each, armor, dust from the burning; and War, who trades men for gold, life for death; and holds his scales where the spear points meet and clash. To their beloved back from Troy, he sends them dust from the flame—heavy dust, dust wet with tears, urns stowed with ashes that once were men."

Cairns: Did you get to Greece directly or did you go by way of Rome?

Miss Hamilton: Oh, I went by way of Rome. My first study was Latin; not Greek. I was very carefully trained in history, and my father put Gibbon's *Decline and Fall* into my hands as a very young child. I just detested it. It seemed to be a chronicle of men killing each other to get something they wanted. . . . I want to digress for a moment. This isn't to the point, but I do think it is a little bit funny. I got something from Gibbon that my father never dreamed of. You see, Gibbon has the habit, when he wants to put a footnote about something peculiarly objectionable in Latin literature—and there is a lot in Latin literature that is peculiarly objection-able—he has the habit of leaving it in Latin. I think his idea was that everybody who knew Latin would be too pure-minded to be hurt by it. But, you see, my father forgot that I could read Latin. And I can truly say I learned the facts of life—as they are called—from Gibbon. I learned a whole lot from Gibbon that wasn't about the horrors of war. Does that answer your question?

Cairns: It answers it exactly.

Miss Hamilton: But, after all, Huntington, all this is pretty incidental to what we were saying about Greece. Greece saw what is fundamental to all human thought and all human action. They were an intellectual nation—the first and probably the only one in the world.

Cairns: What would you say about their clarity?

Miss Hamilton: Of course, that is the peculiar characteristic of the Greek mind. The Greeks had clarity everywhere. In our art, today . . . well? What must strike us, above all, in Greek art is clarity.

Cairns: I would extend that to literature. The playwrights, in the tragedies—there is no doubt about the problem they're discussing and the solution they offer.

Miss Hamilton: No Greek ever thought it was interesting or delightful to write sentences that made no sense.

Cairns: You are referring to modern poetry now?

Miss Hamilton: Not only modern poetry—modern prose. I'm referring to *Finnegan's Wake* and so on—all that kind of thing is un-Greek. Yes, that's a very just way of saying it. We do make problems out of words.

Cairns: Beauty is certainly another characteristic of the Greeks.

Miss Hamilton: I prefer to talk about the Greeks and not talk about beauty. It's often difficult to many of the modern world to have any idea of what the Greeks thought about beauty. I'm always reminded when I speak of Greek beauty of a little story about Epaminondas—a great general of Thebes, a neighboring city to Athens and often at war with her. Epami-nondas had led the Thebans in war against the Greeks and he'd been defeated, and he said, "We'll never be able to conquer the Athenians until we bring the Parthenon to Thebes." You see, the sight of beauty inspired a Greek with a higher spirit—a finer courage—perhaps even to the heights of heroism. The sight of beauty did that. While we have no conception of it today, that was Greece. When we speak of beauty, we're speaking of something we're more or less indifferent to. But I'm not going to talk longer about beauty because I feel we can't understand it as the Athenians did. It is, after all, only half of the shield. There's another side to it, as you know.

Cairns: There certainly is another side and that is the side of thought . . . or mind. Heraclitus said that. And he went on to say that wisdom consists in saying what is true, acting according to Nature, listening to her. That trend runs from Heraclitus through all the Greek thinkers, through Aristotle and Plato.

Miss Hamilton: I keep thinking of what Aristotle called the four cardinal virtues: courage, temperance, justice, and wisdom. Do you remember Plato's definitions?

Cairns: He connected them all together. He defined courage as endurance of the soul. Justice as excellence of the soul. Temperance as health of the soul. And wisdom as communion of the soul with reality.

Miss Hamilton: You can't beat that, can you? Those are four Greek cardinal virtues. After all, the virtue they cared most for was *sophrosone*—they called it that. We have no English word for it.

Cairns: What is your nearest equivalent?

Miss Hamilton: I can describe it best by a negative. The quality the Greeks hated most was insolence, arrogance, self-assertion. Sophrosone was the exact opposite. A man who was sophrosone had a disciplined will. He knew his own weaknesses; he had a kind of modesty of spirit. He had self-control that did not need the control of any other man.

Cairns: But I am surprised you haven't spoken of the Greek notion of excellence which you find all through Homer, through all the Greek playwrights.

Miss Hamilton: I'm glad you reminded me of that—of the Greek notion of excellence—because it does show that the Greeks did not find virtue easy. Aristotle said, "Excellence—much labored for by the race of men." And the Greek poet just after Homer—Hesiod—said, "Before the gates of excellence, the high Gods have placed sweat; long is the road thereto, and steep, and rough."

Cairns: But there is a darker side to Greece that Plato and Aristotle tried to correct. There is the fact of slavery. There was the place of women.

Miss Hamilton: Yes, true. Of course, all through the ancient world slaves were taken for granted. Greece was the first country to question the right of making a man a slave. Plato was made very uncomfortable by it. Plato said that often slaves did better for a man in defending him and his property than his own sons did. And he said it was a very embarrassing possession to own a man. That's where Greece had arrived at two thousand years before we arrived at it.

Cairns: But Plato saw the problem, and tried to—

Miss Hamilton: Plato would have none of it. Plato set exactly the same training for men and women. That is extraordinary, an extraordinary fact. Only the greatest mind in the world would have been capable of that, at such a time.

Cairns: You think he is the greatest mind?

Miss Hamilton: I think Plato is the greatest mind in the world.

Cairns: I wouldn't dispute it.

Miss Hamilton: Certainly not. Plato was a supremely great artist and a supremely great thinker. Of whom else can you say that?

Cairns: What do you say of Aristotle?

Miss Hamilton: Oh, not an artist. He was an artist because he was a Greek. But nothing to compare with Plato; not in profundity of thought. Oh, no. And he knew it himself. He would never put himself on a level with Plato. You know, when I read the *Dialogues,* Athens comes to life as the very best novelist in the world could not surpass. At the same time I realize that the profundity of his thought is equaled by the loftiness of his thought. That's Plato.

Cairns: Nevertheless, Edith, in spite of the ideals of the Greeks—in spite of their greatness—they did put Socrates to death; and Plato said Socrates was the greatest and wisest man that Greece ever produced.

Miss Hamilton: Yes, that is true. I do see a few reasons for that—not that I am apologizing for his death. But Socrates went about trying to make the Athenians see the truth; and he thought no man could see the truth unless he first saw the truth about himself. To show a man the truth about himself isn't exactly a popular procedure.

Cairns: It's very annoying.

Miss Hamilton: Socrates never said, "I know, learn from me." He said, "Look into your own selves and find the spark of truth that God has put in every heart and that only you can kindle to a flame." That procedure aroused a whole lot of enmity. People don't like to be told they are ignorant about themselves. I think the Athenians had been slowly turned against Socrates that way. Then we must always remember that Socrates was put to death when Athens had just been defeated in a terrible war that had lasted twenty-three years. People at the end, defeated in a great war, are not normal. You can't judge the Athenians by Socrates's death.

Cairns: But the great men of Greece, including Plato, were not able to save her in the end.

Miss Hamilton: No. Greece came to an end. Luckily for us, her light did not go out in darkness. Her art and her literature and thought have kept it alive, in part, for us. We have a picture of what happened to Greece. A country to the north of Greece—much the way we regard the Russians, the Greeks did not like their ways at all—came down and conquered Greece. Greece fought, that's true. But not with the old magnificent heroism that had conquered at Martahon and Salamis. Greece was changed.

In every civilization, life grows easier. Men grow lazier in consequence. We have a picture of what happened to the individual Greek. (I cannot look at history, or at any human action, except as I look at the individual.) The Greeks had good food, good witty talk, pleasant dinner parties; and they were content. When the individual man had reached that condition in Athens, when he thought not of giving to the state but of what the state could give to him, Athens' freedom was doomed.

Cairns: You mentioned the ancient world. How do you compare Greece and Rome?

Miss Hamilton: Oh, dear me! Rome is so far below. You know, I really think the best thing that can be said for Rome is that she recognized how good Greece was.

Cairns: What about Rome's other contributions?

Miss Hamilton: I think one of the most magnificent scenes enacted in this great theater of the world was when Paul, an obscure little Jew from a humble town, stood up before the great Roman governor and said, "I appeal unto Caesar." He was a Roman citizen. Everybody born in Tarsus was a Roman citizen. And the great Roman governor couldn't just say to the soldier next to him, "Knock out his brains." He said to Paul what he had to say: "Thou hast appealed unto Caesar and to Caesar shalt thou go." I think that the Roman conception of Roman citizenship which made men equal all over the Roman world was magnificent . . . and unparalleled. I hand that to Rome.

Cairns: We have done a great deal of talking about individuals, about great men in Greece and Rome, and now you have just mentioned St. Paul. I take it that you regard the individual as the principal factor in history?

Miss Hamilton: That is true. We will be saved only by individual people, and that is what Greece never lost sight of. Greece never lost sight of the individual. She never looked at human beings as masses. That is what frightens me about today ever so much more than the sputniks and atomic bombs. I'm afraid we are losing sight of the individual in the mass. Mass production does not produce a genius. The Greeks had a strong sense that each human being is different from another human being. I have often taken a lot of comfort in the fact that my fingerprints are different from everybody else's in the whole world. It is a very reassuring conviction in this world. What I see disappearing today is the individualism of the Founding Fathers that founded our great republic. The Founding Fathers were individualists. I don't know if they had got to Greece or not. But they were trained, educated men. They knew Greece. Perhaps, unconsciously, they imbibed the idea that nobody can really study Greece without getting the idea that·the individual is irreplaceable, and that individual man—individual men—can do almost anything. That's our hope. We can return to all the good that Greece had if we see that there lives what Plato called the spark of good in every man—a spark which St. John called the light that "lighteth every man coming into the world," a light which exists in every human being that lives and which can be kindled into a bright flame to lighten the whole world. That's an enthusiastic statement, but I stand by every word of it.The truth shall make you free. The Greeks saw truth. Now, I want to stop my own foolish inadequate words about them to read you what the greatest of the Greeks said. I know you know it, but you will bear with me.

Cairns: I would love to hear it.

Miss Hamilton: I love the words I am going to read to you more than anything else in all Greek literature . . . Plato, Socrates. You remember, Socrates is in prison. He is going to drink the poison that will kill him in a very few hours. He is going to die, and he is facing the unknown. It would be natural that at that moment he would have a great feeling such as: I must believe in the immortality of the soul; I must comfort myself and my friends. But the Greek in Socrates could not let him do that. His words are: "Remember, in this argument, I am only seeking to convince myself. Do but see how much I have to gain if the immortality of the soul is proved. If it is true, then I do well to believe it. And if there is nothing after death, my ignorance will do me no harm. This is the state of mind in which I approach our argument.

I would ask you to be thinking of the truth, and not of Socrates."

The producer of this conversation, Robert Emmett Ginna, Jr., said when it was ended, "I know that Dr. Suzuki is a holy man."

It is a spiritual and intellectual challenge to follow Dr. Suzuki's uncompromising, poetic, and deeply religious explanation of Zen Buddhism.

Dr. Suzuki's companion was Huston Smith, Professor of Philosophy at the Massachusetts Institute of Technology, who had once subjected himself to the disciplines of a Zen Buddhist monastery.

. . . .

Huston Smith: Dr. Suzuki, when Buddha died what did he leave behind him—primarily a set of sermons or primarily an example?

Dr. Daisetz Suzuki: An example. A sermon is a kind of example, too. When he was about to depart, the last thing he said was, "Work out your own salvation. Do not depend on others." That is the last word he said.

Smith: Does this mean that there is no grace, no cosmic help for man?

Suzuki: That is the way the Theravada Sutra scriptures recalled Buddha's farewell talk—no grace, no help from external source. If any help comes from anywhere it comes out of one's self.

Smith: You mentioned the Theravada. This indicates that there are branches of Buddhism. It has divided?

Suzuki: Yes, yes. That is the case with every religion. Zen is at the root of all Buddhist sects.

Smith: Let me turn to the question of your involvement in Zen. . . . When did you decide that you wanted to make your life study the study of Zen?

Suzuki: When you say study, it's not like studying a science or some other things. A religious impulse, a religious consciousness, is awakened, naturally . . . and unless that problem is somehow settled one cannot feel rested.

James Nelson, *Wisdom for our time* (New York: W. W. Norton, 1961) pp. 137–144.

Smith: Were you born with a religious impulse?

Suzuki: Not born, but it has awakened.

Smith: When did it awaken in you? Do you know?

Suzuki: Well, I do not know exactly. But the starting point was marked, perhaps, when I was sixteen or seventeen. I wanted to get my religious yearnings somehow settled.

Smith: Yes. How long did that take?

Suzuki: It took several years before I thought I was all right. But when I had my own experience, a desire strongly awakened in me that this must also be propagated or given to others.

Smith: Were you studying formally at a college, a university?

Suzuki: No. I was supposed to have been educated in a university, but I did not devote myself very much to the regular curriculum they had given to the students. I absented myself—a kind of delinquent, I suppose; and I shut myself up in a monastery.

Smith: And for how long were you there?

Suzuki: That must have been at least seven or eight years.

Smith: When you decided, when you had come to your own resolution, as you put it, and your own experience, and decided that this should be propagated, did you at once decide to make the West your field of propagation?

Suzuki: No, not necessarily. But my decision was made when I first came to America. That was about sixty years ago. I found out the Western world was quite ignorant of the way Eastern people think and feel. After eleven years of stay in a small American town, I went back to Japan. Then Japanese life, things presented themselves in a quite different light.

Smith: What, for example?

Suzuki: Things peculiar to Japan—such as the tea ceremony, or flower arrangement, or pictures, or such meaningful things.

Smith: And a feeling that there were values in these aspects of Japanese life which the West did not know about?

Suzuki: That's right.

Smith: So, from there, you resolved to give your life to interpreting the East, and Zen Buddhism in particular, to the West?

Suzuki: Yes. Especially in all those branches of art, we might say, which are based on Zen understanding of life.

Smith: Your books were the first books in English about Zen?

Suzuki: About Zen, about Buddhism in general, about the line of Buddhism.

Smith: I wonder what you would say are the reasons why the West has become interested in Zen?

Suzuki: What I suspect is that the West has been giving itself too much to what we call scientific studies. Scientific studies pursue one definite direction; whereas the Eastern way of thinking is just opposite.

Smith: How did Zen start?

Suzuki: Zen is recorded to have started while Buddha was giving a sermon to a congregation. One of his devotees offered a bunch of flowers to Buddha. And Buddha, accepting it, just held it out and showed it to the congregation. Nobody could understand what Buddha meant. But, looking around, Buddha noticed one elderly monk called Mahakasyapa. Buddha smiled. Then he said, "I have a certain precious thing here which I hand over to you." That is the way Zen started.

Smith: In that smile, then, was contained the secret of the Zen perspective?

Suzuki: Not the smile itself, but Buddha's presenting and Mahakasyapa's understanding what Buddha really meant. So the Buddha's mind and his disciple's mind came into one thing.

Smith: Exact identity.

Suzuki: Well, I can't say that. But if we have to explain it, perhaps identity—something coinciding; there was a certain communion between the two.

Smith: The Zen perspective had passed from Buddha's mind to this disciple's mind. This is a very fragile thing.

Suzuki: It's not fragile, in fact. You speak to me; I speak to you. Is that fragile?

Smith: Ideally, the teacher of Zen would be of the same mind and state as—would be a spiritual disciple of—Mahakasyapa who received, who heard (who saw) Buddha's flower sermon.

Suzuki: Yes. *If I raise a finger and you smile, then Zen is transmitted between us.*

Smith: How would you recognize a Zen man if you saw one?

Suzuki: I would say that what distinguishes Zen, psychologically, from all the rest of religious teachings, and from the rest of Buddhist teachings, is becoming conscious of the unconscious. To be attached and not attached. Attachment, yet no attachment. Metaphysically speaking, finite is infinite; infinite is finite. When you understand this, then Zen is understood.

Smith: Dr. Suzuki, you say that morally Zen is characterized by attachment and detachment. What does this mean?

Suzuki: That's a very important part of Zen. In practical life, and so long as we live in a reality world, we get attached to something good or something bad, something beautiful or something not so very beautiful. But in the Bible we read (it was perhaps one of Paul's letters) we live in the world as being not of the world. That expresses the idea of attachment, and yet not being attached. So, as long as we are relative, we get attached to the dualistic view of reality.

But underneath (or in or with the relative world) we have another world which is not relative—a world that I may call the transrealm. In that world, there is no attachment; there is no good, no evil, no guilt, no ugliness. The lotus flower grows out of dirty water, but when it comes out of water how beautiful the flower is.

Smith: What is the method of Zen, as you see it?

Suzuki: Look at, for instance, that image of Dainichi, over there. That Dainichi represents, according to my view, Godhead. Dainichi or Mahavairocana, belongs to Shingon. Dainichi Nyorai is immovable. He does not move, he just sits quiet, eternally quiet.

Every one of us has God, or Godhead, in him. And to come in contact or to come into the presence of this Godhead, God, Dainichi . . . that is what Zen endeavors to lead us to. That is to say, we must come in contact with Godhead and the God-creator. When we come to that, we know what our existence means, what life is.

When Zen talks about ignorance and enlightenment, the ignorance refers to our own intellectual creation and the enlightenment refers to the state of mind in which the cloud of ignorance has been dispersed. This dispersion requires a certain method. That method is taught by Zen.

Smith: You have written that it is indispensable for every seeker to go through a period of commotion in his soul. And, as you were speaking earlier, I understood that in your youth—around the age of seventeen or eighteen—you had this commotion. What precisely was the method of resolution that you followed while you were in the monastery?

Suzuki: It concerns consciousness. Our consciousness is always going this way—up and down, and never quiet. But to gain, to get into the way our mind works, these waves of consciousness must be quieted. That is to say, they must become like a serene ocean without any waves stirring. Or, as Kagonah Sutra says, "like all the stars reflecting themselves on the clean, mirrorlike ocean." That is needed. To reach this mental equanimity, to bring it to realization, we use Koan. It is a problem which is to be experienced, not intellectually interpreted.

Smith: Can you give us an example of Koan, and illustrate how this would function?

Suzuki: The Koan program is so constructed, I might say, as to block every intellectual attempt to solve it. Koan, they sometimes say, is something like an iron bar which cannot be assessed—an iron bar just thrown out before us, demanding what it means or what it is.

I turn to another simile. Joshu was a great master of the Tang Dynasty. A monk asked him if a dog has a Buddha nature. Now, a Buddha nature is supposed to be in possession of every one of us—not only human beings but all beings, nonsentient or sentient. So, the monk's idea was that if everything that exists, or that is, has a Buddha nature, a dog must have a Buddha nature. But the Master denied it, and said no.

Smith: Well, how would you go to work on that Koan? What would you do with it?

Suzuki: The likely approach by the pupil is to attack it intellectually.

Smith: Yes?

Suzuki: The proposition was, if everything has a Buddha nature, a dog ought to have also a Buddha nature. Why did the Master answer it negatively? Then, the pupil who has studied something about logic or dialectic, he might say "is" is "not"; "is not" is "is." "Being" is "not being"; "not being" is "being." So, when the Master said "no," that must mean "yes." A pupil may bring that kind of answer to the Master. The Master will naturally reject it. After a few rejections, the pupil has no way to approach the Master—intellectually nor in any kind of way. The pupil is pushed—somewhat artificially, we might say—into an impasse or corner. He throws himself down. That is to say, he throws down his totality of being. That is a time when he reaches this evenness of consciousness.

Koan brings out that state of mind. Something happens, when everything is so quiet—a wave takes place.

Smith: Do you say that when the mind reaches this deep equanimity, some stimulus is required?

Suzuki: When the state is attained something rises, and this rising, this thing, ought to be experienced.

Smith: This rising, does this involve a coming back to the world of particulars which surrounds it?

Suzuki: Yes. That is, when this level is attained—you may hear it. A physical sound wakes one up. So, generally there is something in connection with the *sense* world. Buddha is supposed to have seen the Morning Star and then somebody heard a knocking at the door.

Smith: Or the broken tile hitting against the bamboo?

Suzuki: Yes, that's it exactly.

Smith: And when the pupil reaches this state of deep serenity—when there can be this little vivid sense experience—then this brings the mind back into the world with an intensity which gives it a new focus.

Suzuki: Yes. That very moment of something coming—this is important.

Smith: That week that I spent in the monastery was the most severe week physically, and I would say mentally too, that I have known—very little sleep, about three hours perhaps a night, the simplest kind of food . . . and if one were drowsing in meditation, there was always the keisaku to swat one and bring one back to awareness. I'm wondering about the place of this severity. Is this necessary in the discipline?

Suzuki: That's more or less artificial. It is not needed. When one is driven to that impasse without having any external agency, it is better.

Smith: Then, Dr. Suzuki, eventually the combination of these methods brought you to a distinctive kind of experience called the *satori,* or the enlightenment experience. What was that like? It was like no other experience you had ever had?

Suzuki: The satori experience is something total.

Smith: The experience of everything?

Suzuki: Not everything. If you say "this, this, this"—that's counting—a serial experience, we might say. But satori experience is something total. It is not one after another. But the whole thing as a whole, intuitively felt. That feeling is not what we call psychological feeling, but something more fundamental. It is when one becomes conscious of one's self—not as subject and object, but self as self.

Smith: So that a true understanding of Zen might bring a renewed freedom to the life of the individual?

Suzuki: That's what I say, yes. Some psychoanalysts talk about freedom being spontaneous, being just "do what you like." That is altogether a great mistake, and one has to be very much on guard against that.

What characterizes Zen is this: simplicity, and sincerity, and freedom. Freedom is very much misunderstood by most people who try to study Zen. They think freedom is something like licentiousness or antinomianism. But real freedom is to see things as they are, to see things in their "suchness," I would say. That is freedom.

Smith: Dr. Suzuki, on the wall, here, is a famous Japanese picture of a monk laughing at the moon.

Suzuki: Yes, yes.

Smith: Does this express Zen feeling? If so, in what way?

Suzuki: There is a story to tell. Is that all right?

Smith: Yes.

Suzuki: It is about that picture on the wall. There was a man, a Zen master, who, one evening, saw the moon coming out of the clouds. And he laughed heartily. And all the villagers around his monastery—where shall I say it was? about ten miles away—heard his hearty laugh. The villagers wondered where that sound came from. Trying to locate it, they finally came to the monastery. There they found that it was the master who had laughed last night, seeing the moon. The picture is that. However loud one may laugh, it is impossible to reach as far as even one mile. But when Zen man laughs, it shakes the universe—more than ten miles, or five miles, or twenty miles. That kind of thing is freedom and free life.

UPWARD BOUND

Leader: Think of yourself ten years from now. Try to picture that. What I'd like you to do is try to describe the picture you have of yourself ten years from now, in any way you can. How would you like to see yourself in ten years?

First Boy: A writer, a reporter, I wouldn't get married, I'd travel.

Leader: So, you'd be a bachelor, a writer, and you'd be traveling around?

First Boy: Yes, I'd write about the people I see, the people I knew. The trouble is right now I don't have anything to write about.

Leader: Is there anything else you can do to clear up the picture? So far I know you're a bachelor and you're traveling around, writing.

First Boy: That's about the general idea.

Leader: Where would you be living?

First Boy: I'd just be traveling around.

Leader: What kind of people would you be associating with?

First Boy: Any kind, I like to meet all types.

First Girl: I want to be a surgical nurse.

Leader: A surgical nurse. Tell me about what else you might look like or be like ten years fron now.

First Girl: I'll be real skinny and real old. I'll be twenty-six.

Leader: Are you going to be married?

First Girl: No.

Leader: Why not?

First Girl: I don't want to get married. I'll get married when I'm about thirty-five.

First Boy: Nobody will want an old woman, an old bag.

First Girl: If you get married when you're nineteen, you'll get tied down and have kids and everything.

G. Weinstein and M. Fantini, *Toward Humanistic Education: A Curriculum of Affect* (New York: Praeger, 1970), pp. 134–145.

Second Girl: I want to be a gym teacher. I don't know why. Like she said, I don't want to get married.

Leader: Ever?

Second Girl: Yeah, but not right now. I want to have fun.

Leader: You do want to get married, but not necessarily ten years from now. What do you see yourself doing besides teaching gym?

Second Girl: I guess going out a lot, not like going out at night, like traveling to schools and teaching.

Third Girl: Sometimes I see myself as a secretary, going to France or something. Then sometimes I see myself as a teacher, teaching either an English class or a steno class, and I'm not married. Sometimes I see myself engaged.

Leader: What's the fear about marriage here? You're engaged but not married.

Third Girl: Because engagements can be broken. But not marriage. Engagements give you a chance to know about the person. Marriage means you're tied down to one person, and you have to know enough about him to make sure you're willing to make sacrifices.

Leader: And don't you think the possibility is good that you *can* know enough about him?

Third Girl: Well, after a while. You can't just tell how someone is when you just meet them. You have to get to know them.

Second Boy: In ten years, I would like to see myself as a chief executive of a profit-making organization or either as a nuclear physicist, because I'm very interested in all types of sciences or that field, because ever since sixth grade, when I started to know what science was, I've become interested in it a lot.

Leader: Well, what about your personal self, that's your professional self.

Second Boy: I'm going to be a bachelor. I don't want no women to be holding me down. This is the changing world of progress, you know. Women would be holding you down. Don't go here, and don't go there. I don't want to hear that.

Leader: You don't have as much freedom?

Second Boy: That's right. They hold you down from a lot of things.

Third Boy: I don't know what I'll do. It all depends on whether I get in college or not. If I get in college, I want to get a real good job and make as much money as I can. I don't want to be a millionaire, but I want to make enough money to live comfortably.

Leader: You don't care what you have to do to make it?

Third Boy: I won't be bloodthirsty or anything, but I want what I guess all people call a good job.

Leader: Anything else about yourself, besides your job, that you'd like to see in ten years?

Third Boy: I guess I'll be married. I don't mind getting married. I may have a couple of kids by then.

Leader: What kind of a house do you see yourself living in?

Third Boy: Kind of suburban. I don't know. I like the city and all, but it's not too good for the kids, although I grew up in the city, and I didn't come out that bad.

Leader: Anything else you see?

Third Boy: I don't know. Not much more. I'll have a nice car and all.

Leader: OK, you kids have told me something you'd like to see happen. You said you want to be a writer and travel around. What do you have to do to get there? You told me what you want to be. What do you have to do to get there?

First Boy: Probably take courses in high school that give you a chance to write, journalism, creative writing. Enter contests that they hold. Write for magazines like maybe *Junior Scholastic.* If you write a story, you might get it in there or in other magazines. You might be getting paid for that, and it would be a start. When you go to college, maybe you could major in English, be in discussion groups, you know. A lot of that kind of thing.

Leader: Do you have a pretty good idea of how you would get to be a surgical nurse, what you'd have to do?

First Girl: After I graduate from high school I'd go to nursing school for four years and study. And every day I'd be at the hospital and learn the routine.

Second Girl: I know I'd have to get a college education for four years. I might as well do it, because your friends are still in school and you might as well go to college. If you get out of high school and don't go to college you'd just be around the streets. It's better for you to go to college.

Leader: Most all of you said that what you want to do would require some college in order to get a good job. What chances do you think you really have of going to college?

Second Girl: Not very big. Unless the government will allow you to take out enough money to put you through college. They won't give you all the money.

First Boy: I thought you meant scholastically, not financially.

Leader: No, anything, whatever it takes to get through college. Do you think you're going to get through, to make it all the way up that line?

Second Girl: I always wanted to be a teacher, but with my marks, I don't even know if I'll get through high school.

Second Boy: I think I'd have a good chance because I've had these two years of biology and chemistry. My teachers both have said that I have a very good chance of going to college, so I think I have a very good chance.

Leader: Do you think you could swing it financially, too?

Second Boy: Oh, yes, I could, because my parents would pay for my college fees and what not.

Leader: Talk to me about the rest of your real chances of making it ten years from now.

Second Girl: Well, I want to go to college, but I don't want my mother to pay for it. I want to pay for it myself. I guess when I get out of school I'll have to get a job and whatever I make, I'll save it all, won't spend nothing of it until I get the amount I need.

Leader: And you think you'll be able to do that?

Second Girl: No, because I know that when I get it and see something I want, I'm going to spend it.

Sixth Boy: My chances are pretty bad scholastically. I got a good IQ and all, but my school marks are very bad. I was doing OK, like passing but not real great. But not this year. It is very bad. It's shot.

Leader: What do you think your chances are?

Sixth Boy: Well, first financially, I want my father to help and my mother to help. My father says he'll help me through college. He wants me to go to college to make the best out of it. And why I want him to help me is because he underestimates me. Like he sees my report card, he sees two seventies or three seventies on it. I'm not failing. But he'd say "Oh, look at this. If you keep this up in high school, how are you going to get to college?" I think that I could make it scholastically. I think my marks are all right.

Leader: Do you think even if they wanted to help you financially they could support you through college? Do you know how much college costs?

Sixth Boy: It varies. You could go to a junior college, maybe.

Leader: What do you do about that? You all have a ten-year dream, and then when I ask you what your chances are of making it, it doesn't sound very positive. How do you live with that?

First Girl: Try to change. Try to better yourself.

Leader: How?

Third Girl: Make sure you know what you're doing.

Leader: How do you do that?

Third Girl: Let's say going to secretary school. Going to that, I have to have steno and typing, definitely, unless I take bookkeeping or some other things. Make sure I know what I'm talking about, what I'm doing, so that after I graduate, I'll be able to get a part-time job or full-time job as a secretary, and sometimes those jobs send you to secretarial school.

Leader: So, you think that's a way out for you, when you say you have to know what you're doing while you're still in high school and get those skills, stenographic skills and so forth? Do you know what you're doing now?

Third Girl: Most of the time.

Leader: So you really don't have to change anything.

Third Girl: Partly, yeah.

Leader: What do you do with that, the dream and the chances?

Second Girl: Once you get out of school, you can try. Trying never hurts. I'm not saying you're going to make it. But at least try. By working, you might just make it. You might be able to pay for the whole thing.

Leader: You know you had your dream and then you told me what your chances were. They didn't sound too good.

First Girl: Chances of going to college or being a nurse? You don't have to go to college to be a nurse.

Leader: Surgical nurse, I thought you said.

First Girl: You have to go to a nursing school.

Second Girl: That's just as bad as college.

First Girl: But it isn't all that hard.

Leader: How do you know?

First Girl: Because my girlfriend's sister is a nurse. She lives in California, and she had to take the exam, right? She took it, and she failed, and they let her take it again. So it can't be all that hard, if they let her take it again. The college boards you can't take over.

Leader: Does she have to pay to go to nursing school?

First Girl: No. I don't know. Sometimes they send you. If you're real good they send you.

Leader: They send you? Are you real good?

First Girl: No. So. I'll have to pay.

Leader: What do you really think will happen with you?

First Girl: I'll be a nurse. My father will send me to nursing school. He wanted me to go to college, and I said. "No," because of my marks.

Leader: And with those marks you can go to nursing school?

First Girl: No, but to be a nurse all you have to do is have chemistry, biology, algebra, and I'm passing them. You know what I got on my biology? A 95.

PRIVATE SCHOOL

Leader: I imagine everyone has a pictue of what they might be doing, of what they might want to be like in the future. So, I'm going to ask you to picture yourself ten years from now. I am sure some of you have the picture already of what you might like to be like or doing at that time. I wonder if you could begin telling me what that picture is like. Yourself—ten years from now.

First Boy: I've changed a lot of times, of course, and now I'm kind of interested in birds, so when I look at the colleges and things like that, I think I'd like to go to Cornell University, which has a program on ornithology there. And then they also have a laboratory where I could continue in that work.

Leader: Can you tell me a little bit about the picture? You'll be going to Cornell and studying ornithology. What else do you see about yourself at that time?

First Boy: I think before getting married I'd like to just live for a while and look around me and things like that before I decide what I want. I'd decide what I want first and then . . . .

Leader: You do intend to get married?

First Boy: Yes.

Leader: Do you think that if you got married before you had a chance to look around, you wouldn't be able to look around?

First Boy: I'd rather look around before I commit myself.

Leader: Can you tell me anything else about where you might be living or what you might be like as a person?

First Boy: I can't really think what I might be like as a person. I think I'd still like to live in New York City, possibly in the Village.

Second Boy: Well, I'm interested in history, so I'd like to go to college and study history and go for a teacher's degree after that. And before I settle down I'd probably like to go to Europe or different places around the world first. Then come back and either live in New York or move out to the West Coast. I really can't say what I'd be like ten years from now. I can't tell now.

Leader: Do you think you'll be married?

Second Boy: Well, I don't know. I guess I'd like to be married, but not too early. I'd like to wait for a while, live by myself for a while.

Third Boy: Well, I'm interested in music, and I kind of picture myself ten years from now traveling around the country and playing in an orchestra and meeting new people. I was sort of considering the Peace Corps for a while, and I think I'd like to go into the army, probably after high school or after college.

Leader: Why the army?

Third Boy: Either the army or the navy, into the service.

Leader: You mean instead of the Peace Corps?

Third Boy: No, I'd like to develop, but I have to serve, so I'd like to get it over with before I go into a career.

Leader: Anything else about who you might be with ten years from now?

Third Boy: I don't want to get married until I really have been around.

First Girl: I've got lots of things. I may be a teacher or join VISTA, and I don't know whether I'll be out of school at that time. Maybe I'll take a master's degree. I want to hitchhike across the country.

Leader: You want to hitchhike across the country. Why?

First Girl: I don't know.

Leader: Do you see yourself settling down at any time with a family or anything?

First Girl: I don't know when.

Leader: Do you see yourself as any different from what you are now, as a person?

First Girl: More experience.

Leader: More experience. What would that be?

First Girl: I don't know. I really can't tell.

Second Girl: I'm really not too sure. I'm interested in fashion designing, so I might go where they have a good art program for fashion. I'd like to live with a roommate for a while, and try for a career and see how it is and then settle down.

Leader: Did any of you mention anything that didn't require college?

Third Boy: I said I wanted to be in the service, and then I want to go to college.

Leader: To study what?

Third Boy: Music and regular college courses, too.

Leader: How clearly can you tell me the steps required to get where you want to be ten years from now? Do you know what you have to do?

First Boy: Well, going to college you have to keep up your marks while you're in high school and your average and things like that. And then, on the entrance exams, do well enough to get in college. And then from there you have to try to learn as much about the field you want to go in and do your own experimenting.

Leader: Is this going to cost you money?

First Boy: Yes, going to college, of course, unless you're going to a city college. Some don't cost anything.

Fourth Boy: My sister's going to college next year, and I can imagine what it's going to be like for me, because she's been looking through catalogues and trying to find a college she would like to go to. She's been taking tests, and she finally decided on one in Ohio. They accepted her, and she had to go out and visit it before she was accepted and make a good impression. I think it's been pretty hard on her. Now this summer, she's going to have to work to save up money for part of the tuition and so it's pretty hard on her.

Leader: What do you think your real chances are of meeting the picture you have of yourselves ten years from now? What do you think will really happen?

First Girl: I guess I'll become a teacher but I don't know about all the other things.

Leader: What makes you think you'll make the teacher thing?

First Girl: Well, I guess because my mother's a teacher.

Leader: Your mother's a teacher, so it seems very possible for you to go through those steps.

Fifth Boy: Well, I think chances really aren't that great to become exactly what I want, because I've changed my mind so many times, and I'll probably change it again.

Leader: But, no matter what you decide, what are the chances?

Fifth Boy: You mean when I finally decide? I'd say they're good.

Leader: How about you?

Third Boy: I really don't know. I think that, first of all, to get where I want to go, I'll have to be recognized by my school and be good in music.

Leader: What do you think the chances are of your being recognized as good?

Third Boy: About 75 percent that I'll be recognized.

Leader: And suppose they recognize you?

Third Boy: Then I'll be able to earn a living and have a family.

Leader: What about your chances, your real chances?

Second Girl: I really don't know. I'm not really sure about fashion design. I've changed my mind so many times that I'm running out of things to be.

Leader: But, assuming that that was it. You didn't change your mind. What do you think are your chances of becoming a fashion designer? With all the things you have to go through to become one?

Second Girl: Not very good.

Leader: Why?

Second Girl: Because I'm not really that good in art, and I know my parents would like me to go to college for things like math, history. I don't think they really want me to try anything like fashion designing. I've told them about it, and they didn't think too much of it.

Leader: What did they want you to try?

Second Girl: They really didn't give me any idea. I wanted to be a teacher, once. They liked that idea. I don't know.

Leader: So what's making the chances difficult, the fact that your parents aren't agreeing to what you'd like to do, or your not being able to decide?

Second Girl: Because of not being able to decide.

Leader: But, do you think that regardless of what you come up with, the chances are good for you to make whatever it is? Do you have confidence about it?

Second Girl: I guess pretty good. No, I don't really have confidence about it.

First Boy: If I don't change again, then I think the chances are pretty good that I would become what I want to be. If I change again . . .

Leader: What makes you think your chances are pretty good?

First Boy: Well, I think that if you want to be something enough that you want to be it, then you have enough control over your life, at least I think I have enough control over my life to become what I want to be.

Leader: What makes you think you have enough control over your life?

First Boy: I don't know what really makes me think that, but nothing makes me think differently.

Leader: Nothing makes you think that you don't have control. In other words, nobody put pressure on you too much, and whatever you decide you can fashion and shape without too much restriction.

First Boy: Well, not so much with my family, but just with my own interests, what I want to continue thinking about or looking into, I would.

A.3.4
MOON
RENDEZVOUS

**NEIL ARMSTRONG,
EDWIN E. ALDRIN,
AND MICHAEL COLLINS**

The Speaker: My distinguished colleagues of the Congress, we are honoring today three men who represent the best in America and whose coordinated skill, fantastic daring, and visionary drive have made history that constitutes a turning point of paramount importance in the journey of mankind. I have the high honor and official and personal pleasure of presenting to you the crew of Apollo 11, who successfully made the historic journey to the moon, Neil A. Armstrong, Col. Edwin E. Aldrin, Jr., and Lt. Col. Michael Collins.

The Chair recognizes Mr. Armstrong.

Mr. Armstrong: Mr. Speaker, Mr. President, Members of Congress, distinguished guests, we are greatly honored that you have invited us here today. Only now have we completed our journey to land on and explore the moon, and return. It was here in these Halls that our venture really began. Here the Space Act of 1958 was framed, the chartering document of the National Aeronautics and Space Administration. And here in the years that followed the key decisions that permitted the successive steps of Mercury and Gemini and Apollo were permitted.

Your policies and the marvels of modern communication have permitted people around the world to share the excitement of our exploration. And, although you have been informed of the results of the Apollo 11, we are particularly pleased to have this opportunity to complete our work by reporting to you and through you to the American people. My colleagues share the honor of presenting this report. First, it is my pleasure to present Col. Edwin Aldrin.

Colonel Aldrin: Distinguished ladies and gentlemen, it is with a great sense of pride as an American and with humility as a human being that I say to you today what no men have been privileged to say before: "We walked on the moon." But the footprints at Tranquility Base belong to more than the crew of Apollo 11. They were put there by hundreds of thousands of

Congressional Record, vol. 115, no. 148, September 16, 1969.

people across this country, people in Government, industry, and universities, the teams and crews that preceded us, all who strived throughout the years with Mercury, Gemini, and Apollo. Those footprints belong to the American people and you, their representatives, who accepted and supported the inevitable challenge of the moon. And, since we came in peace for all mankind those footprints belong also to all people of the world. As the moon shines impartially on all those looking up from our spinning earth so do we hope the benefits of space exploration will be spread equally with a harmonizing influence to all mankind.

Scientific exploration implies investigating the unknown. The result can never be wholly anticipated. Charles Lindberg said, "Scientific accomplishment is a path, not an end; a path leading to and disappearing in mystery."

Our steps in space have been a symbol of this country's way of life as we open our doors and windows to the world to view our successes and failures and as we share with all nations our discovery. The Saturn, Columbia, and Eagle, and the extravehicular mobility unit have proved to Neil, Mike, and me that this Nation can produce equipment of the highest quality and dependability. This should give all of us hope and inspiration to overcome some of the more difficult problems here on earth. The Apollo lesson is that national goals can be met where there is a strong enough will to do so.

The first step on the moon was a step toward our sister planets and ultimately toward the stars. "A small step for a man," was a statement of fact, "a giant leap for mankind," is a hope for the future.

What this country does with the lessons of Apollo apply to domestic problems, and what we do in further space exploration programs will determine just how giant a leap we have taken.

Thank you.

Mr. Armstrong: Now I should like to present Col. Michael Collins.

Colonel Collins: Mr. President, Members of Congress, and distinguished guests: One of the many things I have very much enjoyed about working for the Space Agency, and for the Air Force, is that they have always given me free rein, even to the extent of addressing this most august assemblage without coaching, without putting any words in my mouth. Therefore, my brief remarks are simply those of a free citizen living in a free country and expressing free thoughts that are purely my own.

Many years before there was a space program my father had a favorite quotation: "He who would bring back the wealth of the Indies must take the wealth of the Indies with him." This we have done. We have taken to the moon the wealth of this Nation, the vision of its political leaders, the intelligence of its scientists, the dedication of its engineers, the careful craftsmanship of its workers, and the enthusiastic support of its people. We have brought back rocks. And I think it is a fair trade. For just as the Rosetta stone revealed the language of ancient Egypt, so may these rocks unlock the mystery of the origin of the moon, of our earth, and even of our solar system.

During the flight of Apollo 11, in the constant sunlight between the earth and the moon, it was necessary for us to control the temperature of our spacecraft by a slow rotation not unlike that of a chicken on a barbecue spit. As we turned, the earth and the moon alternately appeared in our windows. We had our choice. We could look toward the Moon, toward Mars, toward our future in space—toward the new Indies—or we could look back toward the Earth, our home, with its problems spawned over more than a millennium of human occupancy.

We looked both ways. We saw both, and I think that is what our Nation must do.

We can ignore neither the wealth of the Indies nor the realities of the immediate needs of our cities, our citizens, or our civics. We cannot launch our planetary probes from a springboard of poverty, discrimination, or unrest. But neither can we wait until each and every terrestrial problem has been solved. Such logic 200 years ago would have prevented expansion westward past the Appalachian Mountains, for assuredly the eastern seaboard was beset by problems of great urgency then, as it is today.

Man has always gone where he has been able to go. It is that simple. He will continue pushing back his frontier, no matter how far it may carry him from his homeland.

Someday in the not-too-distant future, when I listen to an earthling step out onto the surface of Mars or some other planet, just as I listened to Neil step out onto the surface of the Moon, I hope I hear him say: "I come from the United States of America."

Mr. Armstrong: We landed on the Sea of Tranquility, in the cool of the early lunar morning, when the long shadows would aid our perception.

The sun was only 10° above the horizon. While the earth turned through nearly a full day during our stay, the sun at Tranquility Base rose barely 11°—a small fraction of the month-long lunar day. There was a peculiar sensation of the duality of time—the swift rush of events that characterizes all our lives—and the ponderous parade which marks the aging of the universe.

Both kinds of time were evident—the first by the routine events of the flight, whose planning and execution were detailed to fractions of a second—the latter by rocks around us, unchanged throughout the history of man—whose 3-billion-year-old secrets made them the treasure we sought.

The plaque of the Eagle which summarized our hopes bears this message:
Here men from the planet earth first set foot upon the moon July 1969 A.D.

We came in peace for all mankind. Those nineteen hundred and sixty-nine years had constituted the majority of the age of Pisces, a 12th of the great year. That is measured by the thousand generations the precession of the earth's axis requires to scribe a giant circle in the heavens.

In the next 20 centuries, the age of Aquarius of the great year, the age for which our young people have such high hopes, humanity may begin to understand its most baffling mystery—where are we going?

The earth is, in fact, traveling many thousands of miles per hour in the direction of the constellation Hercules—to some unknown destination in the cosmos. Man must understand his universe in order to understand his destiny.

Mystery however is a very necessary ingredient in our lives. Mystery creates wonder and wonder is the basis for man's desire to understand. Who knows what mysteries will be solved in our lifetime, and what new riddles will become the challenge of the new generations?

Science has not mastered prophesy. We predict too much for next year yet far too little for the next ten. Responding to challenge is one of democracy's great strengths: Our successes in space lead us to hope that this strength can be used in the next decade in the solution of many of our planet's problems. Several weeks ago I enjoyed the warmth of reflection on the true meanings of the spirit of Apollo.

I stood in the highlands of this Nation, near the Continental Divide, introducing to my sons the wonders of nature, and pleasures of looking for deer and for elk.

In their enthusiasm for the view they frequently stumbled on the rocky trails, but when they looked only to their footing, they did not see the elk. To those of you who have advocated looking high we owe our sincere gratitude, for you have granted us the opportunity to see some of the grandest views of the Creator.

To those of you who have been our honest critics, we also thank, for you have reminded us that we dare not forget to watch the trail. We carried on Apollo 11 two flags of this Union that had flown over the Capitol, one over the House of Representatives, one over the Senate. It is our privilege to return them now in these Halls which exemplify man's highest purpose—to serve one's fellow man.

We thank you, on behalf of all the men of Apollo, for giving us the privilege of joining you in serving—for all mankind.

[Applause, the Members rising.]

(Thereupon, the flags were presented to the Speaker and to the Vice President.)

The Speaker: I think we would be remiss on this occasion if we did not, in paying the highest honor that the Congress can pay to any person—to invite them and receive them in joint meeting—also honor what might be termed the unseen astronauts, the wives of our distinguished friends. I am going to ask the wives of the Astronauts to rise: Mrs. Armstrong, Mrs. Collins, Mrs. Aldrin.

[Applause, the Members rising.]

The Vice President: On behalf of the Members of the Senate, we are very grateful for the presentation of this flag. We watched with great interest the Apollo program proceed and are conscious of the thrust of the need, in the words of the gentleman who spoke here this morning, the primary need being balance and the need to meet the problems of our society wherever they arise.

I can assure you that this momento will not fall into that category but will be kept and appreciated with the dignity that it deserves.

Thank you very much.

The Speaker: On behalf of the House of Representatives I want to express our sincere thanks to the members of the Apollo 11 for the thought and for the action in carrying this flag, presented to the House, to the moon and flying it on the moon. These two flags are probably two of the most precious flags, not only of our own country, but of any other country. We extend to you the deep thanks of the Members of the House of Representatives and assure you that every care and caution will be taken, because this will be forever one of the most treasured possessions of this great Chamber.

[Applause, the Members rising.]

A.3.5
STRENGTHENING INTERNATIONAL DEVELOPMENT INSTITUTIONS

ADLAI E. STEVENSON

We meet here in Geneva at the midpoint of the Year of International Cooperation and the midpoint of the Decade of Development.* Let us be neither cynical nor despondent about the gap between these brave titles and the fact that at the moment our world community is in fact chiefly notable for minimal cooperation and very lopsided development. Our aspirations are there to spur us on, to incite us to better efforts. They are emphatically not there as a blind or a cover or a rhetoric to suggest that we are really doing very well.

I take as the understood premise of everything I say that as a world community we are not developing as we should and that our record of cooperation is inadequate, to say the least. But I believe—I hope—we can do better and that the nations meeting in 1970 will say: "Ah, yes, 1965 was a kind of turning point. That was the moment at which we began to realize how much better our performance has to be."

How much better can best be registered by a glance at where we are now.

We launched the Decade of Development because we realized, as a world community, that while our wealth was growing, its distribution had become increasingly unbalanced. I need hardly repeat the figures—the developed market economies and the developed centrally planned economies make up about a quarter of the world's population and account for three-quarters of the world's trade, production, and investment.

By the chances of history and geography, these developed nations are largely to be found to the north of the Tropic of Cancer. Ideology makes no difference here. Soviet Russia belongs by income and growth to the developed "north," Ghana to the developing "south" in our new economic geography.

These facts we knew in 1960. In the last 5 years the contrasts have grown more vivid. The developed nations with per capita incomes of above $700 a

*Made before the 39th session of the UN Economic and Social Council at Geneva, Switzerland, on July 9, 1965 (Press Release 170).

Department of State Bulletin, vol. 53, no. 1361, (July 26, 1965), pp. 142–151.

year have grown—the index I use is gross national product per head of population—by not less than 3 percent a year.

Below them a smaller group of nations, which are in the range of $200 to $700 per capita, have grown even more rapidly—by 4 to 8 percent a year.

But at the bottom of the scale at a figure of $200 per head and less, comprising over a hundred nations making up over two-thirds of humanity, the rate of per capita growth has in many instances been less than the average of 2.3 percent of the developing countries as a whole. Population growth has swallowed up their margins, and per capita growth hovers around zero.

THE HIDDEN MISERIES

This is the statistical picture which emerges from the present data about world development. But how bare and uninformative such numbers really are. They tell us nothing about the rates of child mortality—10 times higher among poor than rich. They give us no picture of the homeless migrant living without water or shelter on the fringe of Asian or Latin American cities. We get no feel from them of the dull ache of hunger or the debility that comes from diets without enough protein and vitamins.

These are the hidden miseries about which we talk with our figures of per capita gross national product, our statistical comparisons, our impersonal percentages. We are talking about pain and grief and hunger and despair, and we are talking about the lot of half the human race.

EXPANSION IN THE DEVELOPED SOCIETIES

But we are also talking about another phenomenon—the extraordinary increase in resources available to human society taken as a whole. These 3- or 4-percent increases in the national growth of developed societies mean an unparalleled expansion of new resources.

Under steady and responsible economic management, we cannot see, and we certainly do not want, any end to this process of expansion. Out of the research that is connected with weaponry, with space, and with the whole wide range of needs of our civilian economy, we are constantly making new breakthroughs—new methods, new products, new sources of food or energy or medical relief that increase our capacity to reproduce wealth still further. We have harnessed energy to take us into outer space and to convert saline waters into drink for the thirsty. The isotopes which grow from nuclear experiments can revolutionize medical and agricultural research. And we know not what new, still undiscovered sources of abundance lie ahead.

We have to begin to grasp and digest this new, astonishing liberation of our industrial resources, for only after such an understanding can we hope to act on the scale and with the audacity that our profound problems of poverty and hopelessness and obstruction demand. We shall conquer, no doubt, the dark face of the moon. But I would hope we can with equal confidence conquer the dark face of poverty and give men and women new life, new hope, new space on this planet.

Let's face it: We are nowhere near conquering world poverty. None of us—neither the weak nor the strong, the poor nor the rich, the new nations nor the old—have yet taken seriously enough the contrast between the abundance of our opportunities and the scarcity of our actions to grasp them. It is good that the rich are getting richer—that is what economic development is for. But it is bad that, despite our considerable efforts in the first half of this decade, the poor are still poor—and progressing more slowly than present-day society can tolerate.

What shall we do to improve the trend during the next 5 years? There is something for everybody to do. There are tasks for all of us, and it won't help the poor countries for us to sit around this table blaming the state of the world on each other. There are clear and present tasks for the developing countries in doing what they know is necessary to their own economic growth and social progress. There are tasks, equally clear and equally present, for the industrialized countries. And there are tasks—a growing number of much larger tasks—for U.N. organizations themselves.

I think each of us should come to this table vowing to bring proposals that his nation can—and intends to—do something about. In that spirit I will not rehearse here my views on how the developing nations can better help themselves but will suggest what the wealthier countries can do to help and how the U.N. itself can do more about development and do it better.

A CONVERGENT STRATEGY

Let me suggest first the sense of a convergent strategy for the industrialized nations. Its aim should be to see to it that more of the wealth and purchasing power of our expanding world economy will be used to stimulate economic growth in the developing nations.

We can accomplish this aim only by the coordinate use of a variety of means: by the direct transfer of resources from developed nations to developing nations through effective aid programs; next, by assuring the developing countries greater access to the expanding markets of the world; next, by working to reduce fluctuations in the export earnings of the developing countries; next, by working harder, doing more specific research, on what the more developed countries can do to help the less developed create more wealth faster; next, by helping to slow down the vertiginous growth in the numbers of people which the still fragile developing economies have to support. A steady, overall, 4-percent rate of growth in national income is in itself a difficult achievement. Its effects are tragically nullified if the rate of population growth is 3 percent or even more.

These five strands of a convergent strategy contain no mysteries. We have discussed them over and over again. What has been lacking has been an adequate urgency of purpose and decision and a real determination to face the full costs.

There is no doubt that we can afford whatever direct transfer of resources can really be put to effective use. There are so many manmade obstacles in the developing process that there is a kind of natural limit to the transfer of resources from the richer countries to the poorer countries.

In my judgment, we are in no danger at all of harming our own healthy economies by maximizing our efforts to promote international development. Our problem, rather, is to step up the training of people, the surveying of resources, and the investigation of opportunities—in a word, the preinvestment work—which still sets the ceiling on direct investment, public and private, in the economic growth of most developing countries.

With my next point—improved trading opportunities for the developing countries—I come to all the issues at stake in the continuing work of the new U.N. Trade and Development Board and its committees, and of the GATT [General Agreement of Tariffs and Trade]. These are some of the problems we must face together. Primary prices are unstable, and many have tended downward in the last decade. The tariff structures in the industrial countries hit harder at the processed and manufactured goods than at raw materials. Internal taxes discourage the consumption of tropical products. And finally, there is need for greater effort to improve production and efficiency in the export industries of the developing countries.

Many of the developing countries suffer enormous uncertainties and interruptions of trade, with their unstable, fluctuating export earnings. The world has already put into effect some means of providing compensatory finance and balance-of-payments support to help the developing countries deal with such difficulties. Perhaps we will never find an ideal solution, but I think we have by no means reached the end of the road in dealing with these problems. We must continue to do everything practicable to provide to developing countries resources that are effectively related to the fluctuations in their export trade.

When I say we need a concerted attack on these obstacles, I do not mean a great debate in which the attack is concerted against the governments of the wealthier countries. Complaints about other countries' policies have their place in international politics—they seldom change what the other nations actually do, but they help make the complainant a hero to his own countrymen—and that has its place in politics too.

But when it comes to trade between the world's "north" and the world's "south," we need not a general debate about general principles but concrete proposals, direct negotiations, specific nose-to-nose confrontations about particular ways the developing countries can increase their exports and how the rest of us can really help, commodity by commodity.

RESEARCH ON CAUSE AND CURES OF POVERTY

Another vital contribution the industrialized nations can make to development is to expand their own research into the cause and cures of poverty. Partly this is a matter of putting extra emphasis on those fields of science that are especially relevant to the needs and possibilities of the developing countries. We stand here in the presence of exciting breakthroughs in nutrition, in farming, in water use, in meteorology, in energy. All these are vital, and it is particularly gratifying that the United Nations Advisory Group of Scientists have put the development of water resources and the evolution of new high-protein diets at the top of their list of points needing special attack.

Mr. President, while I am on this subject, I should like to say a special word about the work of the Advisory Committee on the Application of Science and Technology to Development. My Government will make known in due course its detailed views with respect to the specific proposals made by this group in the report which is before us. As to the report itself, I would only say at this time that it is clear, precise, and professional—high testimony to the quality of work that can be done in our international community. On behalf of my delegation, I should like to congratulate all members of the Advisory Committee, the many experts of the specialized agencies who contributed to it, and the members of the United Nations Secretariat under whose supervision the work went forward.

But I have more in mind than the merits of the recommendations put forward and the quality of the report as a whole. I have in mind the background of this report and the process by which these proposals have taken shape for our consideration.

The background of the report, as we all know, is the Conference on the Application of Science and Technology to Problems of the Developing Areas, held here in Geneva in early 1963. That conference was criticized by superficial observers. They said that the whole thing was much too big—too many people, too many subjects, too many papers, too much talk to do any good. They said that the whole thing was much too vague—too general, too unfocused, too disparate—and perhaps there was something in some of this criticism.

But it was a start. And the big thing is that we did not let it die. We maintained the momentum generated at that conference. We went on to the next step. Within a few months after the close of that conference, this Council recommended the establishment of an expert committee of advisers to carry on—to pick up where the conference left off—to sort the important from what is merely useful.

I have no doubt, Mr. President, that what followed was a difficult and tedious exercise for the committee of advisers. But they went about it systematically. They consulted and took evidence. They worked steadily and quietly. And out of thousands of things that might be good to do, they have derived a few dozen of things which it is urgent and necessary to do—which, in fact, it would be outrageous not to do. They have resisted dreams of tomorrow's science and thought hard about today's technology. They have refrained from proposing yet another agency and come to grips instead with existing agencies—what more they might do, what we know they can do better, with foreseeable resources.

So what began as a seemingly unmanageable project has been tamed, mastered, and transmitted into a sensible list of specific proposals of priority value and manageable proportion. This is no small accomplishment in so short a time. And we can all take heart from this exercise. It bodes well for the work of the Council and of the U.N. system at large.

RESEARCH ON URBANIZATION

The Advisory Committee focused of course on science and technology—that is what it was asked to do. But we need research and inquiry fully as much in great areas of social confusion and uncertainty.

I must be content with one vital example. All through the developing world we face an increasing crisis of accelerated and uncontrolled urbanization. Men and women and children are streaming into the great cities, generally the capital cities, from the monotony and all too often the misery of rural life, and they are moving, bag and baggage, long before farming can afford to lose their labor or the city is ready to put them to work and accommodate them properly.

This rootless, hopeless, workless urban poverty is the greatest single cause of misery in the world. Can we lessen or redirect this flow? Can we prepare the urban world better to receive it? Or improve the rural world enough to diminish the flood? We don't know, because we have not sought seriously to find out.

We lack adequate policies, because we have so few facts and so few people trained to develop and implement programs. For too long we have proceeded on the false assumption that people would really rather live in villages than anywhere and that it is better for society if they did. The trouble is they don't—even when the village is modernized and sanitized and electrified, people move into larger towns and cities.

Some countries have in fact recognized that the problem is not less urbanization but more urban area—not just one or two in each country. Some are experimenting with regional development programs—and here I mean regions within countries—in an effort to create new urban centers which will not only deflect migration headed for already overcrowded capital cities but will have an impact on the surrounding countryside and improve rural living in a wide area around the new cities. But the process of decentralization is difficult and complex, and failures—temporary or permanent—are as common as successes.

This is the background against which we helped launch the unanimous decision of the Social Commission to recommend a research training program in regional development, using as a laboratory the current efforts being made in a variety of different lands, political systems, and cultures to deal with the problems of urban in-migration.

With some systematic research perhaps some usable conclusions can be drawn about how best to encourage an appropriate pattern of urban development which will avoid the blight and misery so visible in so many cities throughout the world. This is precisely the kind of research we need if the full weight of modern discovery and modern resources is to be brought to bear on the social as well as the technical problems of the developing world.

POPULATION CONTROL

In this same context—of science applied to an explosive human and social problem—we have to make a wholly new attack upon what President Johnson has called "the multiplying problems of our multiplying populations." It is perhaps only in the last 5 years that we have come fully to realize on what scale they are proliferating. Since 1960, under United Nations auspices, censuses have been held in scores of countries, in nine of them for the first time. They have all underlined the same fact—that population is increasing more rapidly than had previously been imagined and that this accelerating growth, in all developing lands, is eating into the pitiful margins needed to give bread and hope to those already born. We have to find the ways of social, moral, and physical control adequate to stem the rising, drowning flood of people. We need more knowledge, we need more cooperative effort. In fact, much that we do elsewhere will be undone unless we can act in this vital field.

Aid, trade, research, population control—in all these fields we can mount a convergent attack upon the great gap between rich and poor. But we must also mount it together. And that brings me to some quite concrete suggestions about international organizations in the development field—in what direction they should be going and how fast they should be growing.

MERITS OF FUNCTIONAL ORGANIZATIONS

The organizations of the U.N. family perform a rich variety of useful labors. At a moment when one of the central political organs in the U.N. is temporarily hung up on a constitutional hook, it is worth reflecting on the success and growth of the specialized agencies and of the central funds which provide a growing fraction—more than half in some cases—of the resources they apply to the business of development. These agencies are an illustration, and a good one, of the proposition that international politics is not a game in which an inch gained by our player must mean an inch lost by another.

The reality is that international agreements can be reached, and international organizations can be formed, and international common law can be elaborated, on subjects which draw nations together even as they continue to quarrel about the frontiers and friends and ideological frenzies which keep them apart.

So let's look for a moment at the political merits of functional organizations—the kind that work at peace through health, or food, or education, or labor, or communications, or meteorology, or culture, or postal service, or children, or money, or economic growth, or the exploration of outer space—organizations, that is, for the pursuit of some specific and definable task beyond the frontiers of one nation, a task for which the technology is already conceived or conceivable, for which a common interest is mutually recognized, for which institutions can—and therefore must—be designed.

Organizations like these begin by taking the world as it is. No fundamental political reforms are needed; no value systems have to be altered; no ideologies have to be seriously compromised. These organizations start from where we are and then take the next step. And that, as the ancient Chinese guessed long ago, is the only way to get from here to there.

These organizations tackle jobs that can be managed through imperfect institutions by fallible men and women. Omniscience is not a prerequisite; the peace of the world does not stand or fall on the success of any one organization; mistakes need not be fatal.

These limited-purpose organizations bypass the obstacle of sovereignty. National independence is not infringed when a nation voluntarily accepts in its own interest the restraints imposed by cooperation with others. Nobody has to play who doesn't want to play, but for those who do play, there are door prizes for all.

All these special characteristics of the functional agencies are important to their survival value and growth potential. The best example is also momentarily the most dramatic. In the midst of the military, political, and diplomatic turmoil of Southeast Asia, the governments which are working together to promote the regional development of the Lower Mekong Basin have continued to work there in surprising and encouraging harmony.

POLITICAL DISPUTES IN TECHNICAL AGENCIES

But a certain shadow hangs over the affairs of the technical agencies—a shadow which threatens to compromise the very virtues we have just been discussing. That shadow is political controversy, and it has no place on the agenda of the technical agencies.

I shall not attempt to draw sharp lines along the sometimes murky borders between the politicoideological and the functional fields—between just what is doctrinal and just what is technical. The important distinctions are clear enough. The difference between appropriate content for the general debate in the General Assembly and appropriate content for debates on international labor or world literacy or world health does not need much elaboration. We can all recognize that the remaining problems of colonialism have practically nothing to do with the problem of adult literacy—and vice versa. We have organizational arrangements for dealing with both. We have times and places set aside, we have agenda prepared and representatives assigned, for dealing in separate and orderly ways with these and other subjects.

Yet we cannot overlook a disturbing tendency to dilute the proceedings of the technical agencies with ideological dispute—and to steal time, energy, and resources needed to help the developing countries, and divert it instead to extraneous issues calculated to stir everybody's emotions without raising anybody's per capita income.

This limits the value, inhibits the growth, hurts the prestige, and crimps the resources of the technical agencies. It is a wasteful and moreover a futile exercise. It is only to be hoped that these diversionary tactics will fade from our forums so we may get along more promptly with the practical, useful, technical tasks which lie before us in such profusion.

The great spurt in useful activity by the U.N. specialized and affiliated agencies has come about through the good sense of the members, expressed in a series of actions by the Economic and Social Council and in the General Assembly, and designed to provide new resources to break down the main obstacles to development.

Through the Expanded Program of Technical Assistance and the U.N. Special Fund the members have already provided close to $1 billion to help the developing countries organize the use of knowledge and to get ready to make effective use of large capital investments. Now these two programs, on the recommendation of the Council, are to be merged in the 20th General Assembly to become the U.N. Development Program.

We are reaching this year, for the first time, the target of $150 million a year for that program. My Government believes that this has been a useful and efficient way to provide technical assistance and preinvestment capital. The target should now be raised. For our part, we would be glad to see the target set substantially higher.

We also think that the use for development of noncommercial exports of food from some of the surplus-producing countries has been promising. At a meeting in Rome last week we have already indicated that we would be glad to see the World Food Program continued, with a target for the next 3-year period almost triple that of the 3-year experimental period which is just now coming to an end. We hope that other nations which foresee noncommercial surpluses in their agricultural horoscope will join in expanding the World Food Program as another way to transfer needed resources for the benefit of the developing countries.

We are also pleased with the progress of industrial development. The establishment of the Center for Industrial Development in the U.N. Secretariat has clearly proved itself a sound and progressive move. We think the time has come to move further along this line and find much promise in the suggestions made by the distinguished representative of the United Kingdom on this subject. We strongly agree that it will be necessary to secure additional resources for the promotion of industrialization. We believe, however, that rather than to establish yet another special voluntary fund, such resources could best be made available by special arrangements within the framework of the new U.N. Development Program.

INTERNATIONAL DEVELOPMENT PROGRAMS

Beyond raising the target for the Development Program, and expanding the World Food Program, and giving a special push to the work of industrialization, I would foresee another kind of development activity to which I believe every government should accord a very high priority indeed. This is the field which might be called truly international development programs.

So far we have needed to define the word "development" to encompass only the elements of an individual country's economic growth and social progress. Some regional projects have gained favor as well, but clearly visible now on the horizon are programs and projects in which the operating agency will not be a national government or a private company or even a small group of governments in a region—but rather one of the U.N.'s own family of worldwide organizations.

The best example—one that is already requiring our attention—is the World Weather Watch now being planned by the WMO [World Meterological Organization]. In the preliminary design work already underway, it is proposed, for example, to:

—probe into atmosphere from satellites in orbit;
—establish ground stations to read out what the satellites have to say
   and to process and communicate weather information throughout
   continental regions;
—establish floating weather stations to give more coverage to vast
   oceanic areas, particularly in the Southern Hemisphere;
—possibly even launch balloons from international sites which will
   travel around the world at a constant level making weather
   observations as they go.

The major components of the World Weather Watch must continue to be the national facilities, operated primarily for national purposes and also contributing to the needs of the world. But we are speaking here of additional facilities, some of which may need to be internationally operated and perhaps internationally owned and which may be very costly even at the start. Money would have to be raised on a voluntary basis and placed in the hands of an international agency—the WMO, perhaps, or some new operating facility.

Here, then, is a new kind of problem for us to think about before it overtakes us. Here is a great big development project, involving activity inherently international which will have to be financed internationally. We would propose that the U.N. Development Program start experimenting with this kind of development activity, modifying as necessary the rules and procedures that were drafted with national development projects in mind.

Maybe such large projects will have to be financed in some special way. But for a start we would like to see the new U.N. Development Program, with its rich experience in financing various kinds of development, work on this subject and present to its own board, and to this Council, an analysis of the problem of meeting the costs of global international operations.

If all these suggestions for raising our sights—yes, and our contributions—give the impression that the United States believes in the strengthening of international development institutions, you may be sure that the impression is correct. Most of these institutions need to be strengthened to meet, within their respective areas, the challenge of the requirements and aspirations of the developing countries. Equally, and perhaps even more important, their policies and actions need to be harmonized, for there is no room left in this world for narrow parochialism. The various aspects and problems of economic and social development—modernization of agriculture and industrial growth, health and production, education and social welfare, trade and transportation, human rights and individual freedom—have become so closely interrelated as to call for interlocking measures and programs.

These basic conditions in the contemporary world give meaning and urgency to the review and reappraisal of the Economic and Social Council's role and functions which U Thant proposed in this chamber a year ago. The position of my Government is set forth in our submission to the Secretary-General reproduced in document E/4052/Add. 2 and needs no further explanation.

But there are just a few points I want to stress:

With the U.N. system as envisaged in and established by the charter, the General Assembly and ECOSOC [Economic and Social Council] are the two principal intergovernmental organs with overall responsibilites for U.N. policies and activities in the economic and social field, their orderly development and effective implementation.

Whatever the record of the Council in the past—and we believe that it is a good record—it has become evident that the Council faces ever-increasing difficulties in the discharge of its functions due to the ever-widening scope of the United Nations and the multiplication of machinery.

To make the Council fully representative of the total enlarged membership of the U.N., its size will soon be increased by the necessary ratifications of the charter amendment.

We believe that the role of the Council as a preparatory body for the General Assembly, and acting under its authority, needs to be clarified and strengthened. It should make a significant contribution to the work of the General Assembly by drawing its attention to major issues confronting the world economy; by formulating proposals for relevant action; by providing supporting documentation; and in preparing and reviewing programs with a sense of financial responsibilities—and thus assisting in the preparation of budget estimates by the Secretary-General for appropriate action by the committees of the General Assembly.

In stressing the coordination function of ECOSOC every care needs to be taken to encourage rather than to hinder the work of functional and regional economic and social bodies and the activities of the specialized agencies and other related organizations. The role of these functional organizations in achieving coordination within their areas of competence needs to be more fully recognized.

The review and reappraisal proposed by the Secretary-General is a difficult task and adequate time must be allowed for it. Many of the constructive suggestions he made yesterday regarding research, documentation, and sound budgeting are directly related to the work of the Council and deserve most careful thought. It is our hope that the Council at the present session will make the necessary arrangements to facilitate and assure such study in depth and full consideration.

We assume the review will go through several stages, including consideration by both the Council and the General Assembly. The Council will have to undertake thorough preparatory work in order to enable the General Assembly and its Committees II [Economic and Financial], III [Social, Humanitarian and Cultural], and V [Administrative and Budgetary] to reach informed conclusions and to take the necessary actions.

Last but not least, and this I cannot stress strongly enough, the review will require the closest possible cooperation between all members of the Council representing developed and developing countries. The Council will wither away, whatever conclusions are reached by the review, unless there is a will among all of us to make it succeed. And succeed it must as an indispensable organ of the United Nations for the achievement, beyond anything we have experienced to date, of constructive international cooperation in the economic and social fields and as a powerful aid to the promotion of economic development.

Finally, let me say that the need for joint action in the wide field of development is obvious. Whether we are talking about aid, or trade, or research, or urban development, or industrialization—whether we are talking about scientific discovery or about institution building—we hold that there are no monopolies of trained minds and disciplined imaginations in any of our countries.

Joint action is, after all, the final significance of all we do in our international policies today. But we are still held back by our old parochial nationalisms. We are still beset with dark prejudices. We are still divided by angry, conflicting ideologies. Yet all around us our science, our instruments, our technologies, our interests, and indeed our deepest aspirations draw us more and more closely into a single neighborhood.

This must be the context of our thinking—the context of human interdependence in the face of the vast new dimensions of our science and our discovery. Just as Europe could never again be the old closed-in community after the voyages of Columbus, we can never again be a squabbling band of nations before the awful majesty of outer space.

We travel together, passengers on a little space ship, dependent on its vulnerable reserves of air and soil; all committed for our safety to its security and peace; preserved from annihilation only by the care, the work, and, I will say, the love we give our fragile craft. We cannot maintain it half fortunate, half miserable, half confident, half despairing, half slave—to the ancient enemies of man—half free in a liberation of resources undreamed of until this day. No craft, no crew can travel safely with such vast contradicitions. On this resolution depends the survival of us all.

BIBLIOGRAPHY

Abt, Clark C. 1970. *Serious Games.* New York: Viking.

Aly, Bower, and Lucile F. Aly. 1968. *Speeches in English.* New York: Random House.

Ashby, W. Ross. 1963. *An Introduction to Cybernetics.* New York: Wiley.

Auer, J. Jeffery. 1967. *Brigance's Speech Communication.* New York: Appleton-Century-Crofts.

Bagdikian, Ben H. 1971. *The Information Machines: Their Impact on Men and the Media.* New York: Harper & Row.

Baird, A. C., F. H. Knower, and S. L. Becker. 1971. *General Speech Communication.* New York: McGraw-Hill.

Bales, Robert Freed. 1970. *Personality and Interpersonal Behavior.* New York: Holt, Rinehart & Winston.

Barker, L. L., and R. J. Kibler (eds.) 1971. *Speech Communication Behavior.* Englewood Cliffs, N.J.: Prentice-Hall.

Beck, A. H. W. 1967. *Words and Waves.* New York: McGraw-Hill.

Bell, Daniel. 1967. "Toward the Year 2000: Work in Progress," *Daedalus*, vol. 96, no. 3, p. 697.

Borden, G. A., R. B. Gregg, and T. G. Grove. 1969. *Speech Behavior and Human Interaction.* Englewood Cliffs, N.J.: Prentice-Hall.

Brown, H., J. Bonner, and J. Weir. 1963. *The Next Hundred Years.* New York: Viking.

Buber, Martin. 1953. *Good and Evil.* New York: Scribner's.

Buber, Martin. 1958. *I and Thou.* New York: Scribner's.

Buber, Martin. 1967. *A Believing Humanism.* New York: Simon & Schuster.

Buckley, Walter (ed.) 1968. *Modern Systems Research for the Behavioral Scientist.* Chicago: Aldine.

Buehler, E. C., and W. A. Linkugel. 1969. *Speech Communication: A First Course.* New York: Harper & Row.

Byers, B., A. Coladarci, L. S. Harms, and P. Heinberg. 1971. *The Hawaii Communication Test.* Honolulu: State Department of Education.

Carnegie Commission Report. 1971. *Less Time, More Options.* New York: McGraw-Hill.

Casmir, Fred, and L. S. Harms (eds.) 1970. *International Studies Of*

National Speech Education Systems: Volume 1. Current Reports on Twelve Countries. Minneapolis: Burgess.

Cherry, Colin. 1966 *On Human Communication: A Review, A Survey, and A Criticism.* Cambridge, Mass.: M.I.T. Press.

Cherry, Colin. 1971. *World Communication, Threat or Promise? A Socio-technical Approach.* New York: Wiley-Interscience.

Clarke, Arthur C. 1967. *Voices from the Sky.* New York: Pyramid.

Clarke, Arthur C. 1972. *Report on Planet Three and Other Speculations.* New York: Harper & Row.

Clevenger, T., Jr., and J. Matthews. 1971. *The Speech Communication Process.* Glenview, Ill.: Scott, Foresman.

Coates, Joseph, "Technology Assessment," 5, no. 6: pp. 225-231

Cobb, R. W., and C. Elder. 1970. *International Community: A Regional and Global Study.* New York: Holt, Rinehart & Winston.

The Conference Board. 1972. *Information Technology: Some Critical Implications for Decision Makers.* New York: Conference Board.

D'Arcy, Jean. 1969. "Direct Broadcast Satellites and the Right to Communicate." *European Broadcasting Union Review,* 118.

Dechert, Charles R. (ed.) 1967. *The Social Impact of Cybernetics.* New York: Simon & Schuster.

Deutsch, Karl W. 1966. *Nationalism and Social Communication: An Inquiry into the Foundations of Nationality.* Cambridge, Mass.: M.I.T. Press.

Dubos, Rene. 1968. *So Human An Animal.* New York: Scribner's.

Dykstra, G. 1971. *Giant Step: A Pre-School Reading System.* Honolulu: International Learning Systems.

Eichelberger, Clark M. 1968. *The United Nations and Human Rights.* Dobbs Ferry, N.Y.: Oceana Publications.

Fasan, Ernst. 1970. *Relations with Alien Intelligences: The Scientific Basis of Metalaw.* Berlin: Berlin-Verlag.

Feinberg, Gerald. 1969. *The Prometheus Project.* Garden City, N.Y.: Doubleday.

Fitzgerald, Edward. (tr.) 1955. *Rubaiyat of Omar Khayyam of Naishapur.* Berkhamsted, England: Rodale Press

Froehlich, John P. 1969. *Information Transmittal and Communicating Systems.* New York: Holt, Rinehart & Winston.

Fuller, R. Buckminster. 1969. *Utopia or Oblivion: The Prospects for Humanity.* New York: Bantam.

Fuller, R. Buckminster. 1970. *I Seem To Be A Verb.* New York: Bantam.

Geldard, Frank A. (ed.) 1965. *Communication Processes.* New York: MacMillan.

Gerbner, G., O. R. Holsti, K. Krippendorff, W. J. Paisley, and P. J. Stone. 1969. *The Analysis of Communication Content: Developments in Scientific Theories and Computer Techniques.* New York: Wiley.

Goffman, Erving. 1969. *Strategic Interaction.* Philadelphia: University of Pennsylvania Press.

Gray, Giles W., and Claude M. Wise. 1959. *The Bases of Speech.* New York: Harper & Row.

Hall, Peter. 1966. *The World Cities.* New York: McGraw-Hill.

Harms, L. S. 1974. *Intercultural Communication.* New York: Harper & Row.

Harms, L. S., and Joan Y. Harms. 1972. *The Meeting Game.* Honolulu: Harms and Assoc.

Hawkes, Jacuaetta. *The World of the Past.* New York: Knopf, 1963.

Heinberg, P., L. S. Harms, and J. Yamada. 1970. *Speech Communication Learning System.* Honolulu: International Learning Systems.

Heinberg, P., L. S. Harms, W. Nunokawa et al. 1972. *The Preferred Futures: A Report on Measurement of the Capacity of Education to Empower Humans to Achieve Their Preferred Futures.* Honolulu: State Department of Education.

Hellman, Hal. 1969. *Communications in the World of the Future.* New York: M. Evans.

Helmer, Olaf. 1966. *Social Technology.* New York: Basic Books.

Hinchman, W. R., and D. A. Dunn. 1970. *The Future of Satellite Communications.* New York: Twentieth Century Fund.

Jaffee, J., and S. Feldstein. 1970. *Rhythms of Dialogue.* New York: Academic Press.

Jones, Douglas. 1971. *Communication and Energy in Changing Urban Environments.* Connecticut: Shoe String Press.

Keltner, John W. 1970. *Interpersonal Speech-Communication: Elements and Structures.* Belmont, Calif.: Wadsworth.

Kibler, R. J., and L. L. Barker (eds.) 1969. *Conceptual Frontiers in Speech-Communication: Report of the New Orleans Conference on Research and Instructional Development.* New York: Speech Association of America.

Kleinjans, Everett. 1973. "Foundations for East-West Understanding," in Jim Richstad and L. S. Harms (eds.) *World Communication.* Honolulu: East-West Center Press.

Lacy, Dan. 1961. *Freedom and Communications.* Urbana, Ill.: University of Illinois Press.

Lange, D. L., R. K. Baker, and S. J. Ball. 1969. *Mass Media and Violence.* Washington, D.C.: U.S. Government Printing Office.

Lenneberg, Eric H. 1967. *Biological Foundations of Language.* New York: Wiley.

Lerner, Daniel, and Wilbur Schramm. 1967. *Communication and Change in the Developing Countries.* Honolulu: East-West Center Press.

Lerner, Daniel. 1958. *The Passing of Traditional Society.* New York: Free Press.

Lorenz, Konrad. 1967. *On Aggression.* New York: Bantam.

McDonald, R. L., and W. H. Hesse. 1970. *Space Science.* Columbus, Ohio: Charles E. Merrill.

McHale, John. 1969. *The Future of the Future.* New York: Braziller.

McLuhan, Marshall and Quentin Fiore. 1967. *The Medium Is the Massage: An Inventory of Effects.* New York: Bantam.

McLuhan, Marshall and Quentin Fiore. 1968. *War and Peace in the Global Village.* New York: Bantam.

McWhinney, Edward (ed.) 1971. *The International Law of Communications.* Dobbs Ferry, N.Y.: Oceana Publications.

Malmberg, Bertil (ed.) 1968. *Manual of Phonetics.* Amsterdam: North-Holland.

Martin, James. 1969. *Telecommunications and the Computer.* Englewood Cliffs, N.J.: Prentice-Hall.

Maruyama, M., and J. A. Dator (eds.) 1971. *Human Futuristics.* Honolulu, Hawaii: Social Science Research Institute.

Matson, Floyd W., and Ashley Montagu. 1967. *The Human Dialogue.* New York: Free Press.

Mead, Margaret. 1970. *Culture and Commitment: A Study of the Generation Gap.* Garden City, N.Y.: Doubleday.

Meadow, Charles T. 1970. *Man-Machine Communication.* New York: Wiley-Interscience.

Mills, Theodore M. 1964. *Group Transformation: An Analysis of a Learning Group.* Englewood Cliffs, N.J.: Prentice-Hall.

Moles, Abraham. 1966. *Information Theory and Esthetic Perception.* Chicago: University of Illinois Press.

Monroe, A. H., and D. Ehninger. 1967. *Principles and Types of Speech.* Glenview, Ill.: Scott, Foresman.

Mortensen, C. David. 1972. *Communication: The Study of Human Interaction.* New York: McGraw-Hill.

Mowlana, Hamid. 1971. *International Communication: A Selected Bibliography.* Dubuque, Iowa: Kendall/Hunt.

Moyers, Bill. 1971. *Listening to America.* New York: Dell.

Nakamura, Hajime. 1964. *Ways of Thinking of Eastern Peoples.* Honolulu: East-West Center Press.

Nelson, James, (ed.) 1961. *Wisdom for our Time.* New York: Norton.

Neumann, John von. 1963. *The Computer and the Brain.* New Haven, Conn.: Yale University Press.

Newman, R. P., and D. R. Newman. 1969. *Evidence.* Boston: Houghton Mifflin.

Norman, Donald A. 1969. *Memory and Attention: An Introduction to Human Information Processing.* New York: Wiley.

Oceana-United Nations Study-Guide Series. 1963. *Human Rights.* Dobbs Ferry, N.Y.: Oceana Publications.

Peterson, Houston, 1965. *The World's Great Speeches.* New York: Simon & Schuster.

Phillips, G. M., and E. C. Erickson. 1970. *Interpersonal Dynamics in the Small Group.* New York: Random House.

Pool, I. D. S., P. Stone, and S. Szalai. 1971. *Communications, Computers and Automation for Development.* New York: UNITAR Research Reports.

Ramo, Simon. 1970. *Century of Mismatch.* New York: David McKay.

Rao, Y. V. Lakshmana. 1966. *Communication and Development.* Minneapolis, Minn.: University of Minnesota Press.

Reichardt, Jasia (ed.) 1971. *Cybernetics, Art and Ideas.* Greenwich, Conn.: New York Graphic Society.

Rogers, E. M., and R. R. Shoemaker. 1971. *Communication of Innovations.* New York: Free Press.

Rose, Caroline B. 1965. *Sociology: The Study of Man in Society.* Columbus, Ohio: Charles E. Merrill.

Ross, Raymond S. 1970. *Speech Communication: Fundamentals and Practice.* Englewoods Cliffs, N.J.: Prentice-Hall.

Ruesch, J., and G. Bateson. 1968. *Communication: The Social Matrix of Psychiatry.* New York: Norton.

Russell, Bertrand. 1961. *Has Man a Future?* Baltimore: Penguin.

Ruzic, Neil P. 1970. *Where the Winds Sleep.* Garden City, N.Y.: Doubleday.

Schroder, H. M., M. J. Driver, and S. Streufert. 1967. *Human Information Processing: Individuals and Groups Functioning in Complex Social Situations.* New York: Holt, Rinehart & Winston.

Sereno, K. K., and C. D. Mortensen (eds.) 1970. *Foundations of Communication Theory.* New York: Harper & Row.

Shklovskii, I. S., and C. Sagan. 1966. *Intelligent Life in the Universe.* New York: Dell.

Siegman, A. W., and B. Pope (eds.) 1972. *Studies in Dyadic Communication.* Elmsford, N.Y.: Pergamon Press.

Siu, R. G. H. 1957. *The Tao of Science.* Cambridge, Mass.: M.I.T. Press.

Snow, C.P. 1963. *The Two Cultures: And A Second Look.* New York: New American Library.

Sohn, Louis B. 1970. *The United Nations: The Next Twenty-Five Years.* Dobbs Ferry, N.Y.: Oceana Publications.

Sommer, Robert. 1969. *Personal Space: The Behavioral Basis of Design.* Englewood Cliffs, N.J.: Prentice-Hall.

Stevenson, Adlai E. 1965. "Strengthening International Development Institutions," *Department of State Bulletin*, vol. 53, no. 1361 (July 26, 1965), pp. 142–151.

Stewart, Harold. 1960. *A Net of Fireflies: An Anthology of 320 Japanese Haiku Translated into English Verse.* Rutland, Vt.: Charles E. Tuttle.

Theobald, Robert. 1970. *An Alternative Future for America II.* Chicago: Swallow Press.

Theobald, R., and J. M. Scott. 1972. *Teg's 1994: An Anticipation of The Near Future.* Chicago: Swallow Press.

Thibaut, J. W., and H. H. Kelley. 1967. *The Social Psychology of Groups.* New York: Wiley.

Toffler, Alvin (ed.) 1972. *The Futurists.* New York: Random House.

Twentieth Century Fund Task Force On International Satellite Communications. 1970. *The Future of Satellite Communications.* New York: Twentieth Century Fund.

Unesco. 1968. *Communication in the Space Age: The Use of Satellites by the Mass Media.* Paris: UNESCO.

United Nations. 1967. *Human Rights: A Compilation of International Instruments of the United Nations.* New York: United Nations Publications.

Watzlawick, P., J. H. Beavin, and D. D. Jackson. 1967. *Pragmatics of Human Communication.* New York: Norton.

Weinstein, G., and M. D. Fantini. 1970. *Toward Humanistic Education: A Curriculum of Affect.* New York: Praeger.

Welden, T. A., and H. W. Ellingsworth, 1970. *Effective Speech Communication.* Glenview, Ill.: Scott, Foresman.

Wiener, Norbert. 1954. *The Human Use of Human Beings.* New York: Doubleday.

Wiener, Norbert. 1961. *Cybernetics.* Cambridge, Mass.: M.I.T. Press.

Wiener, Norbert. 1964. *God and Golem, Inc.* Cambridge, Mass.: M.I.T. Press.

Winsor, Frederick, and Marian Parry. 1958. *The Space Child's Mother Goose.* New York: Simon and Schuster.

Wooldridge, Dean E. 1963. *The Machinery of the Brain.* New York: McGraw-Hill.

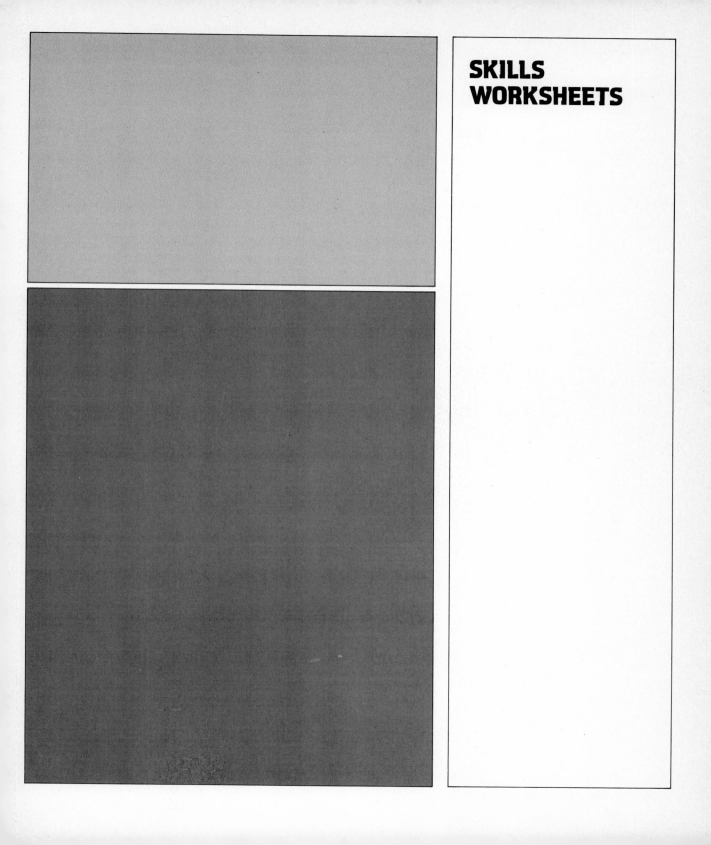

SKILLS
WORKSHEETS

TEMPLATE

Level I

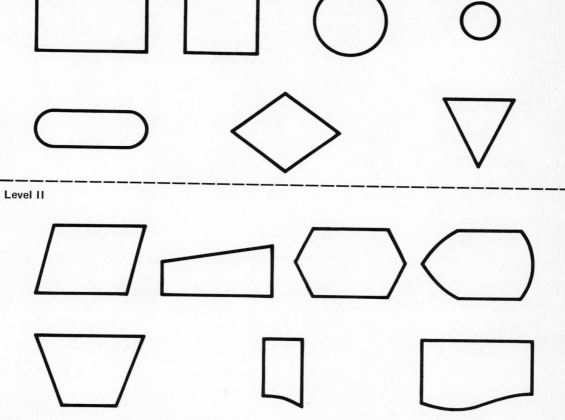

Level II

Level III

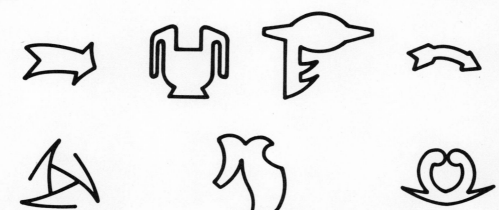

3.S Skills Worksheets: Dyadic Systems in Operation

Transcomnet Link

Begin time: _____ : _____ : _____
                   hr.   min.   sec.

End time: _____ : _____ : _____
                 hr.   min.   sec.

Elapsed time
in seconds: ◯

Matched forms (+1): _____
Mismatched forms (–1): _____
Reliability (–6 to +6): ☐

Telecomnet Link

Begin time: _____ : _____ : _____
           hr.   min.   sec.

End time: _____ : _____ : _____
        hr.   min.   sec.

Elapsed time
in seconds:

Matched forms (+1): _____
Mismatched forms (-1): _____
Reliability (-6 to +6):

Results

	Transcomnet Link	Telecomnet Link	Difference
System reliability	☐	☐	☐
Time in seconds	◯	◯	◯
Average reliability of *several* [°] systems	☐	☐	☐
Average time of several systems	◯	◯	◯
Difference	☐ ◯	☐ ◯	☐ ◯

Based on the above information, state the results in short declarative sentences.

1.

2.

3.

4.

° Add the system reliability scores of each dyad in class and divide by the number of dyads.

4.S Skills Worksheets: Communication Patterns in a Dyadic System

Tutorial: A Tutors B

For the tutorial, A selects 6 shapes, two from each level of the template, and draws a *complete pattern*.
He then instructs B in how to draw the pattern on his paper.

Begin time: _____ : _____ : _____
       hr.   min.   sec.

End time: _____ : _____ : _____
      hr.   min.   sec.

Elapsed time
in seconds:

Matched forms (+1): _____
Mismatched forms (-1): _____
Reliability (-6 to +6):

Tutorial: B Tutors A

Now B selects 6 shapes, two from each level of the template, and draws a *complete pattern*.
He then instructs A in how to draw the pattern on his paper.

Begin time: _____ : _____ : _____
            hr.   min.   sec.

End time: _____ : _____ : _____
          hr.   min.   sec.

Elapsed time
in seconds:

Matched forms (+1): _____
Mismatched forms (–1): _____
Reliability (–6 to +6): ⬜

Interview: A Interviews B

For the interview, B draws a shape, and A asks questions about positioning and so forth. Then A will match B for that shape. The interview continues until A has drawn all of B's shapes. Compare patterns.

Begin time: _____ : _____ : _____
 hr.   min.   sec.

End time: _____ : _____ : _____
 hr.   min.   sec.

Elapsed time
in seconds:

Matched forms (+1): _____
Mismatched forms (-1): _____
Reliability (-6 to +6): ☐

Interview: B Interviews A

For the interview, A draws a shape, and B asks questions about positioning and so forth. Then B will match A for that shape. The interview continues until B has drawn all of A's shapes. Compare patterns.

Begin time: _____ : _____ : _____
           hr.   min.   sec.

End time: _____ : _____ : _____
         hr.   min.   sec.

Elapsed time
in seconds:

Matched forms (+1): _____
Mismatched forms (-1): _____
Reliability (-6 to +6): ☐

Interchange: A and B Interchange

For the interchange, the format will be the same as that used for 3.S. A and B alternate. Both ask and answer questions.

Begin time: _____ : _____ : _____
           hr.   min.   sec.

End time: _____ : _____ : _____
          hr.   min.   sec.

Elapsed time
in seconds:

Matched forms(+1): _____
Mismatched forms (-1): _____
Reliability (-6 to +6): ☐

Results

Dyadic System	Tutorial (TR)	Interview (IV)	Interchange (IC)	Differences
Reliability (0-6) Time (60-?)	AB □ ○ BA □ ○	AB □ ○ BA □ ○	AB □ ○	AB + BA/2
Reliability Time	AB + BA/2 □ ○	AB + BA/2 □ ○	AB □ ○	TR/IC □ ○ IV/TR □ ○ IC/IV □ ○
Average reliability Average time	AB + BA/2 □ ○	□ ○	□ ○	TR/IC □ ○ IV/TR □ ○ IC/IV □ ○
Difference	□ ○	□ ○	□ ○	

1.

2.

3.

4.

5.S Skills Worksheets: Small Group Systems in Operation

Transcomnet Link and/or Telecomnet Link

Begin time: _____ : _____ : _____
            hr.   min.   sec.

End time: _____ : _____ : _____
          hr.   min.   sec.

Elapsed time
in seconds:

Matched forms (+1): _____ °
Mismatched forms (–1): _____ °
Reliability (–6 to +6):

°Compared to model.

Results

Small Group System	Interchange	
	Model/Yours	Full Group Average
Reliability	☐	☐
Time	◯ °	◯ °

1.

2.

3.

4.

° Times will be the same.

6.S Skills Worksheet: The Tutorial Pattern in a Large Group System

Your Data

Information and Interest scores (1.0—10.0) Predicted:

50—Word Summary

Average of all audience members

Information (1.0—5.0)

Interest (1.0—5.0)

Achieved score (1.0—10.0):
Information and Interest

Difference between achieved
and predicted scores

Score:
Achieved score less the difference
between achieved and predicted scores

Your Partner's Data

Predicted

Achieved

Difference between achieved and
predicted scores

Your partner's score

2

*Final
Score
for
Project*

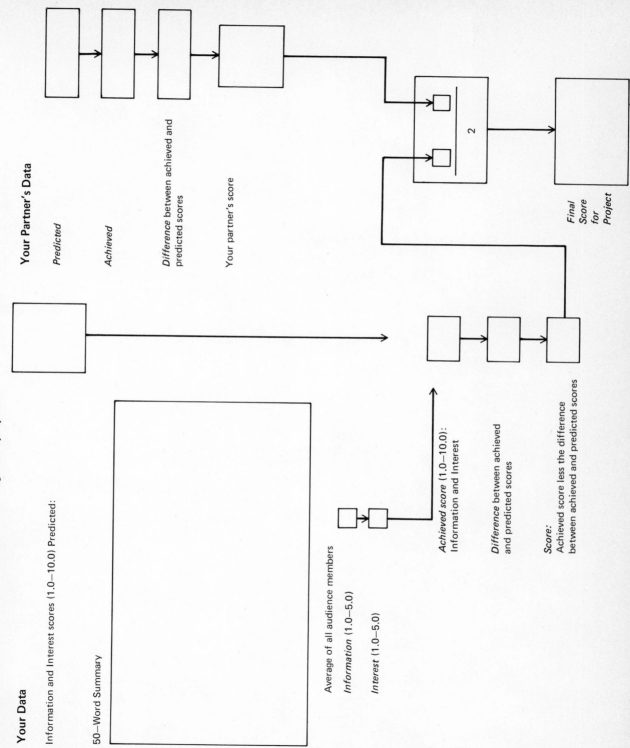

7.S Skills Worksheets: Sentence Intelligibility

Intelligibility Scores

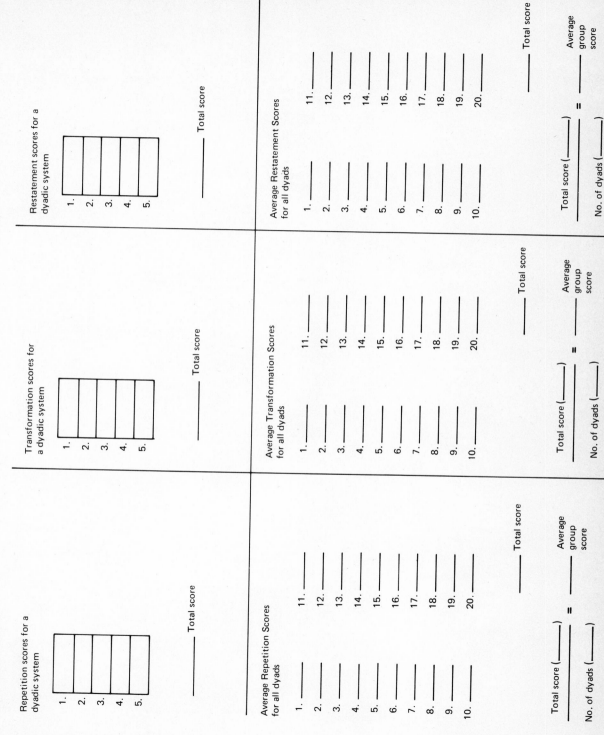

Repetition scores for a dyadic system

1.
2.
3.
4.
5.

_____ Total score

Transformation scores for a dyadic system

1.
2.
3.
4.
5.

_____ Total score

Restatement scores for a dyadic system

1.
2.
3.
4.
5.

_____ Total score

Average Repetition Scores for all dyads

1. _____   11. _____
2. _____   12. _____
3. _____   13. _____
4. _____   14. _____
5. _____   15. _____
6. _____   16. _____
7. _____   17. _____
8. _____   18. _____
9. _____   19. _____
10. _____   20. _____

_____ Total score

$$\frac{\text{Total score} (\underline{\quad})}{\text{No. of dyads} (\underline{\quad})} = \frac{\text{Average}}{\text{group}}\frac{}{\text{score}}$$

Average Transformation Scores for all dyads

1. _____   11. _____
2. _____   12. _____
3. _____   13. _____
4. _____   14. _____
5. _____   15. _____
6. _____   16. _____
7. _____   17. _____
8. _____   18. _____
9. _____   19. _____
10. _____   20. _____

_____ Total score

$$\frac{\text{Total score} (\underline{\quad})}{\text{No. of dyads} (\underline{\quad})} = \frac{\text{Average}}{\text{group}}\frac{}{\text{score}}$$

Average Restatement Scores for all dyads

1. _____   11. _____
2. _____   12. _____
3. _____   13. _____
4. _____   14. _____
5. _____   15. _____
6. _____   16. _____
7. _____   17. _____
8. _____   18. _____
9. _____   19. _____
10. _____   20. _____

_____ Total score

$$\frac{\text{Total score} (\underline{\quad})}{\text{No. of dyads} (\underline{\quad})} = \frac{\text{Average}}{\text{group}}\frac{}{\text{score}}$$

9.S Skills Worksheet: Target Chart Communicative Association

1.
2.
3.
4.
5.
6.
7.
8.
9.
10.
11.
12.
13.
14.
15.

10.S Skills Worksheet: Message Reliability

Record the individual message reliability scores below and calculate the average group reliability scores.

1. _____	11. _____	21. _____
2. _____	12. _____	22. _____
3. _____	13. _____	23. _____
4. _____	14. _____	24. _____
5. _____	15. _____	25. _____
6. _____	16. _____	26. _____
7. _____	17. _____	27. _____
8. _____	18. _____	28. _____
9. _____	19. _____	29. _____
10. _____	20. _____	30. _____

_____ Total

Total _____

_____ = _____ Group Message
Reliability Score

No. of class
members _____

NAME INDEX

SUBJECT INDEX

cost, 69
in home community, 166–167
in world community, 168–169
Teleportation, 75
Telstar, 21
Time, 160–161
real, 43–44
off, 43–44
Time-sharing, 216
in dyadic system, 84–85
in large group system, 112, 121
in small group system, 98–99
Tranceiver, 73
Transcomnet, 60, 69–72
availability, 71
control, 77–78
cost, 71–72

in home community, 166
in world community, 168
Transportation, 62–63
Turing machine, 33–34
Tutorial pattern, 88, 153, 186
in dyadic system, 89–90
in large group system, 115–120
in small group system, 101–104

Universal Declaration of Human Rights, 24, 146, 155, 163

Videophone, 75, 97, 137

World Community, 13, 38, 167–169, 176, 194–195
World WΛn, 199–202